The Côte d'Azur, the symbol of luxury and *dolce far niente*, was at its most fashionable between the two World Wars, as these elegant ladies on the Carlton jetty illustrate. The joyful exhibitionism of the Cannes municipal Casino showgirls is in quite another light.

The beau monde exists side by side with the simple life of the ordinary local inhabitants, like these *bugadières* washing their laundry at the mouth of the Paillon, in Nice, oblivious of the nearby promenade pier, the temple of entertainment.

During the *ferrade* young bulls are branded on the rump with the emblem of the *manade*, or herd. While the *ferrade* is one of the breeder's most important activities, together with weaning and castration, it also constitutes one of the most keenly awaited occasions for festive gatherings. *Gardians* (herdsmen) still exist today, just as in 1920.

Salt was already an important resource in antiquity; its main use today is in the chemical industry. At the beginning of the 20th century salt was still traditionally sifted by hand.

Today, mares in the Camargue are still captured in the same manner as in 1920. This photograph was taken on the Petit Badon domaine.

*Originally published in France by Nouveaux-Loisirs, a subsidiary of
Gallimard, Paris, 1994. Copyright © 1994 by Editions Nouveaux-Loisirs.*

Provence. English
Provence / [Gallimard editions].
p. cm.– (Knopf guides)
Includes bibliographical references and index.
ISBN 0-679-75066-5: $25.00
1. Provence (France) – Guidebooks.
I. Gallimard (Firm) . II. Title. III. Series
DC611.P958P6713   1994
914.4'9 – dc20
CIP 94-8366

First published October 1994
Second edition November 1996

NUMEROUS SPECIALISTS AND ACADEMICS HAVE CONTRIBUTED TO THIS GUIDE.

PROVENCE AND THE CÔTE D'AZUR:
EDITORS: Marie Hélène Albertini-Viennot and Clothilde Lefebvre
PRACTICAL INFORMATION: Florence Picquot, Veronika Vollmer
LAYOUT: Isabelle Roller
PICTURE RESEARCH: Danièle Gillot, Nathalie Beaud, Françoise Thurel and Nicolas Tourlières

NATURE: Michel Albarède, Michel Arnaud, Jean-Marie Triat, Gilles Cotin, Richard Bonnet, Jean-Marie Rocchia, Valerie Jacq, Georges Olioso, René Volot, Gilles Cheylan, Nadine Gomez, Samuel Michel, Alain Robert, Gaëtan Congès, Josette Dejean, Philippe Dubois, Henri Farrugio, Philippe Orsini, Marie-Hélène Sibille
HISTORY AND LANGUAGE: Noël Coulet, René Moulinas, Claude Mauron, Céline Magrini, Henri Moucadel, Martin Borros, Jean-Louis Panicacci, Ralph Schor, Bernard Lacroix
ARTS AND TRADITIONS: Régis Bertrand, Pierre Echinard, Michel Lamy, Claude Martel, Danièle Maternati-Baldouy, André Kaufman, Annie Sidro, Yves Fattori, Danièle Musset
ARCHITECTURE: Erik Fannière, Jean-Luc Massot, Bruno Lallemand, Gaëtan Congès, Jean-Pierre Brun, Nicolas Faucherre, Jean-Loup Fontana, Philippe Genin, Jean Marx, Michel Perreard, Françoise Santinecci-Boitelle, Ivan Yarmola, Henri Raulin, Jean-Christophe Simon
PROVENCE AS SEEN BY PAINTERS: Raphaël Merindol, François Bazzoli
PROVENCE AS SEEN BY WRITERS: Claude Mauron, Ralph Schor, Annick Vigier

ITINERARIES:
IN AND AROUND AVIGNON: Alain Breton, Sylvian Gagnière, Marie-Claude Léonelli, Georges Otioso, Marie-Christine Roquette, Maurice Contestin, Éric Coulet, Laurence Fumey, Alain Fretay, Marie-Hélène Sibille, Claude Sintès, Corinne Frayssinet-Savy
IN AND AROUND ORANGE: Maryse Woel, Michel Bonifay, Joël-Claude Meffre, Monique Bruno, Sylvie Grange, René Bruni, André Kaufman, Isabelle Battez, Georges Olioso, Eve Duperray
IN AND AROUND MARSEILLES: Gilles Cheylan, Pierre Échinard, Émile Témimes
IN AND AROUND AIX: Jean Boyer, Gilles Cheylan, Thierry Durousseau, Bruno Ély, Martine Vasselin, Noëlle Déjardin, Pierre Colomb, Gabriel Demians d'Archimbaud, Yves Esquieu, Raoul Bérenguier, Yann Codou, Jean-Yves Royer, Guy Barruol, Pierre Licutaghi, Léone Caffarel
IN AND AROUND CANNES: José Cucutullo, Pierre Cosson, Pierre Joannon, les Amis du vieux Toulon, Jean-Luc Mordefroid, Karine Lenfant-Valère, Yves Paccalet, Jean Paul Monery, Philippe Orsini, Gil Gianone, Edmonde Soubervie

IN AND AROUND NICE: Bernard Lacroix, Jean-Baptiste Robert, Charles Astro, Rosine Clevet Michaud, Dominique Escribe, Ernest Hildesheimer, Jean-Paul Potron, Ralph Schor, Régis Vian des Rives, Noëlle Desjardin.

CORRESPONDENT IN PROVENCE AND THE CÔTE D'AZUR: Michel Lamy
ADVISORS: Charles Astro, Jean Boyer, Christian Fontaine, Marie-Claude Léonelli, Hélène Vésian, René Volot

ILLUSTRATIONS:
NATURE: Anne Bodin, Frédéric Bony, Jacqueline Candiard, Denis Chavreuil, Jean Chevallier, Gismonde Curiace, François Desbordes, Bernard Duhem, Gilbert Houbre, Alban Larousse, Claire Felloni, Catherine Lachaud, René Metler, Bruce Pearson, François Place, Pascal Robin, Franck Stefan
ARCHITECTURE: Denis Brumaud, Philippe Candé, Nicolette Castle, Benoît Cusson, Sandra Doyle, Chris Fawcey, Eric Gillion, Jean-Benoît Héron, Trevor Hill, Olivier Hubert, Roger Hutchins, Jean-Michel Kacédan, Pavel Kostel, Philippe Lhez, Ruth Lindsay, Arthur Phillips, Maurice Pommier, Christian Rivière, Colin Rose, Michel Sinier, Gabor Szytria, Ed Stuart, Tony Townsend
ITINERARIES: Frédéric Bony, Vincent Bruno, Jean-Philippe Chabot, Gismonde Curiace, Alban Larousse, Claire Felloni, Catherine Lachaud, Jean Chevallier, Jean-Michel Lanusse, Bernard Duhem, Gabor Szytria, François Desbordes, Philippe Lhez, Jean-Michel Kacédan, René Meder, Pascal Robin, François Place, Dominique Mansion, Jean-Benoît Héron, Véronique Marchand, John Wilkinson

PRACTICAL INFORMATION: Maurice Pommier
CARTOGRAPHY: Vincent Bruno, Dominique Duplantier, Jean-Yves Duhoo, Eric Gillion, Stéphane Girel, Frédéric Liéval, Sylvie Serprix
COLORING: Isabelle-Anne Chatellard, Dominique Gros

INFOGRAPHY: Jean-Claude Beronine, Emmanuel Calamy, Kristof Chemineau, Paul Coulbois, Aubin Leray, Cyril Malié, Patrick Merienne

PHOTOGRAPHERS: Philippe Abel, Jean Bernard, Emmanuel Chapsoul, Maryan Daspet, Michel Delgado, Daniel Deschâteaux, François-Xavier Emery, Daniel Faure, François Fernandez, Jean-Marc Fichaux, Yves Gallois, Gil Gianone, Laurent Giraudou, Claude Gouron, Robin Hacquard, Fabrice Lepelletier (L'Oeil et la Mémoire), Michel de Lorenzo, Michel Massy, Pierre Nicolini, Pierre Ricou, Léonard de Selva, Georges Véran,

WE WOULD LIKE TO THANK: Anne Cauquetoux, Pierre-Gilles Bellin, Françoise Thurel and Benoît Laudier.

TRANSLATED BY MICHAEL CUNNINGHAM AND LOUIS MARCELIN-RICE.
EDITED AND TYPESET BY BOOK CREATION SERVICES, LONDON.
PRINTED IN ITALY BY EDITORIALE LIBRARIA.

PROVENCE
AND THE CÔTE D'AZUR

KNOPF GUIDES

CONTENTS

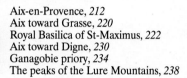

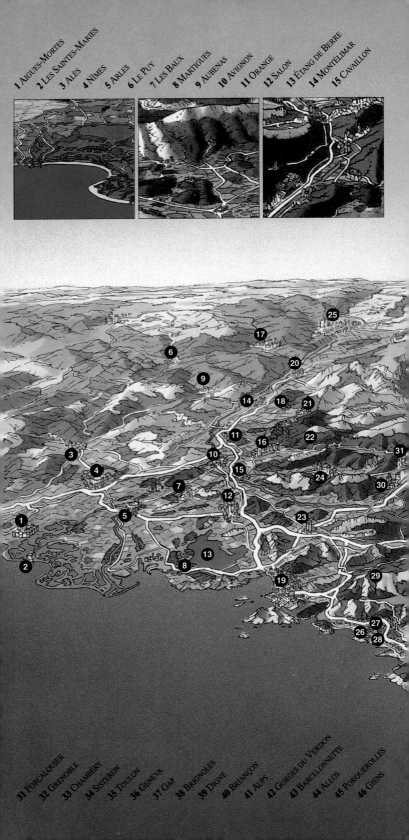

1 AIGUES-MORTES 2 LES SAINTES-MARIES 3 ALÈS 4 NÎMES 5 ARLES 6 LE PUY 7 LES BAUX 8 MARTIGUES 9 AUBENAS 10 AVIGNON 11 ORANGE 12 SALON 13 ÉTANG DE BERRE 14 MONTÉLIMAR 15 CAVAILLON

31 FORCALQUIER 32 GRENOBLE 33 CHAMBÉRY 34 SISTERON 35 TOULON 36 GENEVA 37 GAP 38 BRIGNOLES 39 DIGNE 40 BRIANÇON 41 AUPS 42 GORGES DU VERDON 43 BARCELONNETTE 44 ALLOS 45 PORQUEROLLES 46 GIENS

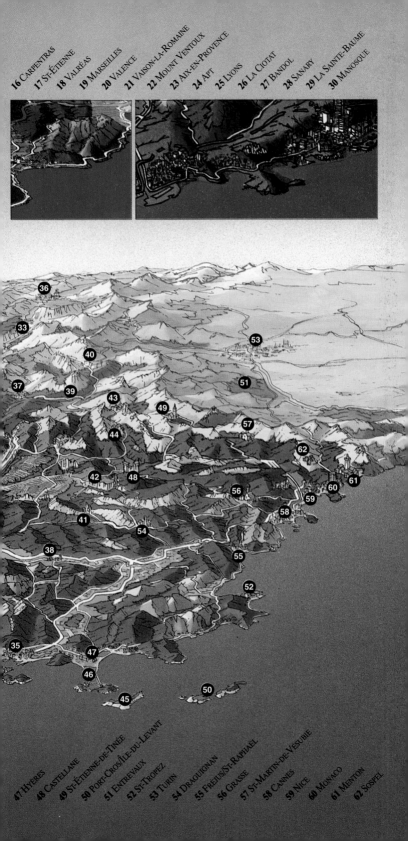

16 CARPENTRAS   17 ST-ÉTIENNE   18 VALRÉAS   19 MARSEILLES   20 VALENCE   21 VAISON-LA-ROMAINE   22 MOUNT VENTOUX   23 AIX-EN-PROVENCE   24 APT   25 LYONS   26 LA CIOTAT   27 BANDOL   28 SANARY   29 LA SAINTE-BAUME   30 MANOSQUE

47 HYÈRES   48 CASTELLANE   49 ST-ÉTIENNE-DE-TINÉE   50 PORT-CROS/ÎLE-DU-LEVANT   51 ENTREVAUX   52 ST-TROPEZ   53 TURIN   54 DRAGUIGNAN   55 FRÉJUS/ST-RAPHAËL   56 GRASSE   57 ST-MARTIN-DE-VÉSUBIE   58 CANNES   59 NICE   60 MONACO   61 MENTON   62 SOSPEL

How to Use this Guide

(Sample page shown from the guide to Venice)

The symbols at the top of each page refer to the different parts of the guide.

■ NATURAL ENVIRONMENT

● KEYS TO UNDERSTANDING

▲ ITINERARIES

◆ PRACTICAL INFORMATION

The itinerary map shows the main points of interest along the way and is intended to help you find your bearings.

The mini-map locates the particular itinerary within the wider area covered by the guide.

CANNAREGIO

Immediately outside the railway station lies Cannaregio, the first of the six *sestieri* of Venice. Situated at the north-west end of the city, this is the second largest *sestiere* after Castello ● *155*, covering an area of 150 hectares. Nearly a third of the population of Venice is concentrated here, amounting to more than twenty thousand people. There are two theories about the origin of the name Cannaregio; according to one, it comes from *Canal regio* (the Royal Canal), meaning to one, it comes from *Canal regio* (the Royal Canal), leading to the second waterway which once provided convenient access to the city from the mainland, by prolonging the lagoon canal of San Secondo (which runs parallel to the railway bridge). The other hypothesis is that the word derives from the reeds and canes which used to abound in this area. In any case, a system of straight, parallel canals, criss-cross this *sestiere*, southwards and linked by *calli*, cross-cross this *sestiere*, workmen's houses interspersed with magnificent palaces to the south, behind the palaces of the Grand Canal, built at the end of the last century. Now the pedestrianized, this street runs from the station to the Campo Santi Apostoli, crossing the *sestiere* from one side to the other and adopting a number of different names as it goes. Few people actually lived in this *sestiere* until the 11th century, and it seems to have been taken form only gradually, as the process of draining and consolidating the site progressed. From the 15th century onwards Cannaregio was a definable quarter, though it was still peripheral to Venice proper. Before the railway bridge and the station were built, manufacturing was the principal industry in the district, despite attempts to create a new area of growth with the Fondamenta Nuove. A similar project in the 16th century, the draining of the Sacca della Misericordia, was also never realized.

● The gateway to Venice, after it is neither the Piazzale, nor the station but the Grand Canal before its churned by propellers such as a great river.
Fernand Braudel, Histor

Santa Lucia Station.

THE GATEWAY TO VENICE ★

PONTE DELLA LIBERTA. Built by the Austrians 50 years after the Treaty of Campo Formio in 1797 ● *34*, to link Venice with Milan. The bridge ended the thousand-year separation from the mainland and shook the city's economy to its roots as Venice, already in the throes of all industrial revolution, saw its dependence on the mainland grow out of all recognition. **SANTA LUCIA STATION.** The present station dates from 1955, but still bears the name of the Renaissance church demolished in 1861 to make way for it. Opposite is the green dome of the Church of San Simeone Piccolo.

Half a day

BRIDGES TO VENICE
The second project for a bridge between Mestre and Venice was laid in 1814. Then in 1841 1846 that construction of the Ponte della Liberta was finally begun. The start of almost 11,500 feet, and included 222 stone arches. On April 25, 1933, the Ponte delle Littorale was opened. Built in less than two years by the engineer Umberto Fantucci, this bridge was intended for use by motor cars.

★ The star symbol signifies that a particular site has been singled out by the publishers for its special beauty, atmosphere or cultural interest.

● ▲ ■ ◆
The symbols alongside a title or within the text itself provide cross-references to a theme or place dealt with elsewhere in the guide.

At the beginning of each itinerary, the suggested means of transport to be used and the time it will take to cover the area are indicated:

🚢 By boat
🚶 On foot
🚲 By bicycle
🕐 Duration

136

THE GATEWAY TO VENICE ★

PONTE DELLA LIBERTA. Built by the Austrians 50 years after the Treaty of Campo Formio in 1797 ● *34*, to link Venice with Milan. The bridge ended the thousand-year separation from the mainland and shook the city's economy to its roots as Venice, already in the throes of the industrial revolution, saw

🚶 Half a day

BRIDGES TO VENICE

NATURE

■ CLIMATE

It is difficult to produce a "still" picture of the mistral, a wind that blows at times in gusts of over 60 miles an hour. This early 20th-century photomontage gives a humorous idea.

Provençal weather is characterized by its remarkably long periods of sunshine and its dry summers. However, temperatures vary enormously over the whole region due to great differences in altitude and the influence of both the Mediterranean and the Alps. Wind and rain, sometimes violent, are an integral part of the climate. The lower rainfalls along the coast gradually increase inland toward the more eastern mountainous areas. The strong, turbulent and gusty mistral brings sudden frosts in the winter but helps to temper the intense summer heat.

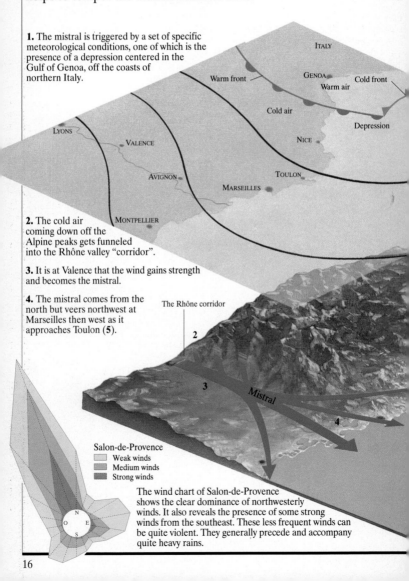

1. The mistral is triggered by a set of specific meteorological conditions, one of which is the presence of a depression centered in the Gulf of Genoa, off the coasts of northern Italy.

ITALY
Warm front
GENOA
Cold front
Warm air
Cold air
Depression
LYONS
VALENCE
NICE
AVIGNON
TOULON
MARSEILLES
MONTPELLIER

2. The cold air coming down off the Alpine peaks gets funneled into the Rhône valley "corridor".

3. It is at Valence that the wind gains strength and becomes the mistral.

4. The mistral comes from the north but veers northwest at Marseilles then west as it approaches Toulon (**5**).

The Rhône corridor

2

3

Mistral

4

Salon-de-Provence
☐ Weak winds
☐ Medium winds
☐ Strong winds

N
O
E
S

The wind chart of Salon-de-Provence shows the clear dominance of northwesterly winds. It also reveals the presence of some strong winds from the southeast. These less frequent winds can be quite violent. They generally precede and accompany quite heavy rains.

It rarely snows on the Côte d'Azur, but when it does the falls are usually heavy because of the proximity of Alps. In February 1956 a snowfall of about 14 inches was recorded at Antibes, while in 1986 there were approximately 10 inches of snow, and 6 inches in 1991.

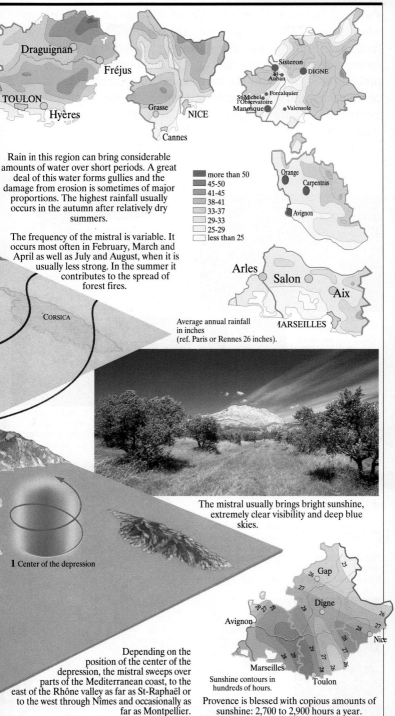

Draguignan

Fréjus

TOULON

Hyères

Grasse

Cannes

NICE

Sisteron

St-Auban

DIGNE

St-Michel l'Observatoire

Forcalquier

Manosque

Valensole

Rain in this region can bring considerable amounts of water over short periods. A great deal of this water forms gullies and the damage from erosion is sometimes of major proportions. The highest rainfall usually occurs in the autumn after relatively dry summers.

The frequency of the mistral is variable. It occurs most often in February, March and April as well as July and August, when it is usually less strong. In the summer it contributes to the spread of forest fires.

- more than 50
- 45-50
- 41-45
- 38-41
- 33-37
- 29-33
- 25-29
- less than 25

Orange

Carpentras

Avignon

Arles

Salon

Aix

CORSICA

MARSEILLES

Average annual rainfall in inches (ref. Paris or Rennes 26 inches).

The mistral usually brings bright sunshine, extremely clear visibility and deep blue skies.

1 Center of the depression

Gap

Digne

Avignon

Nice

Marseilles

Toulon

Sunshine contours in hundreds of hours.

Depending on the position of the center of the depression, the mistral sweeps over parts of the Mediterranean coast, to the east of the Rhône valley as far as St-Raphaël or to the west through Nîmes and occasionally as far as Montpellier.

Provence is blessed with copious amounts of sunshine: 2,700 to 2,900 hours a year.

17

■ ROCKY SEA BED

BARNACLE
These crustaceans, clinging onto the hulls of boats, can travel great distances.

Provence has more than 370 miles of serrated and rocky coasts whose steep cliffs continue under the sea. Reaching dozens of fathoms in depth just off the shore, the sea is 500 to 1,000 fathoms deep only 5 or 6 miles out in the major gulfs. Such precipitous drops show the narrowness, or total absence, of the continental shelf which partly determines the development of marine life. Where the shelf is wide, areas rich in flora and fauna appear.

MORAY EEL. Has an evil reputation due mainly to its aggressive behavior when surprised, and yet it was so highly valued in the most ancient times by the Greeks and the Romans that they kept them in special tanks.

GROUPER OR DUSKY PERCH
Protection measures introduced in 1980 have ensured the conservation of this emblematic Mediterranean species. It can now be seen on certain rocky beds.

TUBULAR SPONGE
It lives on submerged rocks.

MORAY EEL
Spends most of its time hiding in cracks in the rock, showing only its head.

SEA SLUGS
These molluscs display magnificent colors.

MALE SEA PEACOCK

MALE RAINBOW WRASSE

FEMALE RAINBOW WRASSE

WRASSES
These colorful fish have the remarkable characteristic of being transsexual: starting as females they become males with age. They visit the coasts in the summer but live in deep water in the winter.

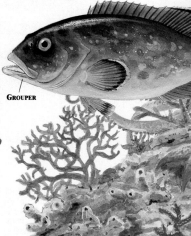

GROUPER

RED CORAL. These are polyps living in colonies. They are much sought after for the jewelry industry.

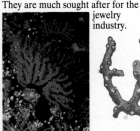

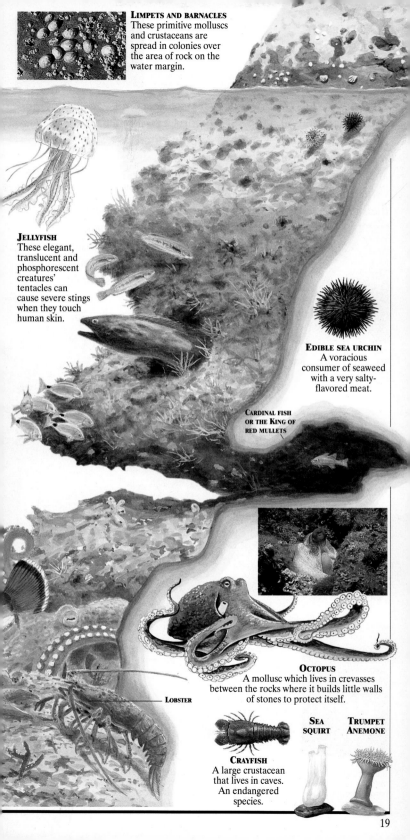

LIMPETS AND BARNACLES
These primitive molluscs and crustaceans are spread in colonies over the area of rock on the water margin.

JELLYFISH
These elegant, translucent and phosphorescent creatures' tentacles can cause severe stings when they touch human skin.

EDIBLE SEA URCHIN
A voracious consumer of seaweed with a very salty-flavored meat.

CARDINAL FISH OR THE KING OF RED MULLETS

OCTOPUS
A mollusc which lives in crevasses between the rocks where it builds little walls of stones to protect itself.

LOBSTER

SEA SQUIRT

TRUMPET ANEMONE

CRAYFISH
A large crustacean that lives in caves. An endangered species.

POSIDONIA

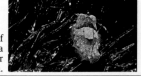

Underwater fields of posidonia provide a perfect refuge for cuttlefish.

The very narrow continental shelf skirting the rocky coasts of the Alpes-Maritimes and the Var supports a posidonia "grassland". Posidonia, otherwise known as Neptune grass, is a seed plant whose flowers ensure its reproduction. Their bushy roots anchoring them to the sea bed form hillocks which shelter a wide variety of animal species and stabilize the marine topsoil. Through their chlorophyll they play a major role in maintaining oxygen levels in these coastal environments. Over the last twenty years pollution has been damaging the posidonia grasslands.

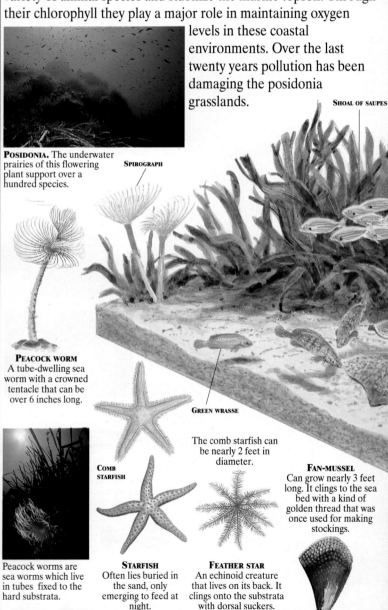

POSIDONIA. The underwater prairies of this flowering plant support over a hundred species.

SHOAL OF SAUPES

SPIROGRAPH

PEACOCK WORM
A tube-dwelling sea worm with a crowned tentacle that can be over 6 inches long.

GREEN WRASSE

The comb starfish can be nearly 2 feet in diameter.

COMB STARFISH

FAN-MUSSEL
Can grow nearly 3 feet long. It clings to the sea bed with a kind of golden thread that was once used for making stockings.

Peacock worms are sea worms which live in tubes fixed to the hard substrata.

STARFISH
Often lies buried in the sand, only emerging to feed at night.

FEATHER STAR
An echinoid creature that lives on its back. It clings onto the substrata with dorsal suckers.

Creatures like this colorful sea slug and the violet sea urchin (left) also find refuge in the posidonia.

PIPEFISH. Also known as the "seaviper", this snake-like fish has a scaleless body like the related seahorse.

CUTTLEFISH. An excellent swimmer that buries itself in the sand to capture its prey. Its color changes to blend with its environment.

SPOTTED PELTODORIS or sea slug is indigenous to the Mediterranean and feeds on sponge organisms.

SEA CUCUMBER. A relative of starfish and sea urchins, it feeds on refuse. It reproduces in July and early August, mostly in the posidonia beds.

POSIDONIA. Gets its name from Poseidon, the Greek god of the oceans. It is a gauge of the quality of marine ecosystems. Flowers rarely and produces fruit known as sea olives.

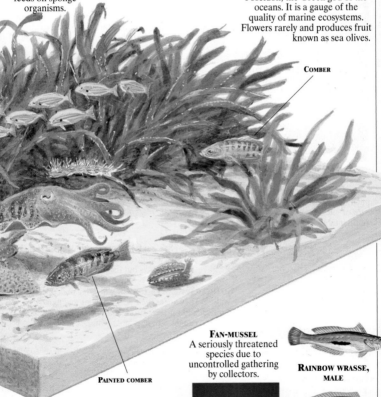

COMBER

PAINTED COMBER

FAN-MUSSEL A seriously threatened species due to uncontrolled gathering by collectors.

RAINBOW WRASSE, MALE

RAINBOW WRASSE, FEMALE

RED MULLET. Lives on the sandy sea beds. The deeper its habitat, the brighter its coloring.

SEA PEACOCK, MALE

SEA VIOLETS AND URCHINS. Their bright yellow meat has a strong salty taste. They are found in the weed beds.

While Provençal fishing is generally on a small scale, it does include some relatively important trawling for bottom feeders on the sandy "shelves" between the delta platform and the rocky sea bed of the Bouches-du-Rhône. However, most of the boats are of the *pointu* type, with a net-hauling wheel installed in the bow, and the local fishing technique is known as *pêche aux petits métiers*. Each net is designed for a specific catch: gill nets for rock fish, seine nets for migratory shoals in open waters, *palangres*, surface or bottom nightlines, for conger eels and other large fish. Special tackle is also used in lobster fishing.

LOBSTER POTS
These handmade wicker cages are baited and the funnel-shaped neck prevents captive lobsters from escaping.

RED MULLET (ROUGET BARBET). Lives in the pebbles or among the rocks down to a depth of 50 fathoms.

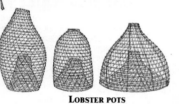

LOBSTERM (LANGOUSTE). This scarce and much sought-after crustacean is caught in traps or gill nets on the coral beds of the continental shelf.

SEA BASS (LOUP). This noble fish is highly prized in Provence. It can reach a weight of 22 pounds, but fish that large are now rare.

GILTHEAD (PAGEOT) are sea bream living in deeper waters. They are at their best in winter and most appreciated for their strong sea flavor. They are caught with nets and nightlines.

WHITING (MERLU)
This highly fertile coastal species thrives in shoals on sandy and muddy sea beds. It is caught by intensive trawling and gill net fishing.

TRAWL
The net sweeps t
sea bed over an area
wide as 2,000 to 2,500 feet.
wood and metal boards keep t
net mouth open, and the frighten
fish seek refuge in the rear pock
of the n

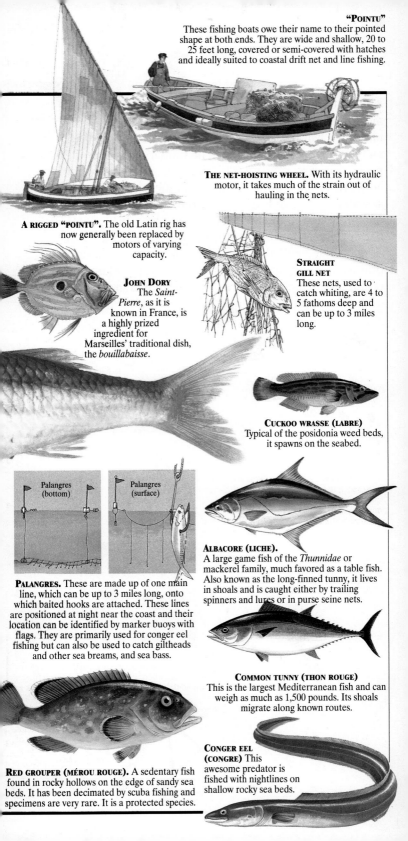

"POINTU"
These fishing boats owe their name to their pointed shape at both ends. They are wide and shallow, 20 to 25 feet long, covered or semi-covered with hatches and ideally suited to coastal drift net and line fishing.

THE NET-HOISTING WHEEL. With its hydraulic motor, it takes much of the strain out of hauling in the nets.

A RIGGED "POINTU". The old Latin rig has now generally been replaced by motors of varying capacity.

JOHN DORY
The *Saint-Pierre*, as it is known in France, is a highly prized ingredient for Marseilles' traditional dish, the *bouillabaisse*.

STRAIGHT GILL NET
These nets, used to catch whiting, are 4 to 5 fathoms deep and can be up to 3 miles long.

CUCKOO WRASSE (LABRE)
Typical of the posidonia weed beds, it spawns on the seabed.

Palangres (bottom)
Palangres (surface)

PALANGRES. These are made up of one main line, which can be up to 3 miles long, onto which baited hooks are attached. These lines are positioned at night near the coast and their location can be identified by marker buoys with flags. They are primarily used for conger eel fishing but can also be used to catch giltheads and other sea breams, and sea bass.

ALBACORE (LICHE).
A large game fish of the *Thunnidae* or mackerel family, much favored as a table fish. Also known as the long-finned tunny, it lives in shoals and is caught either by trailing spinners and lures or in purse seine nets.

COMMON TUNNY (THON ROUGE)
This is the largest Mediterranean fish and can weigh as much as 1,500 pounds. Its shoals migrate along known routes.

RED GROUPER (MÉROU ROUGE). A sedentary fish found in rocky hollows on the edge of sandy sea beds. It has been decimated by scuba fishing and specimens are very rare. It is a protected species.

CONGER EEL (CONGRE) This awesome predator is fished with nightlines on shallow rocky sea beds.

THE CAMARGUE

MARSH HARRIER
The commonest bird of prey in the Camargue. About seventy pairs nest there each year.

The Camargue is undoubtedly France's most remarkable site for the diversity of its bird life. Over 365 species of birds have been observed there and in the neighboring Crau. The Camargue is one of Europe's major overwintering areas for ducks, while in the spring it is home to large breeding colonies of different species of herons as well as gulls and terns. It is also the only place in France, and one of the few in the Mediterranean, where the greater flamingo nests in winter together with such species as the slender-billed gull, the sandwich tern and the collared pratincole, which are very specific to Europe. Mammals, reptiles and amphibians are also widespread in the Camargue.

AVOCET
Breed in the salt marshes where their population can reach six hundred nesting pairs.

BLACK-WINGED STILT
Eclectic in its choice of habitat, it lives both in salt and fresh water marshes or rice fields.

KENTISH PLOVER
Inhabits mainly the salt marshes. Over three hundred pairs come to nest in the Camargue.

HERRING GULL
Extremely common. Several thousand nest in the salt marshes and lakes of the Camargue.

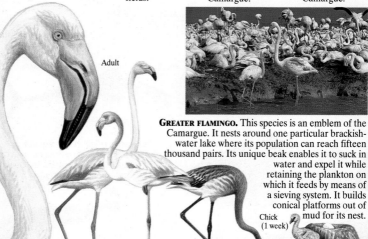

Adult

GREATER FLAMINGO. This species is an emblem of the Camargue. It nests around one particular brackish-water lake where its population can reach fifteen thousand pairs. Its unique beak enables it to suck in water and expel it while retaining the plankton on which it feeds by means of a sieving system. It builds conical platforms out of mud for its nest.

Chick
(1 week)

Immature   Young
(2–3 months)

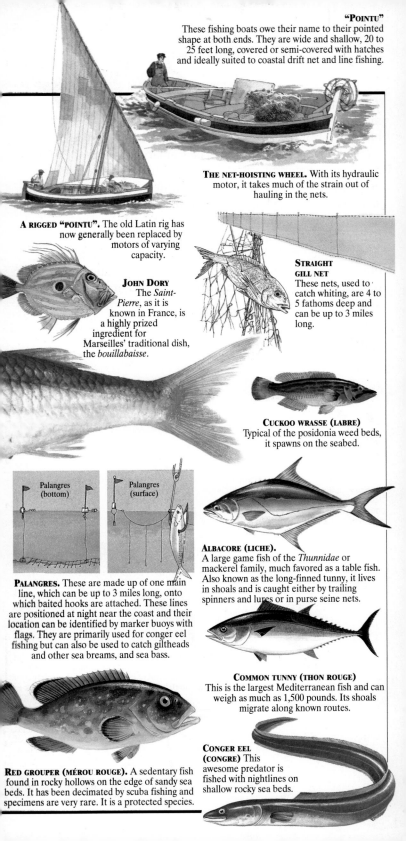

"POINTU"
These fishing boats owe their name to their pointed shape at both ends. They are wide and shallow, 20 to 25 feet long, covered or semi-covered with hatches and ideally suited to coastal drift net and line fishing.

THE NET-HOISTING WHEEL. With its hydraulic motor, it takes much of the strain out of hauling in the nets.

A RIGGED "POINTU". The old Latin rig has now generally been replaced by motors of varying capacity.

STRAIGHT GILL NET
These nets, used to catch whiting, are 4 to 5 fathoms deep and can be up to 3 miles long.

JOHN DORY
The *Saint-Pierre*, as it is known in France, is a highly prized ingredient for Marseilles' traditional dish, the *bouillabaisse*.

CUCKOO WRASSE (LABRE)
Typical of the posidonia weed beds, it spawns on the seabed.

Palangres (bottom)

Palangres (surface)

PALANGRES. These are made up of one main line, which can be up to 3 miles long, onto which baited hooks are attached. These lines are positioned at night near the coast and their location can be identified by marker buoys with flags. They are primarily used for conger eel fishing but can also be used to catch giltheads and other sea breams, and sea bass.

ALBACORE (LICHE).
A large game fish of the *Thunnidae* or mackerel family, much favored as a table fish. Also known as the long-finned tunny, it lives in shoals and is caught either by trailing spinners and lures or in purse seine nets.

COMMON TUNNY (THON ROUGE)
This is the largest Mediterranean fish and can weigh as much as 1,500 pounds. Its shoals migrate along known routes.

RED GROUPER (MÉROU ROUGE). A sedentary fish found in rocky hollows on the edge of sandy sea beds. It has been decimated by scuba fishing and specimens are very rare. It is a protected species.

CONGER EEL (CONGRE) This awesome predator is fished with nightlines on shallow rocky sea beds.

◼ THE CAMARGUE

MARSH HARRIER
The commonest bird of prey in the Camargue. About seventy pairs nest there each year.

The Camargue is undoubtedly France's most remarkable site for the diversity of its bird life. Over 365 species of birds have been observed there and in the neighboring Crau. The Camargue is one of Europe's major overwintering areas for ducks, while in the spring it is home to large breeding colonies of different species of herons as well as gulls and terns. It is also the only place in France, and one of the few in the Mediterranean, where the greater flamingo nests in winter together with such species as the slender-billed gull, the sandwich tern and the collared pratincole, which are very specific to Europe. Mammals, reptiles and amphibians are also widespread in the Camargue.

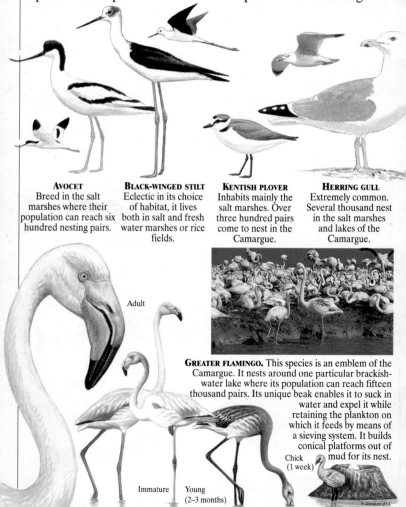

AVOCET
Breed in the salt marshes where their population can reach six hundred nesting pairs.

BLACK-WINGED STILT
Eclectic in its choice of habitat, it lives both in salt and fresh water marshes or rice fields.

KENTISH PLOVER
Inhabits mainly the salt marshes. Over three hundred pairs come to nest in the Camargue.

HERRING GULL
Extremely common. Several thousand nest in the salt marshes and lakes of the Camargue.

Adult

GREATER FLAMINGO. This species is an emblem of the Camargue. It nests around one particular brackish-water lake where its population can reach fifteen thousand pairs. Its unique beak enables it to suck in water and expel it while retaining the plankton on which it feeds by means of a sieving system. It builds conical platforms out of mud for its nest.

Chick (1 week)

Immature   Young (2–3 months)

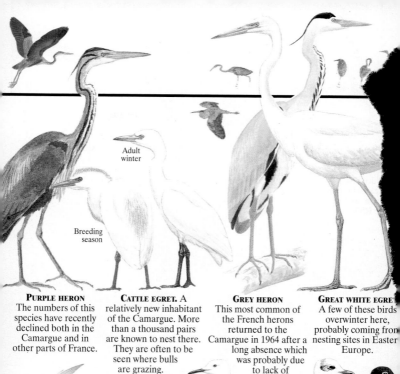

PURPLE HERON
The numbers of this species have recently declined both in the Camargue and in other parts of France.

CATTLE EGRET. A relatively new inhabitant of the Camargue. More than a thousand pairs are known to nest there. They are often to be seen where bulls are grazing.

GREY HERON
This most common of the French herons returned to the Camargue in 1964 after a long absence which was probably due to lack of protection.

GREAT WHITE EGRE
A few of these birds overwinter here, probably coming from nesting sites in Easter Europe.

Adult winter

Breeding season

COMMON TERN
This tern is an irregular visitor to the marshes where it nests on floating vegetation.

SANDWICH TERN
Nests in the Camargue salt marshes on remote islands.

SLENDER-BILLED GULL
The Camargue is the only French breeding site of this gull, which is indigenous to the Mediterranean coasts.

MEDITERRANEAN GULL
Large numbers of this species have been regula winter visitors to the Camargue and neighboring coasts. Some have recently started nesting.

Summer

Winter

Winter

Summer

SHELDUCK
This handsome duck commonly nests in brackish environments. Its young gather in "crèches".

COOT
Large flocks overwinter on the lagoon of Vaccarès, where there can be as many as forty thousand birds.

WILD BOAR
Common, can be seen by day.

COYPU
A wetland species that particularly appreciates the "roubines" (narrow water courses) that flow all over the Camargue.

RED FOX
Plays a major role in eliminating sick animals, particularly in the Rièges woods.

RABBIT
A frequent prey to epidemics of myxomatosis.

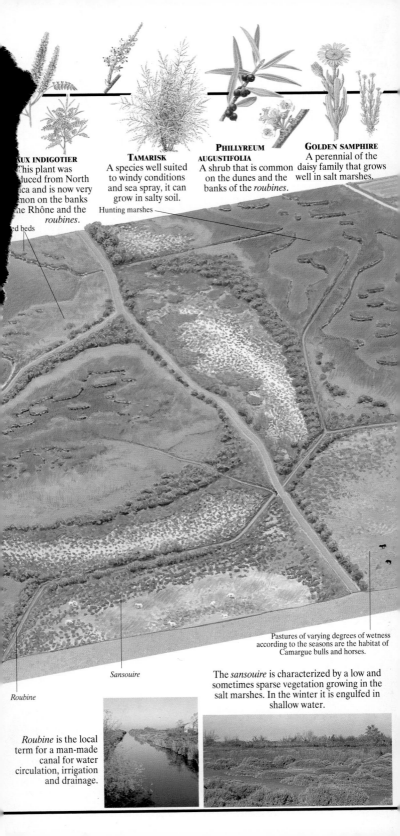

FAUX INDIGOTIER
This plant was introduced from North America and is now very common on the banks of the Rhône and the *roubines*.

Reed beds

TAMARISK
A species well suited to windy conditions and sea spray, it can grow in salty soil.

PHILLYREUM AUGUSTIFOLIA
A shrub that is common on the dunes and the banks of the *roubines*.

GOLDEN SAMPHIRE
A perennial of the daisy family that grows well in salt marshes.

Hunting marshes

Pastures of varying degrees of wetness according to the seasons are the habitat of Camargue bulls and horses.

Sansouire

The *sansouire* is characterized by a low and sometimes sparse vegetation growing in the salt marshes. In the winter it is engulfed in shallow water.

Roubine

Roubine is the local term for a man-made canal for water circulation, irrigation and drainage.

Mixed colonies of various egret and heron species can frequently be found nesting in trees in the quieter parts of the Camargue.

LITTLE EGRET
The elegant silhouette of this species graces the Camargue wetlands where it is very common.

SQUACCO HERON
This small, shy heron is rather rare. It inhabits fresh water marshes, never far from vegetation, and nests in trees.

BITTERN
Its strange "song" is rather like the sound of air being blown over the neck of a bottle or a jug.

NIGHT HERON
A nocturnal bird, not easily seen. It flies over the marshes at dusk, calling with a hoarse croak.

Winter

Breeding season

SPOTTED REDSHANK
Many hundreds of these visit the Camargue in the summer on their way to Africa.

REDSHANK
A few dozen pairs nest each year on islands in the lagoons.

ROLLER
A small nesting population can be observed each year in the Grande Camargue.

BEE-EATER
This summer visitor from tropical Africa feeds avidly on dragonflies.

Female   Male

Female   Male

POCHARD
This non-nesting winter visitor can sometimes be seen in very large numbers, (as many as 21,000 birds) mainly on fresh water lakes.

TEAL
Large numbers of these little ducks overwinter in the Camargue.

Female   Male

RED CRESTED POCHARD
This species migrates from Central Europe to the Camargue, where a small number nest. Up to five thousand birds overwinter here, particularly on the St-Seren marshes.

LADDER SNAKE
This snake is most often found on the *montilles*.

GRASS SNAKE
This harmless snake is particularly fond of aquatic environments.

Everlasting flower

Marran

Sea holly

Marran grass fixes the sand of the newly formed (mobile) dunes whereas the other two plants are also to be found on the older fixed dunes.

EARLY PURPLE ORCHID
An early-flowering orchid which is easy to find at the beginning of spring.

The islands of vegetation in the lagoons provide favorable nesting sites, particularly for terns, gulls and red crested pochards.

Lagoon of Vaccarès

Greater flamingos

Salt *camelles* near Salins-de-Giraud

Developed salt marshes

The *sansouire* consists of a mosaic of plant species that are typical of the Camargue.

Salt production in the Camargue has existed since antiquity and became an industry at the turn of the century. It now accounts for more than one million tons of salt over about 35,000 acres.

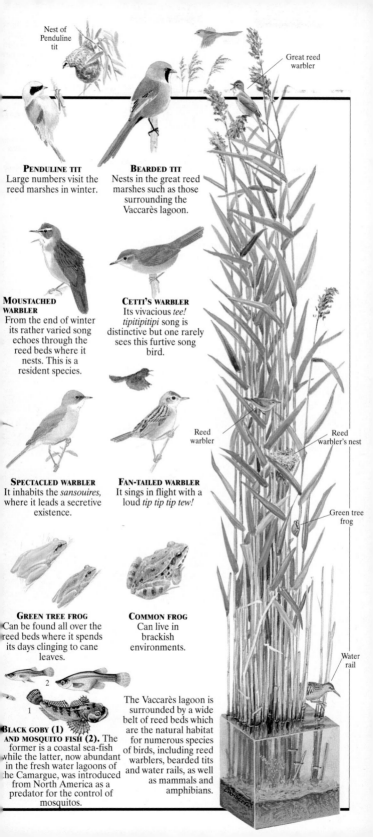

Nest of Penduline tit

Great reed warbler

PENDULINE TIT
Large numbers visit the reed marshes in winter.

BEARDED TIT
Nests in the great reed marshes such as those surrounding the Vaccarès lagoon.

MOUSTACHED WARBLER
From the end of winter its rather varied song echoes through the reed beds where it nests. This is a resident species.

CETTI'S WARBLER
Its vivacious *tee! tipitipitipi* song is distinctive but one rarely sees this furtive song bird.

SPECTACLED WARBLER
It inhabits the *sansouires,* where it leads a secretive existence.

FAN-TAILED WARBLER
It sings in flight with a loud *tip tip tip tew!*

Reed warbler

Reed warbler's nest

Green tree frog

GREEN TREE FROG
Can be found all over the reed beds where it spends its days clinging to cane leaves.

COMMON FROG
Can live in brackish environments.

BLACK GOBY (1) AND MOSQUITO FISH (2). The former is a coastal sea-fish while the latter, now abundant in the fresh water lagoons of the Camargue, was introduced from North America as a predator for the control of mosquitos.

The Vaccarès lagoon is surrounded by a wide belt of reed beds which are the natural habitat for numerous species of birds, including reed warblers, bearded tits and water rails, as well as mammals and amphibians.

Water rail

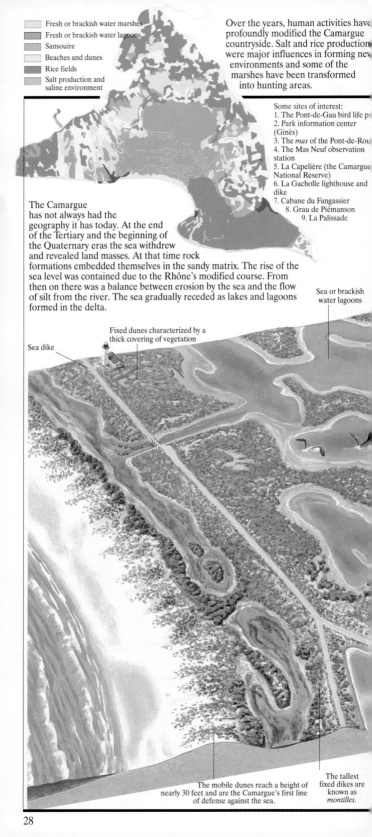

Fresh or brackish water marshes
Fresh or brackish water lagoons
Sansouire
Beaches and dunes
Rice fields
Salt production and saline environment

Over the years, human activities have profoundly modified the Camargue countryside. Salt and rice production were major influences in forming new environments and some of the marshes have been transformed into hunting areas.

Some sites of interest:
1. The Pont-de-Gau bird life p:
2. Park information center (Ginès)
3. The *mas* of the Pont-de-Rou
4. The Mas Neuf observation station
5. La Capelière (the Camargue National Reserve)
6. La Gacholle lighthouse and dike
7. Cabane du Fangassier
8. Grau de Piémanson
9. La Palissade

The Camargue has not always had the geography it has today. At the end of the Tertiary and the beginning of the Quaternary eras the sea withdrew and revealed land masses. At that time rock formations embedded themselves in the sandy matrix. The rise of the sea level was contained due to the Rhône's modified course. From then on there was a balance between erosion by the sea and the flow of silt from the river. The sea gradually receded as lakes and lagoons formed in the delta.

Sea or brackish water lagoons

Sea dike

Fixed dunes characterized by a thick covering of vegetation

The mobile dunes reach a height of nearly 30 feet and are the Camargue's first line of defense against the sea.

The tallest fixed dikes are known as *montilles.*

Rice-growing developed mainly since 1945 and has created major alterations in the irrigation system of the Camargue.

While rice production in the Camargue has existed since the 16th century, this activity now covers over 40 percent of its arable land (nearly 50,000 acres).

Rice fields

Shore vegetation

Rhône

Shrubby seablite

The main species to be found in the *sansouires* are salt marsh plants of the goosefoot family.

Perennial glasswort

Glasswort

Hunting grounds in the marshes have been established with ecology and conservation of the plant species in mind.

Common sea lavender

Herbaceous glasswort

Obione

Block diagram of a *sansouire*.

Block diagram of the vegetation on the banks of a salt water lagoon.

◼ Vineyards

The terraced rows of vines are sheltered from the wind by rows of trees.

Wine has been produced in Provence for 2,600 years. Rosé wine accounts for a major part of the production (65 percent), but there are also red wines (30 percent) and white wines (5 percent). The temperate Mediterranean climate, owing its mildness to the proximity of the sea and the altitude, and the wide range of different soils and grape varieties (*cépages*) explain the diversity and quality of these wines. Due to progress made in regulating the production of *Appellation* wines in the region, Provence now has a wide spectrum of quality wines, from rosé that should be drunk fairly young to red wines which can be aged for a few years and particularly aromatic wines.

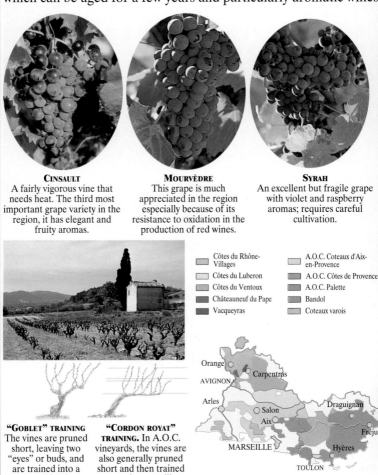

CINSAULT
A fairly vigorous vine that needs heat. The third most important grape variety in the region, it has elegant and fruity aromas.

MOURVÈDRE
This grape is much appreciated in the region especially because of its resistance to oxidation in the production of red wines.

SYRAH
An excellent but fragile grape with violet and raspberry aromas; requires careful cultivation.

Côtes du Rhône-Villages
Côtes du Luberon
Côtes du Ventoux
Châteauneuf du Pape
Vacqueyras
A.O.C. Coteaux d'Aix-en-Provence
A.O.C. Côtes de Provence
A.O.C. Palette
Bandol
Coteaux varois

"GOBLET" TRAINING
The vines are pruned short, leaving two "eyes" or buds, and are trained into a vase or goblet shape.

"CORDON ROYAT" TRAINING. In A.O.C. vineyards, the vines are also generally pruned short and then trained on a wire or trellis.

Orange, Carpentras, AVIGNON, Arles, Salon, Aix, MARSEILLE, Draguignan, Fréjus, Hyères, TOULON

GRENACHE NOIR
This is the basic grape of all the Rhône Valley wines. It is a very robust vine that grows on dry and stony slopes, giving alcoholic content and mellow strength.

CABERNET-SAUVIGNON
This introduced grape has adapted well to the Provence region; it produces a wine that keeps well, but its use is still limited.

MAKING ROSÉ WINE

MAKING RED WINE

The grapes are crushed and the skins are left in contact with the juice in fermentation vats (1, 2, 3); one week for the light red (*rouge de goutte*) (4, 4') to be drunk within two to three years, and two to three weeks for wine that should be kept longer (*vin de garde*) (5, 5').

For rosé (6), the juice to be used is placed in a fermentation vat after only one night of contact with the skins. The grapes must be quite mature for the wine to develop its full aroma.

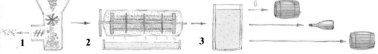

MAKING WHITE WINE

White Côtes-de-Provence are *blancs de blancs*, or white wines made exclusively with white grapes. As soon as they are harvested the grapes are pressed (1) and decanted of impurities (2). The juice is then fermented in vats or in oak casks (3). Provence whites are said to have a golden "robe".

33

THE "GARRIGUE"

BONELLI'S EAGLE
This large bird of prey is now an endangered species in France: only about fifteen pairs still nest in Provence.

The term *garrigue* defines the transitional habitats that exist between the open environments of *landes* and grasslands and the closed environments of oak and pine forests, which cover vast tracts of Provence. The intermediate characteristics of these areas, heavily influenced by their chalky soils and their exposure to the elements, make them rich reserves of different plant and animal species, most of which are well adapted to arid conditions. Unfortunately they are often vulnerable to bush fires.

PRICKLY JUNIPER
Its needles are used for the production of an antiseptic ointment, oil of cade.

SHRUBBY HARE'S-EAR
This evergreen umbellifer can grow more than 6 feet tall.

KERMES OAK
This small variety of oak tree is hardy enough to survive forest fires and grows in poor soil.

HOLM OR EVERGREEN OAK
The saplings of this species can be mistaken for Kermes oak.

COMMON JUNIPER
Found throughout France in sunny areas with chalky soils.

Subalpine warbler

Montpellier snake

Common rosemary

Prickly juniper

Thyme

Rosemary

Rush-like scorpion vetch

Gorse

Thyme

Rock rose

In order to adapt to the poverty of the soil and the aridity certain plants (for example, thyme) have developed tufted capillary roots; others, so as to limit their water loss, produce leaves that are slender and spiky (gorse), hairy, waxy or even rolled up (rosemary).

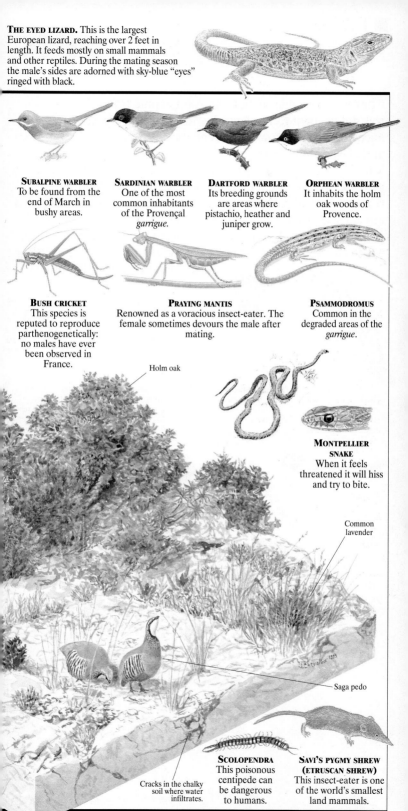

THE EYED LIZARD. This is the largest European lizard, reaching over 2 feet in length. It feeds mostly on small mammals and other reptiles. During the mating season the male's sides are adorned with sky-blue "eyes" ringed with black.

SUBALPINE WARBLER
To be found from the end of March in bushy areas.

SARDINIAN WARBLER
One of the most common inhabitants of the Provençal *garrigue.*

DARTFORD WARBLER
Its breeding grounds are areas where pistachio, heather and juniper grow.

ORPHEAN WARBLER
It inhabits the holm oak woods of Provence.

BUSH CRICKET
This species is reputed to reproduce parthenogenetically: no males have ever been observed in France.

PRAYING MANTIS
Renowned as a voracious insect-eater. The female sometimes devours the male after mating.

PSAMMODROMUS
Common in the degraded areas of the *garrigue.*

Holm oak

MONTPELLIER SNAKE
When it feels threatened it will hiss and try to bite.

Common lavender

Saga pedo

Cracks in the chalky soil where water infiltrates.

SCOLOPENDRA
This poisonous centipede can be dangerous to humans.

SAVI'S PYGMY SHREW (ETRUSCAN SHREW)
This insect-eater is one of the world's smallest land mammals.

35

◼ THE ALEPPO PINE

BLACK RAT
This rat lives wild in the pine forests. The species originated in southeast Asia and first came to Provence in neolithic times.

Contrary to popular belief, the Aleppo pine (*Pinus halepensis*) was not brought to Provence by the returning crusaders: its ancestor used to grow in the region twenty-five million years ago and eleven-thousand-year-old pollens have been found in the Var. This fast-spreading and fast-growing species thrives in the *garrigue*, the *maquis* and on previously cultivated land. It regenerates well after forest fires, thanks to its winged seeds that are carried by the wind. Due to the favorable circumstances of gradual rural exodus and frequent fires the Aleppo pine forests, which covered only 50,000 acres of the South of France in 1850, have now spread over about 500,000 acres.

SCOPS OWL
This tiny insect-eating owl (weight approximately 3½ ounces) breeds in the *pinèdes* and overwinters in Africa.

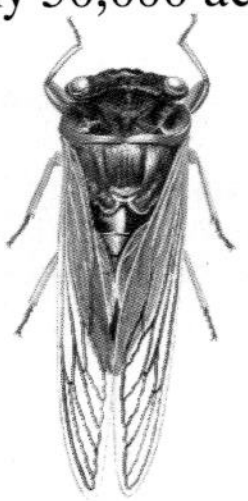

COMMON CICADA. This insect lives for four years underground as a larva; the adult feeds on pine sap and lives only three or four months.

BLACK-VEINED WHITE
This butterfly can be found up to 7,000 feet from May to July.

EUROPEAN ROBIN
A regular winter visitor, it does not nest in the coastal *pinèdes* which are too dry.

SARDINIAN WARBLER
A permanent resident, unmistakable due to its conspicuous red eye-ring. Its preferred habitat is in clearings and thinly wooded *pinèdes*.

Sardinian warbler

BLACKCAP
Large numbers migrate to Provence each autumn and many remain for the winter.

NIGHTINGALE
Arrives in April to fill the woodlands and thickets with its melodious song.

SHORT-TOED TREECREEPER. Present throughout the year. It often nests under the peeling bark of trees.

Kestrel

PINE CONES
The black rat gnaws through these cones to extract the kernel, its favorite food.

THE PINE PROCESSIONARY CATERPILLAR
These caterpillars cause major damage to the foliage when they roam in single file to feed, but they are rarely a serious threat to Aleppo pine forests. They are covered with long, thick hairs that can cause severe irritation to human skin.

This pine, characteristic of the Provençal coast, grows both in sandy and chalky soils. It prefers the latter where other Mediterranean pines cannot compete.

FOREST FIRES

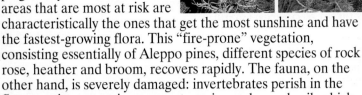

The dramatic topographical features of Provence provide natural wind tunnels which fan the flames.

Each year Provence is plagued by forest fires. The areas that are most at risk are characteristically the ones that get the most sunshine and have the fastest-growing flora. This "fire-prone" vegetation, consisting essentially of Aleppo pines, different species of rock rose, heather and broom, recovers rapidly. The fauna, on the other hand, is severely damaged: invertebrates perish in the flames, micro-organisms cannot survive on burned soil, which leads to the disappearance of birds which feed on insects, spiders, snails, worms and so on.

The *garrigue* can flare up suddenly during the dry season and the flames can be exacerbated by the mistral.

Female

Male

RED-LEGGED PARTRIDGE
Has become scarce due to the disappearance of hill farming. The spaces created by forest fires are suited to their needs until the vegetation recovers.

LINNET
Feeds on the seeds of grasses and likes degraded areas where it can build its nest.

WOODLARK
Thrives on stony plateaux and on barren hilltops.

WEASEL
Hunts the field rodents attracted by the grasses that grow in burnt spaces.

Not all animals are killed by the flames. Many species are suffocated by the gases given off by the fire, like this starling.

KESTREL
This bird of prey is common in the plains. In the hills it remains in sunny treeless open spaces where it finds plenty of its favorite prey of rodents, lizards and insects.

HOBBY
Relatively rare in Provence, where it inhabits river valleys and woods with scattered cork oaks and stone pines.

DWARF IRIS

The frequency of forest fires gives rise to a relatively unproductive and sparse vegetation, barely covering the rocks in these arid landscapes. Bulbs like the dwarf iris are well adapted for survival in bush fires and carpet the windswept hilltops.

39

OLIVE TREES

The olive tree, well suited to a hot, dry climate, is a typical feature of the Mediterranean countryside. It was brought to Provence nearly three thousand years ago by the Greeks who believed its cultivation marked the boundary between the civilized world and barbarity! The fruit, the olive, is harvested at the onset of the first frosts of winter. Green olives are picked in September, whereas some varieties may be picked as late as February, once they are fully ripe, either to be used as table olives or to make olive oil.

AGLANDAU
A high-quality oil olive (Alpes-de-Haute-Provence and Bouches-du-Rhône).

CAILLETIER OR NICE OLIVE. A richly flavored table olive that is preserved in brine and eaten black (Alpes-Maritimes).

GROSSANNE
A popular fleshy table olive. Both the green and the black are eaten (Bouches-du-Rhône).

TANCHE
An olive with an oily flesh, marinated in brine and salted (Vaucluse).

SALONENQUE
A table olive prepared as a green or crushed olive (Bouches-du-Rhône).

PICHOLINE
A table olive eaten green and in brine (Bouches-du-Rhône and Var).

OLIVE TREES produce fruit every other year from their fourth year. They grow to a height of 30 feet and can live several hundred years.

OLIVE GROVES. Olive trees grow on gentle south-facing slopes protected from the wind. They need deep, well-drained soil.

FROM OLIVE TO OIL

1. Olives are first washed in cold water before being crushed under a granite millstone into an oily paste which is then kneaded smooth and pressed.

FLOWERING
Leaves and new shoots appear in March. The trees flower from April to June.

HARVEST
While table olives are still picked by hand, the ripe black olives for the oil presses are now harvested mechanically. The harvesting season varies from September to February.

RIPENING
Only 5 percent of the flowers ripen into olives. The first olives appear in June; they generally ripen fully by October.

OLIVE OIL
Eleven to thirteen pounds of olives are needed to produce a quart of olive oil. "Virgin" olive oil is the pure unblended juice of the olive.

MILLSTONE

SCOURTINS

2. The smooth paste is spread in 4- to 10-lb layers onto *scourtins* – originally round rush mats, now made of nylon. These are then piled in stacks of twenty-five or thirty at a time to be pressed hydraulically.

A distinction is made between *extra virgin* olive oil (acidity < 1 percent), *fine* (acidity < 1½ percent) and *semi fine* (acidity < 3⅓ percent). Olive oil with a higher rate of acidity is called *pure*.

3. The liquid produced by the press is a mixture of oil and water. It is allowed to stand for these to separate. Centrifugal methods are now used in industrial production processes.

41

■ AROMATIC PLANTS

The highly competitive market in lavender essence has driven producers to seek outlets for the dried cut flowers.

The production of lavender and its *lavandin* hybrids, closely associated with the dry hills of Provence, was developed during the second half of the 19th century and reached its peak in the 1920's. Over 100 tons of pure lavender essence were produced in those days whereas in the 1980's the *lavandin* hybrids yielded more than 700 tons of essence. Ninety percent of the land used for aromatic plants is dedicated to lavender production while the rest provides thyme, rosemary, hyssop, sage or savory.

LAVENDER AND "LAVANDIN"
"True" lavender, *Lavandula angustifolia,* grows best at an altitude of 2,000 to 5,000 feet and, being wild, is difficult to cultivate. *Lavandin* hybrids of a lesser quality are easier to manage and grow at a lower altitude, between 1,500 and 2,000 feet.

FIELDS OF BLUE
The "true" and cloned lavender grown at present on 5,000 acres of the Albion plateau currently produces a little more than 20 tons of essence. The *lavandin* grown on about 3,500 acres yields annually over 100 tons.

HARVEST.
This takes place in the summer, under the hot sun, for heat brings the essence up the stem into the flower. Since the 1970's the harvesting process has been mechanized.

LAVENDER ESSENCE
It accumulates in the surface hairs that cover all the annual parts of the plant, especially the flowers.

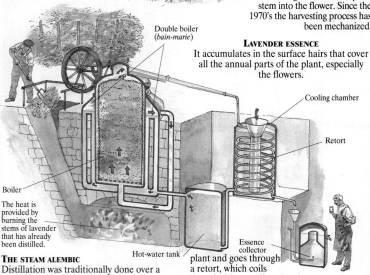

Double boiler (*bain-marie*)

Cooling chamber

Retort

Boiler

The heat is provided by burning the stems of lavender that has already been distilled.

Hot-water tank

Essence collector

THE STEAM ALEMBIC
Distillation was traditionally done over a naked flame, but since World War Two a steam alembic has been in use. Dry lavender is literally steamed in a double boiler. The water vapor draws the essential oils from the plant and goes through a retort, which coils down inside a cooling chamber. Condensation produces a mixture of essential oil and water, which slowly decants into the essence collector.

HERBES DE PROVENCE
Most Provençal herbs are picked from wild plants in the *garrigue*.

HYSSOP (HYSOPE).
Has a bitter, slightly minty flavor. Used in many liqueurs.

COMMON SAGE (SAUGE).
Used in foods, liqueurs, perfumes, and pharmaceutical products.

CLARY (SAUGE SCLARÉE). Properties similar to common sage. Grows in bare and waste spaces.

SAVORY (SARRIETTE).
Properties similar to thyme. The perfect herb for goat cheeses.

OREGANO (ORIGAN). A great appetizer, slightly bitter (medicinal for digestion and in compresses for colds).

FENNEL (FENOUIL).
Grows wild in Provence. Eaten as a vegetable, and essential oils used in aromatherapy.

TARRAGON (ESTRAGON)
Used to flavor soups, sauces, vinegar, and the Bordeaux types of mustard.

BAY (LAURIER). Only the leaves are used in cooking (the flowers have diuretic and digestive properties).

Common lavender   Cut-leaved lavender   French lavender

LAVENDER (LAVANDE)
The dried flowers are sold for culinary uses and herbal cures (good for the intestine), and for their essential oils in the perfume, pharmaceutical and soap industries.

THYME (THYM). A cooking herb, also a disinfectant and a deodorant. As a tea it is a tonic and aids digestion.

ROSEMARY (ROMARIN).
Used for its therapeutic effects on the digestion and as a flavoring, particularly with game.

43

■ EXOTIC PLANTS

VAL RAHMEH
The Menton botanical
garden, established in 1925.

During the 19th century, new botanical discoveries and the fashion for traveling to distant lands triggered a passion for exotic plants. The mild climate, abundant water supplies and sunshine provided perfect conditions for the acclimatization of dozens of tropical species on the Côte d'Azur, in Nice, Antibes and Monaco. Botanical gardens were founded and sea front promenades were planted with palm trees; under the influence of the English, who were frequent visitors to these parts of the Mediterranean, rock gardens and terraces blossomed with lush vegetation.

Over a dozen varieties of palm tree are found in Provence. Most of them, like the sabal palm and the desert fern palm, come from warm parts of the U.S., such as California.

Native to the Canary Islands, the canary palm is the most widespread on the coast, as seen here on the Promenade des Anglais in Nice.

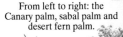

From left to right: the Canary palm, sabal palm and desert fern palm.

BANANA TREE
Ethiopia. Its fruit ripens only in Menton and St-Jean-Cap-Ferrat.

AGAVE. Mexico. A succulent plant without a stalk that flowers once and then dies. Its rigid and spiny leaves grow in a rose pattern.

EUCALYPTUS
Australia. Its hard wood is used for building and cabinet-making. It is also used in pharmaceuticals.

EURYOPS. Southern Africa. A hardy perennial that flowers in winter and spring.

AGATHEA OR BLUE MARGUERITE. The Cape. A perennial of the daisy family.

BARBARY FIG
Mexico. A cactus that flowers in June and July. Has edible fruit.

BOUGAINVILLEA
America. Its "flowers" are in fact modified leaves.

History and language

Early Iron Age axe heads.

PREHISTORY

*40,000 BC
Neanderthal man.*

The *cheval pansu*
(paunchy horse),
Cosquer cave in
Cassis.

*13,000 BC
Lascaux
wall paintings.*

Early Iron Age
clasps.

AROUND 950,000 BC. Traces of permanent hearths dating
from the early paleolithic period in the caves of Vallonet
(Roquebrune, Alpes-Maritimes) and of l'Escale (St-Estève-
Janson, Bouches-du-Rhône) are some of the world's earliest
evidence of man's mastery of fire. All remains dating from the
mid paleolithic times are characterized by pronounced
erosion due to geological phenomena. A number of cave
decorations have thus disappeared. However, the Cosquer

cave, discovered in 1991,
revealed some wall paintings
which can be dated to 2000 BC.
Men hunted horses and
reindeer, except in southern
Provence, where they hunted
bouquetin (wild goat) instead.
Several geological deposits,
such as the ones at Fontbrégoua (Salernes, Var), dating from
the beginning of the neolithic period, reveal major mutations
in the biological species: men began to raise domestic animals
(sheep) and to cultivate the land. With the beginnings of
sedentary life, pottery with "cardial" decorations appeared.
The edge of a seashell, the cardium, was used to produce
these effects. At the end of neolithic times, the cult of the
dead gave rise to the construction of numerous dolmens with
corridors. From the Iron Age (6th–5th century BC) vast
enclosures surrounded the hill dwellings.

900–600 BC. The Ligurians inhabited the region; the arrival of
the Celts in the 8th century gave rise to the term "Celtic-
Ligurian civilization" with reference to the local population.
These were probably the builders of the various megalithic
monuments that exist in Provence, together with the mural
paintings of Mont Bégo and the Vallée des Merveilles.

ANTIQUITY

*Circa 500 BC
The Vix treasure.*

Greek coin,
Marseilles, 2nd
century BC.

Two-headed marble
Herm, 1st century AD.

600 BC. Greeks from Phocaea landed in Lacydon and
founded Massilia (Marseilles). The new
colony spread rapidly: its trade ranged
over the coasts of Provence and
Languedoc, followed the trade route
determined by the Rhône and the Saône
and flourished throughout the eastern
Mediterranean. Other colonies were
founded including Théliné (Arles), Olbia
(Hyères), Antipolis (Antibes), and Nikaïa
(Nice). As a result, the local populations
introduced new crops, planted vines and
olive trees, learned new ways of building
and developed original art forms.

1ST CENTURY BC. The Romans penetrated the Provence
region and settled there. Marseilles had already established
diplomatic relations with Rome, when it appealed for inter-
vention against the threat posed by the Ligurian Celts. During
the conflict between Caesar and Pompey, Marseilles tried to
remain neutral but finally chose Pompey. This led to its being

besieged and conquered by Caesar, losing its independence in 49 BC. The building of Augustus' Trophy at La Turbie in 6 BC marked the end of the pacification of the Alpes-Maritimes.

View of La Turbie by Albanis Baumont.

THE 3RD CENTURY. Christianity spread in Provence. The first monasteries were founded by Saint Honorat on the Île de Lérins and by Jean Cassien in Marseilles at the beginning of the 5th century. Many works of art of that period survive (the baptisteries of Riez and Fréjus and the sarcophagus of Arles) to provide evidence of the rapid Christianization of the area. Constantine's conversion gave privileges to the Church and made Christianity an official religion.

50 BC
The end of the Gallic wars.

496
The baptism of Clovis.

800
Charlemagne is crowned emperor.

THE DARK AGES. At the end of a long period of anarchy the disintegration of the ancient world culminated in the fall of the Roman Empire in 476 AD. The whole of Provence fell under the domination of the Barbarians: Visigoths, Burgonds, Ostrogoths and, in 536, the Franks. From 732 to 739 Charles Martel pacified the area which had been plagued by Moorish raids. In the 9th century Provence became an independent principality under the distant sovereignty of the emperor. The Saracens invaded the Maures coast and from there went on to launch attacks into the Alps. In 974, William the Liberator, Count of Arles, expelled them and extended his authority over Provence, which became a single *comté* (county).

THE MIDDLE AGES

THE COUNTS OF CATALUÑA AND ANJOU. Throughout the 11th century, the authority of William's descendants was challenged by about twenty other families. The end of the male line of the house of Arles was to benefit the counts of Barcelona: in 1112, Raymond Bérenger III became Count of Provence. Throughout the 1300's the counts of Toulouse, who already controlled part of the area as marquesses of Provence, tried to establish rights over the whole county. Alphonse I (1166–91) strengthened the power of this dynasty and made Aix his capital. Freeing himself from the threat from Toulouse by force, Raymond Bérenger V (1209–45) was faced by the communes' desire for emancipation (Arles, Avignon, Marseilles, Nice, Grasse). In 1215 Nice pledged allegiance to the Genoese and in 1229, Raymond II of Toulouse yielded the Comtat Venaissin to the pope. In 1246 Charles of Anjou, brother of Saint Louis and Raymond Bérenger V's son-in-law, started a new dynasty; by becoming King of Naples in 1263, he united the County of Provence to the Kingdom of Naples for over a century.

Saint Honorat, 16th-century polychrome wood statue.

1054
The Schism of the East.

1096–9
The first crusade.

Seal of Raymond VII of Toulouse.

Map of the valley of Barcelonnette
in 1603.

Pope Innocent VI.

1248
*Saint Louis sets sail
for the 7th crusade
from Aigues-Mortes.*

1380
Death of Charles V.

1415
Agincourt.

1431
Death of Joan of Arc.

1453
Fall of Constantinople.

1477
*Death of Charles the
Bold.*

THE POPES IN AVIGNON. From 1309 to 1376, seven French popes ruled from Avignon, a situation that was to last until 1403, under the authority of the two schismatic popes. If the sovereign pontiffs fled Rome because of the anarchy that reigned in the city, their choice of Avignon was motivated by its proximity to the Comtat Venaissin which had been a papal possession since 1274, and by the fact that the Count of Provence, the absolute master of the city since 1290, was also, as King of Naples, a faithful vassal of the Holy See. It was only under Benedict XII, the third French pope, that Avignon became a regular residence and that the building began on the Palace of the Popes, later enlarged by Clement VI. The latter bought the city of Avignon from Queen Joan, Countess of Provence, and thus also became its temporal ruler (1348). In 1367, Urban V tried to take the Curia back to the banks of the Tiber and set off for Rome, but he was unable to stay there because of the continuing disturbances. His dream was made to come true by Gregory XI, whose death in Rome in 1378 brought the series of French popes to a close. Contesting the election of Urban VI, who was a Neapolitan, a faction of the cardinals elected Robert of Geneva, who took the name Clement VII and returned to the Palace of the Popes, while Urban VI remained at the See in Rome. This was the beginning of the great Schism of the West that was to divide Christianity into two obediences. His successor Benedict XIII, who no longer had the support of the King of France, fled to Aragon in 1403; the popes never returned to Avignon.

*Hell
15th-century fresco
by Jean Canavesio.*

King René.

1388, THE FORFEIT OF NICE. The end of the 14th century was a time of misfortunes for Provence: black death, bad harvests, famine, population crisis, plundering by the armed bands of Raymond de Turenne. After Joan I adopted Louis of Anjou in 1380, a group of Provençaux called the Union of Aix supported the rights of Charles de Duras against him. Following the victory of the house of Anjou, Nice and its *viguerie*, Puget-Théniers and the vale of Lantosque surrendered to the Count of Savoy. Henceforth Provence was cut in two. There was a depopulation problem both in Savoy's "Terres neuves de Provence" and in the County of Provence. Local lords negotiated agreements with immigrants so as to rebuild abandoned villages such as Biot (1470) or Pontevès (1477). Such *actes d'habitation* (acts of settlement) continued throughout the first half of the 16th century.

GOOD KING RENÉ.
King René (1434–80), who until then had spent little time in Provence, came to live there in 1471, sharing his time between Aix, Gardanne and Marseilles. The peace he restored brought slow economic recovery to the area. René's nephew and successor Charles III died in 1481, leaving his county to Louis XI. Provence thus became French.

Francis I's interview with Clement VII.

MODERN TIMES

THE SOMBER 16TH CENTURY. Provence, being united with but not attached to France by law, retained its original privileges until 1789 (liberties and exemptions). However, the kings of France gradually brought the Provence institutions into line with those of the kingdom by setting up the great French administrative bodies (the Aix Parliament was created in 1501–3). In 1539, the Villers-Cotterêts statute imposed the use of the French language in all official acts in Provence. From 1524 to 1544 the war between Francis I and Charles V, who was supported by Savoy, had a major impact on these regions. In 1543, the Turkish fleet joined the French king's forces in the siege of Nice. The 1545 massacres of the Vaudois in the Lubéron marked the start of the Wars of Religion that, together with frequent outbreaks of the plague, recurred throughout the last forty years of the century. These events did not prevent a certain degree of population, economic and even artistic growth.

The Edict of Nantes.

THE ANCIEN RÉGIME. The Grand Siècle began in Provence with a conflict between factions in what was called the Provence Fronde (rebellion), which, though separate from the troubles in the rest of France, constituted an uprising that sprang from the rebellion of parliamentarians. Nice became the provincial capital in 1614. Duke Charles-Emmanuel I established a senate in the city to serve both as a court of appeal and a government council; 16th-century Nice contrasts with the incessant unrest in Provence. In 1622 Louis XIII visited Arles, Aix and Marseilles; Louis XIV ceremonially

1515
Marignan.

1517
The Lutheran reformation.

1572
The St-Bartholomew massacres.

1661–1715
The personal reign of Louis XIV.

1701–14
Wars of succession in Spain.

Monseigneur de Belsunce's devoted efforts during the plague in Marseilles, 1720.

49

entered Marseilles in 1660 after it was subdued. The wars between France and Savoy flared up again: the French occupied Nice and its county from 1707 to 1713. With the Treaty of Utrecht, the valley of Barcelonnette became part of Provence while the principality of Orange belonging to the Nassau was gained by France. The 18th century began with the "great winter" of 1709 and the plague of 1720 which started in Marseilles. Industrial production made rapid progress with the appearance of tanneries, soap, paper and textile factories. As for agriculture, the terraces of Forcalquier and the plateau of Valensole became the wheat granaries of Provence. Sheep, horse and mule breeding contributed to the prosperity of the markets of Sisteron, Digne and Seyne.

REVOLUTION AND EMPIRE. In 1787, the meeting of the Provence states in Aix marked the start of pre-revolutionary times. In 1790 Provence was divided into three *départements* (Bouches-du-Rhône, Var and Basses-Alpes); a year later the Comtat Venaissin, annexed to France, became the Vaucluse. Since 1789, Nice, which had become a refuge for emigrating nobility, served as a center for counter-revolutionary propaganda. The Armée du Midi, formed in 1792, recaptured the town; on January 31, 1793 the Convention decreed that this county was French territory, creating the *département* of the Alpes-Maritimes. The revolt of the federalists against Jacobin violence reached the Var in the summer of 1793; in August Toulon opened its harbor to the British fleet. The Bonaparte dictatorship and the reign of Napoleon gave the people of Provence the impression that revolutionary times were over. On April 23, 1814, the County of Nice was given back to Victor-Emmanuel I, King of Sardinia. Paradoxically, the Provence élite were to rally just as enthusiastically to the restored monarchy as they had done to the Empire.

19TH AND 20TH CENTURIES

View of the inside of the Toulon arsenal.

THE 19TH CENTURY. The first half of the century was characterized by amazing economic changes. Transportation improved: about ten suspension bridges were erected to span the Rhône and the Durance between 1813 and 1846; the 1840's marked the beginning of steamer traffic on the Rhône, ports were built and the development of

Soup tureen and bottle cooler, Moustiers earthenware of the second half of the 18th century.

the Camargue began. Industry was modernized and town planning developed: new avenues were built, gas lighting introduced and ramparts demolished. Nice, like Cannes, reaped the benefits of winter tourism as early as 1820. Under the July Monarchy, the Toulon arsenal became the birthplace of the new labor movement. The Var and the Alpes-de-Haute-Provence resisted the coup d'État of Louis Napoleon in 1851. The Second Empire brought Nice back to France in 1860; together with the Grasse *arrondissement*, this formed the new *département* of the Alpes-Maritimes. The Third Republic began during a time of great economic change in Provence: the decline of the population in the southern Alps, the prospering of market gardening in the lower reaches of the Rhône Valley, the creation of specialized agricultural production zones (flowers, perfume plants and wine production) and the spread of tourism.

THE 20TH CENTURY. The beginning of this century was marked by the bloodshed of World War One and rural-urban migration. With the institution of paid holidays in 1936 tourism became more democratic and widespread. This

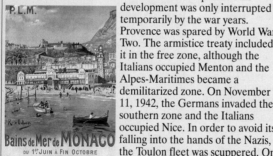

Bains de Mer de MONACO
DU 1er JUIN À FIN OCTOBRE
PLAGE DE SABLE FIN – Etablissement hydrothérapique de premier ordre
relief à la GENDARME à proximité du CASINO DE MONTE-CARLO sur route menant toute l'Année

development was only interrupted temporarily by the war years. Provence was spared by World War Two. The armistice treaty included it in the free zone, although the Italians occupied Menton and the Alpes-Maritimes became a demilitarized zone. On November 11, 1942, the Germans invaded the southern zone and the Italians occupied Nice. In order to avoid its falling into the hands of the Nazis, the Toulon fleet was scuppered. On August 15, 1944 the Allies landed in

several places along the coast. While the hinterland was liberated in one fell swoop, fighting continued in Toulon and Marseilles. Between August 23 and 28 General de Montsabert's troops liberated Marseilles from German occupation. The areas of Tende and La Brigue, which had remained Italian, were returned to France in 1947. In 1956 the state decided to create the region of Provence-Corse-Côte d'Azur. On January 1, 1970 Corsica was detached from it to form a region on its own. The first regional council meeting of the new Provence-Alpes-Côte d'Azur (PACA) region was held on January 8, 1974. This reorganization did nothing to prevent the economic collapse of the coastal area between Toulon and Marseilles, which underwent a process of de-industrialization with the dashed hopes of the Fos complex and the slow death of construction and repair activity in the shipyards. While some industries were declining (the bauxite crisis), a center for high technology developed in the Nice area (Sophia-Antipolis). Mass tourism transformed the countryside and the arrival of the high-speed "TGV" train in Marseilles accelerated this process.

1824
Charles X succeeds Louis XVIII.

Voting ballot for Nice to be reunited with France.

September 4, 1870
Fall of the Second Empire.

1922
The Fascists march on Rome.

1933
Hitler becomes Chancellor of the Reich.

1957
The Treaty of Rome.

IL VEILLE...

SOUSCRIVEZ

National subscription poster.

1958
Birth of the Fifth Republic.

1979
The European Assembly is elected by universal suffrage.

Fos-sur-Mer.

51

THE PLAGUE

On May 25, 1720 the *Grand-Saint-Antoine*, which had left Marseilles for Smyrna on July 22, 1719, returned to port laden with cottons and silks it had taken on board in Syria. On the return trip four sailors and the ship's doctor died of a virulent disease before the ship moored in Livorno.

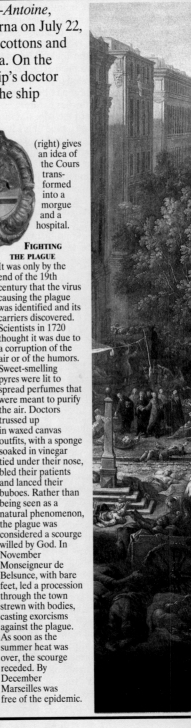

THE ORIGINS OF THE SCOURGE

Since the plague was endemic in the East, all Mediterranean ports, including Marseilles, introduced a protection system designed to control the sanitary conditions on ships. It established the length of quarantine periods for incoming vessels and the fate of the cargo. The crew of the *Grand-Saint-Antoine*, were diagnosed as having "pestiferous fevers". Such a diagnosis should have forced the cargo to be disinfected in the Île de Jarre, but the fragile silks would have deteriorated. By the end of June the toll of suspicious deaths among the stevedores handling the cargo had increased dramatically. On June 20 a woman died in just a few hours. There was a blackish sore on her lip. There were more sudden deaths: this time the bodies had the characteristic swollen glands or "buboes". There was no longer any doubt.

THE HORROR

Fear set in. On July 31 the Aix parliament issued a decree forbidding the Marseillais from leaving the town and the inhabitants of the rest of Provence from having any contact with them. By August there were as many as a thousand deaths a day. There were not enough churches and cemeteries to bury all the dead. Bodies were, at best, placed in common graves after being covered in quicklime or, at worst, left lying on the ground all over the city. The painting by Michel Serre (right) gives an idea of the Cours transformed into a morgue and a hospital.

FIGHTING THE PLAGUE

It was only by the end of the 19th century that the virus causing the plague was identified and its carriers discovered. Scientists in 1720 thought it was due to a corruption of the air or of the humors. Sweet-smelling pyres were lit to spread perfumes that were meant to purify the air. Doctors trussed up in waxed canvas outfits, with a sponge soaked in vinegar tied under their nose, bled their patients and lanced their buboes. Rather than being seen as a natural phenomenon, the plague was considered a scourge willed by God. In November Monseigneur de Belsunce, with bare feet, led a procession through the town strewn with bodies, casting exorcisms against the plague. As soon as the summer heat was over, the scourge receded. By December Marseilles was free of the epidemic.

Tongs for moving cadavers.   Mail tongs.

THE VAUDOIS OF THE LUBÉRON

A 14th-century Vaudois Bible written in Romanic Provençal.

Around 1170 a rich merchant from Lyons by the name of Valdès, also known as Pierre Valdo, decided to forsake all for a life of poverty in accordance with the Gospel. Although he did not directly oppose the Church, his teachings were soon banned. Fleeing the persecutions that had begun in 1230, his followers dispersed to the remote valleys of the Lubéron. After Luther's break with Rome, contact was established between supporters of the Reformation and the Vaudois. At the Chanforan synod in 1532, the Vaudois pledged allegiance to the Reformation.

THE PARABLE OF THE RICH YOUNG MAN
Valdès, taking this parable to heart, sold all his belongings, choosing to live in poverty and preach conversion. He gathered disciples around him who also began to preach the Gospel. But their sermons were soon outlawed by the archbishop of Lyons. The first criminal conviction in 1184 led to the breakdown of relations between the poor of Lyons and the Church. Fleeing from unjust and cruel treatment, the Vaudois went into hiding in the Lubéron.

BIBLICAL FUNDAMENTALISM
As well as refusing to take any vows, they rejected all practises and devotions that were not mentioned in the Gospels, from the cult of saints to the belief in Purgatory. They also rejected the celebration of Mass and the practise of confession. Preachers came sporadically to revive the faith of their brothers living this clandestine existence. This hierarchy of lay apostles meant the Vaudois had much in common with the Cathars and prepared the way for Protestantism.

The temple of Lourmarin (right).

THE SIEGE OF MÉNERBES
This important Vaudois fortress was beseiged by Henry of Angoulême's army for five years, from 1573 to 1578.

JEAN DE MAYNIER
(1495–1558). Baron of Oppède,
notorious for his actions
against the Vaudois, whom
he exterminated.

RELIGIOUS WARS AND PERSECUTIONS

By 1531 the Reformation and the religious wars that inflamed the kingdom of France had started to attract the attention of the authorities to the Vaudois of the Lubéron. Nearly four hundred people were accused of heresy between 1532 and 1539. In April 1546 the parliament of Aix passed a law against the inhabitants of Mérindol, who "were forming Vaudois and Lutheran sects", as well as against those of La Roque-d'Anthéon, of Villelaure and of other neighboring villages. This law condemned them all, by default, to being burned at the stake.

THE CRUSADE AGAINST THE VAUDOIS

The offensive was launched against a number of villages where as many as three thousand Vaudois were living. Against these people Jean de Maynier, the first President of the parliament of Provence (from 1543), raised an army of five thousand men. On April 16 the Baron de La Garde, known as Captain Polin, occupied La Motte, Cabrières and the valley of Aygues while Maynier of Oppède entered Villelaure and Lourmarin. On April 18 it was Mérindol's turn to be razed to the ground. About ten villages were destroyed, over two thousand people were massacred and more than six hundred taken as galley slaves.

SIEGE DE MENERB

THE LANDING OF AUGUST 15, 1944

The decision was taken in December 1943: operation Overlord, the Normandy landing, was to be accompanied by another operation code-named Anvil. It was to be launched on the Mediterranean coast of France so as to immobilize the German troops stationed in the south of the country. The Allied chiefs of staff, who wanted to capture the port of Marseilles, opted for a landing on the beaches of the Maures and the Esterel. However, due to an insufficient number of landing craft, it was not possible to launch the two operations simultaneously. Dragoon, which became Anvil's new code name, was only launched two months after D-Day.

THE SIZE OF THE OPERATION
On August 4 Allied air forces began to bombard Provence. On August 14, 1,200 ships regrouped off Corsica. They carried the American Seventh Army, under General Patch, and the French First Army under General de Lattre de Tassigny.

THE FIRST BRIDGEHEADS
On August 15, at around one in the morning, the first French commandos launched their attack on the cliffs of the Cap Nègre. The German gun batteries, overlooking the beach of Rayol, were neutralized.

THE ALLIED FLEET OFF THE BEACHES OF PROVENCE

By 8am the first assault barges laden with troops, weapons, ammunition and tanks landed on the beaches of Cavalaire, Pampelonne, the St-Tropez peninsula, La Nartelle and further East, near St-Aygulf, the Val-d'Esquières and Les Issambres.

A SPEEDY LIBERATION

After blowing up the St-Tropez harbor installations, shown above with the *Montcalm* in the foreground, almost all the Germans had left, except those occupying the citadel, who were to surrender in the afternoon. Sainte-Maxime fell quickly. Cogolin, Grimaud and La Môle were liberated around 3pm.

SURRENDER AND EVACUATION OF THE TROOPS

August 17 was doubly decisive. General Neuling surrendered at Draguignan and at the same time Hitler ordered his troops to leave the South of France.

THE RIVIERA AND THE CÔTE D'AZUR

The Riviera was made fashionable by English aristocrats who first began appreciating the mild Nice winters around 1750. But it was not until the opening of the Paris-Nice railway line and the coast road, built around 1862–4, that the main resorts appeared. The arrival of American artists and writers in the early 1930's turned these into summer as well as winter resorts, bathing in the sea became popular, and with the introduction of paid holidays, mass tourism developed.

THE PIONEERS
The Duke of Gloucester, the Duchess of Cumberland and the Duke of York established Nice as a winter resort. During the winters of 1784–85 three hundred British subjects were resident in the town, hoping to cure their neurasthenia or respiratory ailments.

COSMOPOLITAN WINTER VISITORS
The tourist activities interrupted by the French Revolution resumed in 1815. Britons, Germans, Italians and Russians would stay in Nice and Cannes from November to May. Most of them would arrive in horse-drawn carriages: the journey from Marseilles to Nice took twenty-four hours. The arrival of the railway in Nice in 1864 and in Menton in 1869 marked the beginning of a new era. The number of winter visitors rose rapidly from 22,000 in 1887 to 150,000 by 1914. Royalty, the well-to-do, business people, famous artists and demi-mondaines all frequented the area, preferring to stay in luxurious palace hotels rather than in villas.

The florid descriptions in Stephen Liégeard's *La Côte d'Azur*, published in 1887, were such a success that the book's title became the accepted term for the area.

VILLEFRANCHE s/MER
PORT DE TOURISME

Taking advantage of prohibition in France, Germany and Italy, Monaco built itself a gambling empire: its first casino opened in 1863 and retained its monopoly on roulette until 1933. The year 1909 saw the inauguration of winter sports in the Nice area: Thorenc, Peïra-Cava, Beuil and Valberg, with the help of the Touring Club de France and the Club Alpin, organized skiing and luge races throughout that winter.

THE GOLDEN AGE
During the late 19th century a number of exclusive resorts developed: Menton, Cap-Martin, Cap-d'Ail, Cap d'Antibes, Beaulieu, Juan-les-Pins, and St-Jean-Cap-Ferrat.

THE CÔTE IN SUMMER
Under the influence of mostly American artists, a new generation discovered the charms of summer in Provence and sea bathing. In 1931 hotels stayed open in the summer for the first time. Chanel launched the "beach pyjama" fashion. With the introduction of paid holidays, workers and the middle classes discovered the Côte d'Azur and mass tourism was born.

Until the end of the 19th century tram and railway companies provided access to the hinterland.

● LANGUAGE

D 6

TRETS

TRÈS
EN PROUVÈNÇO

"INSIDE A CLASSROOM", by François Marius Granet (1775–1849). The spread of compulsory education tended to reinforce linguistic uniformity. The education of girls developed between 1870 and 1880 and had a disastrous effect on the transmitting of Provençal as a mother tongue.

The Provence-Alpes-Côte d'Azur region is characterized by a complex linguistic background and an amazing multiplicity of local languages. The area can be roughly divided into four major language zones: the northern *gavot* or "alpine" Provençal zone, which is part of a large complex that includes the Alpes-de-Haute-Provence, the Hautes-Alpes and the alpine valleys of the Italian Piedmont where Provençal is spoken; to the west a type of language known as *rhodanien* is widespread in the area that includes the Vaucluse, the south of the Ardèche and the Drôme, the eastern part of the Gard and the western half of the Bouches-du-Rhône; to the south, "maritime" or "Mediterranean" Provençal is spoken in the whole of the Var and in the eastern part of the Bouches-du-Rhône; finally, to the east, *Nissart* is spoken around Nice and in the hinterland. To put things more simply, there is an obvious distinction between the development of the County of Provence and that of the County of Nice; the political situation in each was often completely different and this had a major impact on written language.

LE COMTÉ DE PROVENCE

LATIN ORIGINS. Provençal is a Romance language deriving for the most part from vulgar Latin. Reaching Gaul with the Roman colonization, this form of Latin grafted itself onto the basic local languages and was later overlaid by Germanic elements introduced by the invasions that dislocated the Empire. This process was similar to the one which gave birth to the French language further north, with one fundamental difference in that the Latinization in Provence began earlier (2nd century BC), lasted longer and was then less affected by the Frankish influence.

ORAL LANGUAGE, WRITTEN LANGUAGE. Though it became the normal language for oral communication from the end of the Roman

> **"WE ARE NOT SINGING ABOUT THE PAST, AND WE ARE NOT DOING IT IN A DEAD LANGUAGE; OUR LANGUAGE IS ALIVE, IT IS SPOKEN BY A WHOLE PEOPLE, IT HAS ITS GLORY, ITS SCHOLARS, ITS POETS."**
>
> FRÉDÉRIC MISTRAL

Empire, written Provençal emerged only slowly and late (about 1100 AD). Latin, which had been restored by the Carolingian reforms, continued to have great prestige for a long time. And yet it was through its literature that Provençal really developed.

THE SUPREMACY OF FRENCH. It was in the written form, around 1500 AD, that French first began to supercede Latin and also Provençal, which had increasingly been used throughout the 15th century for texts of a local nature. The thrust was facilitated by the integration of Provence into the kingdom in 1481 and was formalized by the Villers-Cotterêts edict (1539), which decreed that official texts should be drafted *en langage maternel françoys et non autrement* (in French mother-tongue and not in any other way). Private writings were soon produced in French, only turning to Provençal for technical or colloquial expressions. In literature French underwent the beneficial influence of the *Pléiade* and later the classical authors of the 17th century, while apart from a few exceptions (Belaud de la Belaudière and Toussaint Gros, for example), Provençal authors from the 16th to the 18th century confined themselves to minor genres.

DECLINE AND SCORN. During the 18th century Provençal continued to decline and its oral usage lessened. To speak the language of the *Encyclopédie*, of the Enlightenment, of the élites became a status symbol so that Provençal became the language of the rural and lower classes and the object of scorn, against which Frédéric Mistral rebelled, seeing it as a portent of impending demise. The first years of the Revolution were beneficial to the *patois* (local dialects): the French Constitution was even translated into Provençal by the Aix *député* Charles François Bouche in 1792. But by 1793 policies turned Jacobinical and restored the supremacy of French. In the 19th century French rapidly penetrated the milieu of the lower classes as a result of population movement caused by wars, railways, the development of the press and education.

RENAISSANCE. In the face of such threats there was a reaction in the middle of the 19th century, which, to some extent, was part of the rise of European nationalism. The great figure of this renaissance was Frédéric Mistral, who was born and died in Maillane (1830–1914). Mistral gave Provençal a simple spelling system that was modern and could convey the nuances of popular speech. He demonstrated it through his writings and in his monumental dictionary, *Lou Tresor dou felibrige*, which he had published in Aix in 1878. In 1855, with his friend Joseph Roumanille (1818–91), an Avignon bookseller, Mistral started a yearly almanack, the *Armana*

TODAY
The efforts of the regionalist movement are mainly focused on education. In 1946, Camille Dourguin and Charles Mauron created the *Lou Provençau* teaching association; more and more candidates started taking the Provençal baccalauréat papers. Stories, poems and novels bear witness to the vitality of the

Provençal language, as exemplified by Joseph d'Arbaud, Max-Philippe Dalavouët, André Degioanni and Pierre Millet.

FRANÇOIS RAYNOUARD (1761–1836)
This lawyer, later to become a *député*, was above all a linguist and writer. He published a *Choix de poésies des troubadours* in six volumes (1816–26). The 13th century was the golden age of the troubadours: Blacas, the lord of Aups, Raimbaut d'Orange, Raimond de Beaujeu and Albertet de Sisteron were among those with the highest reputations.

"Nissart"

Far from being a dialect with Italian roots, *Nissart*, while retaining its own characteristics, is a very Provençal idiom: Frédéric Mistral saw this "Provençality" as one of the causes for Nice's reunification with France in 1860.

Frédéric Mistral

The aim of his work was "firstly to renew and revive this feeling of race that I could see being annihilated under the pressure of the false and unnatural education given in all the schools; secondly to bring about this resurrection by the restoration of the natural and historic language of the land, which the schools are fighting to the death; thirdly to bring Provençal back into fashion by the flow and the flame of divine poetry."

prouvençau: entirely in Provençal and still in print in 1994, it gave rise to a series of periodicals that were to have a lasting impact, especially *L'Aiòli* (from 1891 to 1899) and *Li Nouvello de Provènço*, a bi-monthly magazine which was started in 1989.

Le Comté de Nice

Before it was reunited with France. Because the County of Nice came under the authority of the counts of Savoy the local idiom was protected and retained in hand-written and printed texts. Until the second half of the 16th century one wrote and published in Latin, but also in *Nissart*. In 1562, twenty-three years after Francis I imposed French as the language to be used in the official acts of his kingdom, his son-in-law, Emmanuel-Philibert of Savoy, adopted a similar approach and imposed Italian as the administrative language. However this Italianization took time to spread. The Revolution and the growth of the Empire, with the arrival of emigrants in Nice and the first reunification of the county to France, only promoted the use of French to a limited extent. *Nissart* was alive and doing well, as shown in the *Grammatica nissarda* by Fr. Joseph Niceu; it acquired a new lease of life when the area was again removed from French administrative control in 1814.

From 1860. Its reunification to France opened the way to systematic Gallicization. However, *Nissart* reaped the benefit of the Provençal renaissance movement with the development of a *Nissart* press and of popular dramas. Homage should also be paid to André Compan (born 1922) for his efforts to propagate the *Nissart* language and literature through his *Grammaire niçoise* (1965) and his anthologies of *Nissart* authors.

LIFE IN PROVENCE

THE GAME OF "BOULES"

The game of *boules*, with the sun, pastis and *dolce far niente* (pleasant idleness) has become one of the symbols of life in Provence. The development of clubs, cafés and *guinguettes* (pleasure gardens) contributed greatly to the game's popularity in the 19th century. While the traditional Provençal game of *longue* has now been ousted by the newer *pétanque*, both remain essentially a male preserve. With its challenges and code of honor, the game of *boules* takes place before a lively audience and occasions some priceless verbal exchanges.

BUTABAN AND ROULETTE
The balls used in *boules* were a common sight in the country and in town squares in the 18th century, as the games of *butaban* and *roulette* developed from *quilles* (skittles) and *mail* (pinball).

THE TRADITIONAL GAME. The Provençal game *longue* is played on a stretch of flat ground (50 to 70 feet long). The player takes a run of one stride if he is trying to place his *boule* with his throw, and three if he is aiming to displace another player's *boule*.

A REAL CRAZE
During the First Empire (1804–15), the game reached every corner of Provençal towns. Deemed to be dangerous, after many bystanders complained of being injured on the ankles or the head by heavy boxwood *boules* covered in nails, it was banned on public pathways and confined to *guinguettes*, private gardens and *bastides*.

"PÉTANQUE". This new game is said to have been invented one day in June, 1910 in La Ciotat, when a player, unable to take the three steps, decided to stand with his feet together for the throw.

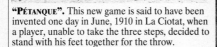

Pétanque is a game for two players or two teams. Each participant has three *boules*. The aim of the game is to get as close as possible to the *cochonnet*, a small wooden target ball that is thrown out 20 to 30 feet at the beginning of each leg of the game. A game is played for a total of thirteen points. The eternal dilemma is whether to *pointer* (to place the boule) or to *tirer* so as to remove an opponent's *boule*. The ideal shot does both at once.

The first *boules* "societies" appeared in 1828. Before long local and even regional competitions were being organized, some of which were even sponsored by the press.

● FESTIVALS

THE FLOWERED "CORSOS"

Flower-covered *corsos* (chariots), successors of papier-mâché carnival floats, are to be seen from February (the mimosa season) to June (carnations). Processions are a feature of all festivals, which are also occasions for competitions. The Nice *corso* consists of twenty flowered chariots, eight hundred *grosses têtes*

In the past, the year was punctuated by a succession of religious festivals that came to a climax at the winter equinox (Christmas) and summer solstice (the feast of Saint John). Reflecting the rural calendar, these also include a series of pilgrimages and blessings of flocks, harvests and farms. Although the de-Christianization of the countryside has reduced the number of these events, Provence still has several genuine and colorful popular feast days. While some have been revived, others have come into being over the last few decades, particularly in the newly developed smaller towns.

THE CAMARGUE COURSE ("CORRIDA")

Course à la cocarde or *course libre* are Camargue entertainments, taking place at Arles and at the Saintes-Maries-de-la-Mer, that are very popular in Provence. The *raseteurs*, who have the task of removing the *cocarde* (tassels and strings) from the bull, are dressed all in white and approach the bull with a technique called the *raset*. Other events include the *abrivado* and the *ferrade*, which coincide with the feast days of the patron saints of Provençal villages.

JOUSTING ON THE WATER

These competitions, which date from the early 15th century, are contests between teams of six oarsmen and a bare-chested, bare-footed jouster. Perched on the end of a projecting platform (the *tintaine*), the jouster, with a lance in his right hand and a shield on his left arm, must dislodge his opponent. Jousting takes place around the national holidays of July 14 and August 15.

(carnival figures), fanfares and brass bands. Each year since 1873 carnival craftsmen have competed for three prizes awarded for chariots, *grosses têtes* and other single figures.

THE BRAVADES

The *bravade*, which was originally a procession in honor of the patron saint of a village or town, still remains a lively tradition in many Provençal communities. The saint is carried through the town accompanied by a guard of honor composed of hussars, musketeers, sailors, horsemen or *turcos*, depending on the place, armed with shotguns or muskets loaded with blanks. Numerous salvos punctuate these ceremonies.

THE CARNIVAL

A pagan feast day taken over by the Church which has added itself into the cycle announcing the Shrovetide of the Middle Ages. The carnival takes place forty days before Easter. Rituals which have been respected for centuries are represented by incredible characters taken from popular mythology, created here by generations of carnival craftsmen.

AÏOLI

This delicious meal is often served at family gatherings or on festive occasions among friends, especially in the summer outdoors (as above in 1930). Whole villages share this convivial meal, generally to mark the end of the feast day of the patron saint.

● CASINOS

**"LES JEUX SONT FAITS?
RIEN NE VA PLUS!"**

The word "casino", the diminutive of *casa* in Italian, has only been used in France since the 19th century.

According to laws of April 3, 1942 and December 23, 1959, "a casino is an establishment with three distinct activities: entertainment, the serving of food and gambling" and can only be opened in places classified as bathing, thermal or climatic resorts. Originally intended for the entertainment of people on health cures, casinos soon attracted tourists who were more interested in roulette wheels and card games than in the beneficial properties of the waters. Seeing trade and tourism prosper, the town councils concerned were favorable to the opening of new casinos. Depending on the season, France has about 134 active casinos in over fifty-one *départements.* The Alpes-Maritimes alone accounts for one-third of the gambling revenue (2.3 billion francs).

THE STAFF

While the term "croupier" is generally applied to all casino employees, there are in fact distinctions between different levels of employment: *chef de table* and *sous-chef de table*, *croupier*, *changeur*, *ravitailleur* and *valet de pied*. To ensure the most scrupulous regularity in the conduct of the proceedings all the staff must have police clearance . . . and wear clothes without pockets.

THE GAMES

The list of authorized games is established by decree. However, each establishment must hold a license, which determines the games it is legally allowed to practice. In 1907 casinos were allowed to have only two-board baccarat, *écarté* and *petits chevaux*, and *chemin de fer* was introduced a short time later. In 1921 the game of *petits chevaux* was replaced by *boule*, and in 1932 roulette was rehabilitated and *trente-et-quarante* was authorized. A decree of 1969 legalized several new games including *vingt-trois*, a variant of *boule*, American roulette, craps and black jack. Finally, in 1987, English roulette, *punto banco* and "one-armed bandits" were introduced.

THE PLAYERS

Lured by the chance of winning and the excitement of the game, the players (adults only) are admitted into gaming halls after purchasing a betting card.

In Provence, the Christmas season traditionally lasts forty days, until Candlemas. This extended period gave rise to the development of some very special ceremonies: the display in churches of complex decorated cribs, the origin of which dates back to the 17th century; the staging of plays known as *pastorales*; and a way of celebrating midnight mass that is unique to Provence. During the ceremony shepherds, fishermen or peasants bring offerings of lambs, fish or *pommes fleuries* as tokens of prosperity.

The *foires aux santons* (crib figure fairs) began in the First Empire.

THREE TYPES OF "SANTONS"
They represent the traditional figures of the Nativity, of the *pastorale* or of village life.

HOW "SANTONS" ARE MADE
The Provençal *santon*, based on the idea of J.-L. Lagnel (1764–1822), is made of fine Aubagne or Marseilles clay. For a simple *santon* the clay is pressed into a two-piece plaster mold; for an articulated *santon*, the individual limbs and accessories are molded separately and assembled. Before it is dried and fired the *santon* is carefully finished by hand, then painted.

CHRISTMAS IN PROVENCE

LE "GROS SOUPER"
This meatless but copious meal is eaten on Christmas Eve and usually consists of fish and vegetable dishes. It ends with numerous desserts and is a true family affair as even the children stay up for midnight mass. Provençal tradition dictates that there be thirteen desserts, a mystical reference to Christ and the Apostles. One of these is the *pompe*, an oil or butter bread that is eaten dipped in *vin cuit*, sweet fortified wine.

THE "PASTRAGE" AT MIDNIGHT MASS
The *pastrage* is the shepherds' offering of a new-born lamb in a highly ritualistic ceremony.

"LA COURONNE DES ROIS" (JANUARY 6–FEBRUARY 2). This brioche is covered with candied fruit and contains a broad bean and a clay figure.
A SCENE FROM THE "PASTORALE". These performances are derived from liturgical *pastorales* in which people from all social levels in a town acted out the Nativity. The first *pastorale* was produced by Antoine Maurel in 1842–4.

● Cults and religion

The furnishings and decorative elements of churches reflect the evolution of religious beliefs over the years and frequently illustrate the difference between official and popular religion. The function of stained-glass windows, frescos and painted altarpieces ordered by the parishes or lay confraternities was to educate the faithful by rendering the teachings of the Holy Scriptures or the Counter-Reformation images. Reliquaries, votive paintings and statues of saints, offered in thanksgiving or to ensure protection against epidemics or natural catastrophes, all express the beliefs and fears of a people who knew tribulation.

RELIGIOUS FEASTS
Pilgrimages and processions are among the most important expressions of popular devotion. In the afternoons of patron saints' feast days, on Good Friday evening, on Rogation Day (March 25) and during the three days that precede the feast of the Ascension, statues and relics are paraded on a platform in an ornate monstrance.

> "The White Penitents [are] referred to as such because they are clothed in long white robes that cover them completely and in which there are only two holes for the eyes"
> Mrs Cradock, 1785

The Penitents

They had devotional and charitable duties, particularly at funerals. After preparing the deceased they would bear the coffin in procession and take charge of the burial.

The Cult of Saints

Saints are regarded as intercessors who can work miracles. People would turn to them not to emulate them but to seek contact with their relics. These were placed in caskets, which often took the form of

Altars and Altarpieces

Prayers are said to the Virgin and other saints, asking for their intercession, because they are considered more accessible than God. People seek to be buried in their vicinity so as to receive indulgences or redemption from sin. There are three main objects of devotion: the Virgin of the Rosary, who replaced the Virgin of Mercy of the Middle Ages after the Counter-Reformation, the Blessed Sacrament and the Souls of the Purgatory.

Votive paintings

These small paintings on wood, canvas or paper, portraying miracles or people in the act of giving thanks, were fashionable from the 17th century to the beginning of the 20th. They express the gratitude of the faithful for protection granted in answer to their prayers when sickness, fires, epidemics or accidents strike.

statues, reliquaries in the shape of an arm or, more usually, busts. Apart from Saint Roch and Saint Sebastian, who were reputed to protect against the plague, the most frequently invoked saints are Saint Joseph and Saint Éloi.

● Faïence

CONTEMPORARY FAÏENCE
Jean Faucon, the descendant of six generations
of potters in Apt, expertly creates new patterns
and produces contemporary pieces using
traditional methods.

The tradition of pottery making in Marseilles dates from Greek times. By the 17th century production had become an industrial enterprise. Having learned the secret of white glazing, the Clérissy family of Moustiers established the first faïence factory in 1679. Polychrome decoration (1738) and *petit feu* or slow firing (around 1760) marked the height of this art, but revolutionary strife caused its decline. Today craftsmen are reviving old styles and adapting them for an international market.

FINE CASTELLET FAÏENCE
With its yellowish-orange glaze, this terrine is typical of 18th-century production. The figure on the lid is characteristic of the fashion of the times.

NEW STYLES
The decorative plate above is an example of the search for new shapes and patterns that marked the 19th century. The piece comes from the Bernard Delacroix factory in Apt and is made of polychrome earthenware. It is adorned with flowers and foliage in high relief.

"FLAMME"
During World War One two workshops managed to reopen in Apt. Léon Sagy and Joseph Bernard developed an innovative mixture of clays known as *"flamme"* (flame). They made reproductions of classical, Moroccan, and Art Deco pieces.

MARBLED EARTHENWARE
Its originality lies in its composition, which consists of different-colored clays fired at the same temperature. This technique is said to have been introduced in Apt by César Moulin's sons around 1775.

THE OLÉRYS-LAUGIER FACTORY AT MOUSTIERS

In 1738, Joseph Olérys, who came from a family of artists in Marseilles, brought back from Spain the technique of polychrome decoration. With his brother-in-law Jean-Baptiste Laugier, he established the second faïence factory in Moustiers.

"GRAND FEU" DECORATION

Between 1750 and 1780 fifteen factories opened up in Marseilles. One potter chose a style of decoration known as "*chinois-fleurs*". Its symmetrical radiating patterns reveal the influence of Rouen pottery. Faïence in the second half of the 18th century was characterized by the widespread use of blue and red decoration.

COPPER-GREEN GLAZE

Honoré Savy from Marseilles later developed a translucent copper-green glaze, as seen on the base of this wall-hung font.

GROTESQUES

Olérys launched the fashion for grotesques, using the caricatured figures by Jean Callot and imaginary animals that were very much in vogue.

"PETIT FEU" DECORATION

This firing technique, developed by the Ferrat brothers in Moustiers from around 1760, enabled potters to use new colors.

BÉRAIN STYLE

This reinterpretation of the grotesque style was a pleasing combination of arabesques, drapes, animals and mythological figures.

THE "ROCAILLE" STYLE

Decoration in blue or manganese monochrome on white or pearly gray was the specialty of Joseph Fauchier, a Marseilles potter.

A master of polychrome statuary and three-dimensional modeling technique, he produced numerous religious figures.

The *adola* is a popular dish throughout Provence. It is made in a *daubière*, a terracotta marmite with a pierced lid. This allows cold water to be added while it cooks, to condense the juices inside the pot and make the meat tender. However, it can also be made in a casserole or a pressure cooker.

INGREDIENTS. 2 pounds of prime beef cut into 3-ounce pieces, 4 ounces of bacon, three onions, two carrots, four whole cloves of garlic, two chopped tomatoes, one bouquet garni (thyme, bay and parsley), one strip of orange peel, salt, pepper and red wine.

1. The day before, marinate the meat in red wine with one onion cut into quarters, one clove of garlic, salt and pepper, thyme and bay leaves.

2. The next day place the *daubière* (or the pot) on the heat (in the *mas*, the Provençal farmhouse, the *potager*, a special cooking alcove in the fireplace, filled with embers, was used). Be sure to place a heat-diffusing mat underneath so as to avoid cracking the terracotta.

3. Add four tablespoons of olive oil, allow it to heat up, then throw in the diced bacon.

4. Chop the carrots and onions into fairly thick rings. Add the onions to the pot.

"The triumph of Provençal cooking is the daube, a carefully prepared piece of beef, flavored and perfumed with all the Provençal herbs, garlic cloves, thyme, *sariette* (savory), bay leaves, shallots, parsley, celery, tomatos and to which no skilled cook forgets to add the peel of an orange, slowly simmered for several hours on the *potager*." (Ferdinand Benoit)

5. When the onions are golden, add the tomatoes and the carrots.

6. Allow all these to sizzle and blend. This is known as the *fond*.

7. When the *fond* is nicely golden, add the pieces of meat and allow them to become well browned.

8. Add an ample glass of red wine and bring to the boil, then add two glasses of water, the garlic, the bouquet garni and the orange peel. Add salt and pepper.

9. Bring to the boil once again and then reduce the heat to very low. Cook slowly for five and a half hours.

Serve on warmed plates with noodles or potatos in their jackets.

● SPECIALTIES

St-Tropez sandals, designed around 1920.

Sault nougat, dark and slightly caramelized or white, creamy and soft.

Pissaladière, an onion tart with *pissala* (a sort of anchovy paste) and black olives.

Bandol A.O.C., Côtes de Provence and Châteauneuf-du-Pape are the prize products of the region's rich wine industry.

The finest olive oil comes from the valley of Les Baux. Marseilles' specialty is pastis, a liquor made from aniseed.

Banon *tomme* is the genuine goat *tomme*, wrapped and matured in vine leaves.

Chestnut purée is produced in the Maures.

Tapenade, a black olive paste seasoned with anchovies, is eaten on bread as an appetizer.

Camargue rice comes in two varieties: the round Cigalon rice and the long Delta variety.

Épeautre is a cereal used to make a unique soup.

Genuine Marseilles soap contains 72 percent fatty acids.

Berlingots have been the pride of Carpentras since 1851.

Crisp almond biscuits are sold in most Provençal *boulangeries*.

The *calisson* of Aix, made of marzipan.

In Nice carnations grown for the cut-flower trade are propagated from cuttings and cultivated in greenhouses.

ARCHITECTURE

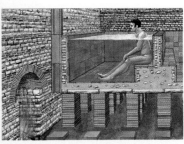

The great public buildings which reflect the social and urban mores introduced and spread by the power of Rome were, with only a few variations, built according to standard plans, using construction techniques the Romans introduced to the region in the 1st century AD: large blocks secured by metal crampons or smaller rubble bound with mortar and used as facing or infill in conjunction with brickwork.

THE HEATED HALLS OF THE BATHS OF CIMIEZ
▲ 291. The floor was built on a succession of small brick pillars holding up large terracotta flags over which concrete was poured. Terracotta tubing set in the walls of the chamber served as chimney flues.

THE TRIUMPHAL ARCH OF GLANUM ▲ 153
One of the main gates of this town. With its sculpted decorations and its shape, it is a classic Roman victory monument.

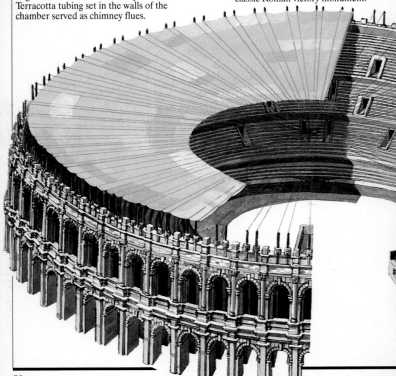

1. Entrance and shops
2. Atrium
3. Tablinium
4. Interior gardens
5. Triclinium (dining room), private baths and living rooms
6. Upper floor, bedrooms

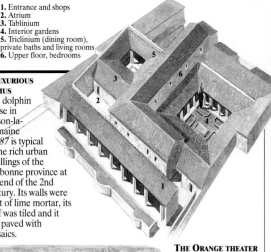

AQUEDUCTS

There was such a demand for water in Roman towns, with their public baths, fountains and drainage systems as standard features, that the first thing the Romans built were gigantic aqueducts. The Fréjus aqueduct, built in the 1st century AD, is over 25 miles long ▲ *252*.

A LUXURIOUS DOMUS

The dolphin house in Vaison-la-Romaine ▲ *187* is typical of the rich urban dwellings of the Narbonne province at the end of the 2nd century. Its walls were built of lime mortar, its roof was tiled and it was paved with mosaics.

THE ORANGE THEATER ▲ *181*

This almost perfect example of the huge Roman entertainment buildings demonstrates the level of social organization (distribution of places according to social rank, sponsorship of performances by local gentry and officials) and the technical excellence of the architecture (gangways for the audience and actors, covered stage and seating, ingenious stage machinery).

THE ARLES AMPHITHEATER ▲ *159*

Amphitheater architecture was standard: an oval arena covered with sand surrounded by the *cavea*, the stone step-seating supported by vaulted arcades. The Arles amphitheater, constructed at the end of the 1st century AD to hold 23,000 spectators, was built of large blocks of local limestone. Two superimposed arcades adorned with columns of the Tuscan order support the stepped seating structure and enclose the access corridors and stairs.

FROM THE SACRED TO THE PROFANE

Greek theaters built on hillsides looked out over the countryside. The performances were of a religious nature. The circular orchestra pit served as a passage for the chorus. Under the Romans, theaters lost their sacred nature and became places for profane entertainments: the chorus disappeared and the stage was backed by a wall with columns and statues, providing genuine architectural scenery in its own right.

Roman theater   Greek theater

During the Middle Ages, with the counts of Cataluña and
Anjou, then the king of France, the count of Savoy, the popes
and the counts of Nassau, Provence was much fought over and
divided. Towns and villages were equipped with ramparts, while
in border territory the warring lords built forts and castles so as
to monitor the enemy. Medieval castles, defensive fortifications
par excellence but also the symbols of seigniorial power, were
replaced by fortified strongholds developed throughout the
alpine ranges according to the designs of Sébastien le Prestre de
Vauban (1633–1707).

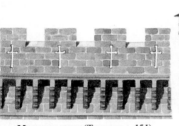

FORTIFIED GUN TOWERS
These were less solid than
proper bastions, but also less
expensive. Used to reinforce
town fortifications, they were
well suited to regions where
heavy cannons could be
moved. With their
pentagonal ground plan
these towers provided
raised gun emplacement
within the ramparts.

MACHICOLATION (Tarascon ▲ *151*)
Before this architectural feature was
invented, if assailants reached the foot of a
rampart, the defending soldiers could not
reach them without leaning out from the
crenelations and making themselves
vulnerable. *Mâchicoulis* made it possible to
shoot downward with greater security.

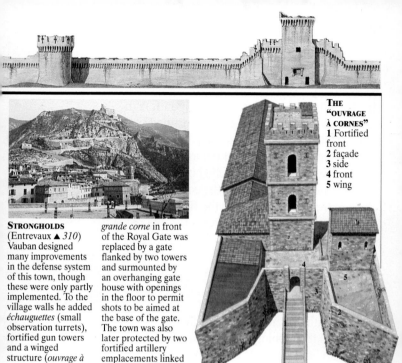

THE "OUVRAGE À CORNES"
1 Fortified front
2 façade
3 side
4 front
5 wing

STRONGHOLDS
(Entrevaux ▲ *310*)
Vauban designed many improvements in the defense system of this town, though these were only partly implemented. To the village walls he added *échauguettes* (small observation turrets), fortified gun towers and a winged structure (*ouvrage à cornes*) to protect the Savoy Gate. The *grande corne* in front of the Royal Gate was replaced by a gate flanked by two towers and surmounted by an overhanging gate house with openings in the floor to permit shots to be aimed at the base of the gate. The town was also later protected by two fortified artillery emplacements linked to the citadel by a path.

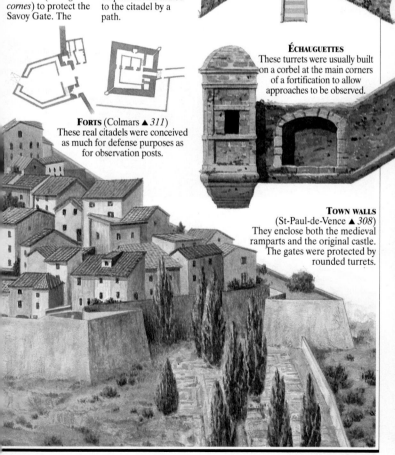

ÉCHAUGUETTES
These turrets were usually built on a corbel at the main corners of a fortification to allow approaches to be observed.

FORTS (Colmars ▲ *311*)
These real citadels were conceived as much for defense purposes as for observation posts.

TOWN WALLS
(St-Paul-de-Vence ▲ *308*)
They enclose both the medieval ramparts and the original castle. The gates were protected by rounded turrets.

● SEA DEFENSES AND FORTIFICATIONS

In the 16th century France called upon Italian
architects for the construction of fortified bastions.
Perched high on steep hills, these buildings were
the first perfect examples of the use of the
bastion. Since there was a need both for
the defense of ports and for the coasts
to be patrolled, islands were the first
sites to be fortified so as to prevent
enemies from using them as
bases for military operations.
Isolated forts or fortresses built
on the ramparts of towns
barred entrance from the sea or,
by dominating them from the hinterland,
prevented them being taken by land forces. As well as
illustrating the principle of defense, these structures
demonstrate the evolution of military strategy and weaponry.

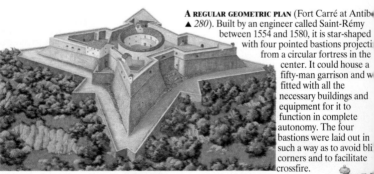

A REGULAR GEOMETRIC PLAN (Fort Carré at Antibe
▲ *280*). Built by an engineer called Saint-Rémy
between 1554 and 1580, it is star-shaped
with four pointed bastions projecti
from a circular fortress in the
center. It could house a
fifty-man garrison and w
fitted with all the
necessary buildings and
equipment for it to
function in complete
autonomy. The four
bastions were laid out in
such a way as to avoid bli
corners and to facilitate
crossfire.

THE ITALIAN STYLE
(St-Elme citadel at
Villefranche ▲ *294*)
The circular and
slightly corbeled
turrets crowning the
projecting bastions of
this fortress are
characteristic of the
Italian architectural
genius for designing
fortifications.

A DOUBLE RAMPART
(Fort St-Nicolas ▲ *200*)
Strategically built at the
entrance of the port, this
fort could aim its batteries
both at the town and at
potential invaders. Its
double ramparts, moats
and bastions show the
adjustments that became
necessary to repel
artillery offensives. The
angled salients allowed
cannons to be moved
into place and
compensated for the
enlarged ramparts
which had recreated
the blind spot
previously eliminated
by the machicolation.

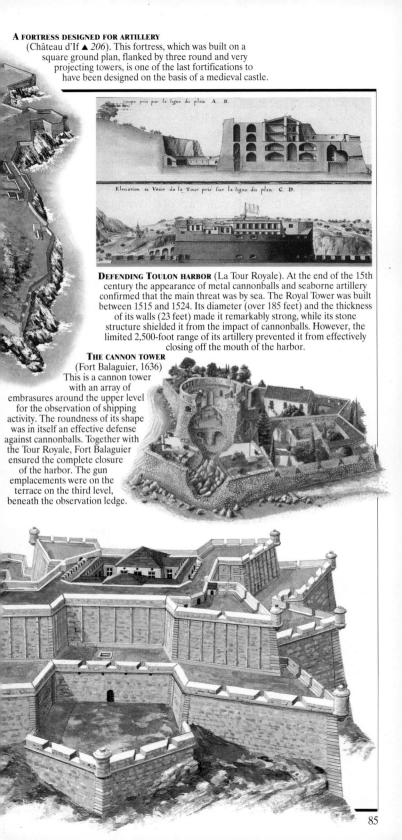

A FORTRESS DESIGNED FOR ARTILLERY
(Château d'If ▲ *206*). This fortress, which was built on a
square ground plan, flanked by three round and very
projecting towers, is one of the last fortifications to
have been designed on the basis of a medieval castle.

coupe pris par la ligne du plan. A. B.

Elevation et Veüe de la Tour pris sur la ligne du plan. C. D.

DEFENDING TOULON HARBOR (La Tour Royale). At the end of the 15th
century the appearance of metal cannonballs and seaborne artillery
confirmed that the main threat was by sea. The Royal Tower was built
between 1515 and 1524. Its diameter (over 185 feet) and the thickness
of its walls (23 feet) made it remarkably strong, while its stone
structure shielded it from the impact of cannonballs. However, the
limited 2,500-foot range of its artillery prevented it from effectively
closing off the mouth of the harbor.

THE CANNON TOWER
(Fort Balaguier, 1636)
This is a cannon tower
with an array of
embrasures around the upper level
for the observation of shipping
activity. The roundness of its shape
was in itself an effective defense
against cannonballs. Together with
the Tour Royale, Fort Balaguier
ensured the complete closure
of the harbor. The gun
emplacements were on the
terrace on the third level,
beneath the observation ledge.

● VILLAGES

The villages scattered all over Provence bear the signs of ancient forms of social organization dating from the Middle Ages or even antiquity. They include hill villages perched like the Roman *oppida*, often displaying signs of a feudal past, valley or plains villages, usually located at staging posts – road or river junctions – and coastal villages set in favorable spots for mooring boats or for fishing. Many of these are examples of surviving forms of rural group habitats established in accordance with a traditional plan and architecture.

THE "ABSOLUTE" HILL TOWN
On hilltops, settlers found sites that were not only easier to defend but also provided a plentiful supply of stone and clean air. They coped with the scarcity of water by building vast cisterns. Many villages of this type were founded at the beginning of feudal times when the inhabitants were forced to live within the fortifications of the fiefdom.

THE "UNDERHILL" VILLAGE
Such settlements had an abundant groundwater supply from the hillside. Cotignac (Var) is a typical example: it grew up at the foot of a cliff whose many caves were first inhabited in the neolithic age. Its security was ensured by a rampart and a castle built on the clifftop.

RIDGE TOWN
As a compromise between hill towns and settlements in the plains, these villages, of which there are many examples, enjoy both the security of being on raised ground and easy access to water supplies. underground

PLAINS VILLAGES
Such villages were created by settlers wishing to live closer to their lands. They came into being when feudal power was no longer strong enough to retain the vassals within the fortified precincts.

A COASTAL VILLAGE (Martigues)
It has three very different quarters – Jonquières, l'Ile and Ferrières – separated by the two branches of the Passe de Caronte. The narrow façades of the fishermen's houses give a harmony to the urban landscape of old Martigues.

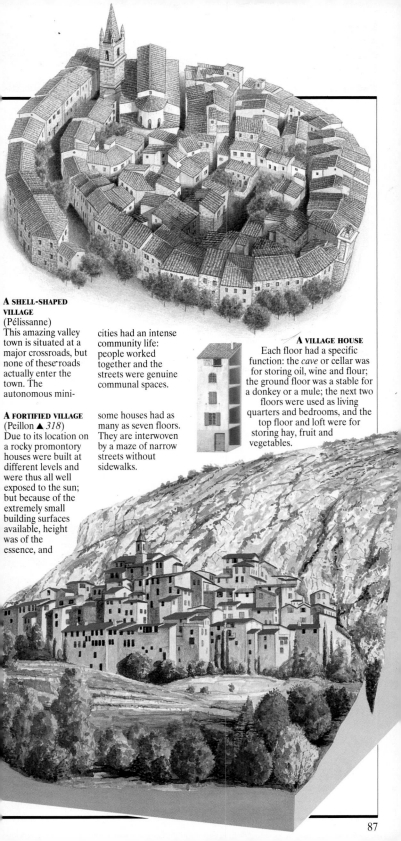

A SHELL-SHAPED VILLAGE
(Pélissanne)
This amazing valley town is situated at a major crossroads, but none of these roads actually enter the town. The autonomous mini-cities had an intense community life: people worked together and the streets were genuine communal spaces.

A FORTIFIED VILLAGE
(Peillon ▲ *318*)
Due to its location on a rocky promontory houses were built at different levels and were thus all well exposed to the sun; but because of the extremely small building surfaces available, height was of the essence, and some houses had as many as seven floors. They are interwoven by a maze of narrow streets without sidewalks.

A VILLAGE HOUSE
Each floor had a specific function: the *cave* or cellar was for storing oil, wine and flour; the ground floor was a stable for a donkey or a mule; the next two floors were used as living quarters and bedrooms, and the top floor and loft were for storing hay, fruit and vegetables.

Provençal rural architecture shows great versatility in satisfying the needs of a population consisting mostly of shepherds and farmers, as well as taking account of the changeable climate. While it includes a wide range of types of buildings (farm, *bastide*, *mas*, *cabane*, *borie*, *cabanon*, pigeon loft), these are always inspired by family and agricultural needs, combining dwelling areas with work spaces in a single structural unit. Construction techniques are closely linked to the available resources of building materials.

THE CAMARGUE "CABANE". Consists of a wooden frame to which reed matting is attached. With its rounded shape at the back, it is designed to withstand the wind.

MODEST MEANS (*fermette* of the Nice countryside). The simplicity of design is compensated for by the use of color. The reddish ocher of the background is set off by the yellowish ocher of the skirting and the shutters. Occasionally a window painted in trompe l'œil is added to restore symmetry to a façade where necessary.

DEVELOPMENT OF THE BASTIDE DE PONTEVÈS

1. 1750 **2.** Before 1840 **3.** 1858 **4.** Second half of the 19th century **5.** Second half of the 19th or beginning of the 20th century

Bastide, or *maison de maître*, is the Provençal term for an agricultural estate belonging to a rich landlord. The functional buildings are organized around the main residence in the center with its transversal roof and its *génoises* (rows of roof tiles set below the eaves to extend the roofing away from the façade).

THE CAMARGUE "MAS". With a blind side to the north and northwest to keep out the gusts of the mistral, these small farmhouses have thick stone and rubble walls to combat the heat in summer. In the example shown above, one of the wings includes a stone pigeon loft.

THE "CABANON". A shelter more than a dwelling, built using dry stone, clay, sand or lime mortar.

PIGEON LOFT. These are usually partly or totally integrated in the structure of a dwelling or farmhouse. When free-standing they are in the shape of a round or square tower. Their single-slope roofs, tiled or plain, are characteristic of the Provençal landscape. Inside, a swivelling ladder on a central "hinge" gives easy access to each level of pigeon holes.

"BORIE" These small dry stone structures – built without mortar – were used as stables, tool sheds or shepherd's huts. The low, narrow door had a wooden or stone lintel. Their vaulted roofs were simply built on the principle of the corbeled arch without any wooden supports.

HOUSES OF THE ALPINE VALLEYS (Pra Roustan). These are characterized by a single large space set into the slope; the main façade, with two or sometimes three levels of windows, is parallel to the slope. Their whole rectangular area is covered by a gabled roof consisting of two or four slopes shingled with gray stone, larch gray slate or flat tiles. The windows are few and narrow. These buildings are built with the local gray stone, which allows thick walls to be erected, either pointed or faced with a rustic cement made from sand and lime.

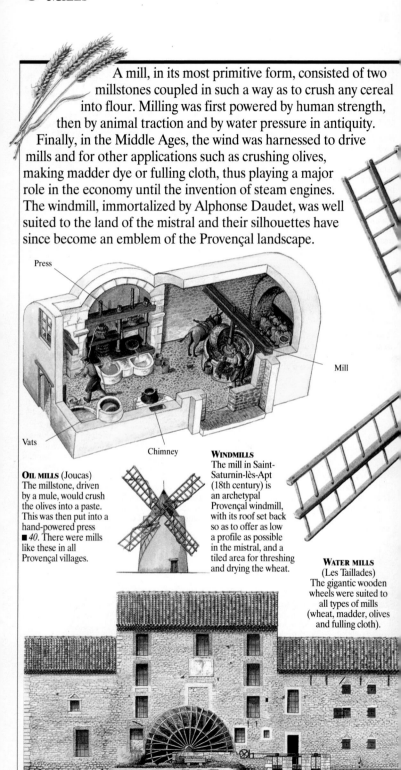

A mill, in its most primitive form, consisted of two millstones coupled in such a way as to crush any cereal into flour. Milling was first powered by human strength, then by animal traction and by water pressure in antiquity. Finally, in the Middle Ages, the wind was harnessed to drive mills and for other applications such as crushing olives, making madder dye or fulling cloth, thus playing a major role in the economy until the invention of steam engines. The windmill, immortalized by Alphonse Daudet, was well suited to the land of the mistral and their silhouettes have since become an emblem of the Provençal landscape.

Press

Mill

Vats

Chimney

OIL MILLS (Joucas)
The millstone, driven by a mule, would crush the olives into a paste. This was then put into a hand-powered press ■ 40. There were mills like these in all Provençal villages.

WINDMILLS
The mill in Saint-Saturnin-lès-Apt (18th century) is an archetypal Provençal windmill, with its roof set back so as to offer as low a profile as possible in the mistral, and a tiled area for threshing and drying the wheat.

WATER MILLS
(Les Taillades)
The gigantic wooden wheels were suited to all types of mills (wheat, madder, olives and fulling cloth).

Millstones are made of an inner layer of soft stone sandwiched between outer layers of hard stone.

The inspection gangway in the roofing enabled the miller to set the sails.

PROVENÇAL TOWER MILLS. The golden age of Provençal windmills was during the 17th and 18th centuries when agricultural development was at its peak. Standing on windswept hillocks on the outskirts of villages, they were built so as to be included in the millers' dwellings. The stone tower serving as a central pivot for the whole structure was designed to make sparing use of large wooden beams, a rare commodity in the area.

The mill's drive shaft.

1. Roof made of chestnut slats
2. Sails that could be set according to the wind strength and direction
3. The milling chamber
4. Drive shaft of the moving millstone
5. Wood casing
6. Moving millstone
7. Fixed millstone with centrifugal radial scores. Centrifugal force was used to expel the crushed produce between the fixed millstone and the wood casing
8. Supporting pillar around which the mill's interior layout was organized
9. Ropes for hoisting sacks of grain
10. Room for sacking the flour
11. Bakery

91

The period of insecurity after the fall of the Roman empire was followed by a time of peace during which the Romanesque style flourished. The characteristics of churches built around the year 1000 included a vaulted arch, simple ground plans, harmonious proportions, few openings, a genuine austerity and perfection in the stonework. A second Romanesque period (12th–13th centuries) was characterized by a lighter style, larger openings for illumination and decorations inspired by antiquity.

ALPINE ROMANESQUE PORTALS (Notre-Dame du Bourg, Digne ▲ *240*). In the Alpine region of Provence Romanesque church portals display an Italian influence with their alternating stones of different colors in the columns: white and dark grey or pink.

CHEVETS (Notre-Dame de Valvert, Allos). They were either flat and barrel-vaulted or semicircular with a *cul-de-four* vaulting.

EPISCOPAL COMPLEX (Fréjus, ▲ *252*)
The episcopal seat combined temporal and spiritual elements, including the bishop's palace, a prelate's residence, the cathedral, the baptistery and the cloister.

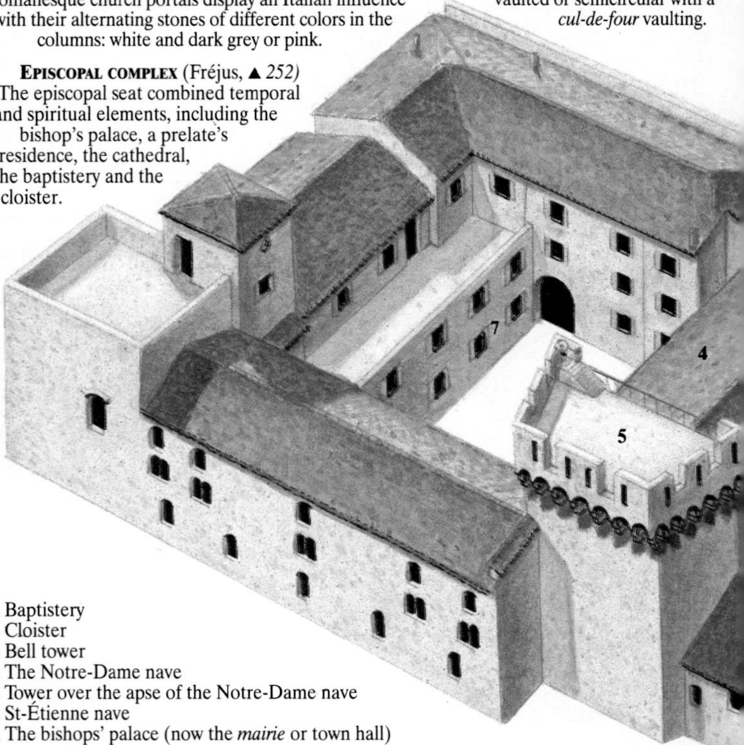

1. Baptistery
2. Cloister
3. Bell tower
4. The Notre-Dame nave
5. Tower over the apse of the Notre-Dame nave
6. St-Étienne nave
7. The bishops' palace (now the *mairie* or town hall)

ROMANESQUE SYMBOL (St-Sauveur Cathedral, Aix ▲ *213*) While the capitals are mostly adorned with the symbols of the Evangelists, they are also decorated with geometrical or floral motifs from antiquity.

THE INFLUENCE OF ANTIQUITY (St-Trophime, Arles ▲ *162*). The triumphal arch design and the opulence of the decorations contrast with the austerity of the façade. It depicts the main themes of sacred history dominated by the figure of Christ in majesty surrounded by the tetramorph.

THE THREE PERIODS OF ROMANESQUE
Romanesque art is characterized by the evolution of the vault, in which there were three periods. The first period was that of the regular semicircular arch (the barrel vault). This changed into the broken or pointed arch. Finally there was the ogee vault (1) formed by the ribbing or ogives converging on a central keystone (2). Supporting arches (3) separated the main bays.

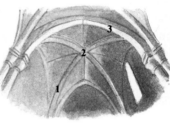

THE EVOLUTION OF GROUND PLANS (St-Donat-de-Montfort) The earliest Romanesque style, characterized by the basilical design, was superseded at a later stage by the single nave plan.

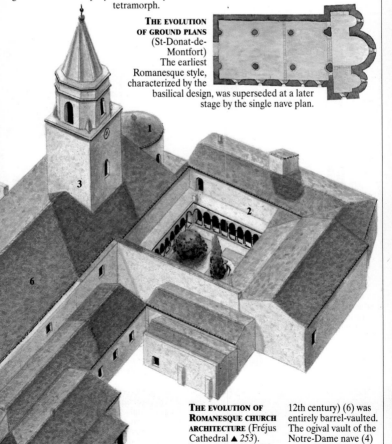

THE EVOLUTION OF ROMANESQUE CHURCH ARCHITECTURE (Fréjus Cathedral ▲ *253*). Long and narrow (18 feet across), the St-Étienne nave (11th–12th century) (6) was entirely barrel-vaulted. The ogival vault of the Notre-Dame nave (4) exemplifies the later period of Romanesque church architecture.

93

● BAROQUE RELIGIOUS ARCHITECTURE

The architecture of the Jésus Church in Nice
is highlighted by opulent gilded and
polychrome stucco moldings ▲ 286.

Not so much a style, Provençal Baroque
was more a way of life that has left
traces we can discover today in the
region's 17th-century buildings. From the
late Renaissance, a frenetic evolution led to
Mannerism and neoclassicism, while the new
orientations of the Church expressed themselves in
the Baroque with spirals, volutes, curves and countercurves in
an endless interplay of convex and concave shapes. These
technical achievements were no doubt influenced by the
mathematical progress of the times.

**THE RIGOR AND BALANCE OF THE
JESUITS' STYLE**
(Jesuit College Chapel, Avignon)
This façade is characteristic of what
became known as *style jésuite*,
inspired by Giacomo della Porta's
Gesù Church in Rome. The two
levels of unequal width, decorated
with Corinthian pilasters and empty
niches, are harmoniously linked by
large volutes.

BAROQUE THEMES (Black Penitents' Chapel,
▲ 137, Avignon). The Baroque exalted new
themes like martyrdom and the ecstasy of
saints. The originality of this composition
resides in the very fine bas-relief in which the
head of Saint John (emblem of the Black
Penitents) is glorified by small angels.

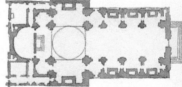

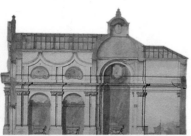

**TWO TYPES OF
GROUND PLAN**
While the larger
churches retained
the traditional
basilical plan, they
generally had an
enlarged central
nave enhanced by
a cupola or a
rotunda.

Smaller churches, on
the other hand, were
usually built "in the
round" or with a
single longitudinal
axis.

ELEGANCE AND THEATRICAL EFFECTS (St-Pons, Nice). The renovation of the original façade has restored this building's elegance, clearly influenced by Juvarra. The chiaroscuro of its porticos, the graceful sweep of its flights of steps and the vitality of their convex curves are echoed by its elliptical vault.

DECORATION
With its special attention to illusion and dramatic effects, the Baroque style was able to express new religious themes and thus renewed the decorative idiom which henceforth included foreshortenings, diagonal lines, perspectives, trompe l'oeil and polychrome effects. Walls and ceilings were covered with angels, masks, caryatids, bowers, drapes and garlands.

FAÇADES (Lambesc Church)
While classical orders of columns – Doric, Ionic and Corinthian – so carefully defined by the Roman architect Vitruvius were retained and raised on a solid base, their superimposition was increasingly replaced by a single colossal order reaching the full height of the walls and conferring powerful unity on the façades.

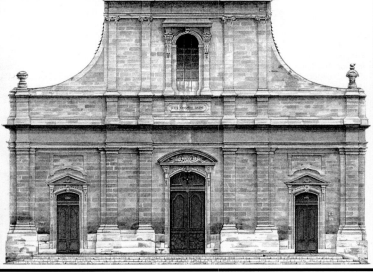

Originally conceived in the Middle Ages as defensive military structures, *châteaux* (castles) underwent major modifications in the Renaissance to adapt them to residential purposes. However, the old quadrangular layout with flanking towers survived for several decades and for many years buildings were updated merely through partial innovations and decorative additions. Models introduced in the Île-de-France were only copied in Provence from the 18th century on. As an extension of the spirit of grandeur "outside the walls", *bastides* are characteristic of the classical period in Provence throughout the 17th and 18th centuries when families sought to assert their position in society by acquiring land. The architectural style was often similar to that of the *hôtel particulier* (townhouse).

RENAISSANCE. The Château d'Allemagne en Provence (16th century) is a fine example of the transition from the defensive medieval castle to the residential Renaissance château. Its superb mullioned windows and Gothic gables are remarkably harmonious.

FROM MANNERISM TO CLASSICISM. With its six great window bays across the façade, the Château d'Ansouis (1645) is a forerunner of classicism in the regularity and sobriety of its composition. Its ornamentation, however, is reminiscent of Aixois Mannerism.

NEW MODELS (Chaffaut) From the end of the 16th century the ancient hill sites (*castra*) were abandoned and plain settlements developed. This made for complexes with more regular plans, in many ways similar to the great châteaux of the Île-de-France.

TRANSITION (Château-Arnoux, c. 1510). While its interior furnishings were designed more for new-found comfort, this building's sturdy structure and gun emplacements show how the mentality was still at a transitional stage in its evolution.

THE CLASSICAL "PAVILLON"
The cubic design of the Château de Tourreau at Sarrians (1747), with its pediments on the façade, bears some resemblance to the considerably older *pavillon* (lodge) Louis XIV had built at Marly. However, the wrought-iron balcony supported by atlantes is distinctly Aixois in style.

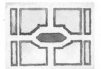

FROM GOTHIC TO THE RENAISSANCE. The Château de Lourmarin ▲ *195* links a 15th-century dwelling (right) with a 16th-century building, clearly influenced by improvements in lifestyle: there are larger rooms, each with a specific function.

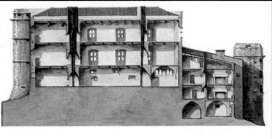

SOBRIETY OF EXTERNAL ADORNMENTS (Pavillon de Lenfant ▲ *219*, 1677, near Aix) While the decorative elements of the interior covered every available space, the ordering of the façades was governed by the simplicity of contrasting shapes, rigorous proportions and a few sculpted features such as ledges, consoles, medallions and brackets.

A MANNERIST DOOR Carpenters were kept busy with the many decorative elements.

THE 18TH-CENTURY FAÇADE (La Mignarde, Aix ▲ *219*). Main façades were usually composed around a central body ordered in a variety of ways: slightly recessed main part, end stones and pediments (arched or triangular). Chain bonds marked the limits of the building.

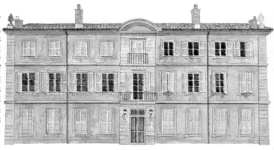

PART "BASTIDE", PART "HÔTEL PARTICULIER" (Pavillon Vendôme, Aix, 1665 ▲ *217*) This "lodge", which was raised by one floor in 1730, has a façade particularly rich in decorations. It is composed around a central body adorned with atlantes and niches. The different floors are separated by carved friezes and pilasters emphasize the vertical ordering into symmetrical bays.

Around 1650 the public and private architecture of Provençal towns revealed all the prosperity of the landed gentry and the upper classes. Modern town planning affected both the older districts and the newly built extensions. The towns grew, their narrow and winding streets were straightened and they were adorned with *cours* (avenues) and squares. The composition of the urban fabric was characterized by fine perspectives, splendid architectural complexes and pedestrian promenades and parks.

A REGULATORY PLAN (Quartier Mazarin 1646, Aix-en-Provence, ▲ 218) The elevation clearly shows the plan's orthogonal design, with broad streets.

The "cours". The origin of the *cours* as a public urban space is Provençal. The first to appear in Paris, "Cours-la-Reine" was designed in 1616 at the request of Marie de Médicis, who brought it from Italy. They were conceived as esplanades for horse-drawn carriages, "courses" or runs outside the city walls. But it was in Aix, with the Cours Mirabeau ▲ 217, built in 1649, and then Marseilles, with the Cours Belsunce ▲ 205, built in 1668, that these spaces became integrated in the urban fabric, as green strips in the town's design, places for outdoor leisure and elegance. They were usually built on the foundations of ruined ramparts and thus became links between the old towns and newly developed areas.

The square (Place Thiars, Marseilles) This square located in the Arsenal district of the town was treated as a functional space in the urban fabric. Since the façades which surround it were not designed specifically for it, this cannot be considered an ordered square.

A NEW DISTRIBUTION
(Hôtel de Caumont, Aix). In the classical period the dwelling area was located between the courtyard and the garden.

The rooms were of regular shapes and carefully proportioned with doors in line with the windows and fireplaces in a central position. Reception rooms generally included a hall, a large antechamber (waiting room), an audience hall (for receptions) and one or more sitting rooms. The family apartments were lower ceilinged, easier to heat and included a hall, a large room, bedrooms, a study and a changing room.

CLASSICAL ORDERING
(the façades of the Cours Mirabeau, Aix, ▲ *217*). The buildings here were used to give a rhythmic cadence to the open space by emphasizing points of importance. Projecting portals supported by atlantes and columns, eye-catching statues in niches and heavy cornices with grotesque masks formed part of the display of public open-air life which animated the tree-lined *cours* filled with mossy fountains.

The fountain of the Hôtel d'Espagnet, Aix.

ATLANTES AND CARYATIDS (Hôtel d'Arbaud, Aix). Atlantes and caryatids inspired by the classical features of antiquity were used instead of plain columns to support entablatures or balconies over portals. The portal of this *hôtel* is adorned with two atlantes, one facing out and one facing in.

BALCONIES (Hôtel d'Arbaud-Jouques, Aix). Enlarged windows inspired the addition of balconies. Wrought-iron work was particularly creative in Provence.

TOWN PLANNER'S RÔLE
The royal inspectors of construction works became ad hoc town planners whose approval was sought for the implementation of projects, the realignment of buildings and the creation of thoroughfares. There were no overall regulations and case-by-case decisions were taken on the spot.

In order to satisfy the whims of nostalgic and well-traveled European aristocrats and bourgeois society, the architecture of the period between 1860 and 1914 was characterized by its eclecticism. It was influenced by such diverse models as Gothic follies, Moorish or Greek villas, Italian palaces, Russian churches and Swiss chalets, and the main concern in choosing building materials was to avoid monotony. However extravagant these buildings were, they never challenged the bourgeois standards of the time: the traditional country house plan was always adhered to and the shape of the rooms was never determined by the external appearance. Palace hotels were of colossal dimensions, with long, repetitive sea-front façades. Rich sculpted decorations adorned their windows, balustrades, pediments and cornices.

A MOORISH VILLA
(Villa Djezaïr, Juan-les-Pins ▲ 275). This neo-Moorish style was a product of the orientalist trend at the turn of the century. The whole range of Islamic decorative elements was used: arches, crenelations, tiles, colors and minarets.

UNBRIDLED LUXURY
(Excelsior Regina ▲ 291)
The ground floor is designed for reception facilities and entertainment, with halls, grandiose staircases, sitting rooms and ballrooms, all luxuriously decorated. The rooms and suites are on the other floors with the best ones facing south, overlooking the park full of exotic plants, the town and the sea. Services and the humble accommodation for the staff are all at the rear, facing north.

THE VOGUE FOR PAVILIONS
Isbas, pagodas, and a wide variety of kiosks, after being used in Universal Exhibitions, were reassembled in these resorts to serve as models for villas.

A NEO-GOTHIC CHÂTEAU
(Château Scott, Cannes ▲ 249)
With its vast irregular plan, this building is typical of an
English *pastiche* of medieval architecture featuring a
central crenelated tower, stone masonry, steep gabled
roofs, a terrace and an arched portico.

BEYOND THE "PASTICHE"
(Château de l'Anglais, Nice)
This fantastic synthesis of a Maharaja's palace and colonial
architecture actually belongs to the India style inaugurated
in 1815 by the Prince of Wales in Brighton, England.

AN ORTHODOX CHURCH
(St-Nicolas, Nice ▲ 289)
While it is inspired by the
five-cupola churches of
Moscow, it differs with its use
of Mediterranean
construction material such as
Italian pink granite, blue
terracotta tiling from
Florence and stone from
La Turbie.

PALACE WITH LONG CADENCED FAÇADES
(Carlton, Cannes ▲ 247)
Flanked by great towers with slate-roofed domes, these
façades are enlivened by projecting window frames, terraces
and balconies, and tall classical pilasters. They frequently
display vertical patterns of decorative brickwork.

GATES AND BELL TOWERS

DEFENSE GATES FROM THE 14TH CENTURY (Porte St-Jean, Tarascon ▲ *151*). Set between two large towers linked by a fortified passage and crowned with machicolated crenelations, this type of gate enabled defenders to catch intruders in a crossfire.

Until the 18th century most Provençal villages were enclosed behind ramparts whose gates controlled access to the village streets. These checkpoints had a triple purpose: security, food and labor distribution, and sanitary inspection. From the 16th century, bell towers or *campaniles* were a characteristic feature of the Provençal urban landscape. Their light structure was designed to let strong winds blow through them. Local blacksmiths and metal workers turned them into works of art to decorate church towers and steeples.

A TRIUMPHAL GATE (Porte de l'Horloge, Salon). On the site of the original rampart a first gate was built in the 17th century. Its influence was Italian, with a triangular pediment, a bossed arch and free-standing columns. The three pyramidal levels with bossed corner stones were added in the 18th century.

RESISTING THE WIND (Bell towers of St-Jérôme, Digne ▲ *240* and of St-Maximin). Their shape is inspired by the *campanula* flower, an 18th-century neologism from the Latin, meaning "little bell".

"HALTE-LÀ" (Château de l'Emperi, Salon). An imposing gate with a drawbridge, portcullis and massive hinged door.

FINE WROUGHT-IRON CAGES (Bell tower of the Couvent des Augustins, Aix). They are spherical, pyramidal or bulb-shaped.

PROVENCE
AS SEEN BY PAINTERS

Painters from Van Gogh (1853–90) and Gauguin (1848–1903) to Pablo Picasso (1881–1973) have been fascinated by the serene and voluptuous light of Arles ▲ 154. When GAUGUIN joined Van Gogh in Arles in 1888, he stayed only from October to December: while the tones and the intensity of the place impressed him, he continued to paint with the technique he had evolved in Pont-Aven, though enriched by the experiments with color that he and Van Gogh had begun to make. This can be seen in *Les Alyscamps* (1).

From his arrival in Provence in February of 1888 to his internment in 1889, VINCENT VAN GOGH's stay in the area represents a crucial phase in his work, when he made the transition between the dark palette of his Dutch period and the intense luminosity of his last works. It was here that he sought to express the harmony "of the golden tones of every shade: green gold, yellow gold, pink gold, bronze or copper colored gold and finally from the yellow of lemons to the lusterless yellow of a heap of thrashed grain". *Les Oliviers* (2), anticipated the Expressionism that was to come.

It was in 1870 that PAUL CÉZANNE (4) (1839–1906), aged thirty and already steeped in the landscape techniques of the Île-de-France, began his exploration of serial painting at l'Estaque ▲ 208. Returning to Aix, his native town, in the 1880's, he tirelessly painted the same set of subjects (the countryside around Aix, the Jas de Bouffan, Mount Sainte-Victoire ▲ 220, Château-Noir) so as to attain a synthesis of forms and a purity of color based on the precepts of Nicolas Poussin. *Great Pine Tree near Aix-en-Provence* (3), in which the composition radiates from the tree, was to become a major source of inspiration for the Cubists.

1	2
4	3

"The shadows of olive trees are often mauve.
They are always moving, luminous,
full of gaiety and life."

JEAN RENOIR

Of the artists whose work is shown here, PIERRE BONNARD (1867–1947), who settled permanently at Le Cannet in 1925, best exemplifies this enchantment with light. In his landscapes, made up of successive and highly contrasting planes – as, for example, *Landscape from Le Cannet* (4) – the interplay of light and shade is expressed by the simple juxtaposition of vivid colors applied in rigorous patterns.

In *Cagnes Landscape* (5), CHAIM SOUTINE (1894–1943), who was little inspired by horizontal landscapes, painted narrow streets and steps reaching up into the sky. He was instantly fascinated by the tones of red – his favorite color – in the stone and the roof tiles.

The Russian-born painter NICOLAS DE STAEL (1) (1914–55) settled in France in 1938 and painted in simple forms and intense colors that he frequently reduced to the limited range of blue, white and red. When he painted *Marine* (2), in the year of his death in Antibes, he had just given up the non-figurative approach and the palette knife in favor of the more fluid effects of the brush. The blinding light of the Mediterranean is conveyed by the interplay of colors: "a little blue and lots of white" is what he had written a few years before with reference to the sun's effect on things.

PICASSO's love affair with Provence particularly imbued the work he produced in the last twenty years of his life. The thick outlines of his *Bay of Cannes* (3) reflect the sharpness of the light.

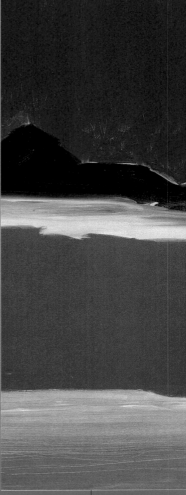

1	2
3	4	5

"THE PAINTER IS DRIVEN TO PAINTING
BY HIS URGENT NEED TO RELIEVE HIMSELF
OF HIS FEELINGS AND VISIONS"

PABLO PICASSO

PURE COLORS
FAUVISM

It used to be said that the Estérel was inhabited only by wild animals, brigands and hermits. Such solitude, bursting with violent color, with ravines dominated by clear blue skies, where reddish rocks seem to cascade vertically down to the sea, was bound to take a hold on the imagination of painters. LOUIS VALTAT (1869–1952) settled at Anthéor in 1899 and stayed there until 1913. *L'Estérel*, which Valtat painted in 1903, is imbued with the rugged harmonies of this coastal region, which only that year had been "tamed" by a road, the *Corniche Sublime*. This painting marks Valtat as one of the *fauves* (wild animals),

painters whose colors the art critic Louis Vauxelles described as "fauve". Like his fellow artists, Valtat was not bound by any particular school but followed his feelings. The reds of the porphyry rocks are enhanced by the dark greens of the forest, seeming to set the painting on fire. Small curved dark lines beneath the rocks and the vegetation create an almost palpable rhythm and convey the force and fierce wilderness of the place in a manner that foreshadows Expressionism. The strong light of the Provençal countryside was leading to a new way of painting.

A work like *Sun over Cassis* (**2**), by the Marseilles artist ADOLPHE MONTICELLI (1824–86), shows how, as a result of this painter's innovative experiments in 1871, the actual features of the countryside are secondary only to the act of painting. His strange landscapes, hovering between Impressionism and Expressionism, opened the way to a brilliant style whose visual effects verged on the abstract. Vincent Van Gogh was an ardent admirer and it was to seek out his work that Van Gogh journeyed to Provence in 1888. In the last twenty years of his life, during which he painted *The Rock at Ganagobie* (**3**), Monticelli developed an individual and violent style. Using short, hard brushes, a cloth to touch in the colors and fingers to spread the paint, he very successfully conveyed the natural contrasts of Ganagobie by means of a tightly woven fabric of contrasting strokes. Following in the traveling tradition of such artists as Delacroix and Stevenson, as well as of Victor Hugo, JOSEPH MALLORD WILLIAM TURNER (1775–1851), the Romantic painter who was a forerunner of the Impressionists, journeyed through the French and Italian Alps filling his notebooks with sketches and a wealth of watercolors. In such works as *Sisteron, Basses-Alpes* (**1**) the details of the landscape are subsumed in a misty and blurred effect that is enhanced by the fluidity of watercolor. The immediate surroundings of Sisteron are thus perceived as though set in the landscape of a sort of German hill town, with an

added glow of luminosity. Half way between Turner's style and Monticelli's, both of which exerted a powerful and persisting influence, a

110

manner of portraying
the Alpes-de-Haute-
Provence developed
that focused on the
almost virginal aspect
of some of its finest
landscapes.
Somewhere between
Impressionism and
Expressionism, with
an occasional touch
of harshness *à la*
Chabaud, this style
was perpetuated as a
form of glorification
of the Provençal
countryside.

R ENÉ SEYSSAUD (1867–1952) was a forward-looking artist who began to anticipate Expressionism in the early 1880's. He divided his painting life between two main locations, the Ventoux and the Étang de Berre. He used color to maximum effect to heighten reality, as in *Reaper at Beaumont d'Orange*, where the reds seem to oppress all the other colors, but actually serve to enhance them by contrast. The density of paint and liveliness of brushstrokes in his work were the essential characteristics of his style.

PROVENCE
AS SEEN BY WRITERS

LIVING IN PROVENCE

RUSTIC LIFE

Petrarch (1304–74) wrote to Francesco of the Church of the Holy Apostles about the time he spent in Provence and the way in which he adapted to the local life.

❝I am spending the summer at the source of the Sorgue. . . . I have so disciplined my palate and my stomach that my plowman's bread often suffices, often even gives me pleasure; and when servants bring me white bread from elsewhere I let them eat it. . . . Grapes, figs, nuts and almonds are my delight, and I take great pleasure in the little fish with which this river abounds. Never do they delight me more than when they are freshly caught; I love to watch them and love to catch them with hooks and nets. What shall I say about my clothing and my footwear? They have all changed. No longer do I wear my usual clothing; I say 'my' because of their exceptional rareness with which, I hope within the limits of modesty and propriety, I once liked to appear conspicuous among my peers. You would call me a farmer or a shepherd, though I still do not lack finer apparel. The only reason for the change is that what I once liked I now dislike. . . . What shall I say about my dwelling? Where I live with one dog and only two servants you would consider the home of Cato or Fabritius. . . .

Here I have acquired two small gardens perfectly suited to my skills and taste. To attempt a description for you would be too long. In short, I believe that no similar spot exists in all the world, and, to confess my unmanly fickleness, I regret only that it is not in Italy. I customarily call it my transalpine Helicon. The one garden is very shady, suitable only for study and sacred to our Apollo. It overhangs the source of the Sorgue, and beyond it lies nothing but ravines and cliffs, remote and accessible only to wild beasts or birds. The other garden, near the house, appears more cultivated, and is a delight to Bacchus. This one, astonishing as it may seem, is in the midst of the very beautiful and swift-running river. Nearby, divided from it by a very small bridge on the further side of the house, hangs a curved vault of native rock that now provides shelter against the summer heat. It is a place that inspires studies, and I suspect is not too dissimilar to the little hall where Cicero used to declaim his orations, except that his did not have a Sorgue flowing alongside. Under this vault, therefore, I spend my afternoons, and my mornings on the hillsides; the evenings I spend in the meadows or in my less cultivated garden at the source where my efforts have conquered nature and cleared a spot under the high cliff in the midst of the waters, narrow indeed but very inspiring, in which even a sluggish mind can rise to the noblest thoughts. What then? I assure you that I could perhaps settle here, except that it is so far from Italy and so near Avignon. Why should I conceal my two weaknesses? My love of Italy charms and tempts me, my hatred of Avignon stings and revolts me, along with its horrible odor that plagues the entire world. Is it any wonder that its excessive proximity pollutes the harmless purity of this country place? I feel the stench driving me away. Now you know my present condition.❞

FRANCESCO PETRARCA, *LETTERS ON FAMILIAR MATTERS*, TRANS. ALDO S. BERNARDO, PUB. JOHNS HOPKINS UNIVERSITY PRESS, 1982

PARADISE

A chronic bronchial condition led Robert Louis Stevenson (1850–94) to search out warm climates beneficial to his health. Here he writes to a friend, W. H. Low, of his house in Hyères.

La Solitude, Hyères, October [1883]

❝My address is still the same, and I live in a most sweet corner of the universe, sea and fine hills before me, and a rich variegated plain; and at my back a craggy hill, loaded with vast feudal ruins. I am very quiet; a person passing by my door half startles me; but I enjoy the most aromatic airs, and at night the most wonderful view into a moonlit garden. By day this garden fades into nothing, overpowered by its surroundings and the luminous distance; but at night and when the moon is out, that garden, the arbour, the flight of stairs that mount the artificial hillock, the plumed blue gum-trees that hang trembling, become the very skirts of Paradise. Angels I know frequent it; and it thrills all night with the flutes of silence. Damn that garden; – and by day it is gone.❞

THE LETTERS OF ROBERT LOUIS STEVENSON, VOL. II,
ED. SYDNEY COLVIN, PUB. METHUEN & CO. LTD, 1921

FOOD

Ford Madox Ford (1873–1939) spent much of the latter part of his life in France and died in Deauville.

❝Shall I, or anyone who was with me, ever forget the exquisite –the *exquisite* – flavour of the huge platter of little birds, with their little claws in the air, with their little eyes disproportionately enormous in their tiny skulls, lying on the tiniest of croûtons of an incredible deliciousness, that we ate in the wine-vault behind the Protestant temple at Nî. . . .

But no! . . . See to what turpitudes local patriotism will lead one! . . . I have enrolled myself under the banners of Frédéric Mistral and of Tarascon against the mendacious hosts of Alphonse Daudet and of Nîmes. At once I find myself about to perjure myself. It is true that in Tarascon I never ate robin, wren, tomtit or nightingale, but neither did I in Nîmes. It was in Arles, the capital of the true kingdom of Provence and the very seat of Mistral and of *félibrisme*, in a wildly clamorous farmers' ordinary that we ate that miraculous platterful of microscopic songsters.

I may formally discuss the cruelty or the reverse of eating tiny creatures when I arrive at my chapter on bull-fighting, football, stage-tumbling, the humane slaughtering of cattle and the slaughter of men in war and my meeting with Mr. Ernest Hemingway . . .

For the moment I will content myself with giving you a menu, some recipes and, since we are about to set out on a journey, some hints as to how to find good restaurants in the country of Provence, where as a whole the cooking is very indifferent.

The South of France – the Midi – divides itself into three zones. In Provence proper – from Mentone to Marseilles – they cook with oil and the products are discouraging. In the territory from the Rhone to Spain which is only by courtesy called Provence you begin to find traces of butter introducing itself into the *cuisine à l'huile*. There are two good restaurants in Marseilles and one in Carcassonne – in a little street in the Basse Ville. But if you want to eat really well there you must order your meal beforehand. By Carcassonne they have already begun to use a little pork-fat. Twenty-one years ago I ate there some *côtelettes de veau à la Maréchal* that were really good.

But it is not until you get to Castelnaudary – of the *cassoulets* – that cooking with goose-fat begins, and *foie gras* and truffles and the real *haute cuisine* of the Toulousain district and the real, high wines of the Bordelais. There too I remember eating. . . . But to say what would be unkind. We have to do the best we can with Provençal food.**"**

FORD MADOX FORD, *PROVENCE – FROM MINSTRELS TO THE MACHINE*,
PUB. GEORGE ALLEN & UNWIN LTD, 1938

BOUILLABAISSE
English chef Simon Hopkinson (b. 1954) was inspired by a meal in Marseilles to create a new recipe.

"I was once enjoying a particularly fine bouillabaisse at a restaurant called Michel in Marseille. This was about ten years ago and I had never eaten this fabled dish before. The unfamiliar fish that were to be included were displayed at the entrance to the restaurant. I had never seen such splendid specimens. Glistening skins and scales, and stiff with rigor mortis freshness. There was rascasse, wrasse, red mullet, John Dory, monkfish, sea bass and a gigantic length of conger eel. All these were included whole or in chunks for my mammoth lunch to come. They were stewed in what I can only describe as a distillation of all things fishy. And this particular fish broth was the burnished terracotta of a Provençal roof tile. There would have been many tomatoes added, some white wine, and of course saffron. The strong and fiery paste called rouille added extra pungency and the dish arrived with some boiled potatoes on the side. These had also been cooked in the soup and were yellow; saffron-stains soaked up by the soft potato.
When I had finished eating the fish, I found myself – as one does – crushing the potatoes into the soup dregs. An interesting thought occurred to me. Mashed potatoes, creamed with saffron, using olive oil instead of butter and adding a little garlic (to account for the remnants of rouille left in the plate) could be a dish in its own right.
Well, all I can say is that it works brilliantly and I urge you to make it.**"**

SIMON HOPKINSON, *ROAST CHICKEN AND OTHER STORIES*,
WITH LINDSEY BAREHAM, PUB. EBURY PRESS, 1994

TRAVELING IN PROVENCE

BY BOAT
The "innocent abroad" described by Mark Twain (1835–1910) endured inexplicable communication problems during his visit to Marseilles.

"Toward nightfall, the next evening, we steamed into the great artificial harbor of this noble city of Marseilles, and saw the dying sunlight gild its clustering spires and ramparts, and flood its leagues of environing verdure with a mellow radiance that touched with an added charm the white villas that flecked the landscape far and near. [Copyright secured according to law.]
There were no stages out, and we could not get on the pier from the ship. It was annoying. We were full of enthusiasm – we wanted to see France! Just at nightfall our party of three contracted with a waterman for the privilege of using his boat as a bridge – its stern was at our companion ladder and its bow touched the pier. We got in and the fellow backed out into the harbor. I told him in French that all we wanted was to walk over his thwarts and step ashore, and asked him what he went away out there for? He said he could not understand me. I repeated. Still, he could not understand. He appeared to be very ignorant of French. The doctor tried him, but he could not understand the doctor. I asked this boatman to explain his conduct, which he did; and then I couldn't understand *him*.**"**

MARK TWAIN, *THE INNOCENTS ABROAD*,
PUB. AMERICAN PUBLISHING CO., 1875

DOWN THE RHÔNE

Charles Dickens (1812–70) traveled across Europe in 1844. Here he describes his approach to Avignon by steamship.

❝Soon after day-break next morning, we were steaming down the Arrowy Rhone, at the rate of twenty miles an hour, in a very dirty vessel full of merchandise, and with only three or four other passengers for our companions: among whom, the most remarkable was a silly, old, meek-faced, garlic-eating, immeasurably polite Chevalier, with a dirty scrap of red ribbon hanging at his button-hole, as if he had tied it there to remind himself of something; as Tom Noddy, in the farce, ties knots in his pocket-handkerchief.

For the last two days, we had seen great sullen hills, the first indications of the Alps, lowering in the distance. Now, we were rushing on beside them: sometimes close beside them: sometimes with an intervening slope, covered with vineyards. Villages and small towns hanging in mid-air, with great woods of olives seen through the light open towers of their churches, and clouds moving slowly on, upon the steep acclivity behind them; ruined castles perched on every eminence; and scattered houses in the clefts and gullies of the hills; made it very beautiful. The great height of these, too, making the buildings look so tiny, that they had all the charm of elegant models; their excessive whiteness, as contrasted with the brown rocks, or the sombre, deep, dull, heavy green of the olive-tree; and the puny size, and little slow walk of the Lilliputian men and women on the bank; made a charming picture. There were ferries out of number, too; bridges; the famous Pont d'Esprit, with I don't know how many arches; towns where memorable wines are made; Vallence, where Napoleon studied; and the noble river, bringing at every winding turn, new beauties into view.

There lay before us, that same afternoon, the broken bridge of Avignon, and all the city baking in the sun; yet with an under-done-pie-crust, battlemented wall, that never will be brown, though it bake for centuries.

The grapes were hanging in clusters in the streets, and the brilliant Oleander was in full bloom everywhere. The streets are old and very narrow, but tolerably clean, and shaded by awnings stretched from house to house. Bright stuffs and handkerchiefs, curiosities, ancient frames of carved wood, old chairs, ghostly tables, saints, virgins, angels, and staring daubs of portraits, being exposed for sale beneath, it was very quaint and lively. All this was much set off, too, by the glimpses one caught, through a rusty gate standing ajar, of quiet sleepy court-yards, having stately old houses within, as silent as tombs. It was all very like one of the descriptions in the Arabian Nights. The three one-eyed Calenders might have knocked at any one of those doors till the street rang again, and the porter who persisted in asking questions – the man who had the delicious purchases put into his basket in the morning – might have opened it quite naturally.**99**

CHARLES DICKENS, *PICTURES FROM ITALY*, PUB. CHAPMAN & HALL, 1844

HEADING SOUTH

In March 1887, John Ruskin (1819–1900) wrote to his young pupil, Rosie, of a journey through France to Nice.

66From Paris we started early on Wednesday morning & travelled all day & all the night in the train – Yes you would have said 'Poor Posie' I was bored But we got over it very well – It was so pleasant to be running after the sun to the south (Dont be Kingfishery) & awaking at about 5 in the morning to see long plains of greyheaded silvery olives and here and there pink perky peach trees dancing among them – And there were groups of dark cool cypress trees pointing upwards, & hills & grey rocks sloping to the sea – the Mediterranean So we shook off our sleepiness, at least Papa Mama and I did for Emily & Adèle still slept; & saw behind those peaks of craggy hills a pink smile coming in the sky telling us that the morning had come really at last So we watched & suddenly there rose (popped w^d be a better word for it really rose in one instant) such a sun – 'nor dim, nor red' (you know the verse) & then dipped back again below the hills It was so beautiful – But I shocked Mama by saying 'Jack in the box' which awoke Emily who declared of course she had been wide awake and had seen it all. Why do people always do that, S^t. Crumpet? This was just before we came to Marseilles. It had been snowing the day before & it was nice to go to sleep & wake up in the summer . . . At Toulon it was like July – I don't like such heat – Transplantation & scorching is too much for an Irish rose – But I sat with Mama and Emily on a rock & sketched Toulon Harbour, (or rather tried to) for you S^t. Crumpet. Then the next we posted, the country was so beautiful some of it & towards evening we saw snowy peaks, they were the mountains of Savoy. I was pretty tired that night & we had to sleep at Frejus such a disagreeable place. . . . I can tell you how the fields were white with Narcissi, how the roads were edged with mauve-coloured anemones & how the scarlet anemones stood up in the meadows tantalizing me in the carriage so much because I wanted to feel them And there were myrtles (wild) growing close to the blue Mediterranean & Mama lay down on them by the seaside at Cannes while Papa and I were talking to a perfectly deaf old French fisherman who gave his † to me as he caught them putting them half alive into my hands, oh, you w^d have been alive there. Well we got here (Nice) on Saturday evening & we climbed up an old Roman Amphitheatre and saw of all sunsets the most glorious. We said it was like Light in the West, Beauvais, and again we thought of you Oh S^t. Crumpet I think of you so much & of all your dearnesses to me.**99**

JOHN RUSKIN, *PRAETERITA*,
PUB. RUPERT HART-DAVIS, 1949

ALONG THE RIVIERA

F. Scott Fitzgerald (1896–1940) first visited the south of France at the invitation of his friends Gerald and Sarah Murphy, and subsequently set part of his novel "Tender Is the Night" there.

66She and her mother hired a car – after much haggling, for Rosemary had formed her valuations of money in France – and drove along the Riviera, the delta of many rivers. The chauffeur, a Russian czar of the period of Ivan the Terrible, was a self-appointed guide, and the resplendent names – Cannes, Nice, Monte Carlo – began to glow through their torpid camouflage, whispering of old kings come here to dine or die, of rajahs tossing Buddhas' eyes to English ballerinas, of Russian princes

turning the weeks into Baltic twilights in the lost caviare days. . . . It was pleasant to drive back to the hotel in the late afternoon, above a sea as mysteriously coloured as the agates and cornelians of childhood, green as green milk, blue as laundry water, wine dark. It was pleasant to pass people eating outside their doors, and to hear the fierce mechanical pianos behind the vines and country estaminets. When they turned off the Corniche d'Or and down to Gaisse's hotel through the darkening banks of trees, set one behind another in many greens, the moon already hovered over the ruins of the aqueducts.**99**

F. SCOTT FITZGERALD, *TENDER IS THE NIGHT*, PUB. THE GREY WALLS PRESS, 1953, FIRST PUB. 1934

BY TRAIN
In his short story "A Canary for One", Ernest Hemingway (1899–1961) describes a train journey through Provence.

66The train passed very quickly a long, red stone house with a garden and four thick palm trees with tables under them in the shade. On the other side was the sea. Then there was a cutting through red stone and clay, and the sea was only occasionally and far below against rocks.
'I bought him in Palermo,' the American lady said. 'We only had an hour ashore and it was Sunday morning. The man wanted to be paid in dollars and I gave him a dollar and a half. He really sings very beautifully.'
It was very hot in the train and it was very hot in the *lit salon* compartment. There was no breeze came through the open window. The American lady pulled the window-blind down and there was no more sea, even occasionally. On the other side there was glass, then the corridor, then an open window, and outside the window were dusty trees and an oiled road and flat fields of grapes, with grey-stone hills behind them.
There was smoke from many tall chimneys – coming into Marseilles, and the train slowed down and followed one track through many others into the station. The train stayed twenty-five minutes in the station at Marseilles and the American lady bought a copy of the *Daily Mail* and a half-bottle of Evian water. She walked a little way along the station platform, but she stayed near the steps of the car because at Cannes, where it stopped for twelve minutes, the train had left with no signal of departure and she had gotten on only just in time. The American lady was a little deaf and she was afraid that perhaps signals of departure were given and that she did not hear them.

The train left the station in Marseilles and there was not only the switch-yards and the factory smoke but, looking back, the town of Marseilles and the harbour with stone hills behind it and the last of the sun on the water. As it was getting dark the train passed a farmhouse burning in a field. Motor-cars were stopped along the road and bedding and things from inside the farmhouse were spread in the field. Many people were watching the house burn. After it was dark the train was in Avignon. People got on and off. At the news-stand Frenchmen, returning to Paris, bought that day's French papers. On the station platform were negro soldiers. They wore brown uniforms and were tall and their faces shone, close under the electric light. Their faces were very black and they were too tall to stare. The train left Avignon station with the negroes standing there. A short white sergeant was with them.**"**

Ernest Hemingway, *The First Forty-nine Stories*,
pub. Jonathan Cape, 1944

Light and color

The Mediterranean

Vincent Van Gogh (1853–90) painted some of his best pictures in the south of France, inspired by the vivid landscapes and jewel colors.

"I am writing to you from Stes. Maries on the shore of the Mediterranean at last. The Mediterranean has the colours of mackerel, changeable I mean. You don't always know if it is green or violet, you can't even say it's blue, because the next moment the changing light has taken on a tinge of rose colour or grey.
A family is a queer thing – quite involuntarily and in spite of myself I have been thinking here between whiles of our sailor uncle, who must many a time have seen the shores of this sea.
I brought three canvases and have covered them – two sea-scapes, a view of the village, and then some drawings which I will send you by post, when I return to-morrow to Arles.
I have board and lodging for 4 francs a day and they began by asking 6.
As soon as I can I shall probably come back here again to make some more studies. The shore here is sandy, no cliffs nor rocks – like Holland without the dunes, and bluer.
You get better fried fish here than on the Seine. Only there is not fish to be had every day, as the fishermen go off to sell it in Marseilles. But when there is any it is frightfully good.
If there isn't – the butcher is not much more appetising than the butcher fellah of M. Gérome – if there is no fish it is pretty difficult to get anything to eat, as far as I can see.
I do not think there are 100 houses in the village or town. The chief building after the old church, an ancient fortress, is the barracks. And the houses – like the ones on our heaths and peat-mosses at Drenthe; you will see some specimens of them in

the drawings. . . . One night I went for a walk by the sea along the empty shore. It was not gay, but neither was it sad – it was – beautiful. The deep blue sky was flecked with clouds of a blue deeper than the fundamental blue of intense cobalt, and others of a clearer blue like the blue whiteness of the Milky Way. On the blue depth the stars were sparkling, greenish, yellow, white, rose, brighter, flashing more like jewels, than they do at home – even in Paris, opals you might call them, emeralds, lapis, sapphires.

The sea was very deep ultramarine – the shore a sort of violet and faint russet as I saw it, and on the dunes (about seventeen feet high they are) some bushes Prussian blue. Besides half-page drawings I have a big drawing, the fellow to the last.**99**

FURTHER LETTERS OF VINCENT VAN GOGH TO HIS BROTHER – 1886–1889,
PUB. HOUGHTON MIFFLIN & CO., 1929

IN PAINTERS' FOOTSTEPS

Crime writer Patricia Highsmith (b. 1921) lives in France, as does the central character in her best-known novels, villain Tom Ripley.

66He came down in a leisurely way from Paris, stopping overnight in Lyon and also in Arles to see the places that Van Gogh had painted there. He maintained his cheerful equanimity in the face of atrociously bad weather. In Arles, the rain borne on the violent mistral soaked him through as he tried to discover the exact spots where Van Gogh had stood to paint from. He had bought a beautiful book of Van Gogh reproductions in Paris, but he could not take the book out in the rain, and he had to make a dozen trips back to his hotel to verify the scenes. He looked over Marseille, found it drab except for the Canebière, and moved on eastward by train, stopping for a day in St Tropez, Cannes, Nice, Monte Carlo all the places he had heard of and felt such affinity for when he saw them, though in the month of December they were overcast by grey winter clouds, and the gay crowds were not there, even on New Year's Eve in Menton. Tom put the people there in his imagination, men and women in evening clothes descending the broad steps of the gambling palace in Monte Carlo, people in bright bathing costumes, light and brilliant as a Dufy watercolour, walking under the palms of the Boulevard des Anglais at Nice. People – American, English, French, German, Swedish, Italian. Romance, disappointment, quarrels, reconciliations, murder. The Côte d'Azur excited him as no other place he had yet seen in the world excited him. And it was so tiny, really, this curve in the Mediterranean coastline with the wonderful names strung like beads – Toulon, Fréjus, St Raphael, Cannes, Nice, Menton, and then St Remo.**99**

PATRICIA HIGHSMITH, *THE TALENTED MR RIPLEY*,
PUB. VINTAGE, 1992

THE LIGHT

Dirk Bogarde (b. 1921) calls the Riviera "a radiant old whore" but finds that he is pulled back to it time and again by the magic and the Light.

66Magic has its components, and the most important of them here is the Light. Without the Light it is fair to say that the Riviera would not exist. In spite of the ruin and the greed along the coastal strip, the Light (and it deserves its capital letter) has not altered. The petrol haze on the seafront has merely dimmed it slightly. It still glows down, sparkling in sequined disarray upon the deceptively clear sea; still scorches the pale bodies unwisely ignoring its

121

power along the artificial beaches. It exaggerates light and shade (shadows here are blacker than pitch) and enhances color – fierce, harsh almost, brilliantly exploding color that one never suspected could exist in nature, so that pink is suddenly carmine, the soft green of the maritime pines is viridian, tiled roofs burst with orange fire, and the dust under one's feet is a rich copper. This, of course, is why Bonnard and Braque, Monet and Renoir, and all the others came here, determined to capture the Light and set it for all time on canvas. My own father was driven to desperation as a painter trying to catch the elusive color of the olive trees. Was it green or was it silver? Was it blue or a mixture of the three? No two painters ever agreed, and my father, alas, never caught it at all. Forever his olive trees were the sorry product of the sodden skies of his native England. They never lost the boiled green of broccoli and were a continuing disappointment to him.**

DIRK BOGARDE, ARTICLE IN *EUROPEAN TRAVEL & LIFE*,
DECEMBER 1988

SPRING

Katherine Mansfield (1888–1923) wrote to her husband on April 12, 1920, of the beauty of the south of France in spring. She was living there at the time in an effort to alleviate her tuberculosis.

**Time seems to be flying this month and I have only 2 more Mondays here after this one. If only the wedder is fine and fayre in May! I don't think it would be possible to have fogs now, do you? The gorgeous air and almost certain sunshine give one quite a horror of such things. Today for instance – its 9 a.m.; it's hot. The sun is pure gold and a great swag of crimson roses outside my window fills the room with a sweet smell. Oh, how I have come to *love* this S. of France – and to dislike the French. The French here don't count; they are just *cultivateurs au bord de la mer*, but it's the voice of la France *officielle* which I loathe so. You should have read *l'Eclaireur* on this last crise; it was a very pretty little eye-opener.

But, Bogey, I do so long for you to know this country in the Spring. It's like the Middle Ages, somehow. I feel it's Elizabethan spring – earlier – far – oh, I don't know *when*. But driving up those valleys and seeing the great shower of flowers and seeing the dark silver olives and the people working in the beanfields – one feels as though one were part of the *tradition* of spring.

Outside my window are two lizards. Sometimes they come in and look at me and their throats pant in a funny way. I wish I could bring them home.

Oh, my dearest, I love the sun. I made a fuss about it at San Remo, but that was because I was ill – but I love it. To WORK and to play in our garden – in woods and fields and on mountains and pebbly shores – with you. And to sometimes draw on thin suède gloves

and go into cities and look at pictures and hear music and sit at a café with a long drink watching the passing show (you with a large parcel of books on the chair by you). That's the life for me – to live like artists, always free and *warm-hearted* and always *learning.* **"**

Letters of Katherine Mansfield to John Middleton Murry,
pub. Constable & Co. Ltd, 1951

Villeneuve-les-Avignon

Violet Paget (1856–1935) wrote her essays, novels and travel pieces under the pseudonym of Vernon Lee.

"The short southern twilight had set in, and cast a delicate, an elegiac veil over the refuse-heaps among the huddled, half-ruined buildings. Above me spread a great white fortress; and towards it, obedient to the cabman and concierge, I took my way up the rough barren hillside. It would be the matter of only five minutes, those out-at-elbows hidalgos had insisted with that southern friendliness eager to make things sound pleasant even at the sacrifice of a little truth; and added, as if speaking of some great avenue of trees: 'Madame n'a qu'à prendre par les amandiers.' The almond-trees were on the brow of the low hill, a stunted grove of almost leafless trees, gnarled and twisted with age. Once past them the path became a slide of loose white stones, not pebbles, but scales of that rock which makes the buildings white and the landscape noble with its sharp stratified cleavage; and among the black, square-cut olive-trees dotted here and there as in an early Corot landscape, the rock came through in great slabs, whiter than ever in the twilight, fringed with vegetation of parched herbs, peppermint, and that minute white candytuft which grows wild all over Provence (I noticed it first in Aucassin's Castle of Beaucaire!), scenting the evening with honey. Rock breaking through the thin soil, stunted aromatic plants, the signs of the real South, of something that is not merely France and Italy, but the whole ancient Mediterranean world! Above, in front, the massy walls and towers of the citadel rose white out of the rock, their corbels and battlements carved with Ionic fairness. And below flowed the great wan river, with a spectral Avignon beyond.**"**

Vernon Lee,
The Golden Keys,
pub. Bodley Head, 1925

HILLS AND VALLEYS

Marcel Pagnol (1895–1974) was born and died in the foothills of the Massif de l'Étoile, not far from Marseilles, and his best-known novels, "Jean de Florette" and "Manon des Sources" lovingly describe the region.

❝He descended toward the plateau that dominated Les Refresquières.

It was a deep valley, mainly hollowed from the blue limestone of Provence by some rugged glacier that had started out during the night of the millenia.

From each side a steep hillside clothed in thick pine woods rose from the bottom of the valley to the foot of the vertical escarpments that sustained the two plateaux. It was a large table of rock furrowed here and there with clefts that the wind and rain had filled with dust, sand, and gravel. The hardy plants of the hills followed the lines of these furrows.

Thyme, rue, lavender, and rockrose had thus formed miniature hedges, and in the larger crevasses cades and junipers, mixed with some twisted pines, had formed little dark green thickets, sometimes burdened with flights of chaffinches.

Right in the middle of the vallon torrential rainfall had carved a bed in the limestone, which was now perfectly bare and polished, like marble, but pierced here and there by circular openings that grew bigger as they deepened, like flattened spheres. They were of all sizes. Many were no bigger than a cooking pot, but others were as much as two meters across.

With every rainfall the vallon received the runoff from the neighboring plateaux. These streams had cut deep ravines down to the bed of rock where the day's torrent rolled and rumbled.

The streams' pounding flight left the holes in the stone filled with bright water, which the birds, the goats, the hunters, and the sun drank dry in a few days.

Because of the storm during the night, all the hollows of the vallon sparkled in the bright rays of the morning sun, and the bigger ones shivered in a breeze that hardly touched the silence.❞

MARCEL PAGNOL, *MANON DES SOURCES*,
TRANS. BY W. E. van HEYNINGEN,
PUB. ANDRÉ DEUTSCH LTD, 1990

THE MISTRAL

Colette (1873–1954) describes the onslaught and aftermath of the mistral at the little house where she spent many summers on the shores of the Mediterranean.

❝The door leading to the vines from the enclosure walled with openwork bricks is straining slightly on its hinges; the wind must be rising. It will swiftly sweep a quarter of the horizon and fasten on the wintry purity of the greenish north. Thereupon the whole hollow of the bay will boom like a shell. Goodbye to my night in the open on the raffia mattress! If I had persisted in sleeping out of doors, that powerful mouth that breathes coldness and drought, deadens all scents and anesthetizes the earth, the enemy of work, voluptuousness and sleep, would have torn off me the sheets and blankets that it knows how to twist into long rolls. What a strange tormentor, as intent on man as any wild beast! Those who are highly strung know more about it than I do. My Provençal cook, when the wind strikes her near the well, puts down her buckets, holds her head and cries: 'It's killing me!'On nights when the mistral blows she groans under it in her little hut among the vines, and perhaps she sees it . . . . A hawk moth from the oleanders is banging against the fine wire netting in front of the french window, returning to the charge again and again until the taut netting reverberates like the skin of a drum. It is cool. The generous dew trickles, the mistral has put off its offensive. The stars, magnified by the damp and salty air, twinkle broadly. Once again the most beautiful of all nights precedes the most beautiful of all days, and not being asleep, I can enjoy it.**99**

COLETTE, *EARTHLY PARADISE*,
TRANS. ENID MCLEOD,
PUB. SECKER & WARBURG, 1966

BEAUCAIRE

Henry James (1843–1916) traveled to Beaucaire to examine a ruined fortress and admire the surrounding country.

66It stands on a foundation of rock much higher than that of Tarascon, and looks over with a melancholy expression at its better-conditioned brother. Its position is magnificent and its outline very gallant. I was well rewarded for my pilgrimage; for if the castle of Beaucaire is only a fragment, the whole place, with its position and its views, is an ineffaceable picture. It was the stronghold of the Montmorencys, and its last tenant was that rash Duke François whom Richelieu, seizing every occasion to trample on a great noble, caused to be beheaded at Toulouse, where we saw, in the Capitol, the butcher's knife with which the cardinal pruned the crown of France of its thorns. The castle, after the death of this victim, was virtually demolished. Its site, which nature today has taken again to herself, has an extraordinary charm. The mass of rock that it formerly covered rises high above the town and is as precipitous as the side of the Rhône. A tall, rusty iron gate admits you from a quiet corner of Beaucaire to a wild tangled garden covering the side of the hill – for the whole place forms the public promenade of the townsfolk – a garden without flowers, with little steep, rough paths that wind under a plantation of small, scrubby stone-pines. Above this is the grassy platform of the castle, enclosed on one side only (towards the river) by a large fragment of wall and a very massive dungeon. There are benches placed in the lee of the wall, and others on the edge of the platform, where one may enjoy a view, beyond the river, of certain peeled and scorched undulations. A sweet desolation, an everlasting peace, seemed to hang in the air. A very old man (a fragment, like the castle itself) emerged from some crumbling corner to do me the honours – a very gentle, obsequious, tottering, toothless, grateful old man. He beguiled me into an ascent of the solitary tower, from which you may look down on the big sallow river and glance at diminished Tarascon and the barefaced, bald-headed hills behind it. It may appear that I insist too much upon the nudity of the Provençal horizon – too much considering that I have spoken of the prospect from the heights of Beaucaire as lovely. But it is an exquisite bareness; it seems to exist for the purpose of allowing one to follow the delicate lines of the hills and touch with the eyes, as it were, the smallest inflections of the landscape. It makes the whole thing wonderfully bright and pure.**99**

HENRY JAMES, *A LITTLE TOUR IN FRANCE*,
PUB. TAUCHNITZ, 1954,
FIRST PUB. 1884

THE PEOPLE

A FAIR

The English writer Arthur Young (1741–1820) saw a different and livelier side of Beaucaire when he visited the town during a fair.

❝The fair of Beaucaire fills the whole country with business and motion; meet many carts loaded; and nine diligences going or coming. Yesterday and to-day the hottest I ever experienced; we had none like them in Spain; the flies much worse than the heat. . . . My quarters at Nîmes were at the *Louvre*, a large, commodious, and excellent inn. The house was almost as much a fair from morning to night as Beaucaire itself could be. I dined and supped at the *table d'hôte*; the cheapness of these tables suits my finances, and one sees something of the manners of the people; we sat down from twenty to forty at every meal, most motley companies of French, Italians, Spaniards, and Germans, with a Greek and Armenian; and I was informed, that there is hardly a nation in Europe or Asia that have not merchants at this great fair, chiefly for raw silk, of which many millions in value are sold in four days: all the other commodities of the world are to be found there.

One circumstance I must remark on this numerous *table d'hôte*, because it has struck me repeatedly, which is the taciturnity of the French. I came to the kingdom expecting to have my ears constantly fatigued with the infinite volubility and spirits of the people, of which so many persons have written, sitting, I suppose, by their English firesides. At Montpellier, though fifteen persons and some of them ladies were present, I found it impossible to make them break their inflexible silence with more than a monosyllable, and the whole company sat more like an assembly of tongue-tied Quakers, than the mixed company of a people famous for loquacity. Here also, at Nîmes, with a different party at every meal it is the same; not a Frenchman will open his lips.❞

ARTHUR YOUNG, *TRAVELS IN FRANCE DURING THE YEARS 1787, 1788 & 1789*, ED. CONSTANTIA MAXWELL, PUB. CAMBRIDGE UNIVERSITY PRESS, 1950

DIFFERENT VALUES

Lawrence Durrell (b. 1912) wrote from Sommières in July 1957 to his friend Alan Thomas.

❝I agree with you about the French; it is the disparity between their character and the character of France itself which is so strange. It is a masterpiece by a grumpy man. But they have a far higher regard for freedom than we have, complete disregard for 'face', and a profound sense of values. I think Claude is right in saying it is because there is still genuine unfeatherbedded peasantry and the values of ordinary life flow from them – in food and similar things. Here one does not feel so bitterly about the mob getting all the gravy – because they spend it unerringly on whatever makes the heart glad. You should see the old workmen spend their wages – the care with which they select a good bottle of champagne – champagne at 12

126

shillings – or even an ordinary rouge at a shilling. You should see them going over a counterful of cheeses with their horny fingers touching them like Menuhin does his Strad. The intellectuals here are really outside ordinary life – nobody looks to them for physical values, only spiritual. It is taken for granted that nobody will do anything to seriously impair the quality of Camembert. *That* will go on. The rest is ideas – and they don't care where the ideas go if they don't get into the wine. Of course the motor-bike and telly barber-shop moronic world is catching up here – but very slowly; and somehow when any lout on a motor-bike can discuss wine and cheese in broken tones with tears streaming down his cheeks you feel less sad about the motor-bike. In England you feel everything is a *cult*, life itself is a sort of ritualistic cult, sex a fertility rite etc. One is conscious of the tabu. And much as I deplore the lack of lavatory sense here I'm convinced that their healthy attitude to ordure is the basis of their psychic balance; the balance in sex relations too. It's good to get men and women using the same lavatory, getting used to the smelliest part of each other; it keeps the crops in perspective. Then there are two other things unique of their kind – the reverence for love and the devotion to artists. There isn't anyone who doesn't gaze admiringly at you if you say you are a painter or poet; even those who can't read. I think these outweigh the bad qualities in a final judgement. I can't think of another nation quite like them at their best. **"**

LAWRENCE DURRELL, *SPIRIT OF PLACE*,
PUB. FABER & FABER, 1969

A SERVANT GIRL

Virginia Woolf (1882–1941) recorded in her diary impressions of two different women she observed in Juan les Pins.

"Yes, I thought; I will make a note of that face – the face of the woman stitching a very thin, lustrous green silk at a table in the restaurant where we lunched at Vienne. She was like fate – a consummate mistress of all the arts of self preservation: hair rolled & lustrous; eyes so nonchalant; nothing could startle her; there she sat stitching her green silk with people going & coming all the time; she not looking, yet knowing, fearing nothing, expecting nothing – a perfectly equipped middle class French woman.

At Carpentras last night there was the little servant girl with honest eyes, hair brushed in a flop, & one rather black tooth. I felt that life would crush her out inevitably. Perhaps 18. not more; yet on the wheel, without hope; poor, not weak but mastered – yet not enough mastered but to desire furiously travel, for a moment, a car. Ah but I am not rich she said to me – which her cheap little stockings & shoes showed anyhow. Oh how I envy you – able to travel. You like Carpentras? But the wind blows ever so hard. You'll come again? Thats the bell ringing. Never mind. Come over here & look at this. No, I've never seen anything like it. Ah yes, she always likes the English ('She' was the other maid, with hair like some cactus in erection). Yes I always like the English she said. The odd little honest face, with the black tooth, will stay on at Carpentras I suppose: will marry?

will become one of those stout black women who sit in the door knitting? No: I foretell for her some tragedy; because she had enough mind to envy us the Lanchester.**99**

THE DIARY OF VIRGINIA WOOLF, ED. ANNE OLIVIER BELL, PUB. HARCOURT BRACE JOVANOVICH, 1982

TOURISM
Edward Burra (b. 1905) wrote of the fashions at the emerging resorts of the Riviera in the 1920's.

66Well my whoreingest. If you could see the jolly men bathing at the bathing beach everyone skilfully undresses on the plage in full view of everyone prizes are given to those who manage to undress and not show the organs only this morning it was won by the celebrated poet of the advance guard William Chappell, Mdlle Ida Rubinstein gracefully gave away the prize which consisted of [a] charmingly fashioned whirling spray which when opened by a secret spring disguised in the spout discloses a tangeè lip stick with powderette & a bottle of Piver's Pompeia. . . . Our hotel is a dream of delight there is a couple that intreeges us no wedding ring my dear the man is very tall and thin & the woman is very small & thin, they have such a twee doggie that violates every puss it lays hands on the chic wear here is ripping red print hankys round the neck & head white linen trews and bathing shoes in blue, white striped or rose pink everyone walks about with drawing books and canvasses the canvasses look a bit futurist you know you cant tell if its the old manse at twilight or death at the festival. We are going to Marseilles on B's birthday you know us men must be satisfied and there aint no facilities here is.n.t it twee all about the Grand Rue where we get our jolly marin ware and linen trousers the guide book says is a veritable ghetto of houses of ilfame my dear I stares into every window hopeing for a thrill but all I see is little Georgette having her nappy changed by loving mothers hands. Billy has come out in a lovely toilette of linen trowsers bathing shoes a pullover & red kerchief and a jolly beret bought at Elli's hatshop Marseilles.**99**

WELL DEARIE! , THE LETTERS OF EDWARD BURRA, ED. WILLIAM CHAPPELL, PUB. GORDON FRASER, 1985

GRASSE
Henry Miller (1891–1980) wrote to Anaïs Nin of a visit to Grasse.

66Nice, June 1939
Monday night
Anaïs –
Got your note this evening on my return from Grasse where I spent the afternoon. If it weren't that there are no buses at night I'd have stayed on. Am thinking of going back there tomorrow and stay overnight, probably leaving this place Wednesday. Grasse is better than all the places I've yet seen! You must go – after I leave. Explore it thoroughly. The old town lies on one side of the main street, in descending layers of labyrinthian coils. Superb decrepitude and very much alive. Hasn't such monuments as Sarlat but more picturesque still. The site is too wonderful. I like the air – very light – about 300 or 400 metres up. Better than Nice – I noticed that immediately. I would like to go back there for a stay in the winter. It's just what I like – the old port which is quite big, or seems so, at first sight. I could kick myself for not having been here sooner. Why don't people talk about these places?
HVM **99**

HENRY MILLER, *LETTERS TO ANAÏS NIN.* EDITED AND INTRODUCED BY GUNTER STUHLMANN. PETER OWEN 1965

ITINERARIES

▲ The Salignac Plateau, near Sisteron. ▼ Forestry plantations near Larche.

▼ The summit of the Lure Mountains, white with frost.

▲ Autumn in Entrechaux.

▲ Orchards in Lubéron. ▼

▲ View of the north side of Port-Cros, from the botanical footpath.

▲ Pointe Ste-Hospice, at St-Jean-Cap-Ferrat.　　　　▼ Cove at Port-Cros.

▲ Black on white, a procession of the bulls at Saintes-Maries-de-la-Mer.

▲ Pink and gray flamingos.   ▼ Camargue bulls among the reedbeds.

▲ Tourettes-sur-Loup, perched on a limestone outcrop.

▲ Old Vence and its ramparts.　　　　　▼ The beautiful village of Peillon.

AVIGNON

▲ AVIGNON

1 St-Bénézet Bridge
2 Palace of the Popes
3 Notre-Dame-des-Doms
4 Petit Palais Museum
5 Tour des Chiens
6 Tour du Châtelet
7 Church of St-Agricol
8 Roure Palace
9 Récollets Convent
10 Carmelite Convent
11 Calvet Museum
12 Requien Museum
13 Old Mint

⏲ Three days

VOULAND MUSEUM
In 1927, a local businessman, Louis Vouland, bought the Hôtel Villeneuve-Esclapon (1882) and filled it with furniture, gold plate, faïence, porcelain, paintings and tapestries. The 18th century was his specialty.

Shortly before the Rhône flows into the Durance, it rounds one final bend where the river is overhung by a rock rising 130 feet out of the water. It was here that the future City of the Popes ● *48* was founded. The earliest signs of human habitation in these parts go back to the 4th millennium BC.

THE ST-AGRICOL DISTRICT

ROURE PALACE ★. This residence was built in 1469 by the Florentine banker Pietro Baroncelli and was to be inhabited by his family until 1909. It contains a notable compilation of written and figurative documentation on Provence, and the

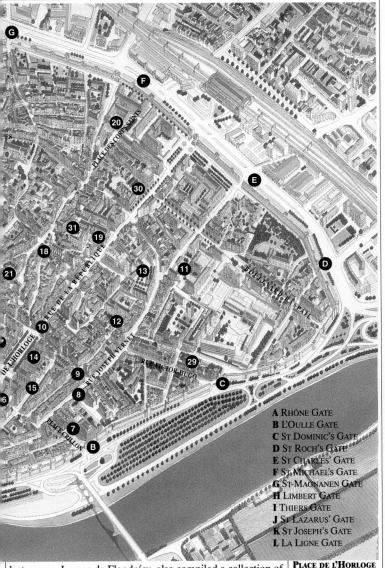

A Rhône Gate
B L'Oulle Gate
C St Dominic's Gate
D St Roch's Gate
E St Charles' Gate
F St Michael's Gate
G St-Magnanen Gate
H Limbert Gate
I Thiers' Gate
J St Lazarus' Gate
K St Joseph's Gate
L La Ligne Gate

last owner, Jeanne de Flandrésy, also compiled a collection of costumes from the region of Arles and the Comtat Venaissin. In addition, there is a fascinating display of *santons* ● *70*, mementos of the cattle dealer Folco de Baroncelli, and Provençal artefacts and furniture.

CHURCH OF ST-AGRICOL. This 14th-century building is now closed to the public. It comprises a massive tower, a nave and two aisles; the façade was built in the 15th century and is a good illustration of the Provençal style of the period. The much-restored statuary is attributed to Ferrier Bernard, a sculptor from Lorraine who lived in Avignon around 1489.

PLACE DE L'HORLOGE
This is situated on the site of the Roman Forum. It was built in 1447 and rebuilt in 1743.

THE "REQUIEN REREDOS" (1450)
The elegant yet monumental art of Enguerrand Quarton was as influential as that of the great master of Aix; it was also decisive for the future of the Avignon School which he tried to liberate from Netherland influences. His adherence to the

THE TOWN HALL. The Town Hall was built in the middle of the 19th century on the site of a former municipal building, which had itself been constructed on land owned by a cardinal in the 1360's. The original building's tower has survived; a jaquemart was added in 1471.

HOUSE OF JEAN VILAR ★. This house occupies premises in the Hôtel de Crochans, a building whose elaborate entrance was designed by Pierre Mignard in 1679. The Hôtel was completed by Franque in the 18th century. Since 1979, it has housed an exhibition of the great stage director's work; it also has a section that recounts the history of the Avignon Festival.

PLACE DU PALAIS ★

This huge open space stands on a slight slope, and is at the center of a magnificent group of monuments. Events are staged here throughout the Festival.

THE AVIGNON FESTIVAL. In 1947, René Char and Yvonne and Christian Zervos organized an exhibition of contemporary art in the Palace of the Popes, and invited Jean Vilar (1912–71), a director best known for his production of Shakespeare's *Richard II*. Vilar, enchanted by the open-air theater, involved himself in the birth of the Avignon Festival. He introduced a theater style that was new and "popular" in the best sense, and broadened the Festival's scope to include mime, dance and music.

ANCIEN HÔTEL DES MONNAIES. This building was constructed during the time of Cardinal Borghese by the Vice-Legate, di Bagni. After the legation was removed, the house was used as a barracks until 1840. Today, it houses the Music Conservatory.

CATHEDRAL OF NOTRE-DAME-DES-DOMS. This cathedral was built on the site of an early Christian basilica and another church consecrated in 1069. The present church dates from the 12th century. The PORCH is influenced by styles dating from Roman antiquity, while the main entrance is surmounted by a tympanum and a pediment decorated with frescos of Christ giving thanks and the Virgin Mary expressing humility; they are by the Italian painter Simone Martini (c. 1340). The square TOWER was partly destroyed in 1405, but was rebuilt shortly afterward without its pyramid-shaped spire.

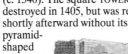

Avignon School is seen here in the grandiose power of his composition, the solidity of the spaces, and the severity of his expressive power enhanced by a striking use of light.

Above: *Prophet* by Simone Martini (c. 1320).

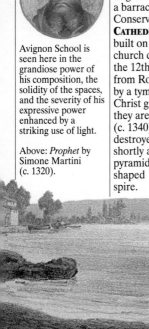

The church has a narthex and a nave with four uneven bays; the APSE was entirely redone in 1671 on plans by the architect Louis-François de La Valfenière (1615–88) who, with his father François (1575–1667), was a major artist of the Counter-Reformation. A gallery in the form of a tribune was added the length of the side walls by François Delbène. The CHOIR contains an *Assumption* (1633) by Nicolas Mignard and some portraits of popes by Garnier (1869).

PETIT PALAIS MUSEUM ★. The Petit Palais itself was built in the early 14th century by Béranger Frédol and Arnaud de Via. Pope Benedict XII bought it in 1335 and turned the Cardinal's Palace into a residence for the bishop. Since 1976, the Museum has owned a number of medieval paintings and sculptures, and some three hundred works by early Italian Masters from the prestigious CAMPANA COLLECTION; there are displays of works of art from Italy in Rooms 3–16 and from Avignon in Rooms 1, 2, 17, 18, and 19. From the early 15th century onward, Florence could be described as a large research laboratory as far as the study of perspective was concerned; however, little survives of the Avignon School, which combined Italian stylization and Flemish realism.

ST-BÉNÉZET BRIDGE ★. This 2,950-foot-long bridge in Villeneuve-lès-Avignon was built between 1177 and 1185, and finishes at the foot of the Tower of Philip the Fair (Tour Philippe-le-Bel). None of it remains except for four of the twenty-four arches that originally straddled the Rhône. Its roadway was made of wood, and this explains how the bridge came to be built so quickly for the period. It was rebuilt in stone in the 13th century, but with one arch fewer as one end of the bridge now formed part of the city wall. The ST-BÉNÉZET CHAPEL, which contains the body of the bridge's founder, is situated over the third pier, and ST NICHOLAS' CHAPEL was constructed on the same site at the end of the 14th century. The arches began to crumble over the years, and it was closed to traffic as long ago as 1633.

CHÂTELET
The covered way, which passes the Tour des Chiens (opposite), the only octagonal tower in the ramparts, was constructed in the late 15th century. The Châtelet was

built around 1345 by Pope Clement VI to control traffic on the bridge and to protect the town. It was rebuilt in 1414; the tower was later raised and watchtowers were added.

PALACE OF THE POPES

During the 14th century, it was normal practise for the Pope to say the hours after rising. He would then say Mass and give audiences in his *studium*. He sometimes took a walk in the garden after signing petitions.

1 Bell Tower
2 Benedict XII Chapel
3 Cloister Courtyard
4 Trouillas Tower
5 Latrine Tower
6 Kitchen Tower
7 Consistory Wing
8 St John Tower

9 Conclave Wing
10 Household accommodation
11 Private apartments
12 Pope's Tower
13 Main entrance
14 Grand Dignitaries' Wing
15 Wardrobe Tower
16 St Lawrence Tower
17 Clementine Chapel
18 Grand Audience Chamber

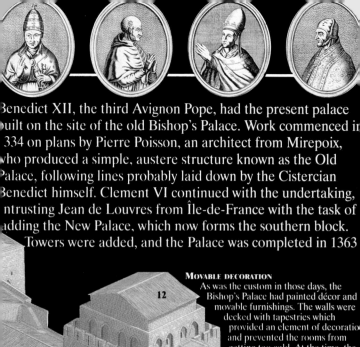

Benedict XII, the third Avignon Pope, had the present palace built on the site of the old Bishop's Palace. Work commenced in 334 on plans by Pierre Poisson, an architect from Mirepoix, who produced a simple, austere structure known as the Old Palace, following lines probably laid down by the Cistercian Benedict himself. Clement VI continued with the undertaking, entrusting Jean de Louvres from Île-de-France with the task of adding the New Palace, which now forms the southern block. Towers were added, and the Palace was completed in 1363

MOVABLE DECORATION
As was the custom in those days, the Bishop's Palace had painted décor and movable furnishings. The walls were decked with tapestries which provided an element of decoration and prevented the rooms from getting too cold. At the time, the tapestries mainly came from the East, Italy, and workshops in Paris and Valenciennes.

The floors of some of the more important rooms boasted colored, varnished and historiated tiles while others had paving stones covered with matting and swathes of freshly cut grass, straw and aromatic herbs. The furniture, of which nothing has survived was simple and was made

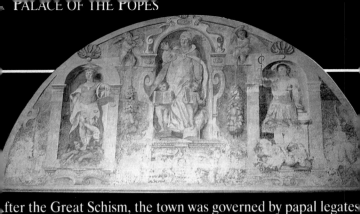

After the Great Schism, the town was governed by papal legates who lived in the palace. François de Conzié, chamberlain to Pope John XXIII (1370–1419), cherished the dream of returning to Avignon and he carried out renovations , but it was Pierre de Foix, the Legate from 1433 to 1464, who was the first to establish himself there permanently. Gradually, the Legates, who were Italian for the most part and related to the popes by marriage, refused to leave Rome, and delegated their functions to vice-legates. The latter had little money at their disposal, and consequently were only able to have much smaller courts.

BARRACKS, THEN A PRISON

The palace was badly damaged during the French Revolution, and was used as a barracks in the early 19th century and then a prison. The Old Palace, already classified as a historical monument, was commandeered in 1871 to store the departmental archives. The first restoration work did not commence until 1906.

MILITARY ARCHITECTURE
This papal residence is situated on the top of a rock, and covers an area of 17,940 square yards; it was simultaneously a fortress and a palace. The walls are flanked by ten square towers, and incorporate pointed equilateral arches supporting the machicolation.

Saint Martial in the Habit of a Bishop, fresco by Matteo Giovanetti (14th century), St-Martial Chapel.

A PRISON DURING THE REVOLUTION

On the night of October 17, 1791, the palace was the scene of the "Galcière" Massacre, a dramatic reaction to the arrests that had followed the murder of Lescuyer, leader of the Revolutionary Party. In 1793, the Convention considered demolishing both the ramparts, as a symbol of the feudal system, and the palace itself. The plan came to nothing, but the palace was pillaged and soon fell into disrepair.

THE MAIN COURTYARD

The earliest productions of the Avignon Festival were performed in this courtyard, and the more prestigious events still take place here. It is bordered to the north and east by Benedict XII's palace, and to the south and west by the two wings constructed by Clement VI. The rectangular plan corresponds to the remains of John XXII's Audience Chamber; the Pope's Tower once housed the Treasury and the Pontiff's Chamber.

THE LOGGIA

The exit from the Clementine Chapel is by way of a double door which opens to the north onto the loggia, a kind of porch mainly lit by the "Indulgence Window"; the restoration of this large window in 1913 was controversial. From here, the Pope used to give his triple blessing to the crowds assembled in the palace courtyard. At the Pope's coronation, it was in this loggia that the *triregnum*, a tiara ornamented with three crowns, was placed on his head.

ST JOHN'S CHAPEL (ST JOHN'S TOWER)

God Blessing Herod and these women's faces are among the frescos executed by Matteo Giovanetti in 1347 on the walls of St John's Chapel, an elegant shrine with ribbed vaulting. The paintings on the north and east walls relate the life of Saint John the Baptist, and

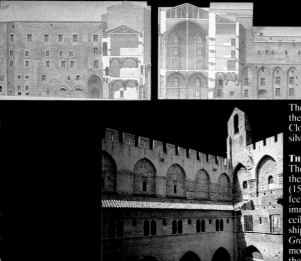

The bell tower below the Benedict XII Cloister contains a silver bell.

THE GRAND TINEL

The enormous size of the Banqueting Room (158 feet long by 34 feet wide) and its immense wooden ceiling shaped like a ship's keel make the *Grand Tinel* one of the most striking rooms in the entire palace. Matteo Giovanetti's frescos were destroyed in the fire of 1413. The fireplace with a canopy, which has now been rebuilt, was used to reheat food that had come up from the kitchens situated in the towers; this task was carried out in the *dressoir* concealed behind a stone arch, and the dishes were then brought to the Pontiff's table.

ST-MARTIAL CHAPEL (ST JOHN'S TOWER)

The walls and ribbed vaults of this chapel are covered with charming frescos executed by Matteo Giovanetti in 1344–5. These paintings miraculously escaped the fire of 1413 and, for the most part, the vandalism that occurred subsequently; despite some obvious anachronisms, they depict with great verve and poetic imagination the life of Saint Martial, the Apostle of Limousin. Limousin was also notable as Clement VI's birthplace. It is possible to follow the saint's life story by referring to the letters which mark the panels.

▲ PALACE OF THE POPES

These small carved brackets in the Grand Audience Chamber are decorated with representations of animals. They are objects of superb artistry.

THE POPE'S BEDCHAMBER (ANGELS' TOWER)
The walls are notable both for the fresh yellows and blues of the richly decorated foliage painted in tempera and for the originality of the motifs. In the upper part of the room, the frieze includes a succession of quadrilobes, and the dado consists of red drapery held up by rings. The window embrasures are adorned by empty birdcages. The original polychrome joists still support the ceiling, but a floor made of painted and varnished tiles has been rebuilt on the basis of 14th-century models.

THE GRAND AUDIENCE CHAMBER
This masterpiece by Jean de Louvres is 170 feet wide by 50 feet high, and is divided by naves separated by five central pillars arranged in the customary manner for a lower room in a castle. Light comes through two large bays in each of the gabled walls and five tall windows in the south wall. The Rote Tribunal, which derives its name from the wheel-shaped surrounding wall, used to meet near the east chevet.

146

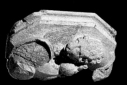

THE STAG ROOM (WARDROBE TOWER)

Clement VI's love of lordly splendor is exemplified here in the *studium* by the originality and opulence of the mural decoration. The themes, a far cry from the pious images one might have expected to find in a Pope's apartments, illustrate the pleasures of hunting and of falconry. The frieze adorned with a charming landscape full of animals is next to the Pontiff's family coat of arms.

SALOMON   DAVID

FRESCO OF THE PROPHETS

Matteo Giovanetti produced this famous fresco of twenty Old Testament figures in 1352 and 1353. It is in the Grand Audience Chamber on a section of the vault in the double bay where the Tribunal used to sit. The scene of the Last Judgement was sadly destroyed by the military government in 1822, and only traces of red remain of the *Crucifixion* which once adorned the east wall. A tierce-point door leads to the Lesser Audience Chamber where the ceiling is decorated with 17th-century trompe l'oeil paintings of military themes.

▲ AVIGNON

"CARRYING OF THE CROSS"
This marble reredos was commissioned by King René in 1478 from the Dalmatian artist Francesco Laurana for the Celestine Church in Avignon. It now hangs in the Church of St-Didier

ESPRIT RÉQUIEN (1788-1851)
This native of Avignon is considered to be the founder of botanical geography. He carried out the first inventory of Corsican flora and the first survey of the terracing on Mount Ventoux. A friend of the writer Prosper Mérimée, Réquien also made a name for himself through the stout defense he put up on behalf of the city ramparts. He was curator of the museum from 1839 to 1852. Since 1940 the museum has occupied an 18th-century mansion and houses a herbarium of immense scientific importance containing about 300,000 specimens. The disciplines of geology and paleontology are also well represented.

PLACE DES CORPS-SAINTS
This square is shaded by delightful plane trees and is adorned by a fountain. It is very popular with students, who go for walks here between lessons.

RUE DE LA RÉPUBLIQUE

CHURCH OF ST-DIDIER. This southern Gothic church, built between 1356 and 1359 on the site of an earlier church, has a single nave with six ribbed bays, ending with a pentagonal apse lined with chapels next to a massive tower topped by an octagonal spire. The frescos were rediscovered in 1950 in what is now the baptismal chapel; they are attributed to a 14th-century Florentine workshop.

LAPIDARY MUSEUM ★. This museum of stone artefacts has been housed in the Jesuit Chapel (1620-61), a typically Counter-Reformation building with a single nave, since 1933. The museum provides an almost complete history from the Gallo-Roman civilization of the Tène culture (c. 500 BC–AD 1000) to the period of the Roman Empire, and also displays elements from Greek and Egyptian civilizations.

CALVET MUSEUM. Since 1833, this museum has occupied the Hôtel de Villeneuve-Martignan, built by the Franques around 1472. The Museum was founded thanks to the generosity of Esprit Calvet (1728–1810), a Professor in the Faculty of Medicine at the University of Avignon, who bequeathed to the town his library and collections of paintings, furniture and antiquities. The museum is currently closed for repairs.

AROUND ST PETER'S CHURCH

SYNAGOGUE. The Jewish quarter was located near St Peter's Church as early as 1221. The synagogue was rebuilt in the 18th century and, after it burned down in 1845, Bondon, the town's architect, rebuilt it, producing the only synagogue in France on a circular ground plan.

ST PETER'S CHURCH ★. Although this church was not completed, it was much restored in the 15th century. The richly decorated west façade was done between 1512 and 1520, and the choir is adorned with fourteen paintings depicting the Life of Saint Peter and Doctors of the Church; these are set in opulent gilt wainscoting (1634). The best paintings include those by Simon de Châlons and Nicolas Mignard (*The Holy Family*, 1641) and an 18th-century cycle representing Saint Anthony of Padua by Pierre Parrocel.

CARMELITE CONVENT. Only the church (14th and 18th centuries) and the cloister remain. The church contains superb paintings by Pierre Parrocel and Nicolas Mignard.

148

"CORONATION OF THE VIRGIN MARY"
The Municipal Museum moved into the residence of
Peter of Luxemburg in 1986. The museum's greatest
work is this magnificent reredos by Enguerrand
Quarton ▲ *138*, dated 1454.

VILLENEUVE-LÈS-AVIGNON ★

LA CHARTREUSE DU VAL DE BÉNÉDICTION. In 1356, Pope Innocent VI decided to found a charterhouse on land he owned in Val de Bénédiction. Only the *tinel*, a large rectangular room, and the chapel survive. The building was intended for use by monks and was consecrated in 1358. The CHURCH was enlarged on many occasions, and the apse was demolished during the French Revolution. The chapel closest to the choir contains Pope Innocent VI's tomb. The MONASTERY CELLS are grouped around the CEMETERY CLOISTER and ST JOHN'S CLOISTER. The monastery was restored and acquired by the state in 1909; it houses a national center of writing for the stage.

FORT ST-ANDRÉ. In the early Middle Ages, St Andrew's Hill (Colline St-André), then known as Mount Andaon, was still an island; it was the site of a hermitage, and later a monastery. A fortified wall, begun in the 13th century and finished around 1372, protected both township and monastery. Today, it only encloses the STE-CASARIE and NOTRE-DAME-DE-BELVEZET CHAPELS, the latter an elegant Romanesque building heavily restored in the 19th century, the remains of the 18th-century abbey and some dwellings. Troops loyal to the King of France occupied the fortress until the late 18th century. ST ANDREW'S MONASTERY, now private property, probably dates back to the 7th century. In 1063–87 when Saint Pons was abbot, it prospered and the buildings spread as far as the small fortified town on Mount Andaon.

COLLEGIATE CHURCH OF NOTRE-DAME. Cardinal Arnaud de Via, a nephew of Pope John XXII, had a palace built here in 1322 and later founded a chapter of canons. The chapter then became collegiate, a cloister was established in the courtyard, and the tower was turned into a steeple. The carved, historiated décor of the consoles on which the arches rest is remarkable, and some of the scenes of the Life of Christ still preserve their original polychrome design.

A DEFENSIVE, RELIGIOUS AND ARTISTIC ROLE
In 1292, although opposed by Avignon and the Comtat, the King of France founded a "new town" (*ville neuve*) at the foot of Colline St-André, behind the monumental construction at the exit to the stone bridge straddling the Rhône. All that remains is the square tower, known as the Tower of Philip the Fair; at one time, the hospital and the Châtelet were nearby. When the Comtat was returned to France, this defensive function was no longer required; Villeneuve became a religious place dominated by St Andrew's Monastery, the Collegiate Church and the Charterhouse. Since the 19th century, it has been an important artistic center.

PONT-DU-GARD ★

On the way from Villeneuve-lès-Avignon to Nîmes, near Remoulins, do not miss this 2,000-year-old Roman bridge commissioned by Emperor Augustus's son-in-law. Magnificently located, it stands 150 feet above the waters of the river Gard.

▲ AVIGNON TOWARD NÎMES

1 AIGUES-MORTES
2 SAINTES-MARIES-DE-LA-MER
3 NÎMES
4 ÉTANG DE VACCARÈS
5 ARLES
6 SALINS-DE-GIRAUD
7 BEAUCAIRE
8 TARASCON
9 BAUX-DE-PROVENCE

⏱ One week
🚗 186 miles

STONE CONSTRUCTIONS
Beaucaire has looked to stone and water during much of its history: stone has provided the village with excellent material for building defenses, and water has brought prosperity through trade.

ST MAGDALEN'S FAIR
Beaucaire has been famous for its Fair since the 15th century. It starts on July 22, the feast of Saint Mary Magdalen, the town's patron saint, and lasts until July 27 or 28. Three public holidays and possibly a Sunday are added to the three days of the Fair, and goods are tax free on these days.

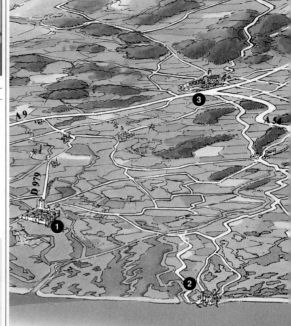

BEAUCAIRE

A MEDIEVAL CASTLE ★. This castle was the fief of the counts of Toulouse in the early Middle Ages, and was restored by the kings of France in the mid-13th century. The upper part of the building is open to the public only when there are organized exhibitions of falconry. The castle now houses the MUNICIPAL MUSEUM.

THE OLD TOWN. PLACE DE LA RÉPUBLIQUE is situated midway between the town's shopping streets, which are lined with lovely 17th- and 18th-century buildings, and the nearby fairground which, from the 16th century onward, included huts where the entertainers lived. In the early 18th century, the COLLEGIATE CHURCH OF NOTRE-DAME-DES-POMMIERS replaced a Romanesque chapel dedicated to the Virgin Mary: a Romanesque frieze on the outside (above), which probably dates from the 12th century, illustrates eleven scenes from the Passion.

Tarascon

THE CASTLE ★. The present building was
constructed around 1400 by Louis II of Anjou,
the father of Good King René ● *49*; the latter
had the work completed in 1449. The lower
courtyard to the north stands between four
square towers and includes the medieval
kitchens; one of these towers contains the
apothecary's shop of St Nicholas' Hospital and
its 250 pieces of 17th-century faïence. The
castle's round towers once housed the seigniorial
apartments.

COLLÉGIALE STE-MARTHE ★. The castle's
homogeneity contrasts with the eclecticism of the
Collegiate Church of St Martha, a 12th-century
building restored at the end of the 13th century; the
tower, sacristy and flying buttresses were also
restored in the 15th century. Most of the decoration
in the choir is of scenes in the life of Saint Martha; it
includes works by Mignard, Vien and Parrocel.

ARTISTS AT WORK. The workshops were founded in
1882 and revived by Charles Démery in 1916. They
may be visited by appointment ★.

THE "TARASQUE"
In the 1st century
Saint Martha
delivered the
inhabitants of
Tarascon from the
Tarasque, a monster
which hid in the
Rhône and terrorized
the region. Seven
centuries later,

Tarascon, now a
frontier town under
the Count of
Provence, grew larger
than Beaucaire,
which belonged to the
King of France.

**THE SEIGNIORIAL
LODGINGS**
The arms room is on
the left by the
entrance; a staircase
opposite leads to a
terrace, the chapel,
and a dining room
which has high
windows for reasons
of defense. This huge
room covering an
area of 2153 square
feet is repeated on
the two stories above:
today, these contain a
series of 18th-century
tapestries
representing the
Roman General
Scipio Africanus.
From a terrace at the
top, it is possible to
appreciate the castle's
strategic importance.

151

Opposite: A Bonelli's eagle,
ephedra and shadberry.

**TARTARIN DE
TARASCON**
The Villa Tartarin is
in the Faubourg
Condamine. It is an
old olive press built in
1761, and was used by
Alphonse Daudet on
the jacket of his novel
Tartarin de Tarascon.

THE ALPILLES ★

Marvelous farming land and mild winters have enabled this
region to grow wheat since ancient times. In the Middle Ages,
farmers took over from the monks of Montmajour, drained
the marshes in the valleys and overcame the problems of the
hills by means of terracing which contained the earth on
particularly steep slopes. They planted olive ■ *40*, almond and
apricot trees, all of them well adapted to the arid soil, as well
as growing cereals; higher up, windmills ● *90* turned the
cereals into flour. There are fewer almond and apricot trees
these days, but there are still plenty of olive trees, especially
in the Baux Valley. The slopes of the Alpilles are shaded by
Scotch firs and kermes oaks, and patches of reddish earth are
the only sign of the bauxite that was once mined here.

ST-RÉMY-DE-PROVENCE

THE "PLANET", OR PLACE FAVIER ★. The HÔTEL MISTRAL DE
MONDRAGON, which now houses the Alpilles-Pierre-de-Brun
Museum, was once the residence of the Mistral family, lords
of Croze in Dauphiné. The building was constructed around

**THE ALPILLES ON
FOOT**
The GR 6 (Grande
Randonnée, or
marked walking path)
crosses the massif
from Aureille, keeps
to the high ground
until St-Rémy,
continues to Les
Baux, and drops
down to the plain as
far as St-Gabriel.

1550 and enlarged over the remaining years of the century. In
1599, Paul de Mistral appropriated two houses that stood
opposite, and had them pulled down to accommodate a
"planet"; it became a public park in 1647. The Museum ★ is
devoted to local history. The HÔTEL DE SADE situated
opposite has been turned into a museum of archeological
objects found at Glanum. The remains of ST PETER'S
CHURCH, a shrine since the 11th century, are at the end of a
blind alley on the eastern side of the "Planet". The HÔTEL
ESTRINE, once the Prince of Monaco's court, is now the
Présence Van-Gogh art center.

Les Baux-de-Provence ★

The village is perched on a rocky spur that rises to 804 feet and overlooks two fertile valleys. The Renaissance façades of the houses date from the 16th century.

Pavillon de la reine Jeanne ★. This elegant Renaissance pavilion (right) lies in the Vallon de la Fontaine near the former wash-house in a garden that once belonged to the counts of Les Baux. The building is traditionally known as

Glanum
This town expanded during the reign of Augustus, and acquired a number of public monuments including a triumphal arch and a mausoleum. However, it declined from the 1st century AD before disappearing altogether around 270 in the face of Barbarian invasions. The ancient town was much larger than the site that has been unearthed to date.

Queen Jeanne's Pavilion; the poet Frédéric Mistral (1830–1914) had a copy made for his tomb.

Hôtel de Manville ★. Built in 1571 by a Protestant family, this mansion is the most beautiful Renaissance house in the town. Today, it houses the Museum of contemporary Art.

Hôtel des Porcelets ★. This elegant late 16th-century residence is now the Yves Brayer Museum, and contains seventy-five of Brayer's paintings from his Italian period (1930). Yves Brayer (1907–90) lived in Les Baux and was buried here. The 17th-century Penitents' Chapel opposite is decorated with Nativity frescos by Brayer (1974).

St Vincent's Church. This church dates from the 12th century, and was enlarged in 1609 by means of a clever Romanesque pastiche. The façade was restored in the 19th century by Henri Révoil. On Christmas Eve a popular ceremony called the *pastrage* ● *70* takes place during Midnight Mass.

The citadel (12 acres) ★. The 15th-century Tour-de-Brau House stands at the entrance to the citadel; it is the oldest

Montmajour Abbey ★
In the 11th century the counts of Provence chose Montmajour as their burial-place, and it became one of the most important abbeys in the region. Decline set in from the late Middle Ages, and the Order of Saint Maurus was given the task of reforming the church. It was sold as a stone quarry during the French Revolution, but it was then purchased by the painters Réattu and Révoil and restoration commenced in 1862.

mansion in Les Baux and is now a Museum. Adjoining the 16th-century Hôpital Quiqueran is the 12th-century Romanesque St-Blaise Chapel which contains the tiny Olivier Museum. The remains of the old fortress are overlooked by the 12th-century dungeon, while the Sarrasine, Paravelle and Bannes Towers, and the stone tower in the shape of a dovecote ★ rise from the external wall. Archeologists have uncovered the 16th-century rampart and remains of medieval houses.

1 NOTRE-DAME-DE-LA-MAJOR
2 AMPHITHEATER
3 INTERNATIONAL
   PHOTOGRAPHY ENCOUNTERS
4 ROMAN THEATER
5 SUMMER GARDEN
6 CHURCH OF ST-TROPHIME
7 RÉATTU MUSEUM
8 ROMAN BATHS
9 TOWN HALL
10 MUSEUM OF PAGAN ART
11 PLACE DU FORUM
12 MUSEON ARLATEN
13 MUSEUM OF CHRISTIAN ART
14 ESPACE VAN-GOGH
15 ST JULIAN'S CHURCH

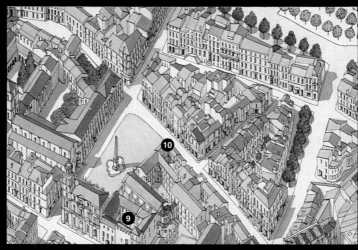

9 TOWN HALL   **10** PAGAN ART MUSEUM

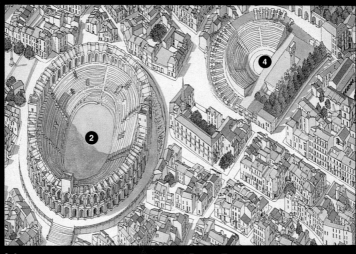

2 AMPHITHEATER   **4** ROMAN THEATER

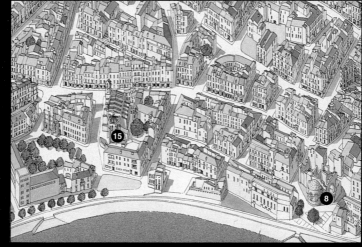

15 ST JULIAN'S CHURCH   **8** ROMAN BATHS

"HE HAD ONLY TO OPEN HIS ENCHANTED CAPE FOR THE CROWD
TO CEASE BREATHING IN ANTICIPATION OF A MIRACLE"
RAYMOND GUÉRIN

PORTE DE LA REDOUTE

BOULEVARD ÉMILE COMBES

1

2

3

PLACE
VOLTAIRE

15

REMPARTS

PORTE DE LA CAVALERIE

PLACE LAMARTINE

GRAND RHÔNE

WATCHTOWERS
During the Middle Ages, the amphitheater's defenses were improved by the addition of the three famous towers. They contribute significantly to the building's unique appearance.

ARLES: HISTORY

Arles was a Greek colony ● 46 from the 6th century BC, but did not prosper until the period of Roman domination. There were two phases of construction: first, the reign of Augustus around 30 BC, when the forum, theater, baths and public places were built; second, about one hundred years later under the Flavian dynasty, when the circus, amphitheater and port installations were added. Expansion came to a halt at the end of the 3rd century following a succession of Barbarian raids. However, as early as the 4th century, with the backing of Emperor Constantine, Arles became an Imperial residence, the main town of the Seven Provinces, and the Prefecture of Gaul. The town did not escape the troubles which beset Provence in the late 6th century ● 46. From the 9th century onward, periods of prosperity alternated with recession. In the 12th century, Arles was again an important town in Provence, but by the 15th century its status had been undermined first by the plague and later by war; then, after rediscovering affluence during the 16th century, Arles was once more ravaged by the plague in 1720 ● 52. After 1825, the ruins became fashionable and the monuments began once more to command serious attention. Today, Arles has opted for tourism and also hosts top-class international exhibitions; these include the celebrated International Photography Meetings held in the town since the 1970's.

THE HAUTURE DISTRICT

THE ROMAN AMPHITHEATER ★. The Amphitheater, which dates from the 1st century AD, occupies an enormous space hewn out of the rock on the north side of the hill. It has a characteristically elliptical shape, measuring 446 feet at its longest; it covers an area of about 13,754 square yards and is the twentieth biggest amphitheater in the Roman world. The tiered upper seats have been destroyed. The Amphitheater maintains its links with the past by hosting bullfights and the celebrations of the Confraternity of Gardians (herdsmen); this guild was founded on January 2, 1512, and the festivities are held on the Sunday after Saint George's Day (23 April) ▲ 165.

FROM IRON-BRANDING TO BULLFIGHTS
The different stages in the process of rearing bulls have always been treated as occasions for celebrations; in the Camargue ▲ 164, for instance, the task of branding is followed by the *ferrade*. Bulls are natives of the Rhône Delta, and this love of everything associated with them gave rise after 1838 to a fashion for *ferrades* held in public. When the houses that filled the Arles Amphitheater were cleared away in

1830, a bull race was organized to celebrate the Taking of Algiers. After 1869, the introduction of Spanish bulls and cows into the herds belonging to Joseph Yonnet, and then those of Lescot and Pouly, encouraged the presentation of Spanish spectacles, and finally of modern bullfights.

THE SARCOPHAGUS AVENUE ★

This avenue was laid out in the 18th century by the Minimes brothers at Les Alyscamps, at a time when a Museum of Antique Art devoted to objects found in the cemetery was being planned. It was pillaged in 1793 by lovers of antiquities, but many of the carved sarcophagi are now on display at the IRPA ▲ 163. This curious path, lined with abandoned tombs and shaded by cypress trees, made such a deep impression on Van Gogh that he painted it four times during his stay in Arles in 1888.

THE "FERIA"

(Easter weekend) The *feria* is an opportunity for the public to watch bullfights with *matadores de toros* (experienced bullfighters) and *novillades* (young matadors still learning their profession). The spectacle, which lasts three days and nights, also includes bulls being released into the streets, exhibitions on subjects related to bulls, and street performances by brass bands called *peñas*.

PHOTOGRAPHIC MEETINGS. The photographic exhibitions take place on the right of the amphitheater. They were started by Lucien Clergue in 1970, and are now held every July. Arles is also the home of the National Photography School.

NOTRE-DAME-DE-LA-MAJOR. This church to the east of the Amphitheater was built in the 12th century and has been considerably restored since then. The traditional Gardians' Mass is celebrated here every year.

LES ALYSCAMPS ★

AN ANCIENT CEMETERY. The name "Alyscamps" comes from *Alysii campi*, or Elysian Fields, the Kingdom of the Dead where valiant warriors were taken after they died. It is one of the most celebrated cemeteries from the Middle Ages, and is venerated as the burial place of Saint Genesius. The cemetery once extended well beyond this avenue, but some of it was destroyed when railway workshops were set up during the 19th century. The Church of St-Honorat is at the end of the avenue.

Death of Alcibiades by Jacques Réattu.

CHURCH OF ST-HONORAT. In the 12th century, work commenced to replace a basilica dedicated to Saint Genesius, but it was never completed. In the Middle Ages, the tower was known as the "lantern of the dead"; it resembled a lighthouse and contained a light which announced the proximity of a cemetery to all those in the vicinity.

THE ROMAN THEATER ★

The Roman Theater in Arles was built on the top of the Hauture Hill during the reign of Augustus. The tiered seats are placed over a system of substructures consisting of concentric galleries and radiating vaulted halls. Some of the external portico can still be seen on the garden side where a bay has been inserted in the medieval southern rampart. The tiers were partly rebuilt in the 19th century to enable stage events to be put on, but the lower rows of seats still give a good idea of the facilities the Romans enjoyed. The floor of the *orchestra*, which was reserved for the chorus, is made of green cipolin set in pink breccia marble. The stage can still be seen, as can the stage wall which was originally decorated with a hundred or so columns; all that remains are two marble columns topped by a fragment of an entablature (below).

AROUND THE ROMAN BATHS

CONSTANTINE'S BATHS. These thermal baths ● *80* were used as a swimming pool, public baths and a meeting place. The northern baths are the best preserved, but baths are also known to have existed in the south of the town on the site of the Esplanade and it is thought that remains of a third establishment were uncovered under the Place de la République in the 18th century. The baths in the north, known as Constantine's Baths, were built in the later years of the Empire; they are made of alternating brick and limestone rubble.

THE RÉATTU MUSEUM ★
The building was the property of the Knights of Saint John of Jerusalem in the 14th century; it was rebuilt in the 16th century, and then, in 1797, was bought by the painter Jacques Réattu (1760–1833) who installed his workshop there. When he died, his daughter left the house to the town of Arles on condition that a public museum devoted to painting be founded there. The museum has most of Réattu's paintings; he was Marseilles' official painter under the Directoire. It also contains a large collection of contemporary art and fifty-seven drawings donated by Picasso in 1971; a portrait of the artist's mother, *María Picasso López*, and *Lee Miller in Arlesian Dress* were presented later. The Hôtel de Ste-Luce ★ contains the largest collection of photographs of all the provincial museums.

PLACE DU FORUM
This square is now lined with lively cafés. The remains of a pediment suggest that the central area of the ancient Forum was provided with a decoration of monumental proportions, probably a large entrance.

This gate represents
the theme of the Last
Judgement. Man-
eating lions beneath
the feet of Saint Peter
and Saint Paul tell the
story of Deceit being
crushed by Faith;

above, the symbols of
the Evangelists
surround Christ in all
His majesty. On the
lintel, there are
carvings of the Elders
of the Apocalypse, as
portrayed in Saint
John's Gospel.

THE FORUM

THE CRYPTOPORTICUS ★. The city plan of Arles, like that of
all Roman colonies, was organized around the forum; it was
situated slightly to the south of where the square of the same
name now stands. The only part that can still be seen is the
cryptoporticus, an enormous horseshoe-shaped area 2952 feet
long and 197 feet wide, made of three underground galleries
at right angles to one another. It is not clear what the
cryptoporticus was used for, but it probably gave some
solidity to the foundations of the Forum proper,
which resembled a huge courtyard laid with
paving stones.

PLACE DE LA RÉPUBLIQUE

This square was originally called
Place du Marché; it was rebuilt in
the 17th century.
CHURCH OF ST-TROPHIME ★. This
gem of Romanesque art was built on
the site of the 5th-century Basilique St-
Étienne. The present church dates from
the 12th century, when it was dedicated to Saint Trophime
who brought the gospel to Provence and whose remains are
kept here. The church was completed around 1180 by a
TOWER in the Lombard style. The interior is remarkable for
the height of the building compared with the narrowness of
the aisles, and for the contrast between the Romanesque
sobriety of the nave and the Gothic exuberance of the choir.
The adjoining ARCHBISHOP'S PALACE dates from the Middle
Ages; it was restored in 1669 and given a new façade in the
18th century. The Passage de l'Archevêché leads to the
CLOISTER. The north and east galleries are 12th century, while
the rest dates from the 14th century. The north gallery is
decorated with sculptures representing the Resurrection and
the origins of the Christian Church in Arles; Saint Trophime
and Saint Stephen adorn the corner piers.
THE TOWN HALL. This building was designed by Jacques
Peytret and constructed by Jules Hardouin-Mansart; the latter
also redesigned the hall's vaulting. The design of the Town
Hall was influenced by Versailles; it includes a 16th-century
tower, and was finished in 1676. The square was completed by
the installation of an obelisk brought from the Roman Circus.

<table>
<tr><td>

LA ROQUETTE
This part of the town, surrounded by a rampart at the end of the 12th century, was from the Middle Ages to

</td><td>

the present day inhabited by sailors, porters and other workers. La Roquette had its own autonomous administration.

</td></tr>
</table>

THE MUSEON ARLATEN ★

This private house, built by Honoré de Castellane, contains a museum of Arles life. It is a fine example of the local families' taste in the early 16th century.
In 1648, it was sold to the Jesuits who turned it into a college and altered the entrance.

A FOLK POET. In 1895, Frédéric Mistral conceived the idea of founding an ethnographic museum that would recount the history of Provençal life and thought. It contains some twenty thousand objects and documents, ranging from costumes and furniture to objects of piety and agricultural tools.

ESPACE VAN-GOGH ★. The former Hôpital Van-Gogh, which acquired its name after the painter spent some time there, is in Rue du Président-Wilson. The courtyard of this old hospital (1573) is surrounded by a charming garden laid out exactly as it was in the 19th century with the help of Van Gogh's own paintings, drawings and letters.

THE ROMAN CIRCUS AND THE IRPA

THE ROMAN CIRCUS IN ARLES. This circus built at the end of the 1st century has seating for about twenty thousand spectators. Its colossal size (1476 feet long by 361 feet wide) meant that it had to be constructed outside the town walls, and this partly explains why it was totally destroyed when stones were needed to strengthen the defense wall at the end of the Empire. The circus contained a huge track divided in two by a long wall decorated with marble sculptures and a decorative scheme of dolphins spitting into the water which told the spectators how many laps the chariots had completed. The large obelisk stood in the center of this wall.

THE IRPA (*Institut de recherche sur la Provence antique*). The Research Institute for Ancient Provence occupies an extraordinary blue triangular building designed by the architect Ciriani. It is also a museum devoted to the town's antique collections, which include 4th-century sarcophagi, sculptures and mosaics from the surrounding area, and statuary of Hellenistic inspiration from the period of Augustus discovered in the ruins of the Roman Theater.

THE VENUS OF ARLES
This statue was discovered in the Roman Theater in the 17th century by a courtier eager to present it to Louis XIV. When the king made it known to the consuls that he would be happy to acquire it, the people of Arles agreed, hoping thus to be exempted from taxes. They were disappointed. Two hundred years later, Frédéric Mistral complained about those local worthies who had "handed over their beautiful Venus in exchange for a Saint-Louis Cross. The Venus of Arles is now in the Louvre, and the plaster copy is in Arles. It serves them right!"

THE ARLÉSIENNE
The Museon Arlaten has many examples of the Arlesian style modified by women every day, and whose originality was based on a coiffure with

headbands surmounted by a ribbon fringed with lace. Above: Arlesian style from the period of Louis-Philippe.

THE CAMARGUE: HISTORY

Gardians' huts painted by Van Gogh.

The Rhône Delta is an accumulation of alluvial deposits and unstable land which has always discouraged human habitation. It did, however, interest foreign powers: both the Ligurians and the Greeks were attracted by the transport facilities, salt production and fishing. The Romans also planted vines and cereals. When the Roman Empire fell, the Camargue was subjected to frequent pillaging, and its fortunes did not revive until the Middle Ages when the Cistercians and then the Templars settled here, tilled the land and worked the saltpans. By the 15th century, the region had become quite prosperous. Later, major hydraulic works were undertaken along the delta and companies were set up to clear away the salt. The construction of dikes on the Rhône in 1869 marked a turning point for the region which acquired a totally artificial appearance. The development of Salin-de-Giraud ▲ *166* led to the laying of a railway which opened in 1892 and served the entire Camargue. It was closed down during the 1950's.

THE GARDIANS' SKILLS
The trident, known as a *ferre* or *ficheroun*, is made of wrought iron; the shaft is made of the wood of a chestnut tree. It is used only for encouraging stubborn animals and for protection in the event of being attacked by a bull.

THE CAMARGUE TODAY

SPARSE HABITATION. Apart from some houses at Les Saintes-Maries-de-la-Mer and a few hamlets, there are hardly any dwellings, and most of these belong to larger properties. The Camargue *mas* (farmhouse) ● *88* is often hidden behind a wood to protect it from the *mistral* ■ *16*; huts ● *88,* older and more modest in design, were inhabited by fishermen, salt-workers and *gardians.* Today they are used by tourists or as residential property.
THE ECONOMY. The Camargue produces rice (formerly used to desalinate the land) and wine (of only moderate quality so far). The marshlands are also exploited: the reeds that grow there are harvested for cattle (fodder and straw) and the construction of huts. Horses are extremely important; they are the constant companions of the *gardians* whose job it is to watch over the bulls in the wetlands. For a long time, the rearing of bulls was the only way of eking out a living from land which could not be cultivated.

FISHING IN THE ÉTANG DE VACCARÈS
Professional fishermen who use stretches of the reserve make a living out of catching eels, grey mullet and atherines. They use *trabaques*, nets which include a section that is perpendicular to the bank; this drives the fish toward

FAITH OF THE BULL. The *gardians* riding across the marshes and the *sansouires* ▲ *166* have a true faith, the *fe di biou*, or faith of the bull, a real religion that claims many adherents from Provence to the Languedoc. The first official rules of the *gardians'* arduous work go back to 1512 when the Confraternity of St George ▲ *159* was formed. The beginning of the 19th century saw the appearance of the first *manades*, herds of horses from which the best would be selected for games involving bulls. These games, which derive from a very ancient bullfighting tradition, are based on a Camargue race that went from the courtyard of the *mas* to the village square, and then onto the bull ring. Animals were never killed in any of these games; the aim was simply to remove emblems placed on, and between, the horns of six bulls which ran one after the other. In addition to these strictly codified and ritualized races, there were games for amateurs such as the *abrivado* and the *ferrade*; these used to be played on the days when farmers in Provence held large celebrations in which local people participated.

PARC NATUREL RÉGIONAL DE CAMARGUE. The Camargue Nature Park was founded in 1972 and takes in the commune of Les Saintes-Maries-de-la-Mer and that part of Arles near the delta; except for sections of the reservation that are fenced off, access is unrestricted over an area of 210,000 acres. Apart from protecting the land, the park's objective is to show to advantage the unusually fragile natural and cultural heritage of the region.

groups of three-hooped nets called *coeurs* (hearts).

ARLES TO SALIN-DE-GIRAUD (D 36)

THE VACCARÈS ★. The Vaccarès, the *pièce de résistance* of the Rhône Delta's hydraulic system, is a vast lagoon of some 230 square miles. Its shallow waters (under 6½ feet), the winds that ruffle the surface almost incessantly, and the long hours of sunshine provide it with an exceptional capacity for purification. That property enables the Vaccarès to absorb safely over 52,315,000 cubic yards of water which is destined for the rice fields; it has been

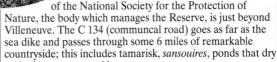

THE SANSOUIRES
These are dominated by marsh-samphire, fleshy plants that are common in salt-producing regions.

In damp weather, the ground is usually flooded; in dry weather, it cracks and covers itself with a coat of salt from the rising salty ground water. The combustion produced by the marsh-samphire once provided some of the soda required in the manufacture of Marseilles' soap.

Red behen, a plant much venerated by the people of the Camargue, often adorns tombs and mausoleums.

essential for the lagoon's survival ever since the dikes stopped the Rhône from overflowing. The salinity level varies between ⅟₁₆ and ¾ oz of salt per pint, and the flora and fauna include water milfoil, sea wrack, carp and sea bream. It is also a spot much frequented by fish-eating birds, and by the pink flamingos ■ *24* for which the delta is so well known.

THE NATIONAL RESERVE ★. The Reserve covers an area of 32,400 acres stretching from the north of the Vaccarès Lagoon to the sea. It was built in 1927, and is an astonishing mosaic of freshwater and brackish wetlands. The only access for the public is by the sea dike and at Capelière Estate. LA CAPELIÈRE, the information center of the National Society for the Protection of Nature, the body which manages the Reserve, is just beyond Villeneuve. The C 134 (communal road) goes as far as the sea dike and passes through some 6 miles of remarkable countryside; this includes tamarisk, *sansouires*, ponds that dry up in the summer, and lagoons.

THE SEA DIKE ★. The sea dike is 12 miles long and was built in 1857–8. Access by motorized vehicles is forbidden; visitors coming by car should drive off the road and onto any of the dikes that are accessible in dry weather. First, there are several miles of salt production in huge evaporation basins where sea water pumped in at Beauduc is gradually concentrated. The steady level of sea water from March to September attracts large numbers of birds which come here every spring to mate in colonies on the little islands. At this point, cars must be left at the COMTESSE car park. This is Lower Camargue, famous for its salinity levels, and marked by exceptional summer dryness and winter floods. One-and-a-quarter miles after the

Gacholle Lighthouse, the Chemin des Douanes leads down to the sea through the dunes and across a beach 718 yards wide. The dunes were recently threatened by the rising level of the sea, but they are now protected by wooden fencing. There is a 5-mile coastal route as far as Les-Saintes-Maries. The first section takes in the IMPÉRIAL LAGOON which is popular with seabirds ■ *24*; after that, follow the C 140 road to La Bélugue at the Salin-de-Giraud/Bac-de-Bacarin crossroads. At the fork which leads to BEAUDUC, go toward Salin. Finally, pass FARAMAN, and continue in the direction of Salin-de-Giraud.

SALIN-DE-GIRAUD

This village grew during the second half of the 19th century to meet the needs of the salt and chemicals industries, and Marseilles' soap industry. It is notable for its architecture which was influenced by northern mining villages.

A SOUTHERN "MINING VILLAGE". Before the factories came, Giraud Lagoon was fished and the surrounding area was used for the rearing of livestock. Later, the Solvay and Péchiney companies were obliged to build houses to attract workers to this out-of-the-way spot; it soon became a modern workers'

Avignon toward Nîmes
The Camargue

AVIGNON CASTLE
This castle boasts superb wainscoting, Aubusson and Gobelins tapestries,

outstanding paintings, marbles and exceptionally beautiful furniture.

THE CHURCH AT SAINTES-MARIES
This church contains the processional ship of the Holy Marys (opposite), the saints' *oreiller* (a piece of marble said to contain their bones) and a fine collection of ex-votos.

GYPSIES AT SAINTES-MARIES
They arrive every year, one week before the feast of May 24. It is an opportunity for them to be baptised in a holy place and to perform rites associated with asking for a hand in marriage.

city. Salin is as remarkable for its architecture as for the diverse range of nationalities working there; they include Italians, Greeks, Armenians, Spaniards and Turks. On entering the town, visitors should turn right at the roundabout, pass the post office and, at the end of the straight line, follow signs to PIÉMANSON BEACH on the D 36 road. After 1¼ miles, there is an observation table which is accessible by car.

VIEW OVER THE SALT PANS. Salt has been exploited in these parts since ancient times. In the 19th century, the salt marsh (*salin*) at Giraud grew to be the largest in Europe. From the platform provided by a local salt industry firm, the *Compagnie des salins du Midi et des salines de l'Est*, there is a fine view out over the marshlands, the collection areas and the storage spaces. The salt is used in the chemicals industry, mainly factories in Fos.

FROM ARLES TO THE SAINTES-MARIES (D 570)

THE CAMARGUE MUSEUM. The *Fondation du Parc Naturel Régional de Camargue* bought the Pont-de-Rousty *mas* in 1973, and a Museum stands in the sheepfold belonging to this typical Camargue farm. The Camargue Museum, an ecology museum, tells the story of the Rhône Delta from its geological formation to the present day, through displays demonstrating a variety of human activities. The museum works in association with a discovery path 2¼ miles long which passes through cultivated land, grazing land and marshland belonging to the Mas de Rousty.

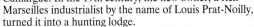

AVIGNON CASTLE ★. This castle has been owned by the Council since 1984, but it is managed by the *Parc Naturel Régional de Camargue*. In the 13th century, Joseph-François d'Avignon Arlatan built the first section of the present residence, and it later became the biggest in the whole of the Camargue. In the 19th century, the new owner, a rich Marseilles industrialist by the name of Louis Prat-Noilly, turned it into a hunting lodge.

PONT-DE-GAU BIRD SANCTUARY ★. This 150-acre sanctuary was opened in 1949 and is featured at the nearby GINÈS INFORMATION CENTER. Its large aviaries, marshes and lagoons offer a pleasant nesting site for both native and migratory birds ■ *24*. A little further on, the D 85 skirts the Petit Rhône and arrives at the Saintes-Maries.

AVIC
▲

LES-SAINTES-MARIES-DE-LA-MER

The village of Notre-Dame-de-la-Mer was once situated at the very end of the delta, on a tiny stretch of sandy land that was forever at the mercy of the Mediterranean waves. Although it is now the most important village in the Camargue, it was quite isolated for a long time. In the Middle Ages, it stood over ¾ mile off the coast, and was a fortified township that spent much of its time trying to defend itself against the pirates who ravaged Provence as they sailed up the Rhône. The village took its present name in the 19th century, which refers to the three Marys: Mary the sister of the Virgin, Mary Magdalen, and Mary Salome.

THE CHURCH ★. The church was built in the 12th century over a former Gallo-Roman sanctuary, and was fortified during the Hundred Years' War to enable it to withstand the attacks of plundering mercenaries. The interior is noted for capitals adorned with plants from which human forms emerge. The crypt, built in 1448, contains the tomb of Saint Sarah who is covered by a large number of robes and mantles.

THE BARONCELLI MUSEUM. This small local museum, named after the Marquess Folco de Baroncelli, contains collections relating to local history, regional folklore (costumes and furniture) and Camargue zoology.

A PILGRIMAGE. The 1315 Constitution of the Confraternity of Les-Saintes-Maries demonstrates the fervor with which Saint Mary, the sister of the Virgin, and Saint Mary Salome were venerated at the time. Indeed, there were so many pilgrims that, in 1343, the Bishop of Paris, Foulques de Chanac, ordered their feast days, May 25 and October 22, to be celebrated throughout his diocese. Archeological excavations organized a hundred years later by René of Anjou ● 49 in the Church of Notre-Dame-de-la-Mer unearthed their remains. These are now in twin reliquaries in the high chapel dedicated to Saint Michael. Since 1448, ceremonies have been held on May 24–25, October 22 (nowadays on the nearest Sunday) and December 3 to commemorate the days of their canonization.

THE GYPSIES. There is no historical written evidence relating to the gypsies' devotion for Sarah, the patron saint of gypsies; nor has she been recognized by the Church. The devotion is largely based on their presence at Beaucaire Fair ▲ 150 and among the pilgrims to Santiago de Compostela.

FROM SAINTES-MARIES TO MÉJANES. Cacharel, a farm best approached along the D 85 road, is the starting point for a wonderful journey to Méjanes via the Cinq-Gorges Dike. The view over the lagoons, *sansouires* and marshlands teeming with wading birds is quite spectacular.

THE SAINTS
After the death of Christ, Mary the sister of the Virgin Mary, and Mary Salome, mother of the apostles James and John, were forced to leave Palestine. They were accompanied by their servant Sarah, Lazarus, his sister Martha, and Mary Magdalen. After a sea crossing, they landed on the shore of the Camargue. When their companions departed to preach the gospel in Provence, the saints, who were older, settled where the present village church now stands; they are also said to have built an altar here.

169

View of Aigues-Mortes by Frédéric
Bazille (1841–70)

AIGUES-MORTES: HISTORY

BY ROYAL DECREE. Aigues-Mortes was founded around 1240 in the middle of a vast plain of lagoons and marshland some 9¼ miles west of the Rhône Delta. The new king, Louis IX, ordered it to be built to provide the port he needed to implement his Mediterranean policies. Aigues-Mortes had been well known to navigators for a long time; from a military point of view, this strip of land was ideally located as it was cut off from *terra firma* by an impenetrable line of marshes.

A NEW TOWN. To encourage settlers to come to such an unyielding area, a Foundation Charter was granted to the town in 1426 exempting the inhabitants from tolls, forced loans, port tax and tallage. A high causeway was built over the marshland to connect the town to dry land. Within a few years, the port of Saint Louis had become one of the most important staging-posts between the fairs of Champagne and the Italian cities, and between Northern Europe and the Levant. A large Genoese colony settled here, and it was also from this port that Saint Louis' two Crusades departed in 1248 and 1270. Paradoxically, it was the same forces of nature which had fashioned the port of Aigues-Mortes that brought about its demise; nothing could be done to arrest the Rhône's alluviation. The passageways built to link the Gulf of Aigues-Mortes to the inland basins had been warping since the 14th century, and the incessant work of dredging the channels was swallowing up most of the port's revenue. Competition from Marseilles, which became French in 1481, was the last straw.

LA TOUR DE CONSTANCE

A HUGE LIMESTONE CYLINDER. This tower was originally known as the King's Tower (Tour du Roi) and was completed in 1248; the town wall was not constructed until twenty years later. The tower overlooks the Aigues-Mortes Lagoon from a height of 131 feet. It stands on its own in the middle of a circular moat with a fortified wall running round the outside, and has two doorways and two bridges that extend across the moat. The tower is made of very smooth stone; the only exceptions to this abstract presentation, the embrasures of the arrow-slits that defended the building, are associated with death.

TOWERS AND GATES
The Salt and Wick Towers stand in splendid isolation on the northern flank of town wall; the Villeneuve, Powder and Bourguignons Towers are clustered round the corners of the ramparts. At the Gardette, St-Anthony, Queen's, Moulins and Marine gates, there are two round twin towers on either side of the

entrance. All these gates were equipped with a double portcullis, and the space in the middle was used as an entrance area overlooked by a break-back trap. However, some of the gates, such as the Cordeliers, Arsenal, Organeau, Galions and Remblais gates, were much less well defended: they had to make do with a single portcullis, and instead of having two large round towers, they were only provided with four small polygonal towers.

The parapet, which was given a rounded design in the 16th century, was surmounted by a crenelated covered way and supported an upper hoarding; the latter consisted of a series of overhanging skeleton galleries containing loopholes and trap-doors. The small tower straddling the parapet was originally the lighthouse that had stood in the port, and the wrought-iron casing was the lamp.

A MASTERPIECE OF GOTHIC RATIONALISM. The skill of the unknown engineer responsible for the Constance Tower lay in ensuring that the stairways, emergency exits, wells, fireplaces and items of defense could fit within the framework of a regular, twelve-sided ground plan; other elements that had to be incorporated included the firing lines of the arrow-slits and the vaulting of the halls.

A WAR MACHINE
The circuit wall has two levels of arrow-slits: a lower level at the foot of the wall which gave a good view into the bottom of the moats (which are now filled in), and a higher level more suitable for firing arrows over longer distances. The round towers of Aigues-Mortes overhang the adjacent walls by

THE TOWN WALLS ★

A HOMOGENOUS DESIGN. Philip III is credited with building these splendid walls, work on which probably finished around 1290–1300. Despite work being interrupted on a number of occasions, the walls were completed in forty years at the most, and they represent the most comprehensive synthesis of work by the King's engineers in the late 13th century.

BUILDING TECHNIQUES. The limestone was brought from deposits in Beaucaire and used as rubblestone; this consisted of two facings of dressed stone containing a quantity of tightly packed loose stones and sand. The facing was then embossed, but neither side of the stone was given a smooth finish and this served to give the walls a particularly powerful appearance. The work was completed by Philip the Fair. Many of the keystones and corbels were decorated with carved figures or plant motifs at a time when embossing was becoming less and less common. Even the structure of ceilings was changing: they had previously been mounted on four ogees, but now, according to the schema adopted in the church's chevet, they were on six, or even seven.

more than 26 feet. They are adapted for "outflanking", that is to say firing to one side. This function was performed through two lateral arrow-slits at the lower level. They were later replaced by the cannon.

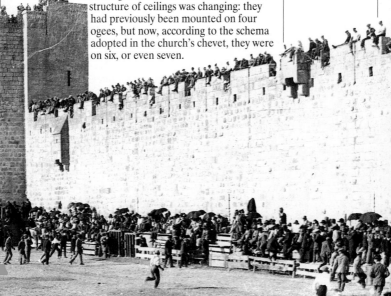

1 JARDIN DE LA FONTAINE   2 TEMPLE OF DIANA   3 TOUR MAGNE   4 ST PAUL'S CHURCH   5 LYCÉE   6 PLACE DU MARCHÉ   7 CARRÉ D'ART   8 MAISON CARRÉE   9 AMPHITHEATER

IN THE CENTER OF THE MEDIEVAL TOWN Nîmes only retains a very small stretch of wall from this period; at this time, the town covered an area of only 75 acres encircled by a rampart. Nîmes was ruled by the Count of Toulouse, but there were other powers erecting boundaries

at the same time. One was the bishop who had walled the quarter called the "Enclos du Chapitre" (Chapter Enclosure) next to the Cathedral; another comprised the more influential inhabitants of the town who, in the course of the 12th century, began to reject the viscount's authority.

NÎMES: HISTORY

A "FRENCH ROME".
The existence of a permanent spring, known as the Fontaine Spring, as early as the 6th century BC persuaded a Greek tribe known as the Volcae Arecomici to build a fortified town here. It was called "Nemos" after the god to whom the spring was dedicated. However, it was in the period of Roman domination under the Emperor Augustus that Nîmes enjoyed its greatest prosperity. Barbarian invasions in the 3rd century led to a decline in the town's fortunes, and the inhabitants withdrew to a small number of buildings that were easy to defend; these included the amphitheater, which was hurriedly turned into a fortress.

NÎMES IN THE MIDDLE AGES. Nîmes gradually established itself as an important market town, providing outlets for products from the hinterland, and producing wool and leather goods. Following the Crusade against the Albigensians in the 13th century, Nîmes came under the rule of Louis VIII of France. Years of prosperity were then followed in the 14th century by a period of crisis. The departure around 1330 of the town's Italian merchants, who had been subjected to excessively high taxes, and the expulsion of the Jews marked the beginning of an economic recession; this was exacerbated by a series of natural calamities and by pillaging by mercenaries during the Hundred Years' War.

THE WARS OF RELIGION. The 16th century was notable for the adoption of the Protestant Reformation; this was to have a major impact on events in the region for many years to come. Following the establishment of the Consistory of Nîmes in March 1561, Protestants gradually began to dominate the Consulate. The Catholic counter-offensive supported the power of the monarchy, and this was pursued vigorously during the reigns of Louis XIII and Louis XIV. In 1632, the Protestants were removed from the Consulate and the Jesuits took control of education. Locally, the textile industry supplanted agriculture, Nîmes became a city of workshops and, before long, it was one of the leading manufacturing cities in the kingdom, specializing in the production of silk.

THE END OF THE ANCIEN RÉGIME. Economic prosperity led to an increase in the population, with many people living outside the city walls. It was about this time that the Fontaine district was built.

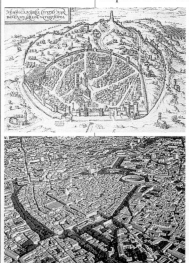

RUE DE LA RÉPUBLIQUE

NÎMES TODAY
For a long time, the economy relied mainly on small and medium-sized companies. The arrival of repatriated settlers from Algeria in the 1960's brought in fresh capital, and the successes of the Éminence and Cacharel companies brought great prosperity to Nîmes. Jean Bousquet, the managing director of Cacharel and mayor of Nîmes since 1983, is involved in this economic revival through a policy of major works (development of the city's ancient heritage, together with the setting up of the Safeguarded Sector in 1985) and encouraging companies to open offices in the city.

The French Revolution also revived old antagonisms between the progressive views of the Protestants and the conservatism of the clergy and the Catholic aristocracy. Initially, Nîmes adhered closely to revolutionary ideas, but opted for the federalist counter-revolution in 1792.

CHANGES IN THE 19TH CENTURY. Major building works included clearing up the amphitheater in 1809–11, restoration of the area around the Maison Carrée, now transformed into a museum, completion of the theater, and the afforestation of Mount Cavalier around 1820. The arrival of the railways in 1840 made Nîmes a communications center. Textile production had been crucial until 1850, but was now in decline. However, the weaving of fabrics, carpets, shawls, and hosiery remained the most active and diversified industrial sector. Moreover, by 1860, Nîmes was the second most important city in France for the wine trade.

173

AROUND THE MAISON CARRÉE

A VARIED HISTORY. This house appears to have been used for public functions in the 9th century. From the 11th century, when Nîmes was ruled by the counts of Toulouse, it was used as the city's Consular Building. It became private property in the 16th century then was acquired in 1670 by the Augustinians who made it into a church. Finally, after the Revolution, it housed the Departmental archives before becoming the first Town Hall in 1823. Excavations carried out during restoration work in 1816–22, and then again in 1991, have revealed the level of the floor in ancient times and the remains of a portico that encircled a temple on three sides.

THE CARRÉ D'ART
This simple, classical building, designed by Sir Norman Foster and opened in 1993, is something of an imitation of the Maison Carrée. It includes a Museum of Contemporary Art, which is on the two upper floors to take best advantage of the natural light, and a

A SURVIVING ROMAN BUILDING. As we can see from the inscription on the north face, the temple was dedicated to the Roman Empire, and more particularly to the Caesars, the adopted sons and heirs-at-law of the Emperor Augustus. The Maison Carrée is a perfect example of Imperial architecture in the Narbonnaise during the time of Augustus, and it was a major influence and model for architects and builders in the region. It has a pseudo-peripteral ground plan, marked particularly by a *cella* whose doors are articulated by engaged half-columns. The sobriety of the architrave, the irregularity of the foliage frieze, and the proportions and outline of the cornice provide stylistic and chronological evidence that the building was constructed at the very end of the 1st century BC or the early years of the Common Era. Such a conclusion is corroborated by the inscription and archeological finds. The Maison Carrée today contains a small Museum of Antiquities.

reference library for contemporary art. The collection of some 250 works is organized around three major themes: firstly, art in France from 1960 to 1990 with all its different trends (new realism, supports-surfaces and free figuration) and groups gathered round artists like Claude Viallat, Martial Raysse and Christian Boltanski; secondly, a Mediterranean focus bringing together artists from Spain, Italy and the South of France; and thirdly, German, British and American art including works by artists like Polke, Dorner and Schnabel.

ST PAUL'S CHURCH. This church, which was built between 1838 and 1848, is typical of the movement toward the rediscovery the Middle Ages and a range of regional

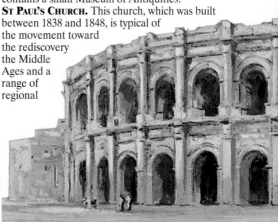

Romanesque styles. The interior décor by Hippolyte Flandrin is evocative of Byzantine art; it includes encaustic frescos and representations of figures against gold backgrounds.

AROUND THE AMPHITHEATER

THE ALPHONSE-DAUDET LYCÉE (right) Since 1883, this school has had premises in the former General Hospital, which was built in 1694. When the *boulevards* were laid out in 1811, the school's façade was rebuilt by Durand; it has preserved a degree of neoclassical severity, the sole decorative element being a coping frieze with alternating triglyphs and metopes decorated with scenes. The first-floor arcades were originally open and contained small shops.

THE AMPHITHEATER ● *80.* The late 1st-century Nîmes Amphitheater is one of the best preserved from the Roman Empire. It is elliptical in shape and seated twenty thousand people. The façade, built of courses of large stones, is ostentatiously articulated on the lower periphery by sixty bays, and higher up by two rows of regular arches topped by a small attic story. The first-floor arcades are decorated with Tuscan pilasters without a base, while those on the next floor are adorned with engaged columns standing on plinths; two-thirds of the shafts protrude. The attic story was simply decorated with small, short, narrow pilasters. At the time of the Barbarian invasions of the 4th century, the arches were closed up and the amphitheater turned into a fortress; they were surmounted by two square crenelated towers until the beginning of the 19th century. For a long time, the building looked like an enclosed quarter of the town with its alleyways, its two chapels, its wells and its cellars full of fine wines. It was cleared of debris in 1812 and restored, and was then turned into a site for staging spectacles ◆ *345*; initially, it was used for games involving bulls and then, from 1863 onward, for Spanish bullfights.

PLACE DU MARCHÉ
The Crocodile Fountain has stood in this pedestrianized square since 1988; it was designed by Martial Raysse and built by Silvio and Vito Tongiani. The fountain is a combination of marble and bronze and, in a single humorous structure, brings together the crocodile in the Nîmes coat of arms, the water which played a part in the founding of the town, and a truncated column, the symbol of ancient monuments.

A Visit by Francis I to the Monuments of Nîmes, 1838, by Alexandre Marie Colin.

FINE ARTS MUSEUM. The city's collections of works of art were first established in 1823 in the Maria Theresa Museum, which was founded in the Maison Carrée as a complement to the School of Drawing that had opened in 1820. After spending a brief time (1880–1) in a short-lived Palace of Arts, the collections found a home in another building which was replaced in 1907 by the present museum. The architect Max Raphel constructed the main hall around a representation of Admetus' Marriage, a huge mosaic found in Nîmes in 1882; alterations to the interior were carried out in 1986 by Wilmotte. The collections are dominated by French art of the 19th century, but there has been substantial diversification. There are about three thousand works altogether and, until recently, the museum has concentrated on past and present local artists in its purchases and exhibitions. However, it will soon receive a new encyclopedic collection of works dating from 1869, with a bequest by Robert Gower of over four thousand paintings of the Flemish, Dutch and Italian Schools.

AROUND THE CATHEDRAL

THE MUSEUMS OF ARCHAEOLOGY AND NATURAL HISTORY. The building housing these museums was once a Jesuit college and an imperial *lycée* and then a royal *lycée*; it has often been enlarged and renovated, and the façades giving onto Boulevard Amiral-Courbet and Grand'Rue still bear traces of this work. The museums were established here after 1888.

DENIM JEANS
As early as 1730, there were commercial references to "nims", a fine fabric that was exported to North America. However, modern denim ("de Nîmes") jeans were developed during the gold rush in the United States in the 1850's. At that time Levi Strauss, a recent immigrant, was importing from Nîmes a tough fabric which he initially sold as a kind of canvas or wagon cover, but soon began to use to make trousers. The product was improved by Jacob W. Davis who reinforced the pockets with studs, and went into business with Levi Strauss in 1872.

VILLARET CROQUANTS
Another Nîmes specialty is the *croquant*, a crispy biscuit made of almonds and honey, and scented with orange blossom. It has been made since 1775 at the Villaret bakery at 15 Rue de la Madeleine.

The Jesuit chapel and college in Grand'Rue serve as a permanent reminder of the city's first university. This was the Collège ès Arts, which was granted its charter by Francis I and stood on this very site. The cloister, which is articulated by wide arches, was built between 1680 and 1736.

The MUSEUM OF NATURAL HISTORY AND PREHISTORY provides a detailed account of the prehistory of the region and includes large displays of ethnological, zoological and geological artefacts; the MUSEUM OF ARCHEOLOGY is noted for its collections that run from the Iron Age to the end of the Roman era. In particular, the pre-Roman period includes the Marbacum Torso, which was discovered at the foot of the Tour Magne, and a large amount of funerary objects. The Roman era is illustrated by numerous everyday items such as tools, jewels, pieces used in games, and crockery; they, too, were unearthed in local digs.

THE CATHEDRAL. The Cathedral was consecrated in 1096 by Pope Urban II while on his way to start the First Crusade. The building bears the signs of successive restoration work and enlargements. Elements from the Roman period include the pediment which was inspired by the Maison Carrée. The restoration work was linked to the need to rebuild the Cathedral which had been destroyed on two occasions, in 1567 and 1621, as a result of religious strife. Only the left-hand side of the façade was spared, and that was thanks to the tower which had been erected in the Gothic period and turned into a watchtower by the Protestants. The Protestants took control of the town after the "Michelade" of 1567 when two hundred Catholic clergy and dignitaries were massacred on Saint Michael's Day, and nearly all the convents and churches destroyed, together with the Bishop's Palace. Monseigneur Cohon, who led the Catholic revival for much of the 17th century, had the Cathedral rebuilt between 1636 and 1646. Then, in 1669, he had the Rosary Chapel added behind the choir; this Baroque chapel was dedicated to the veneration of the Virgin Mary. Lastly, Henri Révoil, the Architect of Historic Monuments, provided the interior with new decoration in a neo-Medieval style dominated by Gothic elements; these included vaults with intersecting ribs and, running along each aisle, a triforium surmounted by bays with Gothic arches.

MUSEUM OF OLD NÎMES. This museum is housed in the former Bishop's Palace next to the Cathedral. It was built between 1683 and 1685 by the local architect Jacques Cubizol to plans by Alexis de La Feuille. Its classicism is emphasized by the horizontal lines and symmetrical organization of the façade. This building is one of the few examples in the region of the use of the ground plan of a private Parisian mansion between courtyard and garden. The original design for the palace was not properly completed until 1760 by Pierre Dardailhon, the town architect; the Bishop's Chapel, which was once directly connected to the palace, and the great staircase, with its typical Louis XV vaulted ironwork, date from this period. The museum was founded in 1920 on the initiative of Henri Bauquier; it has collections of items from local history.

LITTRÉ ISLAND
This tiny island, in a small river called the Agau, has been associated with the textile business since the Middle Ages. The banks used to be lined with workshops used by the dyers. Even the street names remind one of the past: Rue de la Gaude (yellow weed) and Rue de la Garance (madder-wort) recall tinctures long abandoned, and Rue des Flottes (skeins) evokes the hanks ready to be dyed. Carders, weavers and cloth shearers lived on the side streets. Although rehabilitated in the 1980's, The Îlot Littré is one of several old craft districts whose decline coincided with that of the textile trade in the 19th century.

JARDIN DE LA FONTAINE

A FRENCH GARDEN. This garden was originally designed in the 18th century to improve the town's water supply. The initial plan involved clearing a large number of mills from the area surrounding the spring. However, when preliminary work was carried out in 1738, remains of a temple were discovered; this sanctuary had surrounded the spring in ancient times, although the only trace so far visible was the Temple of Diana. The utilitarian aspect of the undertaking was now matched by a new concern for providing the spring with a suitable setting; the task was entrusted to the engineer Mareschal. He designed the space in the traditions of the French Garden (1745–55), concentrating on an abundance of trees and flowers and a symmetrical organization based on the central grotto.

THE AUGUSTEUM. This portico consisting of three aisles and two naves stands at the foot of Mount Cavalier and surrounds the springs of the fountain. Although the Augusteum enclosed a piece of holy land, it also provided a link between a theater in the northeast and a large vaulted room, the pseudo-temple of Diana, in the west. In the middle, there was almost certainly an altar dedicated to Rome and Augustus; all that remains is a fragment of masonry.

THE TEMPLE OF DIANA. This sanctuary dates mainly from the first phase of building under Augustus. A vast central hall with two corridors on either side still include some of its original vaulting which consists of courses of large stones; some protrude strongly, resembling transverse ribs. The side walls, of which the northern ones have been perfectly preserved, were decorated with monolithic columns with composite capitals and molded plinths; these columns support an entablature whose cornice is decorated with denticles. Twelve niches once adorned the inner walls, topped by alternately curved and triangular pediments. The temple was probably used as a library and a site for celebrations in honor of the Emperor.

THE MAGNE TOWER. The 3¼ miles of town wall enclose an area of 550 acres. The Tour Magne ("large tower"), with its facing of rubble stone and extensive use of courses of large boulders, has long been a source of fascination. It incorporated a pre-Roman tower that was pulled down in the 17th century to provide missing casing; just above the crepidoma, there is an octagonal tower of sober design, whose decoration serves to break the monotony of the stonework.

ORANGE

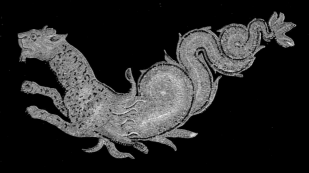

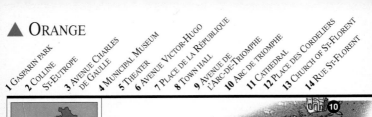

▲ ORANGE

1 GASPARIN PARK
2 COLLINE ST-EUTROPE
3 AVENUE CHARLES DE GAULLE
4 MUNICIPAL MUSEUM
5 THEATER
6 AVENUE VICTOR-HUGO
7 PLACE DE LA RÉPUBLIQUE
8 TOWN HALL
9 AVENUE DE L'ARC-DE-TRIOMPHE
10 ARC DE TRIOMPHE
11 CATHEDRAL
12 PLACE DES CORDELIERS
13 CHURCH OF ST-FLORENT
14 RUE ST-FLORENT

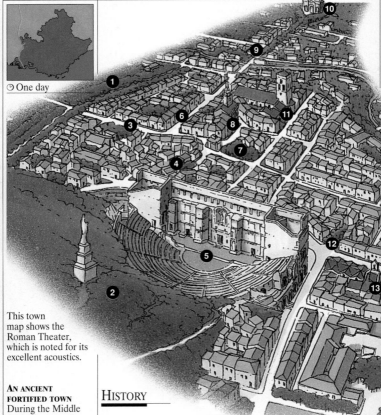

⊙ One day

This town map shows the Roman Theater, which is noted for its excellent acoustics.

AN ANCIENT FORTIFIED TOWN
During the Middle Ages, the town withdrew inside the ramparts which were strengthened by a castle that stood on the hill. At the time, Orange had three monasteries and some religious buildings clustered round the Basilica of St-Eutrope.

HISTORY

A ROMAN COLONY. The Romans colonized this area in 35 BC, and distributed the land to veterans of the 2nd Legion. The town was later encircled by a large hexagonal rampart which cut the hill in half; the triumphal arch in the north and the amphitheater in the west were thereby left outside the town's boundaries. Archeological digs have revealed residential zones consisting of streets crossing at right angles, and small blocks of dwellings whose area corresponded to the length of the amphitheater wall.

A BISHOPRIC AND A PRINCIPALITY. The Bishopric of Orange was founded in the 4th century. In 1096, when Rambaud de Nice, the ruler of the city, followed Peter the Hermit to the Crusades, his daughter, Tiburga, set up the principality as a vassal state of the Holy Roman Empire comprising Orange, Jonquières and Courthézon. In 1173, Orange passed to the House of Baux, before finally coming under the

rule of John I of Châlon and then of his descendants.
DUTCH AND PROTESTANT ORANGE. The principality was bequeathed to the House of Nassau which, after its conversion to Protestantism, turned Orange into a haven for Protestants who had been forced to flee neighboring countries. In the early 17th century, Maurice of Nassau made Orange into one of the most powerful strongholds in Europe thanks to the plans of the Dutch architect Servole. It was subsequently razed to the ground in 1672 on the orders of Louis XIV, who was still at war with William of Orange over the United Provinces. Six years later, William took back the principality under the Treaty of Nijmegen; then, under the Treaty of Utrecht, Orange finally became part of France.

AROUND THE ROMAN THEATER ★

MUNICIPAL MUSEUM ★. This museum, which has been located in a private house since the 17th century, tells the story of the city from prehistory to the 18th century. It provides information on how administrative affairs were conducted, including the role of the ROMAN REGISTER which set out the terms of ownership of land distributed to the colonists. In 1949 416 fragments were discovered carved on stone, dated between 25 BC and 10 AD, and coming from three different registers. The WETTERS ROOM contains five paintings that once hung in the drawing room of a house in Rue de la Fabrique, executed in 1764 by Gabriel-Maria M. Rossetti for the Wetter brothers who owned the printed calico factory in Orange. They present a remarkable picture of factory life at the time, and include all phases of production. The first printed cotton from the Indies arrived in Europe on ships owned by the East India Company.

ROMAN THEATER ★. This is considered to be one of best-preserved theaters surviving from Roman times. It was constructed in the time of the Emperor Augustus, and has survived the vagaries of the weather because it has continued to be used for events in the city. The theater has been restored on many occasions, and is now classified as a World Heritage Site. The northern façade of the stage wall is 121 feet high, and was described by Louis XIV as "the most beautiful wall in [his] kingdom". At the base, there is a series of arches, some of which are blind, and three doors standing under a portico. At the top of the wall, there is a row of projecting corbels pierced with holes which fit the consoles, themselves pierced with cylindrical holes; the corbels were used to support poles holding up the hawsers for the *velum* (or awning) which provided shelter for the spectators. The great hollow in the ground formed by the *cavea* could hold nine thousand people; access was by way of *vomitoria* leading away from the two main entrances.

WILLIAM III OF NASSAU (1650–1702)
William opposed the Sun King and, while Stadholder of the United Provinces, became King of England, Scotland and Ireland in 1689 through his marriage to Mary Stuart.

TREASURES IN THE MUNICIPAL MUSEUM
The Museum contains many superb ancient pieces, including this fragment of a marble plaque on which the register has been carved (above).

The Printing Workshop, painted for the Wetter brothers. On the left is one of the earliest printing presses that used rollers; on the right is an area for hanging printed fabrics.

▲ ORANGE

Decorative theme
on the Arc de
triomphe
illustrating the
Roman victory

OPERATIC FARE. Renewed interest in Orange's theater during the last century encouraged the idea of using such a beautiful setting for theatrical presentations. Thanks to Jean Vilar, Avignon already had an international reputation for theater, and in 1970 the "Nouvelles Chorégies d'Orange" decided to specialize in opera. It has since acquired an enviable reputation, and the festival attracts some of the world's greatest singers.

THE AMPHITHEATER. It is likely that this vast paved area bounded by a high semi-circular wall on St-Eutrope Hill had some connection with a temple situated on the side of the hill, destroyed in 1911 when a water reservoir was being constructed. It appears to have been an *augusteum* dedicated to the cult of the Emperor and extended by the forum.

DECORATION
The walls were originally covered with a marble facing and niches containing statues; an example of the latter is the statue of Augustus which is set in the largest niche of all just above the Royal Gate. The stage wall included seventy-six grey and white marble columns.

THE STAGE
The stage resembled the one used nowadays for the "Chorégies". It was made of pieces of wood about 3½ foot-high, encircled by the stage wall and its side extensions, and covered by a roof. Single-story rooms called *basilicae* were to be found on either side of the stage.

A view from Colline St-Eutrope: *Road Climbing up the Hill*, a painting by Paul Surtel (1949).

COLLINE ST-EUTROPE. This hill was laid out as a public park at the beginning of the 20th century, and contains a number of important archeological remains. The cross which has been at the entrance since the 17th century marks the site where St-Eutrope's Basilica stood in the 12th century. The PRINCES OF ORANGE CASTLE looks out over the theater; this castle was built over the ruins of a former *castrum* in the northern section of the hill. It was altered and then enlarged, and its continually improved defenses eventually included the great works undertaken by Maurice of Nassau who added eleven bastions. Wide moats made access difficult in the south, and a steep slope provided good protection on the side where the

town is situated. Such military architecture struck Vauban as so effective that he used the plans to strengthen the kingdom's frontiers. Two of the four groups of dwellings can still be made out in the west and south. The Powder Tower (Tour des poudres) was restored in the 17th century, and contains a vaulted lower room with an ENTRÉE EN BAIONNETTE which is extremely difficult to get access to. Further to the south, there are the remains of large bastions with a moat and a counterscarp.

AROUND THE CATHEDRAL

CATHEDRAL OF NOTRE-DAME-DE-NAZARETH

Orange was the site of a bishopric for nine hundred years from the 4th century onward. The present-day Cathedral was built in the 12th century, was consecrated in 1208, and has been renovated many times since then. In the south side of the Cathedral, there is a 12th-century doorway that gives

onto Place Clemenceau; this was altered somewhat in the 17th century through the addition of a double door topped by a triangular pediment. The Romanesque church consists of a single nave with four bays, and its ceiling is in the form of a Gothic arch. Monseigneur du Tillet, Bishop of Orange at the end of the 18th century, had the Cathedral restored and added embellishments to the stalls in the chapter and to the high altar. The painted decoration was the work of two Italian craftsmen, Zanetti and Perratoni; it is dated 1809.

FORMER TOWN HALL. When the Commune was founded in 1282, the Council met in leading citizens' homes or in the rooms of the Cathedral cloister. As the archives grew in size, it became increasingly difficult to move them about, and in

1389 a house was purchased in Rue Puits-Balanson; this was Orange's first town hall. The 12th-century building is still there: its façades are pierced with gemeled bays with elegant columns surmounted by florid capitals and standing on a molded band.

L'ARC DE TRIOMPHE ★. This triumphal arch is situated in the north of the modern city, but outside the town's former limits. Recent research suggests that the arch was built between 20 and 25 AD in honor of the Roman general Germanicus. It has been restored on many occasions, for instance in the 13th century when it was used as part of the town's defenses. No visit to Orange would be complete without a walk from Rue St-Martin to Cours Aristide-Briand. It is also well worth spending time in the picturesque Place aux Herbes, the large Protestant church, Impasse de la Cloche, and in Gasparin Park, which has a 19th-century theater situated next to it.

⊙ Six days

🚗 155 miles

FERDINAND REVOUL AND HIS CARDBOARD BOXES
One day, while repairing boxes for a friend who was a silkworm breeder, this Valréas businessman realized that he could make much better ones. He started selling to the pharmacy, jewelry and confectionery trades. When he died in 1864, new workshops opened up and the printing business took off at much the same time.

CAFÉ DE LA PAIX ★
This café has preserved its early 20th-century décor and architecture.

NOTRE-DAME-DE-NAZARETH
This church has two towers: an octagonal campanile with three bays, and an arcaded tower that also has three bays, although one of them is now walled up.

VALRÉAS

MUSEUM OF CARDBOARD AND PRINTING ★. In the 19th century, Valréas launched itself successfully into the cardboard and printing industries. This museum is situated in an old commercial building; it describes the history of the processes in manufacturing cardboard boxes.

PLACE GUTENBERG. Situated in this square are the 16th-century HÔTEL D'AGOULT, with a fine Gothic door, and the 13th-century DELPHINAL CASTLE, whose façade still includes the corbels of the original machicolation. The castle became a papal house after 1317.

HÔTEL DE SIMIANE ★. At the suggestion of Pauline de Grignan, a granddaughter of Mme de Sévigné who married into the Simiane family, the house was renovated. This elegant building has three façades organized around a main courtyard. The drawing room has a painted ceiling and is decorated with 18th-century frescos; there is also an oratory and a library.

CLOCK TOWER. The square dungeon is all that remains of this castle built by the Ripert family in the 11th century. The dungeon gained its clock tower in the 16th century.

NOTRE-DAME-DE-NAZARETH. This primitive church was constructed in the early 12th century and at the end of the century aisles were placed in the nave and the south door was added. In 1477, when the church was enlarged, a whole series of bas-reliefs were used as arch-stones in the pronaos; some chapels were built later.

WHITE PENITENTS' CHAPEL ★. This church was built in 1585, and was then further decorated in the 18th century with the addition of wainscoting, together with a coffered ceiling made of painted wood adorned with blue and gold rose windows and trompe l'oeil paintings.

184

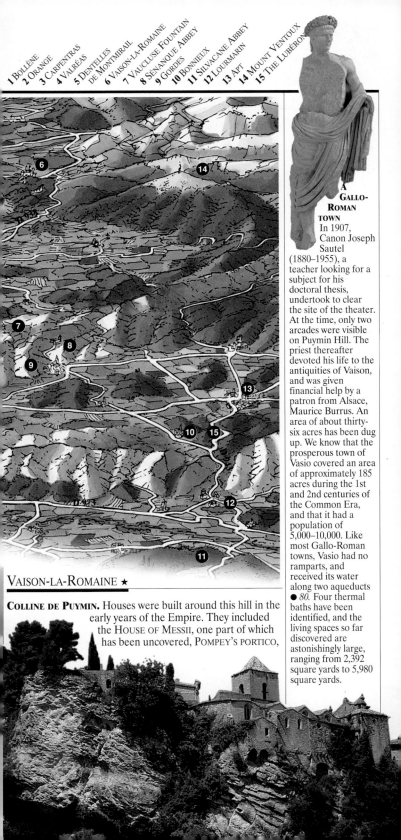

A GALLO-ROMAN TOWN In 1907, Canon Joseph Sautel (1880–1955), a teacher looking for a subject for his doctoral thesis, undertook to clear the site of the theater. At the time, only two arcades were visible on Puymin Hill. The priest thereafter devoted his life to the antiquities of Vaison, and was given financial help by a patron from Alsace, Maurice Burrus. An area of about thirty-six acres has been dug up. We know that the prosperous town of Vasio covered an area of approximately 185 acres during the 1st and 2nd centuries of the Common Era, and that it had a population of 5,000–10,000. Like most Gallo-Roman towns, Vasio had no ramparts, and received its water along two aqueducts ● *80*. Four thermal baths have been identified, and the living spaces so far discovered are astonishingly large, ranging from 2,392 square yards to 5,980 square yards.

VAISON-LA-ROMAINE ★

COLLINE DE PUYMIN. Houses were built around this hill in the early years of the Empire. They included the HOUSE OF MESSII, one part of which has been uncovered, POMPEY'S PORTICO,

THE PEACOCK HOUSE
This residence from the early years of the Roman Empire is on the edge of the town; it takes its name from its decorative bird motifs. Five polychrome mosaics are in the museum in Vaison; they belong to the Rhône School, which appears to have developed at the end of the 1st century.

ANTIQUITY
The long-buried stones evoke the atmosphere of a town in antiquity. They include remains of the basilica and the House of the Silver Bust.

THE THEATER
The *cavea* was rebuilt in 1930. All the original tiers carved out of the rock have survived.

encircled by colonnades but still largely buried underground, RUE DES BOUTIQUES, a public park, and the PRÉTOIRE THEATER and the PRÉTOIRE HOUSE; the latter was an enormous *domus* organized on terraces on the side of the hill. A series of glazes are painted on clay walls.

THE VILLASSE DISTRICT. This part of the town bears the name of a 17th-century bourgeois house in the center of the district. It was here that Canon Sautel conducted archeological digs, discovering not only one of the city's most beautiful residential areas but also the RUE DES BOUTIQUES, the large room in the THERMAL BATHS, the HOUSE OF THE SILVER BUST (a huge dwelling incorporating a peristyle surrounded by a colonnade, a garden with a pool and reception rooms), and the DOLPHIN HOUSE which was built around 40 BC and subsequently enlarged in the 2nd century.

ST-QUENIN CHAPEL. This was built over a vast, early medieval cemetery to the north of the town. The stone structure and the ancient-looking decoration fooled historians into thinking it was a Roman temple. The west façade includes the coat of arms of Bishop Joseph-Marie de Suarès, who had the chapel built in the 17th century, and contains 5th-century remains. The chevet is triangular.

FORMER CATHEDRAL OF NOTRE-DAME-DE-NAZARETH. This was constructed around 1040 on the ruins, of a Gallo-Roman building which are still visible at the base of the chevet. The original design comprised a large nave and bays with six aisles, covered by a coving on square pillars; there is also an apse preceded by a bay in the choir and framed by two apsidioles in a half-dome. The last bay in the nave is covered by an octagonal cupola on squinches with representations of the four Evangelists.

CLOISTER. The cloister was built around 1160 to the north of the Cathedral, and the bishop lived in the nearby

palace which has now disappeared. External arcatures with semicircular vaults open out into the gardens; the interior was restored in the 19th century.

ROMAN BRIDGE. The bridge was constructed on a rock in the early years of the Empire at the narrowest point of the River Ouvèze. This structure has survived the many occasions when the river has flooded; only the parapets, which were rebuilt this century, were carried away in the floods of 1992.

OLD TOWN. The medieval gate topped by a 16th-century belfry and a cast-iron campanile made in1786 leads into a maze of narrow, cobbled streets. The CATHÉDRALE DE LA HAUTE-VILLE, which is not open to the public, dates from 1464. Apart from the façade which was restored much later, the church has an ogival nave to which two chapels were added in 1601. The OLD PRESBYTERY, with its stone door and elegant balustraded balcony of wrought iron, stands next to STE-CONSTANCE CHAPEL; all that remains of this chapel is a stone door topped by a small tower.

CASTLE (not open to the public). The buildings were organized around a tall 13th-century dungeon, and above the blind ground floor there is a vaulted upper floor with a small number of bays; it is extended by a fortified terrace. The interior courtyard is bounded by the curtain walls.

MOUNT VENTOUX ★

A MOUNTAIN. While masses of black pine trees on the steep, north face of Mount Ventoux plunge down as far as the bed of the River Toulourenc, the south-facing flanks are much more gentle. Orchards and vineyards abound on the lower slopes, giving way to thickets of green oak trees and other species of oak with deciduous leaves, including durmasts. Higher up, there are Atlas cedars and black pines. Above 5,250 feet, only a few junipers grow in the chalky soil, while in springtime, *Iberis candolleana* and poppies manage to grow among the stones.

A SPIRITUAL HOME. In 1336, Petrarch climbed Mount Ventoux and later described his experience. In the 15th century, the Bishop of Carpentras had the STE-CROIX CHAPEL built on the summit; it was a popular place of pilgrimage until the beginning of the 20th century. Hikers can repeat this journey by taking the GR 91 which skirts the foothills of the mountain to the north of Bédoin, and then following a path signposted in blue just after the village of Fébriers. The whole walk takes five hours.

A RANGE OF SPORTS. The hills of Mount Ventoux are ideal for skiing, and all kinds of rides and walks; what is more, the chalets built in the 1950's and 1960's on the north slopes of Mount Serein have lost none of their rare charm. The Cabane du Contrat just outside the resort is a suitable starting point for an ascent of the north face along the GR 4; the climb takes one hour.

CARPENTRAS

AROUND LA CHARITÉ. Today, LA CHARITÉ houses the cultural center. The chapel dates from 1672 and the building was enlarged between 1730 and 1747. In the late 18th century, the institution was moved to the hospital and the

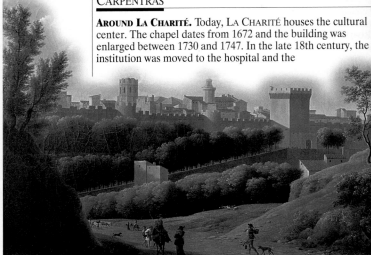

JOSEPH DOMINIQUE D'INGUIMBERT (1683–1757)
D'Inguimbert was born in Carpentras, and was a pupil of the Jesuits and then the Dominicans before completing his education in Aix-en-Provence and at the St-Jacques Novitiate in

Paris.
After a long stay in Italy, he was appointed Bishop of Carpentras in 1735. His untiring charitable work for the poor led him to build the huge Hôtel-Dieu (general hospital) and, keen on making knowledge freely available, he also founded an extraordinary museum-library that was open to all. Both establishments, to which he gave all his money, are still in existence.

premises were used successively as an orphanage, a girls' school and council offices. The CHURCH OF NOTRE-DAME-DE-L'OBSERVANCE was built in 1590 by the Franciscans; during the Revolution, the monastery was sold and the church was not reopened until 1802. The choir and neo-Gothic tower date from 1882.

THE ORANGE GATE. This fortification no longer has its ravelin, but it is still the only surviving section of the 14th-century wall. It is surmounted by an equilateral arch in a tower 82 feet high, and opens on the town side.

LAPIDARY MUSEUM ★. This museum has been housed in the Baroque chapel ★ of the former Visitandine Convent since 1936. The décor of marble and gypsum, the pulpit, the glory and reredos which once surmounted the vanished altar, and the wrought-iron communion table are from the mid 18th century. The high altar of gilt wood was originally the high altar in the Cathedral. The museum contains artefacts belonging to Monseigneur d'Inguimbert and objects discovered locally.

BELFRY ★. The covered passageway has a coffered ceiling, with remains of 16th-century mural paintings and traces of the fire of 1723. The basket-handle arched door leads to the spiral staircase, which in turn leads to the upper floors and belfry. The bell tower ● *102* was commissioned in 1577.

SYNAGOGUE ★. In the 16th century Jews made up almost one-tenth of the population of Carpentras. The first floor of the synagogue was probably built no earlier than the 15th century, and the façade and the vestibule with its monumental stairway date from 1890. The Main Hall, the Women's

ECONOMIC ACTIVITY
Agriculture was the
principal means of
earning a living,
particularly after the
Carpentras irrigation
canal was built.
Crystalized fruit and
preserves
transformed
agricultural produce,
and the canning and
wooden box
businesses provided
packaging. People
still come to the
St-Siffrein Fair on
November 27 on their
barges, and the
Friday market is
entertaining.

Section and the bakery open onto an internal courtyard. The
Prayer Room on the first floor was rebuilt after 1741. To the
east is the Ark containing the Torah Scrolls, and to the west is
the *tebah* where the Rabbi stands to read the
Torah. The galleries were reserved for
women. Other objects include the Throne of
the Prophet Elijah, everlasting lamps, ritual
chandeliers and candelabra.

ROMAN ARCH. This arch ● *80* dating from
the first ten years of the Common Era is the
only vestige of the town's ancient history. It
consists of a single bay and is decorated with
bas-reliefs representing captured Barbarians.

BISHOP'S PALACE. The palace was built
between 1646 and 1652 to plans by François
des Royers de La Valfenière; it was turned
into the Law Courts in the early 19th century. The ceremonial
chamber and the main reception room have retained their
17th- and 18th-century decorations
respectively.

THE JEWISH GATE
The gate was the
work of Blaise
Lescuyer, who

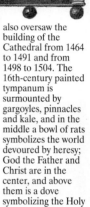

also oversaw the
building of the
Cathedral from 1464
to 1491 and from
1498 to 1504. The
16th-century painted
tympanum is
surmounted by
gargoyles, pinnacles
and kale, and in the
middle a bowl of rats
symbolizes the world
devoured by heresy;
God the Father and
Christ are in the
center, and above
them is a dove
symbolizing the Holy
Spirit.

CATHEDRAL OF ST-SIFFREIN ★. From the
square it is possible to see all that
remains of this 12th-century
Romanesque cathedral which collapsed
around 1400. A new cathedral in the
Gothic style was built after 1404. Beyond
the Gothic cathedral's chevet, which
stands on the site of the Romanesque
cloister, is the JEWISH GATE through
which Jewish converts passed before they
were baptized. The décor on the composite west façade was
done by Isnard between 1615 and 1618. The tower was pulled
down in 1875 and rebuilt by Révoil between 1899 and 1902 in
the neo-Gothic style. The nave with its six ogival bays
supported by buttresses is extended by a narrower and lower
choir and a seven-sided apse. The Cathedral contains 18th-
century ironwork, gilt wood decoration in the choir and
numerous paintings; in the treasury there are paintings on
wood, liturgical ornaments, and gold plate, and in the nave
there is the Balcony of St-Clou, built to thank Providence
for saving the town from the plague of 1721 ● *52*.

**INGUIMBERTINE LIBRARY AND THE DUPLESSIS-COMTADIN
MUSEUM ★.** The former contains 250,000 volumes, 5,000
manuscripts, correspondence of the Humanist scholar
Nicolas-Claude Fabri de Peiresc, drawings, prints and
musical scores; it is one of the most valuable libraries in the
province. The museum houses Monseigneur d'Inguimbert's
collection of paintings, furniture and
artefacts from the Comtat Venaissin.

HÔTEL-DIEU ★. The long façade of this
general hospital built in the Italian style is
topped by a balustrade adorned by six
flame ornaments. The furnishings of
the apothecary's dispensary in the west
wing have been preserved; they were
decorated by Duplessis in 1762. The
first-floor gallery with its flat ceiling
and walls covered with DONATIFS leads
to the chapel.

FONTAINE-DE-VAUCLUSE ★

EXCEPTIONAL BEAUTY. The closed valley (*Vallis clausa*) gave its name first to the village and then to the département. The village largely owes its existence to the mysterious spring and to the River Sorgue from which Saint Véran chased away the dragon that haunted the fountain grotto. From the 15th century onward, paper mills sprang up in the area, and the paper industry made the village prosperous for many decades.

LAURA AND PETRARCH
The fountain is the source of the River Sorgue, which drove the mills built on its banks. Petrarch was utterly charmed by the countryside, which was very wild at the time, and he bought a house nearby. He made

frequent visits between 1337 and 1352. The house stood on the site of the modern Petrarch Museum; it was destroyed by looters in 1353, but by this time Petrarch had returned to Italy with his daughter. He greatly missed the region during the rest of his life.

There is a good view from the path that leads up to the castle of the Bishops of Cavaillon, rebuilt in the 13th century.

CHURCH OF ST-VÉRAN ★. St-Véran was built in the 11th century on the site of an ancient shrine and a Carolingian building that contained Saint Véran's tomb. All that remains is a few elements now used for other purposes, fragments of the 8th-century chancel, a 6th-century carved altar in a 1st-century funerary slab, and a 6th-century sarcophagus, allegedly that of Saint Véran. The church was restored in the 12th century, and on many occasions subsequently. The Descent from the Cross Reredos was presented to the church by the Guild of Papermakers in 1654. In 1803, a column was erected in honor of Petrarch (1304–74) in the square at the end of the bridge.

PETRARCH MUSEUM-LIBRARY ★. This museum-library, which was founded in 1927, contains drawings and prints relating to Petrarch, Laura, Avignon and Fontaine-de-Vaucluse, as well as a fine collection of old editions of Petrarch's works. There is also a small exhibition of modern art.

CALL TO FREEDOM MUSEUM ★. This museum deals exclusively with the period 1939–45, and recalls the activities of the French Resistance in Vaucluse through a splendid collection of posters, artefacts, clandestine publications, and militant magazines.

UNDERGROUND WORLD OF NORBERT CASTERET ★. The museum bears the name of one of the founders of modern speleology, and contains an exhibition of materials used in the study of caves, a reconstruction of various sites, and a magnificent collection of crystallizations.

VALLIS CLAUSA CRAFT CENTER. The Vallis Clausa papermill ★ still manufactures paper using methods employed in the 16th century, specializing in the incorporation of flower petals. A guided tour of the facilities is available.

THE FOUNTAIN ★. The earliest explorations of the well took place in 1878, and the lowest point of 1,010 feet below the surface was not reached until 1985. The spring pours out at the base of a calcareous and karstified system.

GORDES

A CHARMING VILLAGE. In the 17th and 18th centuries, this village on the edge of the Vaucluse Plateau was well known for

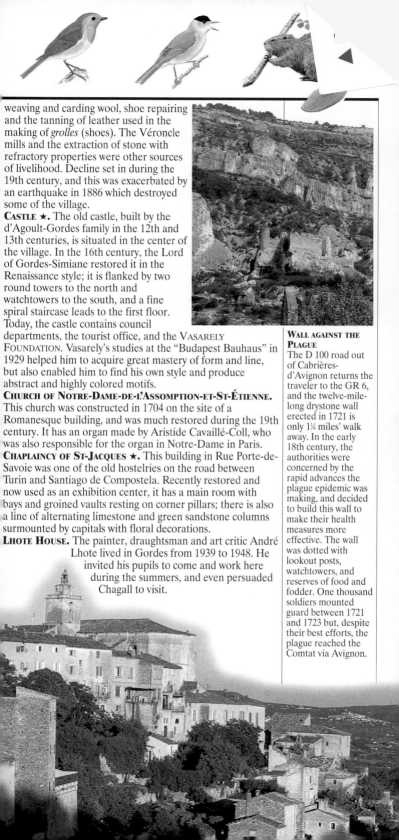

weaving and carding wool, shoe repairing and the tanning of leather used in the making of *grolles* (shoes). The Véroncle mills and the extraction of stone with refractory properties were other sources of livelihood. Decline set in during the 19th century, and this was exacerbated by an earthquake in 1886 which destroyed some of the village.

CASTLE ★. The old castle, built by the d'Agoult-Gordes family in the 12th and 13th centuries, is situated in the center of the village. In the 16th century, the Lord of Gordes-Simiane restored it in the Renaissance style; it is flanked by two round towers to the north and watchtowers to the south, and a fine spiral staircase leads to the first floor. Today, the castle contains council departments, the tourist office, and the VASARELY FOUNDATION. Vasarely's studies at the "Budapest Bauhaus" in 1929 helped him to acquire great mastery of form and line, but also enabled him to find his own style and produce abstract and highly colored motifs.

CHURCH OF NOTRE-DAME-DE-L'ASSOMPTION-ET-ST-ÉTIENNE. This church was constructed in 1704 on the site of a Romanesque building, and was much restored during the 19th century. It has an organ made by Aristide Cavaillé-Coll, who was also responsible for the organ in Notre-Dame in Paris.

CHAPLAINCY OF ST-JACQUES ★. This building in Rue Porte-de-Savoie was one of the old hostelries on the road between Turin and Santiago de Compostela. Recently restored and now used as an exhibition center, it has a main room with bays and groined vaults resting on corner pillars; there is also a line of alternating limestone and green sandstone columns surmounted by capitals with floral decorations.

LHOTE HOUSE. The painter, draughtsman and art critic André Lhote lived in Gordes from 1939 to 1948. He invited his pupils to come and work here during the summers, and even persuaded Chagall to visit.

WALL AGAINST THE PLAGUE
The D 100 road out of Cabrières-d'Avignon returns the traveler to the GR 6, and the twelve-mile-long drystone wall erected in 1721 is only 1¼ miles' walk away. In the early 18th century, the authorities were concerned by the rapid advances the plague epidemic was making, and decided to build this wall to make their health measures more effective. The wall was dotted with lookout posts, watchtowers, and reserves of food and fodder. One thousand soldiers mounted guard between 1721 and 1723 but, despite their best efforts, the plague reached the Comtat via Avignon.

THE VILLAGE OF BORIES ★. These drystone huts (*bories*) ● *88* go back to neolithic times. The Théâtre National Populaire actor Pierre Viala fell in love with the place and undertook to restore it. The village stands a little way outside Gordes; alleyways, paddocks, pigsties and wine cellars have all been restored, and the presentation is completed by a display of objects and working tools.

THE CLOISTER
The semicircular vaults are punctuated by square beams that mark the center of each gallery (all of

which are terraced) and the four corners of the cloister. Like the rest of the cloister, the capitals are decorated with great simplicity. There was once a section in the south inhabited by lay members, but this was burned down by local people in 1544; it was rebuilt in the 18th century and turned into abbey accommodation and a guest house. The washbasin opposite the refectory door disappeared, and a copy was made in the 19th century.

SÉNANQUE ABBEY ★

CISTERCIAN ABBEY. Together with the abbeys of Silvacane ▲ *196* and Le Thoronet ▲ *225*, Sénanque is one of the three "Cistercian sisters of Provence". Its foundation owed much to the reforming spirit of Cîteaux Abbey, and is architecturally marked by a return to the Rule of Saint Benedict, according to wishes expressed by Saint Bernard in 1130. Twelve monks built the abbey in 1148 and cultivated land given to them by the lords of Gordes. After a long period of decline, the abbey was rebuilt around 1600 by the Commendatory Abbot, who had the south wing added. After being sold to the French state at the time of the Revolution, Sénanque enjoyed a revival in the mid 19th century; then, after being abandoned, it was acquired by the monks of Lérins in 1988.

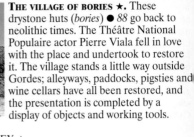

THE MONKS' WING. The broken barrel-vaulting of the MONKS' DORMITORY is an extension of the ceiling in the church transept. The whole building is lit by twelve semicircular windows. The monks devoted their lives exclusively to spiritual endeavors and lived quite separately from lay people. The CALEFACTORY, which has preserved one of its two original fireplaces, has groin-vaulting which rests on a central column; it was used as a reading room in winter, but also provided working space for the copyists. The CHAPTER HOUSE was where the monks met; it has ribbed vaulting supported by two pillars. Apart from the leaf motifs on the capitals, there are very few decorative elements.

THE CHURCH. The nave is lined with bays and has broken barrel-vaulting. At the transept crossing, the tower is supported by an octagonal cupola on squinches, most unusual in the Cistercian tradition; the arms of the transept lead to the two apsidioles. The choir is closed off by a semicircular apse with a half-dome and lit by semicircular bays.

APT

HISTORY. *Apta Julia* was founded at the end of the 1st century
BC, and was an important resting place along the Via
Domitiana ▲ *237* which linked the Rhône Valley and Italy.
Few original buildings have survived, although the basements
of the museum contain vestiges of the theater's tiers. The
impact of ecclesiastical power, which took the form of the
cathedral, baptistery and chapter, built between the 5th and
11th centuries, altered the urban landscape, while reusing the
main site of the Roman town and the foundations of some
ancient buildings. The prosperity the town enjoyed in the
modern era is reflected in the façades of the 17th- and 18th-
century aristocratic residences and in the Bishop's Palace,
which dates from the mid 18th century. The manufacture of
crystalized fruit and conserves proved as successful as the
production of faïence ● *74* and, despite a number of crises,
continues to the present day. In the late 19th century, the
mining and refining of ocher became the third element in the
area's process of industrialization, and contributed to a major
transformation of the landscape.

FORMER HOSPITAL OF LA CHARITÉ. The main façade of this
institution, which was built between 1690 and 1713, has a
pediment topped by a statue of the benefactor of these
hospices. A Baroque chapel was built in the west wing around
1700; it has preserved its high altar made of gilt wood, and a
superb reredos with four
Corinthian pilasters and
a curvilinear pediment.

PLACE DE LA BOUQUERIE. In the
Middle Ages there was a small

**CAPITALE MONDIALE
DES FRUITS CONFITS**

suburb in this area that contained a wide variety of different
houses. Most of the present cafés were originally inns that
stood close to the city gates.

FORMER BISHOP'S PALACE ★. This palace, thought to be one
of the earliest in Christian Provence, was occupied by famous
prelates including Saint Stephen. Since the Revolution, it has
housed the Sub-Prefecture, council offices and the Tribunal.

RUE DES MARCHANDS. This road more or
less follows the line of the Roman road,
the *Decumanus maximus*, and crosses
from one side of Apt to the other; the
road beneath the vault of the
CLOCKTOWER, built between 1561 and
1568, provides a line of communication
between east and west. The tower is
crowned by a *campanile* containing a
clock showing the faces of Christ and
Saint Peter.

**OCHER QUARRIES IN
ROUSSILLON**
Helpful notices along
the route through the
ancient quarries
explain the process of
mining ocher and
enable the visitor to
appreciate this
unique landscape of
vermilions, whites
and yellows and the
emerald green of the

pine trees. The
possibilities of ocher
were discovered by a
man from Roussillon,
Jean-Étienne Astier,
who marketed it in a
powdered form.
Intense production
for more than a
century brought
prosperity to the
region, with exports
of ocher going all
over the world.

APT (Vaucluse)
Fabrique de Fruits Crist
La Fabrication

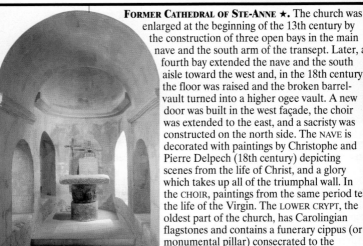

FORMER CATHEDRAL OF STE-ANNE ★. The church was enlarged at the beginning of the 13th century by the construction of three open bays in the main nave and the south arm of the transept. Later, a fourth bay extended the nave and the south aisle toward the west and, in the 18th century, the floor was raised and the broken barrel-vault turned into a higher ogee vault. A new door was built in the west façade, the choir was extended to the east, and a sacristy was constructed on the north side. The NAVE is decorated with paintings by Christophe and Pierre Delpech (18th century) depicting scenes from the life of Christ, and a glory which takes up all of the triumphal wall. In the CHOIR, paintings from the same period tell the life of the Virgin. The LOWER CRYPT, the oldest part of the church, has Carolingian flagstones and contains a funerary cippus (or monumental pillar) consecrated to the memory of C. Allius Celer, a *flamen* (priest) of *Apta Julia*. The CHAPEL OF ST-JOHN THE BAPTIST contains an early Christian marble sarcophagus from the Pyrenees, and the CHAPEL OF STE-ANNE leads to the Treasury.

MUSEUM OF ARCHEOLOGY AND HISTORY ★. The museum is in the former Curial House (1778), and contains collections of archeology, and sacred and decorative art by the faïence makers Moulin, Bernard, Sagy, Esbérard and Delacroix.

MAISON DU PARC. The Hôtel Trouchoc de la Sablière (18th century) became the headquarters of the Parc naturel régional du Lubéron in 1977. It houses a GEOLOGICAL MUSEUM.

SAIGNON GATE. This is one of Apt's medieval entrances. It was altered and enlarged in the 18th century, and surmounted by a clock and a pinnacle in the form of a *campanile* ● *102*.

A LONG HISTORY
There has been a Church of St Mary and St-Castor on this spot since the 11th century. At one point, it was completely destroyed and had to be rebuilt by Bishop Alphant; it was altered again in the 12th century. The church was in the form of a Latin cross, and consisted of a nave with three bays, a choir and a transept. All that remains is the upper crypt, the transept crossing covered by an octagonal cupola, the first part of the choir, the south end of the transept and the south apsidiole.

Above: The lower crypt.

BONNIEUX

THE CASTELLAS GATE ★. The village of Bonnieux lies at the foot of the spur on which a town of the same name once stood. Entry is by the 12th-century Castellas, or Chèvres, Gate opposite the entrance to the castle.

OLD CHURCH ★. Nothing remains of the 12th-century church except the three bays on the west side of the nave and the north part of the transept. The ancient door to the south is topped by an arch

PLACE ST-PIERRE AND ITS FOUNTAIN
This is the site of the former fortress and principal residence of the counts of Apt. Under the Ancien Régime, several Apt families

from the nobility and upper bourgeoisie owned private mansions in this square. Today, the 19th-century Fontaine St-Pierre stands in the center of the square.

with floral decoration and an eagle, the symbol of the fourth Evangelist, Saint John.

THE VILLAGE. Since 1859, the council offices have been in the HÔTEL DE ROUVIL, a mansion that has preserved its door with 17th-century metopes and triglyphs. The *campanile* comes from the former Tour de l'Horloge. The small square in front of the door is lined with 16th- and 17th-century houses that have low, embossed doors.

BAKERY MUSEUM. This museum occupies a 17th-century building that was used as a bakery in the 19th century; it is devoted to the history of bread and the growing of wheat.

THE NEW CHURCH. The new church was built in 1870 and resolves the problems of gaining access to the old church. The broken barrel-vaulting covers a nave with two bays, and contains four early 16th-century wooden panels depicting episodes from the Passion.

Robert-Laurent Vibert by Vignol (1914). Vibert bought Lourmarin Castle and set up an artists' foundation in 1925. Exhibitions and concerts take place there in the summer.

Below: *Street in Lourmarin* (1866) by Paul Guigou (1834–71).

LOURMARIN

HISTORY. Lourmarin grew around two hills: La Colette, where the castle stands, and La Colinette where the village was built. It was an important commercial staging post as early as the 11th century. Following outbreaks of pillaging and epidemics of the plague in the 14th century, the village was abandoned by its inhabitants until approximately 1470 when Fouquet d'Agoult, the lord of the manor, brought some Vaud families to repopulate the area and work the land. Subsequently, despite opposition from neighboring lords and persecutions prompted by the Wars of Religion, the community became one of the most important in the region. The town also prospered thanks to agriculture, and later to the silk which was produced and processed locally. Since the middle of the 19th century, vines, fruit and vegetables have been Lourmarin's major economic resource.

THE CASTLE. The present building consists of two interlocking

RENAISSANCE ARCHITECTURE
The superb spiral staircase (below) is the castle's pièce de

résistance. It connects two sets of apartments inside a square tower that links the Old Castle and the New Castle.

195

THE LUBÉRON
This range of mountains lies half-way between the Alps and the Mediterranean, extending 31 miles between Manosque, Cavaillon, the lower valley of the Durance and its tributary, the Calavon. The Lourmarin Comb at Apt divides the chain in two. The Grand Lubéron, a rounded massif, rises to 3,690 feet, while a large projecting shelf to the east, the Carpentras Plateau, backs onto

the great Bonnieux massif as far as Castellet. The Petit Lubéron in the west is more undulating, and

consists of two plateaux. The limestone plateau rises to 1,968–2,296 feet and is dotted with gorges, ravines and sheer cliffs. The other plateau, with an average altitude of 984 feet, has its back to the south face; it is called *les craus*. A line of hills bordering the Calavon Valley forms the southern edge of the Vaucluse Mountains opposite the Lubéron.

groups of buildings: the Old Castle and the New Castle. The former (1470) was a humble rural dwelling which was turned into a castle with an internal courtyard, galleries, a dungeon, an embossed tower with loopholes and, to the northwest, a large kitchen which served the newer buildings. The design of the New Castle is quite different, and was influenced by that of châteaux on the Loire. It has an extra tower and it opens out onto a terrace; this was originally closed off by a curtain wall which was strengthened to the south by a third tower. The New Castle was eventually abandoned and by 1920 was simply a ruin. It was about to be sold as a stone quarry when it was bought by Robert-Laurent Vibert ▲ *195*.

PROTESTANT CHURCH. The architect Penchaud was responsible for this church's austere yet beautiful appearance. It was built between 1806 and 1816 and has a rectangular porch in the front; the large hall is lit by numerous bays and is covered by a coffered ceiling.

BELFRY. This tall structure dominates the little town. It was built in the 17th century on the site of an early castle; the clock dates from 1732.

ST ANDREW'S CHURCH. All that remains of this 12th–13th-century building, dedicated originally to Saint Trophime, is the north walls of the first two bays. After the village was repopulated at the end of the 15th century, the church was restored and a chapel was also added, of which the last two bays of the aisle survive.

SILVACANE ABBEY ★

This was the last of the "three Provençal sisters" ▲ *192* to be built. The abbey was constructed between 1175 and 1300 on a Cistercian plan that was characterized by great sobriety and harmoniously combined Romanesque and Gothic styles. The church itself was built between 1175 and 1230, and consists of a nave flanked by aisles opening onto a transept lined with chapels, and a rectangular choir; the nave and the choir are barrel-vaulted. The lower-lying cloister, whose galleries with their powerful semicircular arcades encircle a wide courtyard decorated in one corner with a circular washbasin, stands between the left-hand aisle and the refectory, a large room with four bays with ribbed vaulting. Behind the east wing are the monks' hall, the chapter house (its ribbed vaults springing from columns) and the small sacristy with broken barrel-vaulting. The abbey suffered pillaging during the Wars of Religion, and its decline continued into the 17th and 18th centuries. After the French Revolution, the land was used for farming and the building was frequently damaged, but it has been gradually restored since being acquired by the State in 1846.

MARSEILLES

1 PALAIS DU PHARO   2 FORT ST-NICOLAS   3 FORT ST-JEAN   4 BASILIQUE ST-VICTOR   5 OLD PORT   6 PIERRE PUGET GARDENS   7 NOTRE-DAME DE LA GARDE   8 LAW COURTS   9 LA CANEBIÈRE   10 PRÉFECTUR

⊙ Three days

OLD MARSEILLES
The town occupied almost exactly the same amount of space in the 17th century as it had in Phocaean times.

A GREAT COSMOPOLITAN PORT
In the 18th century, the city's maritime activities stretched way beyond the Mediterranean, reaching as far afield as the Antilles and the South Seas.

HISTORY

Marseilles was founded around 600 BC by Greeks from Phocaea in Asia Minor. It was conquered by Caesar in 49 BC, and exerted little influence for several centuries. Christianity established itself in the 3rd century around what was later to become the Abbaye St-Victor. After being successively overrun by the Franks, the Saracens and the Aragonese, Marseilles benefited from a revival in the Mediterranean's commercial fortunes in the 15th century. It had joined the Catholic Leagues opposed to Henry IV, and aroused the wrath of Louis XIV by requesting independence. A virtual monopoly of trade with the Levant granted by Colbert encouraged commerce which was seriously disrupted by the plague of 1720 ● *52*. The Revolution found expression in a series of rebellious actions, and Marseilles' federalism in 1793 led to the town suffering severe repressions. The conquest of Algeria in 1830 and the opening of the Suez Canal in 1869 gave trade a boost; later on, the building of the railways and of the Durance canal prompted the construction of factories. After the war, the town saw the disappearance of the old industries and the arrival of immigrants and repatriated settlers from North Africa.

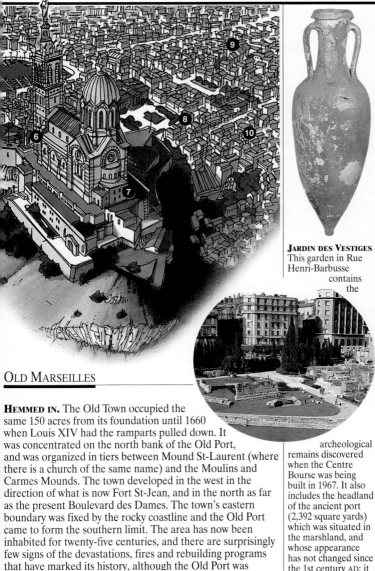

"I AM OVERWHELMED BY THE SINGULAR
BEAUTY OF THIS TOWN"

MME DE SÉVIGNÉ

JARDIN DES VESTIGES
This garden in Rue
Henri-Barbusse
contains
the

OLD MARSEILLES

HEMMED IN. The Old Town occupied the
same 150 acres from its foundation until 1660
when Louis XIV had the ramparts pulled down. It
was concentrated on the north bank of the Old Port,
and was organized in tiers between Mound St-Laurent (where
there is a church of the same name) and the Moulins and
Carmes Mounds. The town developed in the west in the
direction of what is now Fort St-Jean, and in the north as far
as the present Boulevard des Dames. The town's eastern
boundary was fixed by the rocky coastline and the Old Port
came to form the southern limit. The area has now been
inhabited for twenty-five centuries, and there are surprisingly
few signs of the devastations, fires and rebuilding programs
that have marked its history, although the Old Port was
destroyed by German bombs in 1943. Only a few buildings
around the Town Hall survived.

MUSEUMS. The HISTORY MUSEUM, which was opened in 1983,
provides a history of the city going back to ancient times. It
also contains the *Épave de la Bourse*, a 2nd-century ship
discovered in the Old Port in 1975 and still in excellent
condition, and a large model of life in Marseilles under the
Phocaean Greeks. Behind the Town Hall, the ROMAN DOCKS
MUSEUM ★, which was opened in 1963 and renovated in 1985,
houses the archeological remains of the 1st-century AD
Roman docks *in situ* and a collection of amphoras (above).
Containers of this type have been found all along the coast.

archeological
remains discovered
when the Centre
Bourse was being
built in 1967. It also
includes the headland
of the ancient port
(2,392 square yards)
which was situated in
the marshland, and
whose appearance
has not changed since
the 1st century AD; it
was still in use until
the 3rd century, at
which point it sank
into the mud. Other
treasures include
remains of a fresh-
water basin, the
town's eastern
fortifications, and
other constructions,
including roads and
necropoles, dating
from Greek and
Roman times.

199

THE OLD PORT
This was once the economic hub of Marseilles. It is now a very lively district, and is the focus of much of the city's charm. Until the 19th century, all maritime activity was concentrated in this area, and fishermen living around the St-Jean district would set sail every morning for the *calanques* of Sormiou and Niolon. The Old Port now welcomes pleasure crafts, and is also noted for its fish and seafood specialties.

AROUND THE TOWN HALL

TOWN HALL. The Town Hall was the first Baroque building in Marseilles, and was constructed on plans provided by the city's official architects, Gaspard Puget and Mathieu Portal, between 1665 and 1674. It was divided into a *Loge* (market), reserved for merchants, and a first floor used by the elected members. The back of the building was enlarged in the late 18th century by the architect Brun.
MAISON DIAMANTÉE ★. This house behind the Town Hall derives its name from the bosses carved in diamond-point on the façade. Work commenced on its construction in 1570 for a merchant of Spanish extraction, Pierre de Gardiole. The interior is one of the few examples of Mannerism in Marseilles. It contains the MUSEUM OF OLD MARSEILLES which has displays of furniture, costumes, cribs and *santons* (ornamental Christmas figures) ● *70*

QUAI DU PORT

Quai du Port contains the postwar buildings by Fernand Pouillon. It leads to the CONSIGNE SANITAIRE ★, originally a floating dock that was built as a permanent structure in 1716, the final component in the Frioul Archipelago's health system.
FORT ST-JEAN ★. At the end of the 12th century, the Knights of the Order of the Hospital of St John of Jerusalem settled in the Old Port on a rocky promontory that served as a bastion; the courtyard of the fort still contains remains of their church. The King René Tower was added in the 15th century and the Fanal Tower in 1644. In 1666, Louis XIV had fortifications put up around the port and the town; the Knights were ejected and the citadel rebuilt at the same time as Fort St-Nicolas was being constructed opposite. Eight years later, Vauban had a moat built to separate the fort from the town; in 1938, the moat was filled in.

THE MAJOR CATHEDRALS

THE OLD MAJOR ★. This cathedral was built from 381 onward and is one of the most beautiful Romanesque buildings in Provence. It is an unusually refined structure which has been restored on numerous occasions. Inside, there is a bas-relief attributed to the Della Robbia brothers.
THE NEW MAJOR. This is the largest French cathedral to be built since the Middle Ages. It was constructed between 1852 and 1893, and is in the Byzantine style.

THE PANIER DISTRICT ★

From the 13th to the 18th centuries, the upper town was situated on the *buttes* (mounds) and was mainly inhabited by clerics whose livelihoods were often linked to the trading of prisoners. All that remains of the medieval layout with its narrow, winding streets is to be found in the Panier district on the *Butte des Moulins* (Mound of the Mills). This can be reached through PLACE DE LENCHE, formerly a Greek *agora* and now a market place. While walking up the MONTÉE DES ACCOULES ★ it is possible to see above PLACE DES MOULINS two towers that are the last surviving archeological remains of the town's fifteen windmills.

VIEILLE CHARITÉ ★

A BAROQUE MASTERPIECE. This is the only public edifice built in Marseilles by the architect Pierre Puget. It was intended to provide accommodation for the poor. After it fell into disrepair, the hospice was eventually renovated and it now houses a number of leading institutions.

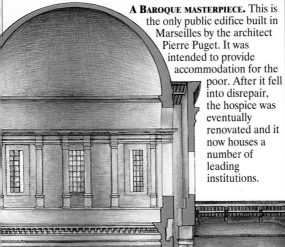

HÔTEL DAVIEL (BELOW)
This private mansion housed the Law Courts from the 14th century, but is now a Town Hall annex. The present building was constructed in 1743 by the Gérard brothers, while the sculpture is by a local artist, Jean-Michel Verdiguer. The overall design of the façade recalls that of the Town Hall itself (left). The ironwork is characteristic of the "Marguerite" style that was common in Marseilles.

VIEILLE CHARITÉ
This four-sided building has three floors opening onto internal galleries. There are no pillars or cornices, and the building is dominated by a gallery topped by a simple elliptical dome. The hospice was finished in 1679; it was made of pink limestone and is a magnificent example of Provençal Baroque.

▲ MARSEILLES TOWARD NOTRE-DAME DE LA GARDE

La Canebière was laid out in the 16th century, and takes its name from the rope makers and hemp merchants who lived in the area. The Provençal word *canebiero* means a place where hemp is sold.

1ᵉʳ Arrᵗ
LA CANEBIERE

ARCHEOLOGICAL MUSEUM ★. This museum's Egyptian collection is the second most important in France after that in the Louvre. Classical antiquities are dominated by some important collections, including Cypriot and Etruscan objects. The museum is also noted for its display of carved and painted items of the 3rd century BC from the site at Roquepertuse.

MUSEUM OF AFRICAN AND OCEANIAN ART ★. This museum opened in 1992 and has been the recipient of various bequests. They include Pierre Gauche's collection of West African art, and that of Professor Henri Gastaut which specializes in the cranium.

THE KING'S SHIPS
The docks were built in 1488, but were not expanded until 1666 when they were renovated by Nicolas Arnoul. The dock area was a town within a town, covering 25 acres and providing

THE OLD DOCKYARDS

The city area that climbs up from Quai de Rive-Sud to the lower slopes of La Garde Hill was built during the reign of Louis XIV. After the construction of Fort St-Nicolas, Louis had the naval dockyards modernized and the southern districts enclosed. In 1748, after the galley slaves departed for Toulon ▲ *270*, the dockyard was closed down and the buildings fell into disrepair. They were finally pulled down in 1780, and only one building, at 23 Cours d'Estienne-d'Orves, survived. In 1784, a plan to replace these buildings was entrusted to the Marseilles architect Joseph-Henri Sigaud. The area was

accommodation for twenty thousand people, mainly galley slaves (Turks, common criminals and Huguenots), free seamen and officers.

marked out in vast rectangles of buildings organized around closed courtyards; the severe appearance of the embossed façades makes this one of the best examples of local neoclassical architecture.

ST VICTOR'S BASILICA

THE CRYPTS OF ST VICTOR'S BASILICA ★
The 13th-century crypts incorporate the 5th-century ruins, and constitute a true underground church. A line of chapels and niches containing medieval and Baroque sculptures links the 4th-century pagan and Christian sarcophagi and 11th–12th-century tombstones. The crypts are dominated by a 13th-century black Virgin who is carried aloft in the Candlemas Procession ● *70*.

This is one of the city's most important monuments for its historical associations and for the beauty of the architectural remains. It originally incorporated a quarry which was turned into a necropolis in the 3rd century. An early monastery was founded in the 5th century by Saint John Cassian; a few remains are to be found in the crypt dedicated to the Christian martyr Victor. The abbey was to become one of the most famous religious centers in Gaul. In the 10th century it passed to the Benedictines and had its golden age in the 11th century. Renovations were carried out in the 13th and 14th centuries, and the high windows in the nave were added in the 17th century. The surrounding wall was pulled down in 1660 and the monastery was razed to the ground during the Revolution. The Basilica contains a painting of the Virgin by Michel Serre and a 5th-century altar table.

EX-VOTOS FROM NOTRE-DAME ● 72
This collection is one of the biggest
in the Bouches-du-Rhône. It ranks
with the collections in the museum
at Martigues and the church at
Saintes-Maries-de-la-Mer ▲ 169.

NOTRE-DAME DE LA GARDE

La Garde Hill used to be a lookout post
over the sea, and in the 13th century a
chapel was built there. The church later
became a priory belonging to the monks
of St Victor, but was rebuilt in the 15th
century. In the 16th century, the building
was fortified in response to threats of an
invasion by the armies of Charles V of Spain. In 1851 Léon
Vaudoyer drew up plans for a basilica in the Romanesque-
Byzantine manner, and the construction was entrusted to
Henri Espérandieu; the work took from 1853 to 1899 to
complete. The gilt Virgin on the top of the building was made
in the workshops of the celebrated Charles Christofle.

LA CANEBIÈRE ★

STOCK EXCHANGE. This building, constructed in 1860, is a
model of classicism. Today, it houses the Maritime Museum.
A SYMBOLIC ROLE. The road known as the Canebière has
made the city famous. The best time to go
there is when the Santons Fair ● 70 takes
place on the Allées Gambetta and endows
the area with gaiety. The majestic
buildings that line the Canebière are a
reminder that the elders of the Second
Empire wanted to produce a style of
architecture that comprised freestone
houses conforming to a popular model.

THE CITY CENTER
AROUND LA CANEBIÈRE

CANTINI MUSEUM ★. This museum is situated in the building
formerly occupied by the Cap-Nègre company (1694);
abstract, figurative Cubist and Surrealist works are on display.
OPERA HOUSE. The Opera House was opened in 1767, but
was later destroyed by fire. It was rebuilt between 1919 and
1924 by the architect Castel in the Art
Deco style.
COURS PUGET ● 98. The area
around this road was very elegant
during the Second Empire,
and was a favorite
meeting place for the
commercial
bourgeoisie.

THE BONNE MÈRE
The old fortress's tall
tower, drawbridge
and bastion, all of
them vestiges of the
Basilica's defensive
architecture, contrast
with the overall
elegance of the
spaces, themselves
emphasized by the
polychrome motif
decoration. The
richness of the

materials (marble and
lapis lazuli) and the
subtlety of Henri
Révoil's mosaic
decorations,
contribute to the
beauty of this shrine
dedicated
to the
Marian
Cult.

▲ THE ST-CHARLES DISTRICT OF MARSEILLES

1 PORT DE LA JOLIETTE 2 NOTRE-DAME-DE-LA-MAJOR 3 HÔTEL-DIEU 4 TOWN HALL 5 OLD PORT 6 AIX GATEWAY 7 LA CANEBIÈRE 8 ST-CHARLES' STATION 9 PROTESTANT CHURCH 10 PALAIS LONGCHAMP 11 FORMER Z...

PROTESTANT CHURCH
Owing to a lack of money, the only ornamentation on the façade is a rose window.

FOUNTAIN OF THE DANAÏDES (1907)
Local sculptor Jean Hughes makes use of mythological subjects in this paean on the theme of water.

ECLECTIC ARCHITECTURE
This water-tower-cum-museum is influenced by a variety of styles, from a Roman triumphal arch, Bernini's gallery in St Peter's in Rome and Italian *palazzi*. It is an illustration of the 19th century's infatuation with eclecticism.

THE TOWN IN THE 19TH CENTURY

PROTESTANT CHURCH. This church, built on the site of a former Monastery of Reformed Augustinians, is remarkable both for its size and for its large neo-Gothic façade. It was designed by the architect Reybaud. Work was begun in 1855, but the church was not completed until 1868.

BOULEVARD LONGCHAMP ★. Opened in 1834, this is one of the most delightful avenues in the city. Some of the houses bear marks of 19th-century eclecticism, such as Renaissance medallions in the Florentine style that alternate with the sober "triple windows" which had characterized Marseilles' architecture since the end of the previous century.

GROBET-LABADIÉ MUSEUM ★. This private house was built on plans by the architect Gabriel Clauzel. It contains examples of 18th-century furniture, medieval sculptures, paintings from various periods, and a collection of musical instruments.

PALAIS LONGCHAMP ★

A SPECTACLE OF STONE AND WATER. In 1839, faced with a growing population and droughts, the town decided to build a canal that would bring water from the River Durance into Marseilles. Later, by way of celebrating the water's arrival, the town erected a water tower that also served as a commemorative monument. The result was the Palais Longchamp (1862–9), a structure with Baroque references designed by the Nîmes architect Henri Espérandieu.

MUSEUM. The natural history section in the right-hand wing of the Palais

Longchamp houses paleontology and mineralogy collections, objects from Provençal prehistory, and local flora and fauna.

THE FINE ARTS MUSEUM ★. This museum in the left wing of the Palais was renovated between 1970 and 1980, when it gained a mezzanine and a drawing section. There are many examples of European painting and sculpture of the 16th–19th centuries, but the main body of the collection is made up of paintings from the French School of the 17th and 18th centuries.

FROM THE PALAIS TO THE COURS BELSUNCE

ST CHARLES' STATION. The station's staircase is justly famous both for its size and for its décor; broad flights of steps, metal linkways and Baroque-style decoration give it a 1900's feel although work was not started on it until 1923.

PORTE D'AIX. The Triumphal Arch of the Porte d'Aix (Aix Gateway) was constructed by the architect Michel-Robert Penchaud; it was started in 1823, but not completed until 1839. The decoration was carried out by David d'Angers and Jules Ramey, a commemoration of military victories being preferred to the eulogy of the Bourbons that had been originally planned.

COURS BELSUNCE ● 98. This road, which was built in the reign of Louis XIV, leads from the Aix Gateway to La Canebière. Louis wanted to make Marseilles the port that served his kingdom toward the east, and resolved to build a new city that would attract officers and merchants. The old ramparts were demolished in 1666 and new roads laid out; Marseilles grew to the south and east, and expanded from 175 to 480 acres.

COURS BELSUNCE
It is still possible to make out the façade and glass canopy of the celebrated "Alcazar", a theater and music hall. Raimu, Fernandel and Yves Montand have all performed here.

▲ MARSEILLES TOWARD CASSIS

1 MARTIGUES **2** ÉTANG DE BERRE **3** MARIGNANE **4** ÎLES DU FRIOUL **5** ÎLE D'IF **6** L'ESTAQUE **7** LA CORNICHE **8** MARSEILLES **9** CALANQUES **10** CASSIS **11** LA CIOTAT

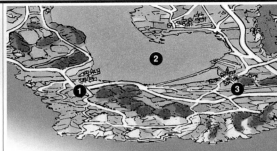

⊙ Two days
🚗 31 miles

A WALK TO THE ISLANDS
There is a boat service from Quai des Belges to the Frioul Archipelago (the islands of If, Pomègues and Ratonneau) that lies 1 mile off the coast.

These islands have played an important strategic role over the centuries. The island of If was fortified at the end of the 16th century, and was the first line of defense along France's southern coast. Pomègues was used exclusively for quarantined ships, and played a leading part in protecting the region's health.

THE NEW PORTS

The port of Marseilles is the third biggest in Europe after Rotterdam and Antwerp, and has long been identified with the Lacydon. However, a new town grew up in the 19th century with the opening of the BASSIN DE LA JOLIETTE, a new basin which shifted maritime activity to the north of the city. Over the years, more than 11 miles of new docks gradually extended as far as the Étang de Berre. Nowadays, more trade takes place in the port installations of Fos, Marseilles' real docks having been slowly abandoned.

THE SOUTH OF MARSEILLES

BORÉLY CASTLE ★. The exterior of this building, particularly the central fore-part flanked by two wings ending in slightly projecting pavilions, is in a marked classical style. It is in marked contrast to the interior décor which has been almost completely preserved, and largely consists of stucco and gypsum decoration and marvelous paintings, mostly in the Parrocel Gallery, the Salon Doré and the Chapel.
LA CITÉ RADIEUSE ★. Le Corbusier's famous tower block of multiple dwellings (1952) is at 280 Boulevard Michelet. The Cité Radieuse is made of reinforced concrete, and rests on thirty-eight stilts each supporting a load of 2,000 tons. This prototype was greeted with skepticism, and while it was under construction, there was much talk locally of the *maison du fada* (crazy man's house).

206

THE MAGALONE
The garden statuary symbolizes the seasons, and dates from the late 17th century.

THE MAGALONE ★. The Magalone is opposite the Cité Radieuse, and is one of the few remaining *bastides* (Provençal country houses) ● 96 which adorned this suburb of Marseilles in the 18th century. Much of the Magalone's originality lies in the 2,152 square-foot hall which takes up the entire ground floor, and a stairway that closes off the perspective at either end of the room.

THE CORNICHE ★

COVE OF THE CATALONIANS ★. The former St-Lambert district lies between Pharo Park and the Place du 4-Septembre; it takes its name from the Catalonian fishermen who lived there at the end of the 18th century.
CORNICHE DU PRÉSIDENT-KENNEDY ★. A road which starts beyond the Cove of the Catalonians overlooks the foothills of the La Garde Massif, whose final spurs follow a coastline indented with little coves. At the end of one of them is the picturesque Vallon des Auffes ★: this narrow creek takes its name from the Provençal word *aufo*, or Esparto grass, which was used for weaving baskets and was left out to dry here.
ENDOUME ★. The Promenade cuts across the promontory in the Endoume district, leaving above and below a whole maze of tiny streets, some of them very steep, which give unexpected views of a stretch of sea or blue sky. Here and there, there are rows of luxurious and more modest houses, all simply decorated.

BORÉLY CASTLE
This castle was constructed in the second half of the 18th century on plans by Marie-Joseph Peyre, director of the King's Buildings, and Esprit-Joseph Brun for a businessman, Louis Borély. The interior decoration is the work of Louis Chaix, a painter from the nearby village of Aubagne.

207

...llage of L'Estaque has long been ...pular among the residents of ...arseilles for Sunday walks. It is also considered by some to be one of the birthplaces of 20th-century art. Cézanne (1839–1...) ...ed here in 1871 after managing to avoid the Franco-Pru...an War, and found in L'Estaque the support he needed for his studies into ways of simplifying pictorial spaces. He returned frequently until the mid-1880's, on each occasion developing his revolutionary ideas of perception and representation. He later brought his friend Renoir, who also painted the countryside around L'Estaque, while remaining faithful to Impressionism. Then, after 1907, some young painters, mainly Cubists and particularly Georges Braque (1882–1963), discovered Cézanne and revisited his life as a way of prolonging his influence.

"L'ESTAQUE, EVENING EFFECT"
Cézanne's synthetic concerns are clearly evident in this painting where the backlighting accentuates the way in which color is used to build up form and line. Cézanne was more interested in the process than in the subject matter; for him, backlighting was above all a painting problem. This view inspired a number of other painters after Cézanne's death.

"THE TERRACE, L'ESTAQUE" (1918)
One of the last people to paint L'Estaque after Braque, Dufy and Matisse was Albert Marquet, a painter so captivated by Marseilles that he returned there frequently for many years. He was not concerned with Cézanne and Cubism, but the serenity that emanates from this picture, which abounds in bold lines including high-angle views and distortions, proves that the lessons had not been lost.

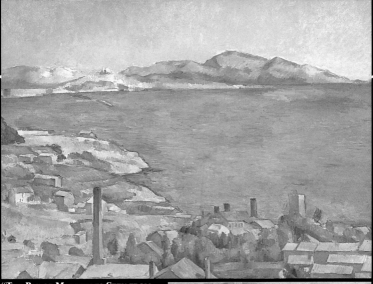

"The Bay of Marseilles Seen from L'Estaque" (1883–5)
In a letter which Cézanne wrote to Pissarro in 1876, he described L'Estaque as "a card to be played – red roofs on a blue sea".

Braque at L'Estaque
Georges Braque, whose love of Fauvism had already been nourished in the countryside of La Ciotat, brought about the idea of a Cubist L'Estaque. Braque's use of color ranged from flamboyant reds (*L'Estaque*, 1907, above) to ochers and natural greens. Form also came from his use of undulating brush strokes and geometrical simplifications (*Houses at L'Estaque*, 1908, left). Cézanne's influence, as well as the new ideas that Picasso was investigating, are evident here.

▲ MARSEILLES TOWARD CASSIS

Some of the *calanques*, including Callelongue and Sormiou, have *cabanons*, old fishermen's shelters that were constructed over a period of many years.

A FRAGILE BALANCE
Arid countryside of this sort is not found anywhere else in France; it is due to the combined action on the chalky rocks of the sun, the mistral and the summer's dry heat. The result is an extraordinary diversity of flora and fauna: over a thousand plant species, and numerous colonies of birds, including Bonelli's eagles and peregrine falcons.

THE CALANQUES ★

The *calanques*, or rocky inlets, form a classified zone covering 12,100 acres; the word *calanque* comes from the Provençal *calenco*, or "steep". The ground is mostly rocky, and the *garrigue* is only now beginning to recover its lost ground.

HOW TO GET THERE. It is only possible to get to the *calanques* by boat or on foot: GR 98b departs from Parc Adrienne-Delavigne at bus stop 19 just beyond the Église de la Madrague. Laid out in 1973, this path takes eleven hours to complete and takes you from Marseilles to Cassis along the coast and over the hilltops. There are many walking routes which join up with the "Sentier de grande randonnée" along the way; they include Mazargues, Luminy, Les Baumettes and La Gineste, which are further to the east and inland.

FROM CALLELONGUE TO PORT-MIOU ★. The path leads from the picturesque hamlet of GOUDES ★ to the narrow *calanque* of Callelongue, the first of a series of deep indentations which cut into the rock where the Marseilleveyre and Le Puget Massifs reach the sea; the best known of these are Sormiou (where the Cosquer cave ● *46*, discovered in 1991 and since walled up, contains exceptional examples of paleolithic rock art), Morgiou, Sugiton, L'Oule, En-Vau (spectacularly jagged stones), Port-Pin (a fine sandy beach) and Port-Miou (longest beach). From the path from Callelongue to Col de Sormiou, there are superb views out over the Riou Islands ★; this tiny archipelago is carpeted with mastic trees, oleasters, rosemary and arborescent mallow, and inhabited by seagulls, and Cory's and Mediterranean shearwater.

PORT OF CASSIS
A fishing port in the 19th century, it became a holiday resort in the early 20th century. The village is sheltered by the Gardiole cliffs and Cap Canaille, and its population rises to 35,000 during the summer.

CASSIS ★

Cassis, made famous by Frédéric Mistral ● *61* in his poem *Calendal*, was an old Roman fishing port that is now a lively seaside resort.

CASSIS CASTLE (not open to the public). The castle, which dominates the village, was built in the 13th century by the counts of Baux whose emblem, a star with sixteen points, adorns a stone above the entrance. The upper part of the towers were pulled down at the end of the 18th century as part of a plan to restore the building.

WALKS. The whole of the port is equally appealing, as are the little streets that run down to it; these are lined with houses dating back to the 17th century, and include the Town Hall, once a private house belonging to the Moustiers family.

AIX-EN-PROVENCE

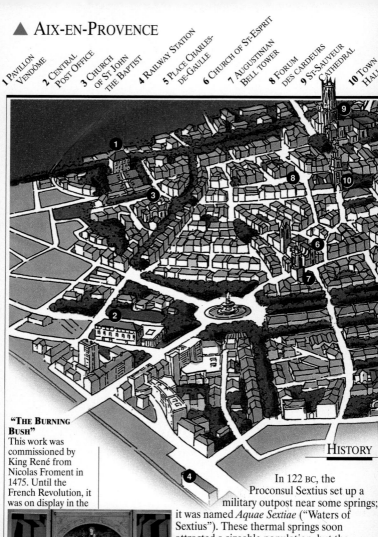

"THE BURNING BUSH"
This work was commissioned by King René from Nicolas Froment in 1475. Until the French Revolution, it was on display in the church of the Monastery of the White Friars. One might say that *The Burning Bush* is ablaze, but by no means burning itself out. The painting symbolizes the Virginity of Mary; the side panels depict the donors at prayer.

HISTORY

In 122 BC, the Proconsul Sextius set up a military outpost near some springs; it was named *Aquae Sextiae* ("Waters of Sextius"). These thermal springs soon attracted a sizeable population, but the township later suffered great destruction. At the end of the 12th century, the counts of Provence moved their residence here, but it was mainly thanks to Louis II of Anjou, who founded the university in 1409, and his son, King René, that Aix became a major center of artistic creativity. The Parliament set up in 1501 to defend the autonomy of the Three Estates against the monarchy held its sessions in Aix, and the city was soon home to a refined and cultivated society. A period of economic isolation followed, but Aix's cultural reputation, largely deriving from its university, was never challenged.

LE BOURG ST-SAUVEUR

The old township of St-Sauveur was in the middle of the ancient, medieval city of Aix-en-Provence. This Roman settlement was organized around the forum, which was itself later buried beneath the cathedral. The town gradually expanded toward the west but, at the first sign of incursions, the population would withdraw from this area and retreat up onto the hill. A new town grew up in the early Middle Ages

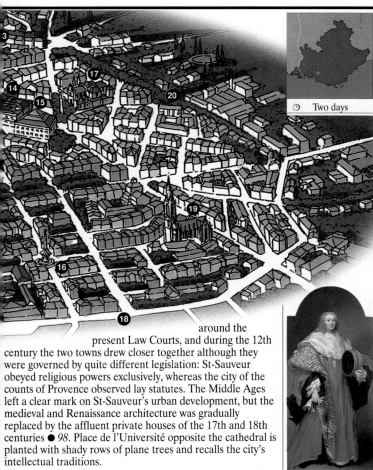

Two days

around the present Law Courts, and during the 12th century the two towns drew closer together although they were governed by quite different legislation: St-Sauveur obeyed religious powers exclusively, whereas the city of the counts of Provence observed lay statutes. The Middle Ages left a clear mark on St-Sauveur's urban development, but the medieval and Renaissance architecture was gradually replaced by the affluent private houses of the 17th and 18th centuries ● *98*. Place de l'Université opposite the cathedral is planted with shady rows of plane trees and recalls the city's intellectual traditions.

ST-SAUVEUR CATHEDRAL

This cathedral, frequently altered between the 5th and 18th centuries, is a combination of several different buildings; this can be easily observed from the façade. To the right, the 12th-century Romanesque portal marries antique decoration with a smooth wall and is next to the reused remains of a Roman wall; to the left, there is a Gothic portal built between 1477 and 1505 and adorned with pictures of the twelve Apostles. Only Saint Michael, who dominates this particular group, was spared by the Revolution; this representation of the

THE BAPTISTERY
The eight columns come from an earlier building. The cupola was rebuilt in 1577.

▲ AIX-EN-PROVENCE

THE FOUNTAINS IN AIX
Some forty public fountains quench the thirst of the population of Aix, gushing warm and cold water out of the ground through stone spouts and bronze pipes. Some of them are attached to finely balanced aristocratic façades; others stand next to the Roman columns and classical pyramids that adorn the city's squares and crossroads

THE CLOISTER ★
The 12th-century cloister is unusually ethereal and elegant. It contains an astonishing variety of small, fluted,

wreathed columns adorned with plant motifs or carved with fabulous animals, caryatids or atlantes; one of the latter is of Saint Peter holding the keys of Heaven. They support capitals showing scenes from the Old and New Testaments.

archangel wearing a Phrygian hat and slaying the devil came to symbolize the Revolution overcoming Tyranny. Around 1830, when the cathedral was used once again for worship, it was restored and its statues "redone". The north side is attached to the tower, work on which had lasted from 1323 to 1425, although the pinnacles were added in 1880; there is a small lapidary museum containing various carved fragments by the entrance on the right. A little further on is the baptistery, whose original ground plan dates from the early 5th century.

THE ROMANESQUE NAVE. The nave runs the length of the baptistery; it was built in 1180. The transverse arches and protruding pillars are typical of the late Provençal Romanesque.

THE GREAT NAVE. This was constructed between 1285 and 1515. The choir radiates around the high altar whose current appearance dates from the early 19th century. The choir also boasts an exceptionally fine series of tapestries depicting the life of the Virgin Mary; this was executed in 1511. A second row of decorations includes an elegant painting in grisaille of the *Annunciation* which conceals beneath its volets the *Buisson ardent* (Burning Bush) reredos ★, one of the greatest examples of French painting ▲ *212*.

THE NAVE IN NOTRE-DAME-DE-L'ESPÉRANCE. This was built between 1694 and 1705 and is based on three lateral Gothic chapels. It reaffirms the cathedral's fundamental symmetry.

THE ARCHBISHOP'S PALACE ★

Place des Martyrs-de-la-Résistance, also known as Place de l'Archevêché, was redesigned from 1739 onward to give greater prominence to the newly renovated Archbishop's Palace. The Espéluque Fountain (1618) (the word comes from *espeluco*, the Provençal word for "cave") has stood on the north side of the square since 1756; the east side is dominated by the palace's imposing Regency façade.

THE TAPESTRY MUSEUM. This museum has occupied the first floor of the Archbishop's Palace since 1910. It houses a collection of 17th- and 18th-century works including Beauvais tapestries of unusual beauty; they include the *Grotesques*, which date from 1689 onward, a single-piece *Life of Don Quixote* (1735–44) and *Russian Games* from 1769–93. A section of contemporary textiles alternates with temporary exhibitions. There is also a Museum of Theater Arts which displays the work of distinguished

A REGENCY PALACE
The building dates from the early 18th century. The door is attributed to the sculptor Toro.

stage designers who have been involved in the Aix-en-Provence Festival; this museum has not yet been completed.

THE INTERNATIONAL FESTIVAL OF MUSIC AND LYRICAL ARTS. The Aix-en-Provence Festival takes place every year in the Archbishop's Palace. In 1948, the Countess of Pastré and Gabriel Dussurget decided to found a music festival which would adopt a novel approach to Mozart and to modern composers such as Darius Milhaud and Olivier Messiaen. Since 1974, the repertoire has included *bel canto*, performed by some of the world's greatest singers. Mozart has also been well served with performances of little-known vocal pieces, in addition to his seven greatest operas which have been performed ever since the festival opened.

RUE GASTON-DE-SAPORTA ★

This street is one of the last to survive of the city's original octagonal plan. In the 17th and 18th centuries, it was the main thoroughfare of Bourg St-Sauveur and was inhabited by important families who had exchanged their medieval parcels of land for large *hôtels* (mansions) which gave onto courtyards and gardens. The HÔTEL DE CHATEAURENARD at no. 19 contains a superb staircase with trompe l'oeil decoration and ceilings (above) with illusory reliefs carried out by Jean Daret in 1654.

MUSEUM OF OLD AIX ★. The façade of the late 17th-century Hôtel d'Estienne-de-St-Jean is remarkable for its colossal display of fluted columns surmounted by Corinthian capitals; this is probably the work of Laurent Vallon. The severity of the façade is in sharp contrast to the finely carved door which opens into a spacious hall. The house has preserved some of its original décor including the painted ceilings, friezes and furniture, and since the 1930's it has housed the Museum of the Arts and Popular Traditions. In addition to the Corpus Christi Screen, there are two 19th-century pieces: the Talking Crib and the Corpus Christi marionettes.

THE CORPUS CHRISTI SCREEN
This screen consists of ten double-sided panels painted on canvas. It is the oldest representation of the Corpus Christi celebrations, a ceremony that has had deep significance in Aix for many centuries. This anonymous painting from the first half of the 18th century was executed for Jean-François de Galice, a counselor in the parliament of Provence.

THE OLD TOWN

The belfry marks the beginning of the Old City which encircles the palace of its founders, the counts of Provence.
THE CLOCK TOWER. This stands on a rubblestone Roman wall. It was once a symbol of the communal franchises, and partly closed off the town during the 12th century. It was rebuilt in 1510 to house the archives, but only four figures representing the seasons remain of the planetary tower of 1555.
TOWN HALL. The Town Hall is shown to advantage in a square which dates from 1750 and also boasts the Chastel Fountain (1756–8) on the south side. The Town Hall has occupied the same spot since the 14th century, the present building having been constructed between 1655 and 1671. Beyond a railing with a surbased arch lies the former arsenal with its vaulted arch and the double-spiral staircase of 1655, the first of its kind in France.
GRANARY ★. Corn taxes were one of the town's principal sources of income. In the 17th century, a permanent granary was built on the site of the marketplace; the work was carried out by the Vallons, father and son, who completed the southern half in 1720 and then the northern section in 1760.
LAW COURTS. The Counts' Palace housed the parliament, the audit office and the prison before it was pulled down in 1786 due to its poor state of repair. Claude Nicolas Ledoux then designed a new palace, but his plans were shelved as too expensive. The present building is the result of a renovation which Michel Penchaud carried out between 1822 and 1832 at the same time as he was constructing the prison at the back. The Esplanade in front of the Town Hall ends at Place des Prêcheurs, a square built by Good King René around 1450.
CHURCH OF STE-MARIE-MADELEINE. Behind the façade built by Henri Révoil in 1855 stands a former chapel to a Dominican convent. The interior, constructed by Vallon between 1691 and 1703, preserves the early Gothic building's original plan. It contains a fine *Annunciation* ★ (left) dating from 1444; this is the central panel of a triptych attributed to Barthélemy d'Eyck, a painter and King René's manservant. The volets are on display in museums in Brussels and Rotterdam.

THE FASHION FOR ATLANTES
Atlantes derive from the giant, Atlas, who carried the terrestrial globe on his back. Baroque artists in Aix adopted this theme in a wide variety of styles. Examples include these carved atlantes on the Hôtel d'Arbaud; they date from around 1670.

PLAÇO DEI TRES OUME

PLACE DES TROIS ORMEAUX

AROUND PLACE D'ALBERTAS ★

The Albertas family was one of the most important in Aix during the 18th century. In 1724, Henri d'Albertas had Laurent Vallon renovate his house and then, between 1735 and 1741, he bought the houses opposite and had them pulled down. In 1742, his son commissioned Georges Vallon to use the area for a square which would further enhance his own residence; the result was an imitation of the Parisian fashion for royal squares.

THE MUSÉUM ★. Close by is the magnificent Hôtel Boyer-d'Éguilles which was built between 1672 and 1675 by Louis-Jaubert in BIBÉMUS stone for Magdeleine de Forbin d'Oppède. The marvelous Baroque façade, with its colossal fluted pilasters, overlooks a courtyard to which there is access through a monumental entrance designed for coaches. The Muséum has traditional collections of geological and paleontological specimens, but its reputation mainly rests on its remarkable displays of dinosaur eggs, found at the foot of Mount Ste-Victoire ▲ *220*.

PAVILLON DE VENDÔME ★

The Pavillon de Vendôme, built in 1665 for Louis de Mercoeur, Duc de Vendôme, once stood outside the ramparts. Nobody ever lived in this folly, and it was renovated at the beginning of the 17th century and turned into a pavilion. A second story was then added and covered with convex tiles, and the first-floor bays were closed up. Of the interior's original décor, only the late 17th-century allegorical painted ceiling and the early 18th-century horseshoe staircase remain. The pavilion also contains an exceptionally beautiful chest signed by Foullet, and other furniture including ceramics from Moustiers and painted leather.

GRAND COURS ★

Grand Cours, or Cours Mirabeau, was laid out in 1649 between the New Quarter and the Old Town along the outer extremity of the old city wall. It was the first large public area, and for a long time was a setting for the upper classes in their private houses; much later, it became the peaceful city-center promenade it is today. The dwellings

VALLON, FATHER AND SON
Laurent Vallon (1652–1734) was a leading Baroque architect who had a profound influence on design in Aix. His last work was the Hôtel d'Albertas. His son, Georges (1688–1767), continued in the style developed by his father.

HÔTEL D'ALBERTAS
This is an example of Baroque themes as reinterpreted by Vallon; it includes a balcony supported by two tritons, and a facing of joint lines and pilasters.

CHURCH OF ST JOHN OF MALTA

The elegant Gothic tower has a tall spire standing on a base surrounded by gables. The church was rebuilt in 1272 and was the first Gothic monument to be constructed in Provence. The chapels beside the single vaulted nave were added in the 17th century. Before the French Revolution, the transept contained the tombs of the counts of Provence from the House of Barcelona.

on the north side of the Grand Cours, which backed onto the Old Town, were cramped and had an urban feel about them; on the south side, by contrast, architects had more space to play with and the houses were much deeper, with fronts overlooking the street while the backs gave onto gardens. Halls, galleries and antechambers were only attached to rooms dating from the 16th century, but the most elaborately decorated features of houses in Aix were the staircases: they started in the entrance halls and, on the first floor occupied much of the breadth of the façade; they were also proportionate to the width of the doorways.

HÔTEL MAUREL-DE-PONTÈVES ★ (NO. 38). This is unquestionably one of the most sumptuously decorated houses in all Aix. It is attributed to Jean Lombard, and dates from 1647.

HÔTEL DE FORBIN (NO. 20). This house, built in 1656 and restored in the 18th century, is one of the biggest on Grand Cours and was designed by Pierre Pavillon.

HÔTEL GANTES (NO. 53). This house is best known for its café, *Les Deux Garçons*, whose interior still has reminders of the fashionable meeting place it was in the early 19th century.

HÔTEL DU POËT ★ . Built in the first half of the 18th century, the Hôtel du Poët is noted for its sculptures (grotesque masks and agraphia) and ironwork decorations.

THE MAZARIN DISTRICT ★

ORIGINS. In 1646, the Archbishop of Aix, Michel Mazarin, brother of the more famous cardinal of the same name, was granted permission by the king to surround the St-Jean district with a wall. Mazarin entrusted the task to the investor Jean-Henri d'Hervart, who was also responsible for Aix's third expansion in modern times after Villeneuve and Villeverte. Jean Lombard, who created the design, had to bear in mind two constraints: to the east, the Church of St John of Malta and the surrounding district, and to the west the Benedictine Convent. He focused on two main thoroughfares, Rue du Quatre-Septembre and Rue Cardinale, placing the small Place des Quatre-Dauphins where the two roads met, and constructed a mostly regular patchwork design of three to five roads at right angles. The district, which is kept cool by walled gardens, took a century and a half to complete; it was initially inhabited by artisans, and later by the nobility.

THE GRANET MUSEUM. The 13th-century Church of St John of Malta, the former fortified chapel of the Knights of the Order of the Hospital of Saint John of Jerusalem, stands on one side of PLACE ST-JEAN-DE-MALTE; the former Palais de Malte is on the other side. The

house which once contained the Commandery of the Knights of Malta was built between 1671 and 1676 by the geometrician Alphonse Dumas, for Prior Jean-Claude Viany. When it was turned into the Granet Museum, its severe façade was superbly restored, and adorned by protruding cornices, frames round the bays, and gargoyles. The Granet contains one of the finest collections of paintings in any museum in Provence. It is located above rooms given over to archeological remains from Aix (Gallo-Roman mosaics and murals) and from Entremont, a small town 1¼ miles north of Aix where Celto-Ligurian tribes ● *46* built their capital city prior to the Roman conquest. The Celto-Ligurian statuary forms one of France's leading collections.

OUTSIDE THE WALLS OF AIX

MÉJANES LIBRARY ★. The basis of this library was a bequest made by the Marquess of Méjanes, a learned bibliophile who, in 1786, donated his collection of eighty thousand books. For many years, the "Méjanes" was in the Town Hall; it has now been transferred to a former match factory.

THE VASARELY FOUNDATION. Since 1976, Jas de Bouffan Hill has been dominated by the black and white façades of an architectural center founded by the painter Victor Vasarely. It contains some forty monumental works which trace Vasarely's studies into the links between painting and architecture.

THE BASTIDES ROUND AIX. The *bastides* ● *96* of Provence once provided summer accommodation for members of parliament and their families. In the 18th century, however, new *bastides* began to be designed in a severe, four-square manner, and they no longer had the appeal of the fortified houses of a century earlier. The more elegant apartments now moved to the first floor, and the second floor was reserved for private dwellings. The best examples of the *bastide* are the PAVILLON DE LENFANT ★ on the N 96 road with its restrained façade contrasting with the pomp of its interior décor (ceilings, plaster moldings, a Van Loo cupola and a horseshoe staircase), LA MIGNARDE (D 63 road), a 17th-century house restored around 1770, and LA GAUDE (D 63 road), a building set off by terraces and parterres.

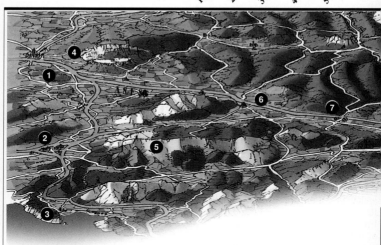

MOUNT STE-VICTOIRE ★

The massive splendor of Mount Ste-Victoire makes a
powerful impression on the traveler as it looms up out of the
Aix countryside. A mantle of *garrigue* on its north face extends
all the way to the summit in an uninterrupted riot of greenery.
A path goes from the lake at the Bimont Dam (1946) to the
summit where there is a chapel and the ruins of a convent
built in 1657, and a metal cross, the PROVENCE CROSS, which
is 62 feet high and was erected in 1871 to fulfil a vow made
during the Franco-Prussian War. Below lies the GARAGAI
CAVE, the ceiling of which is covered with stalactites.

**"MOUNT STE-
VICTOIRE FROM
THOLONET ABBEY"
(1904)**
The first
representations of the
the purple crests of
Mount Ste-Victoire
date back to the 17th
century when painters
started to include the
mountain in their
compositions as a
piece of simple
scenery lost
somewhere in the
background. Mount
Ste-Victoire appeared
as a subject in its own
right in 18th-century
paintings by artists
such as Jean-Antoine
Constantin, and his
pupil François-
Marius Granet.
However, this
magnificent
mountain was truly
immortalized by
Cézanne, who
executed more than
sixty paintings of it.

THE STE-BAUME MASSIF ★

THE MASSIF. The rocky ridge of Ste-Baume is some 7½ miles
long and rises to more than 3280 feet above Basse Provence.
This mountain was formed during the Secondary Era, and

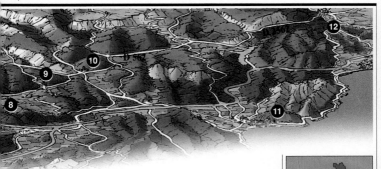

crumpled during the Tertiary Era when the older geological strata began to overlay the newer ones. The abundance of water in these parts makes the massif into a virtual water tower for the region. A forest on the Plan d'Aups Plateau (alt. 2460 feet) slightly to the north of the rocky ridge somehow escaped the worst rigors of the Ice Age; this sacred wood covering 300 acres has never been felled, and is a favorite destination for hikers using the GR 98.

🕐 Three days
🚗 155 miles

ST-PONS PARK ★. This park, endowed with abundant vegetation, contains the 13th-century CISTERCIAN ABBEY OF ST-PONS and the nearby 12th-century St Martin's Chapel, together with ruins of glassworks and various mills. The present church is the side nave of a shrine that once had three naves, and whose remains can be seen to the north. The abbey was larger than Le Thoronet ▲ 225.

THE MARY MAGDALEN GROTTO. The grotto is a natural cave some considerable way up a sheer cliff over 330 feet high. (The word *baume* derives from the Provençal word for "grotto".) A terrace in front of the grotto opens onto the forest and provides a spectacular view. The Dominicans have significantly contributed to the area's celebrity; it now boasts a marble altar, and a statue from the charterhouse at Montrieux. The trail to ST-PILON reaches an altitude of almost 3,280 feet, and from it, on a clear day, it is possible to see as far as the coast.

MARY MAGDALEN
Tradition has it that, after Mary Magdalen disembarked at

Saintes-Maries ▲ 169 and converted the people of Provence, she retired to Ste-Baume and was buried at the Basilica of St Maximinus where her tomb was found in 1279. There have been pilgrimages to the grotto said to have been her hermitage since the 13th century.

THE GROTTO
The grotto is visited by large numbers of people. Access is by a path, called Way of the Cross, laid out in the early 20th century.

ST-MAXIMIN-LA-STE-BAUME ★

ROYAL MONASTERY ★. Work was started on the monastery and the basilica ▲ 222, which it adjoins to the north, in 1296, but the former was not completed until the 18th century. The Dominicans settled here in 1316. The present Mayor's Office was once an 18th-century guest house (or hospice). It formed the southern part of a U-shaped courtyard; the other wing was occupied by a theological college.

The Royal Dominican Basilica of St Maximinus is unusual for Provence, a region marked by a preponderance of Romanesque styles and an almost complete absence of Gothic. On the outside, the basilica is squat in design and very southern in appearance. The interior, however, is much influenced by the great Gothic churches of northern France. The nave is almost 100 feet wide and 268 feet long, and was enormously popular with the crowds of pilgrims who came to Ste-Baume, one of the very first places of pilgrimage in the whole of Provence.

"MARY MAGDALEN" by Boisson (1797). Mary Magdalen was the first person to whom Christ revealed himself after his resurrection. "Do not hold on to me," Jesus said to her. "But go to my brothers and say to them, 'I am ascending to my Father and your Father, to my God and your God.' " According to legend, Mary Magdalen, Martha and Maximinus were sent by the Apostle Peter to preach the Gospel in Provence. Mary Magdalen is said to have withdrawn to Ste-Baume.

The cloister probably dates from the 15th century. It measures 135 by 135 feet and has rib-vaulted galleries. In accordance with the customary monastic layout, its east wing contained the chapter house and the sacristy, which is attached to the basilica. The cells and refectory are in the north.

"HOLY PLACES ARE TO THE WORLD WHAT THE STARS ARE TO THE FIRMAMENT. A SOURCE OF LIGHT, WARMTH AND LIFE."
HENRI LACORDAIRE (1802–61)

The crypt is a 4th-century Christian cave containing the 4th- and 5th-century sarcophagi of Saint Maximinus, Saint Sidonius Apollinarus, Saint Marcella and Saint Susanna. Mary Magdalen's tomb is made of very fine marble from the Imperial quarries in the Sea of Marmara.

FURNISHINGS
The basilica has been presented with outstanding furnishings in honor of Mary Magdalen. These include the choir stalls (1692), the wooden pulpit carved by Louis Gudet in 1756, the 18th-century Liétaud Glory (above), Jean-Esprit Isnard's organ (1773), a Crucifix Reredos by Antoine Ronzen(1520), and a 17th-century Reredos of the Rosary in the south apsidiole. To the left, Saint Dominic (17th century).

A GOTHIC BASILICA?
The Basilica of St Maximinus is in the architectural tradition of northern France in that it has three naves. The axis of the polygonal chapels terminating the side naves to the east is at an angle of 45°. The absence of a transept and the three levels of ribbed vaulting recall Bourges Cathedral.

ROMANESQUE SIMPLICITY
The basilica's squat appearance, its simple porch, the absence of a corridor along the arches and the tall windows are reminiscent of the Romanesque style.

Statue at the entrance to the choir.

A SELF-CONTAINED UNIVERSE
The cloister is said to enclose the body in
such a way as to give greater freedom to
the soul. Elsewhere, the architecture of
the abbey provides space for the various
activities of monastic life.

BRIGNOLES

Rue Louis-Maître
and the porch of a
majestic 16th-century
mansion where the
Duc d'Épernon once
lived.

**"THE GREAT
STAIRWAYS OF
BRIGNOLES"**
The stairways in these
paintings by a local
artist, Gabriel
Suzanne (1917–66),
lead to Place Caramy
in the medieval
center of Old
Brignoles.

HISTORY. Brignoles lay on the
Roman road that connected Rome
and Narbonne, and in the 12th
century it came under the jurisdiction
of the counts of Provence who built a
castle there; all that remains is a tower
enclosed within the presbytery. When
Charles I of Anjou, the brother of
Saint Louis, became Count of Provence in
1245, he left the old palace to his mother-in-law
and, around 1260, started work on the present
palace where the museum is now housed. Brignoles
was defeated and occupied by troops under Charles V of
Spain in 1536. It adopted the principles of the Revolution, but
did not experience the excesses that took place elsewhere in
France. In the 19th century, the town concentrated on the
extraction of bauxite, and around this time the growing
population overflowed beyond the three sets of ramparts.
HÔTEL DE CLAVIER ★ (top of RUE DU PALAIS). This residence
was constructed between the 13th century and the end of the
18th century; it is notable for its gypsum decoration which
typifies 16th- and 17th-century design and is remarkably well
preserved. The house has been frequently altered, and is now
a mixture of styles: 13th-century vaulted cellars, a
Renaissance patio (originally open-air), and a magnificent
room with a ceiling decorated in the French manner, a small
theater and a 17th-century fireplace with carved dolphins.
ST-SAUVEUR CHURCH ★. This Gothic church to the north of
Rue des Lanciers has a single, broad nave; when it was being
enlarged in the late 15th century, it incorporated earlier
chapels. On the right, near the entrance to one of the chapels,
is a reredos that includes a *Crucifixion* done by Balthazar
Lomellin in 1587; it is painted in an old-fashioned style, and is
now in poor condition. Further on is a *Descent from the Cross*
by Barthélemy Parrocel which exploits the contrasts between
light and darkness, thereby illustrating Caravaggio's influence
which was now well established in
Provence, even in the smallest towns.
**THE COUNT'S CASTLE AND THE
BRIGNOLES MUSEUM ★.** This 13th-
century building is extremely beautiful;
its gardens, laid out at a lower level to the
south, were once the ditches in the
second line of fortifications. A vaulted
hall on the first floor and some casemates
come from the original structure. The
rest of the castle, including the second-
floor ceiling decorated in the French
manner, is more recent. ST-LOUIS'
CHAPEL is attached to the palace, and the
Black Penitents who lived here had a
door constructed around 1600. It now
forms part of the BRIGNOLES MUSEUM,
which has some remarkable pieces,
including a 6th-century cippus-altar, and
the La Gayole marble sarcophagus ★
made in Greece around 270–90.

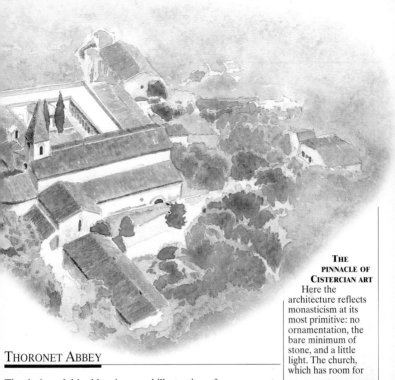

THORONET ABBEY

The design of this abbey is a good illustration of a movement that swept through Europe in the 11th century and clamored for a return to Christianity's original values. This movement led not only to the reforms proposed by Pope Gregory VII, but also to the foundation of the Cistercians, an Order that argued for a strict application of the Rule of Saint Benedict. Saint Bernard came to Cîteaux in 1112 and founded 160 monasteries before his death in 1153. In 1146, the Cistercians settled on the site of what is now Thoronet Abbey, an area that had been inhabited and cultivated since the 11th century. The monastery was completed by 1175. Beyond the CHURCH, STOREROOM and LAY MEMBERS' DORMITORY, the CLOISTER opens onto the church to the north, and the library, CHAPTER HOUSE and locutory to the east. The MONKS' DORMITORY is linked directly to the church.

THE PINNACLE OF CISTERCIAN ART
Here the architecture reflects monasticism at its most primitive: no ornamentation, the bare minimum of stone, and a little light. The church, which has room for eight hundred people, is in the form of a Latin cross. Two barrel-vaulted aisles flank the nave with broken barrel-vaulted bays. The fourth bay is at a somewhat higher level and forms the transept crossing. The transept supports the rectangular tower which is pierced with a semicircular bay on each side, like the spire above it. This simple, unornamented church is completed by a half-domed apse lit by three small bays.

THE TOWN OF THE DRAGON
The etymology of Draguignan is uncertain. It may have been a Roman called Draconius who gave his name to the town. Tradition also has it, however, that Saint Hermentaire, Bishop of Antibes, delivered the region

from the grip of a terrible dragon. This local interpretation of history is challenged by the troubadour, Féraud, who attributed the deed to Saint Honorat.

Draguignan in the 19th century.

DRAGUIGNAN

HISTORY. Fréjus, where the Bishop's Palace had long been located, rapidly became the religious capital, but the role of administrative capital was given to Draguignan. A turret was erected on the rock overlooking the area in 1235; its dual purpose was to protect the inhabitants and stand guard over a town which had risen up against the counts' authority only a few years earlier. Later, ramparts were added and, by the middle of the 13th century, Draguignan had become the sixth most important town in Provence. Two hundred years later, when the population had risen to almost 6,000, Draguignan ranked fourth and, by the time of the Revolution, the town had long since spread beyond the second line of its fortifications. The Revolution was warmly welcomed and, in 1797, the town was awarded the Prefecture of Var, an honor that Toulon had been refused for surrendering to the English in 1793. The Artillery School and Army Arsenal were transferred from Toulon in 1974 and today, with the military camp at Canjuers, Draguignan has the biggest barracks in France.

EAST OF THE OLD TOWN. A MUSEUM has been installed in the summer residence of the Bishop of Fréjus, Monseigneur du Bellay, in Rue de la République. It contains fascinating items such as the manuscript of the *Romance of the Rose*, and a painting by Peter Paul Rubens, *Personnages in the Garden of Love*. At one end of PLACE AUX HERBES stands one of the 14th-century CITY WALL GATES, the grooves of its portcullis still intact. The second turning to the right off RUE DE L'OBSERVANCE ★ which, with Grand'Rue, circumscribed Draguignan's prosperous district, leads to a square containing the MINIME CONVENT CHAPEL (1707): this church is in the classical style, and has a reredos and some 18th-century paintings.

CLOCK TOWER. The clock tower replaced the turret in 1660. The platform of the municipal belfry is 60 feet high and is flanked by four corner watchtowers; it supports a wrought-iron campanile installed in 1723.

WEST OF THE OLD TOWN. The second gate in the 13th-century city walls, the PORTAGUIÈRES GATE, is approached along RUE DE LA JUIVERIE; this road contains a 14th–15th-century house called the SYNAGOGUE; at one time, many small Provençal towns had Jewish communities. RUE DE L'ANCIEN-THÉÂTRE leads to

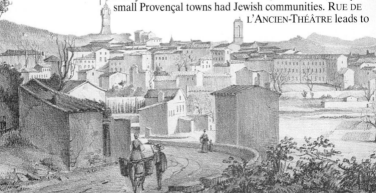

> "YOU'RE NEVER QUITE SURE WHERE YOU ARE. ONE MOMENT, YOU THINK YOU ARE AT SOME OBSCURE PLACE IN THE MIDDLE AGES...; THE NEXT MOMENT, YOU SUDDENLY FIND YOURSELF IN 16TH-CENTURY ITALY" FRANCIS DE MIOMANDRE

ST MICHAEL'S CHURCH, built by Révoil in 1869 in the neo-Gothic style. After 1807, the TOWN HALL incorporated the house of the King's Prosecutor; this was enlarged by the annexation of part of the Cordelier Convent.

ST-HERMENTAIRE CHURCH. Built mostly in the 13th century although the accoladed doorway is from the 16th century; the exterior elevations date from antiquity (6th century). St-Hermentaire is a good example of the rural Christian church of the period; it has an apse and a baptistery. The Gallo-Roman baths unearthed in the 19th century are only a few dozen yards away. There used to be a *bravade* ● *66* on the feast of St-Hermentaire.

GRASSE

HISTORY. During the Saracen raids in the 9th century, the people of Grasse used to take refuge behind an enormous tuff-stone rock. The situation of this new town at an important communications crossroads, together with the development of the perfume trade in the 16th century, helped Grasse to grow prosperous and it soon became a regional capital. Most of the episcopal buildings, including the tower, palace and cathedral, were built around 1244, the year in which Pope Innocent IV transferred the Bishopric of Antibes to Grasse.

CATHEDRAL ★. This consists of a nave with six bays flanked by aisles terminating in semicircular apsidioles; the vaulted choir is at a slightly lower level. The nave is lit by tall windows and is connected to the aisles by huge arches resting on massive cylindrical limestone pillars; the tribunes date from the late 17th century. The exuberant St-Sacrement Chapel was built between 1738 and 1744; it contrasts with the extreme austerity that characterizes the rest of the building. The Rubens paintings were commissioned directly from the artist, who was not yet known in Italy, by the Archduke Albert for the Church of Santa Croce di Gerusalemme in Rome. *Christ Washing the Feet of the Apostles* (1754) by Jean-Honoré Fragonard ▲ *229* is somewhat conventional, and gives few hints of the lighter style that this pleasure-loving painter was later to acquire. In the choir, there is also an *Assumption of the Virgin Mary*, a fine reredos attributed to Louis Bréa.

THE BISHOP'S PALACE. Today, this houses the Town Hall. Although the palace has been restored on many occasions, it has preserved a number of medieval elements: one of them is the oldest building, a high tower made of tuff-stone, known as the Bishop's Tower,

RESTRAINED AND UNORNAMENTED
The cathedral is typical of Romanesque art of the east of Provence. It was originally built of local white limestone, but has been restored on many occasions.

OBJECTS OF VENERATION, OBJETS D'ART
The St-Honorat Reliquary, a small 16th-century walnut chest, once contained the remains of the founder of Lérins Abbey

▲ *274*. The sides and lid are decorated with scenes of Saint Honorat's life; the polychromy has retained an extraordinary freshness. The 15th-century reredos attributed to Louis Bréa depicts Saint Honorat with Pope Clement and Saint Lambert, the Bishop of Vence from 1114 to 1154. *The Crown of Thorns* is one of three youthful Rubens paintings in Grasse; the *Descent from the Cross* is a copy and *Saint Helen* is temporarily on display in the council offices.

INTERNATIONAL PERFUMERY MUSEUM

A building with a fine Second Empire façade contains the reconstruction of a traditional perfume factory. The exhibition shows the various processes of distillation, explains certain techniques (including the *enfleurage* of more delicate plants), and includes a display of various tools and equipment. There is also a collection of perfume bottles designed by Guimard and Lalique.

THE ORIGINS OF PERFUME-MAKING

Perfumery was closely linked to the tanning industry which flourished throughout the city during the 13th century, but it was of little importance of its own until the 16th century when there began to be a fashion for

perfumed leather. Apothecaries and perfumers then settled in Grasse, attracted by the micro-climate which encouraged the growth of the most delicate flowers. The Guild of Glovers and Perfumers published their statutes in 1729, but the early 19th century saw stiff competition from companies like Guerlain. Grasse nonetheless became the perfumery capital under the Second Empire.

which looks down over Le Puy from a height of 85 feet. When the cathedral and Bishop's Palace were under construction in the 13th century, the tower was linked to the new buildings by a portico of which three arches and a column survive. The second-floor chapter house, which is now used as the Municipal Chamber, has preserved its original walls, and the marriage room next door, once the bishops' private chapel, is still intact.

CLOCK TOWER. This ancient tower of the counts in Place du 24-Août recalls the agreements signed between Grasse, when it was a free commune governed by a consulate, and the Count of Provence to whom the tower was given.

MEDIEVAL TOWN. Grasse extended rapidly around Le Puy between the 11th and 13th centuries, and the steep rock in its turn encouraged the construction of convents and monasteries outside the walls. Around 1300, the town added a new rampart with seven gates flanked by towers; however, to cope with the increasing population, taller buildings had to be constructed, and houses were even put up in courtyards and gardens. The absence of a building policy produced a town of narrow, winding streets punctuated occasionally by tiny squares and filled with irregularly aligned houses. The first shops opened by perfume merchants in the 17th century are to be found in RUE RÉITREL, one of the narrowest and most picturesque streets in Grasse.

Parfums aux Fleurs de Grasse

JEAN-HONORÉ FRAGONARD (1732–1806) Below: *Portrait of Mme Fragonard*. Left: *The Progress of Love in Young Girls' Hearts*, one of a series of panels commissioned by the Comtesse du Barry for her pavilion at Louveciennes. When the paintings

were delivered, the countess realized that they contained obvious allusions to her liaison with Louis XV, and she refused to accept them. When

Fragonard visited a cousin of his, he took the canvases with him and hung them in the house that was to become the Fragonard Museum; he then added the floral paintings. They were sold in 1898 after an excellent copy was made by the Lyons painter La Brély; the originals are now in the Frick Collection in New York. The second floor is devoted to the work of Fragonard and members of his family, including his son Alexandre, his grandson Théophile, and his sister-in-law Marguerite Gérard.

THE PERFUME INDUSTRY TODAY. In recent years, the perfume industry has abandoned the manufacture of finished products and opted increasingly for natural essences, as well as the synthetic perfumes launched by François Coty. Local factories are now competing with increasingly sophisticated processes of analysis and synthesis, and are turning to new markets like aromas for the food industry.

MUSEUM OF PROVENÇAL ART AND HISTORY ★. This mansion was built between 1770 and 1776 by the Marquis de Clapiers-Cabris. The unusually elegant interior décor includes polychrome wainscoting commissioned from Rousseau, the King's cabinet-maker. A subscription in 1921 enabled the house to be turned into a museum: it traces the evolution of Provençal furniture, and contains a fine collection of Moustiers faïence.

NAVY MUSEUM. This naval museum situated in the cellars of the Hôtel de Pontèves includes a large number of objects from the life of the Lieutenant-General of the Navy, the Count of Grasse (1722–88), as well as a collection of model ships.

FRAGONARD MUSEUM ★. The painter Fragonard and his family stayed in this late 17th-century private house in March 1791 during their only visit to Grasse. The town purchased the house in 1875 and has installed a reception room and the museum.

1 PARC REGIONAL 2 SIMIANE-LA-ROTONDE 3 MANOSQUE 4 GRÉOUX-LES-BAINS 5 OBSERVATOIRE-DE-HAUTE-PROVENCE 6 FORCALQUIER 7 LURE MOUNTAIN 8 VALENSOLE 9 GANAGOBIE PRIORY 10 SISTERON 11 DIG

⏱ Four days

🚗 162 miles

COATS OF ARMS
The origin of the four hands in the Manosque coat of arms is unknown. The hand (*main* in French) possibly represents the first syllable of Manosque, and the number of hands might refer to the town's four medieval quarters.

A SOBER FAÇADE
The façade of St-Sauveur Church, which is only decorated by three oculi and a Gothic door, overlooks a charming square adorned with a fountain. Although a number of documents refer to the existence of this church as early as 1235, it was not consecrated until 1372. The original structure consisted of a single central nave, a transept, a cupola over the transept crossing, and three pentagonal apses. The aisles were added in the 17th century. At one time, in the south of the transept, there was a bay which gave access to the Blue Penitents' Chapel; this chapel was pulled down in 1922.

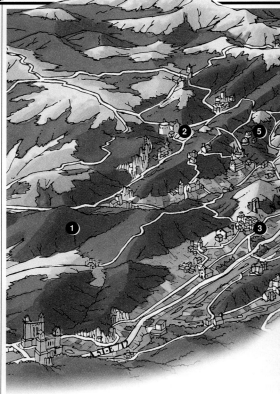

AROUND ST-SAUVEUR CHURCH

SAUNERIE GATE ★. Only two of the six 14th-century gates, the Saunerie Gate and the SOUBEYRAN GATE, have survived. The word "saunerie" comes from the Provençal *saou*, meaning "salt", and salt stores stood on this spot during the Middle Ages; "soubeyran" means "superior", and this gate stands at the highest point in the village.

ST-SAUVEUR CHURCH ★. This church contains lovely paintings from the 18th century (*Baptism of Christ* and *The Holy Family*) and the 17th century (*The Ascension of*

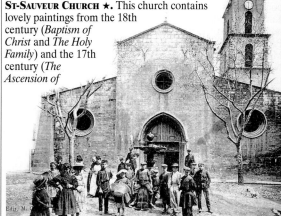

Christ, Saint Peter Receiving the Keys to the Kingdom, The Descent of the Holy Spirit on Mary and the Apostles and *Saint Catherine*). The organ, which was built by the Meyssonier brothers in 1625, was installed on one side of the choir as is the custom in Provence. It was rebuilt in 1826 in the Italian tradition and placed at the head of the tribune.

AROUND NOTRE-DAME-DE-ROMIGIER

THE TOWN HALL ★. The Town Hall's classical two-story façade is characteristic of the 18th century. The second floor is articulated by elegant balconies and by five tall windows, the arches of which are decorated with a carved arch-stone.
CHURCH OF NOTRE-DAME-DE-ROMIGIER. The original 10th-century building was much restored over the centuries. The nave, which has four groined vaults separated by semicircular and Gothic transverse ribs, ends at a ribbed, pentagonal apse whose keystone is decorated with a relief representing the Paschal Lamb. The 5th–6th-century high altar was originally a Roman marble sarcophagus; according to tradition, a 6th-century statue of the Virgin in polychrome wood was once concealed in it when the village was being plundered.
HÔTEL D'HERBES. The Hôtel d'Herbes houses the Manosque Archives. This collection of almost four hundred medieval papers is one of the most valuable in France, and includes municipal proceedings since 1360.

OUTSIDE THE TOWN WALLS

CARZOU FOUNDATION. Between 1985 and 1991, the Armenian painter Carzou completed a cycle of murals entitled *My Apocalypse*, inspired by his fear of modern means of destruction.
JEAN GIONO CENTER. This library-cum-video-center provides visitors with copious information about the writer's life and work.
LOU PARAÏS ★. Jean Giono lived in his house in the Lou Paraïs quarter of Manosque from 1929 to 1970 when he died. His delightful garden overlooks the town.

FOUR DISTRICTS
The four districts of Manosque used to surround the Church of Notre-Dame-de-Romigier in the center of the town. They were called Les Ébréards, Le Palais, Les Payans and Les Martels, and each had its own church, oil crusher, bread oven and ditch. The Ébréards district almost certainly derives its name from a leading Jewish family, Le Palais takes its name from the former palace of the

Knights of Saint John of Jerusalem, Les Payans was restricted to peasants (*paysans*) and Les Martels was solely inhabited by artisans who worked with hammers (*marteaux*).

JEAN GIONO (1895–1970)
This lyric poet and skilled novelist portrayed the countryside and people of Haute Provence with great affection, and daily indulged his taste for enjoyment.

PIERRE MAGNAN
This writer of detective novels was born in Manosque in 1922. All of his characters live in his native Haute Provence.

231

HISTORY

During the 13th century, a series of marriages united the county of Forcalquier and the counties of Provence, and then the counties of Anjou ● *47*; the latter ruled until 1480. Louis XI captured the town of Forcalquier with the help of bombards (an early form of cannon) which he fired from a hill since known as La Bombardière. The town has always been of a rebellious nature, which manifested itself with particular virulence in 1851 when Forcalquier led the Republican revolt against Napoleon III's coup d'état. During the last war, Forcalquier was also a hotbed of Resistance activity.

AROUND THE CATHEDRAL

THE CATHEDRAL OF NOTRE-DAME-DU-MARCHÉ. Most of this church was completed in 1217. Its tower was very large for the period, and might have been a copy of the fortified tower, still partly standing, of the CHURCH OF ST-MARI. The nave, a classical, Provençal, Romanesque vessel with a broken-barrel vault and bays separated by transverse ribs, contrasts with the richly decorated Gothic choir and transept. The nave is only Gothic in so far as the spaces are treated in the Romanesque manner. This original synthesis of styles prefigures what was known as the "southern Gothic". The only furnishings to survive are a beautiful tondo, a statue of Saint Pancratius and a large, wooden, 17th-century statue of Christ.
THE MARKET. The local market, one of the most important in Provence, is held in PLACE DU BOURGUET; it attracts about three hundred stall-holders every Monday morning, more for the big Easter and St Pancratius fairs.
VISITANDINE CONVENT. This Baroque church, painted by the Italian artist Barrofi, belonged to a convent built for the Visitandines in 1630. It now houses the MUNICIPAL MUSEUM.
CORDELIER MONASTERY. Like the cathedral, this monastery is a superbly skilled synthesis of Romanesque and Gothic styles. It gives some indication of the influence exerted by the Franciscans; around this time, the order was charged by the pope to represent the Inquisition in the counties of Provence and Forcalquier.

A HISTORIC COUNTY
Forcalquier basin is the result of geological movements in the Lure and Lubéron mountains and the Durance and Calavon rivers. Forcalquier itself is situated by the side of an old Roman road, the Via Domitiana ▲ *237*; it was long a vital trading-post. In the 11th century, a branch of the family of the count of Provence settled in the village and took the title of counts of Forcalquier.

AROUND THE CITADEL

RUE ST-MARI. The street is surfaced with *calades*, or stones placed on their sides and secured with a mortar of lime and sand. It is marked by shrines of the Way of the Cross, and leads to the remains of the CITADEL which used to overlook the town. The buried ruins of one round tower are the only vestiges of the fourteen towers that once existed. Only a few walls of the ROMANESQUE CHURCH OF ST-MARI survive; at the end of the street, there is part of the turret built in the apse of the church, which itself formed part of the ramparts.

CHURCH OF NOTRE-DAME-DE-PROVENCE. This neo-Byzantine church (1875) stands on Citadelle Hill. It once claimed to be the national sanctuary of Provence.

TOWARD RÉCOLLETS CONVENT

RÉCOLLETS CONVENT. This convent once incorporated St Peter's, a church with a humble Romanesque façade; it was saved from demolition by a town planning program. The ceiling of the sacristy has 17th-century gypsum decorations.

THE PROTESTANT CHURCH. The ideas of the Reformation won over some inhabitants of Provence including the people of Vaud ● *54* in 1489 and the Lutherans in 1538. After the Edict of St-Germain of 1576, Forcalquier and Mérindol were the only towns in Provence where Protestant worship was authorized.

THE OLD TOWN
Forcalquier's 17th-century mansions all have three basic elements: a hall, a courtyard and a spiral staircase.

FORCALQUIER'S FOUNTAINS
The Good Fountain existed in Roman times, and it still provides water for a series of fountains and washhouses, most of which date from the 15th century. St Michael's Fountain (1512) is the oldest in the region; the Joan of Arc Fountain dates from 1900.

THE CORDELIER CLOISTER
This charterhouse is accessible only to the monks. It opens onto the cloister through a door and two Romanesque windows.

233

Ganagobie Priory is of particular interest for its setting and its magnificent architecture. The priory's origins are undoubtedly Carolingian, although only a few Romanesque buildings have survived; these include the church, the cloister and the monastery buildings. It stands on a hill high above the Durance Valley. It was founded in the 10th century by John III, Bishop of Sisteron, and was shortly afterward attached to the powerful Abbey of Cluny. Following restoration work in the 1960's, Ganagobie has rediscovered its ancient splendor. It has housed a monastic community since 1993.

A SOBER 12TH-CENTURY CHURCH
The priory church is dedicated to Our Lady. It has a nave with three transverse ribs to the east and a double transept opening into three semicircular apses. It is entirely faced, both inside and out, with finely pointed stonework and is particularly striking due to the balance of its interior layout, its splendid masonry and the ordering of its west façade. The interior of the *priorale* is curiously unadorned.

AN EXTRAORDINARY DOORWAY

This door is deeply embedded in the wall. It consists of an arch with five Gothic archivolts which frame a tympanum dominated by Christ in his majesty surrounded by symbols of the four Evangelists. The twelve Apostles are placed under eight arcatures and are depicted on the lintel. The festoons that decorate the archivolts and engaged piers are the product of a montage executed in the 16th century using elements of small recycled columns.

This compact, solid block on a square ground plan consists of four barrel-vaulted galleries. The bays are decorated with small twin columns topped by capitals adorned with stylized leaves.

MOSAICS : ASSYMMETRICAL AND BALANCED COMPOSITIONS

The monastery choir (the apse and the east transept) has a group of floor mosaics of exceptional size and iconographic splendor; they are the most important mosaics in France.

The dazzling white, red and blue coloring of the floor was executed around 1125; it is part of the superb décor which includes valiant knights and soldier saints fighting evil monsters, alongside representations of fabulous animals weaving in and out of geometrical figurations.

A BOUNDARY MARKER
Sisteron is a doorway between two
countries, Provence and Dauphiné,
and two climates. Dominated by
the citadel, the town overlooks
one of the most impressive
valleys of the Durance.

NOTRE-DAME-DES-POMMIERS
The façade is

THE CITADEL

HISTORY. The town is overlooked by numerous
structures that date from many periods. The
upper rampart, or covered way, and the
13th-century turret were built by the
counts of Provence ● *47*. In the 16th
century, following damage to the north
and south of the town sustained during
the Wars of Religion, a level of defenses
fortified with bastions was added and
linked to the 14th-century rampart
encircling the town. These fortifications
were the work of Henry IV's engineer,
Jean Érard, who also designed the
crenelated defenses. Of Vauban's
ambitious project of 1692 to provide
Sisteron with a vast defense system
incorporating both fortress and town,
only the powder magazine and a ditch
were completed. The underground
stairway (350 steps) linking the fortress
and the town's north gate was carved out
of the rock between 1842 and 1860.

articulated by two
thick buttresses
which correspond
to the internal
dividing walls.

TOUR OF THE CITADEL. The south gate leads to the first circuit
wall of two 14th-century bastions overlooking the entrance:
the Notre-Dame Bastion is on the right; the King's Bastion is

on the left. A narrow gateway leads to the second circuit wall, which dates from the 14th century; this is part of the 16th-century Government Bastion cut by crosspieces to the west. The view out over the valley is outstanding. Steps lead to the third circuit wall where the garrison's barracks once stood, and lastly a final series of stairways ascends to the upper rampart; this is a narrow, 13th-century covered way lined by walls that were once crenelated and are now punctuated by the turret and the Notre-Dame Chapel. The 15th-century church has been restored and is now used for exhibitions. Access to the upper terrace is by way of a steep staircase; the north face is little more than a narrow hideout, a final refuge for the inhabitants when under siege, and two 16th-century walls at a lower level. One final staircase leads to the 17th-century Devil's Watchtower perched on top of the rock. The return journey takes in the extraordinary underground stairway on the first north wall. As the visitor approaches the south face, Vauban's powder magazine is on the right.

AROUND THE CATHEDRAL

NOTRE-DAME-DES-POMMIERS (right). This 12th-century church was built on a plan influenced by early Romanesque design; it was one of several episcopal buildings which included the Church of St-Thyrse, the baptistery and a cloister. In the 16th century, the bishop had this austere building embellished by providing the chapels with reredoses and paintings (*The Holy Family*, 1643, by Nicolas Mignard) and acquiring precious liturgical furnishings such as a high altar.

THE TOWERS. The towers are all that survive from the enceinte built in 1370. This fortification consisted of high walls punctuated by towers, and of gates well defended by drawbridges, portcullises and barbicans.

OLD SISTERON MUSEUM (visits by arrangement only). This museum provides a history of Sisteron through its collections of objects found in local excavations, and engravings and drawings of the town.

LA BAUME DISTRICT

PLACE DU DAUPHINÉ. This square overlooks the River Durance between the citadel and La Baume Rocks. This is where the Dauphiné (an old French province) finishes and Provence starts. Nearby is the extraordinary La Baume Rock, its vertical ridges of Tithonian limestone alternating with softer banks of limestone weakened by erosion. A good, though narrow and stony, route along the southern face of the rock leads to the "Silver Hole" grotto. Access is also possible along the GR 6 hiking path; the whole trip takes 4¼ hours.

THE VIA DOMITIANA
This road was built after *Provincia* had been established by Proconsul Domitius Ahenobarbus, the founder of Narbonne. It first crossed the western Alps at the Mont-Genèvre Pass, reached the Rhône Delta along the Durance and Calavon Valleys, passed through the plains of Mediterranean Languedoc and Roussillon, and crossed the eastern Pyrenees at the Perthus-Panissars Pass. The Via Domitiana formed the foundation of Roman power: it was the route taken by Roman armies, functionaries, merchants and travelers; it was used by the Imperial post, the *cursus publicus*; it enabled the regions of the Empire to develop in an extraordinary way. And Sisteron was a compulsory staging-post on it.

THE LURE MOUNTAINS

At about 5,250 feet above sea level near the Lure Refuge, the forest abruptly gives way to the heath and grasslands of the summit. This open area is very alpine in character despite its relatively low altitude; this is because it has been frequently deforested and used for grazing. "From the top of the Lure, you can see the whole of upper Provence spread out before you. This land... of lavender, brambles and ancient customs smokes, snorts, grunts, sleeps and is flattened by the wind." (Jean Giono)

THE LANDSCAPE

The Lure landscape consists of heathland growing juniper, rocky, graminaceous grasslands and enormous scree slopes that have a somewhat sterile appearance but in fact abound in numerous plants that have adapted to the poor, unstable soil. Juniper also adapts to the altitude and adopts a prostrate habit. In May, the grasslands are dotted with the light purple and pale yellow of a most beautiful type of orchid known as the elder orchid, with spikes of purple flowers arranged in a spiral form, the little spring gentian with its deep blue flowers, the orangey-yellow southern tulip, and the fritillaria of the Dauphiné, a pale wine-colored, bell-shaped flower. They are all protected species.

The raven

BIRDS. Ravens breed in solitary pairs on the cliffs of the northern slopes, and from late winter onward the largest of the European crows engage in spectacular display flights. The short-toed eagle is a small species of eagle which, after returning from tropical Africa in late March, spends its time searching for grassland snakes and lizards.

The short-toed eagle

F. Desbordes

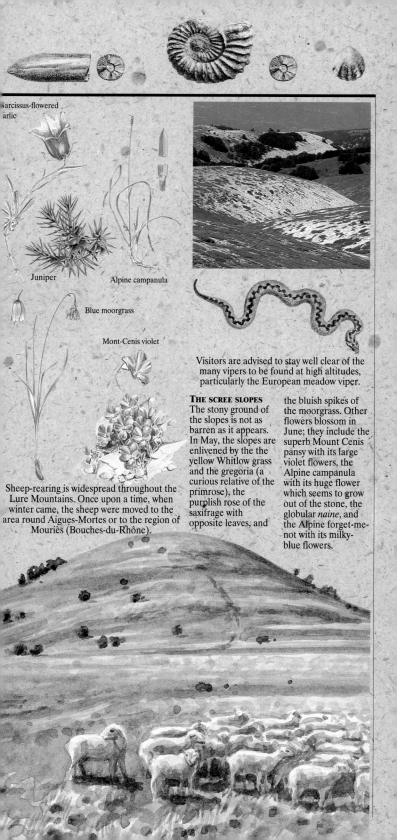

Narcissus-flowered garlic

Juniper

Alpine campanula

Blue moorgrass

Mont-Cenis violet

Sheep-rearing is widespread throughout the Lure Mountains. Once upon a time, when winter came, the sheep were moved to the area round Aigues-Mortes or to the region of Mouriès (Bouches-du-Rhône).

Visitors are advised to stay well clear of the many vipers to be found at high altitudes, particularly the European meadow viper.

THE SCREE SLOPES

The stony ground of the slopes is not as barren as it appears. In May, the slopes are enlivened by the the yellow Whitlow grass and the gregoria (a curious relative of the primrose), the purplish rose of the saxifrage with opposite leaves, and the bluish spikes of the moorgrass. Other flowers blossom in June; they include the superb Mount Cenis pansy with its large violet flowers, the Alpine campanula with its huge flower which seems to grow out of the stone, the globular *naine*, and the Alpine forget-me-not with its milky-blue flowers.

Étienne Martin's *Le Pré de Foire* evokes an atmosphere that th
modern pedestrianized streets have managed to preserve. Some of th
street names – Rues des Tanneurs (tanners), Chapeliers (hatters) and
Plâtriers (plasterers) – are a reminder of the wide range of busines
once conducted by artisans and merchants in the Old Town

HISTORY

A NEW ROLE FOR THE TOWER
The clock tower had to be pulled down before St Jerome's Cathedral could be built. It was later integrated into the completed cathedral, heightened and, in 1620, was topped by a wrought-iron *campanile*.

The prefecture of Alpes-de-Haute-Provence is located in a wonderful setting surrounded by mountains and at the confluence of the valleys of the rivers Bléone and Mardaric and the Eaux Chaudes Torrent. Christianity first came to Digne in the 4th century, but no bishopric was established until 506. Later, the dislocation of the Carolingian Empire opened up an era of uncertainty, and the surrounding hills became the inhabitants' only refuge from marauding Saracens. In the 11th century, the bishops of Digne had a fortified castle built on a rocky hillock; although it has now disappeared, it was around this fortress that a new city grew up and replaced the fortified township. In the 13th century, the new city was in its turn encircled by high walls protected by fifteen towers, and in 1490 a new cathedral was built close to the castle. The Wars of Religion, and then a terrible epidemic of the plague in 1630, did much damage to Digne just as it was moving into a period of prosperity, and at the beginning of the 18th century, the town was still enclosed within its ramparts. When the monasteries were acquired by the state after 1789, they were substantially altered and turned into institutions of the Republic. Digne itself began to expand in the early years of the 19th century with the construction of Boulevard Gassendi but experienced a period of economic stagnation throughout the Third Republic. Today, Digne is one of France's leading thermal resorts; Old Digne, too, has been renovated, and festivals and fairs attract large numbers of tourists every year.

THE OLD TOWN

PIERRE GASSENDI (1592–1655)
Gassendi was not only a theologian, philosopher, Provost of the Chapter of Digne and historian, but also a naturalist and astronomer. His thoughts and ideas, best known for being opposed to those of Descartes, influenced such men as Charleton, Locke and Newton.

ST JEROME'S CATHEDRAL (open every afternoon except Mondays and Fridays). Built in 1490, this church was greatly enlarged and decorated after 1851. Its monumental design and neo-Gothic influence are splendidly illustrated by the square in front of the church, and by the southern façade inspired by Chartres Cathedral. The complicated ground plan shows the various enlargement projects implemented since 1490. In the 16th century, the church was provided with a sacristy which, in 1601,

became the Corps-Saints Chapel. Then a new chapel was added next to the nave in 1650; this is the location of the recumbent statue of Antonio Capissuchi of Bologna, Bishop of Digne from 1602 until his death in 1615. The only element surviving from the 17th century is the small reredos by the local sculptor Honoré Maïsse; it was restored in 1989. The stained-glass windows installed in the choir in 1855 were the work of the glassworker-painter Alphonse Didron and depict scenes from Christ's Passion, the life of the Virgin and the life of Saint Jerome told in the manner of Jacques de Voragine's *Légende Dorée*.

DEPARTMENTAL MUSEUM OF RELIGIOUS ART ★. This museum is situated in the former Blue Penitents' Chapel. It contains precious objects of religious art including reliquary busts, *santons*, priestly ornaments and collection plates. A copper plate dating from the 16th century is shown below.

DIGNE IN THE 19TH CENTURY

BOULEVARD GASSENDI. This long avenue dates from the First Empire. In the middle, there is a huge square which contains a bronze statue of the celebrated philosopher Pierre Gassendi which was erected in 1851. The TOWN HALL, a former hospice, was built in 1720, abandoned, and renovated in 1987. On the other side of the square is a marble fountain made by MARIA SZUSZA DE FAYKOD in 1989. Every other year in June, Digne hosts a SYMPOSIUM OF CONTEMPORARY SCULPTURE which attracts many artists and their works.

DIGNE MUSEUM. This museum is both an art and natural history museum and, as such, faithfully reflects the eclectic passions of its early 19th-century founders. The work of Pierre Gassendi is given due prominence in a gallery devoted to the 19th century and the teaching of science. The second-floor ethnological collection consists mainly of butterflies, while the third floor contains works by painters of the Italian and Flemish Schools and by a number of charming regional artists; the latter include the painter Étienne Martin (1858–1945)

THE HAUTE PROVENCE GEOLOGICAL RESERVE
This reserve, which was opened in the 1980's, is the largest in Europe and covers an area of some 370,000 acres in the *département* of Alpes-de-Haute-Provence. Its purpose is the study, protection and exploitation of all traces of the Earth's history. The remains in the subsoil of the southern Alps are of great importance; they include plant life from the Primary Era, ammonites, large reptiles that prove there was marine life during the Secondary Era, and birds from the Tertiary Era.

and his son, the watercolor artist Paul Martin. The whole collection provides a comprehensive survey of the Provençal landscape school of the 19th century.

THE OUTSKIRTS

NOTRE-DAME-DE-BOURG ★. It probably required the whole of the 13th century to complete work on this church; it was later destroyed by fire. The original building was constructed on the site of the city in Gallo-Roman times, and a mosaic with a geometric design, some cellars and parts of the early Christian structure have survived from that period. Despite its great size, this Romanesque church is endowed with a remarkable unity of style: the nave has four large bays and a large broken-barrel vault, and the rectangular choir has a flat apse. The surviving fragments of the 14th- and 15th-century mural paintings are superb: the side walls have an *Annunciation* to the north and, to the south, a *Last Judgement* accompanied by Vices and Virtues and punishment in hell. These magnificent works were in poor condition for a century, but they are now being restored.

ALEXANDRA DAVID-NEEL FOUNDATION ★.
The Foundation is just past the "Total" garage on the road leaving Digne in the direction of Nice. The celebrated orientalist and explorer of Tibet wrote many of her books in this house, which she bought in 1928. She would stay in the house between expeditions, and only settled here permanently in 1946 when she was already seventy-eight years of age. The town of Digne was left this remarkable woman's entire estate and, in 1977, it set up a FOUNDATION to renovate the building and assist Tibetans living in exile; the Foundation also provides additional research study facilities. The house is open to the public who may walk round with a recorded commentary as guide. Some of the rooms contain objects of oriental art of exceptional beauty; they include Ming Buddhas, 18th-century Japanese incense time-keepers, painted banners ("tankas"), ritual objects from Tibet and "tsa-tsas" made of the powdered bones of the dead. All were given to the explorer in the course of her expeditions. She used to keep them inside a small temple built in one of the rooms of her house. *My Journey to Lhasa*, her best-known book, contains fascinating anecdotes about some of these amazing objects. Other cases contain personal belongings and items she took on her travels.

ALEXANDRA DAVID-NEEL (1868–1969)
Alexandra David-Neel spent much of her life on the roads of Asia. At the age of twenty-seven, she traveled to Hanoi and then crossed Tibet on foot in eight months; she was the first European woman to enter the forbidden city of Lhasa. In 1946, she returned to Digne, where she lived with her adopted son, the Lama Yongden, and then with her secretary Marie-Madeleine Peyronnet.

UNITY OF DESIGN
Much of the façade's beauty derives from the rose window with its large annular archivolts much influenced by Gothic design, and the statues at the entrance in the Lombard style.

CANNES

▲ CANNES

1 CROIX-DES-GARDES **2** MÉDIATHÈQUE **3** VILLA ÉLÉONORE-LOUISE **4** VILLA VICTORIA **5** CHÂTEAU DES TOURS **6** LE SUQUET **7** TOWN HALL **8** OLD PORT **9** PALAIS DES FESTIVALS **10** NOTRE-DAME-DE-BON-VOYA-

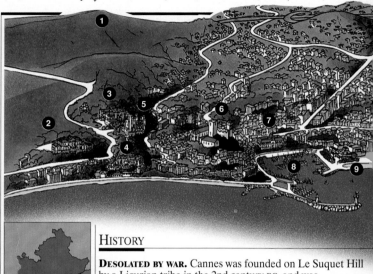

⏱ Two days

Wooden statue from the Marquesas Islands.

HISTORY

DESOLATED BY WAR. Cannes was founded on Le Suquet Hill by a Ligurian tribe in the 2nd century BC, and was subsequently colonized by the Romans in 154 AD. The town then entered a long period of upheaval which was dominated by Saracen raids and lasted until the year 1000. During the wars between Francis I and Charles V of Spain (1524–36), Cannes was invaded on two occasions, and it again came under attack when Louis XIII went to war with Spain in 1635. The town was conquered by Victor Amedeus II, Duke of Savoy, in 1707, and was then occupied in 1746–47 by Imperial Troops during the War of the Austrian Succession.

A HOLIDAY RESORT. Enchanted by Cannes in 1834, Lord Brougham, an English aristocrat, decided to settle there. This marked the beginning of the town's affluence, with luxury residences springing up to provide winter accommodation for the international nobility. Some smaller houses were also built, initially in the town itself, and later by the sea. From 1930 onward, Cannes became a summer resort, and extended westward into the area known as La Bocca. The local economy had traditionally relied on fishing and the growing of mimosa, but this soon was replaced by tourism ● 58.

THE OLD PORT
At the turn of the century, the Quai St-Pierre at the foot of Le Suquet was devoted exclusively to fishing. Today, it plays host to beautiful luxury yachts.

244

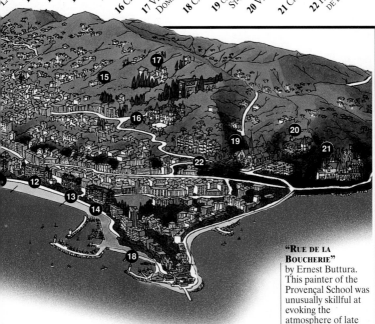

"RUE DE LA BOUCHERIE" by Ernest Buttura. This painter of the Provençal School was unusually skillful at evoking the atmosphere of late 19th-century Cannes.

LE SUQUET ★

MUSÉE DE LA CASTRE. This museum has been housed in the former Cannes Castle since 1922. It was founded in 1877 with a collection donated by Baron Lycklama, a Dutch scholar and humanist; this included ethnological items from five continents. The museum also contains an extraordinary collection of three hundred musical instruments from all over the world. The theme of the history of the human race runs through the entire exhibition: the 12th-century Chapel of Ste-Anne is used for temporary exhibitions, while other rooms are given over to the history of man, religion and mythology. Provence itself is represented by works of the 19th-century Provençal School. The museum's central courtyard is dominated by the 11th–14th-century SUQUET TOWER. This watchtower, last line of defense in the event of an attack, is 72 feet high; access to the first floor is by way of an external staircase. A vaulted passageway that has survived from the former ramparts leads to the square in front of the CHURCH OF NOTRE-DAME-DE-L'ESPÉRANCE, an austere building dating from the late Provençal Gothic period (1521–1648). It contains two items of interest: an 18th-century Virgin in carved wood in the choir, and a 15th-century CHRIST DE LA BONNE MORT.

THE HÔTEL MAJESTIC
This hotel was built in 1926 on plans by the architect Théo Petit. The Majestic has always been considered to have some of the best facilities in the region.

View of La Croisette at Cannes by Pierre Bonnard (c. 1925).

THE PROMENADE DE LA CROISETTE IN 1928
Although La Croisette was opened in 1871, it was not until 1961 that it acquired its present appearance. Major works have been undertaken to keep the sea back, but the roadway is frequently damaged by storms.

THE BACK STREETS OF OLD CANNES. Rue Panisse-Coraille leads into RUE ST-ANTOINE. This is the main thoroughfare of Old Cannes, and bears the name of a medieval chapel dedicated to Saint Anthony and now a residential building. This street has retained its low houses, which were once inhabited by fishermen and their families, and old vaulted outhouses; it boasts a genuine Provençal charm. Some of the streets still bear the names of the families that once lived there, such as Pons, Panisse and Preyre; when a family moved on, the street was given a new name.

THE OLD PORT. The use of the port by pleasure craft is a recent development; there are already four yachting harbors. Fishing has always been the main economic activity because the land around Cannes is unsuitable for agriculture. The waters of the nearby coast have always been richly abundant, and fishing rights have been the subject of lengthy and bitter negotiations between the people of Cannes and the abbots of Lérins ▲ 272.

THE FORVILLE DISTRICT. This is where the Forville Market is held. The quarter was built after 1870 to respond to the needs of a city already expanding at great speed, and the market still sells locally grown fruit, vegetables and flowers. Fishermen also come up from the port to sell their catch.

BOULEVARD DE LA CROISETTE

BURIED UNDER THE SAND. At the headland of the cape which marks the end of the Bay of Cannes and separates it from Golfe-Juan, there is an unprepossessing monument surmounted by an ancient cross much venerated by the people of Cannes. It is this cross, or *crocetta*, that gave its name to the promenade, and then the *boulevard*, which runs along the coast. At the end of the 18th century, the perimeter of the bay was overrun by sand, and the former Royal Road that originated in Antibes disappeared under the dunes. In 1850, the local counselors saw the need to construct a road round the bay; they also wanted something similar to the Promenade des Anglais in Nice to attract the winter clientele. It took twenty years for the Boulevard de la Croisette to be completed, and for palm trees to be planted along its route.

THE PALAIS DES FESTIVALS. The Palais des Festivals was built at one end of La Croisette. It is the venue for the Cannes Film Festival every year in May; other events that take place there include the International Record and Music Publishing Market, the International Television Programmes Market and numerous other conferences. The Palais comprises the Grand Auditorium and 150,700 square feet of exhibition space, and the west wing houses the casino, gaming rooms and night club.

THE INTERNATIONAL FILM FESTIVAL. The Cannes Film Festival was established to counter the Fascist ideology that lay behind the Venice Film Festival, but it was not held in its first year owing to the outbreak of war in 1939. The Festival's official opening at the Municipal Casino did not take place until September 20, 1946. Ever since then, except for 1948 and 1950, the festival has been held annually, initially in September and from 1951 onward, in May. It usually lasts for about a fortnight. In 1947, new premises were built on the site of the old Cercle Nautique, and the festival has met with even more success ever since.

THE OLD CASINO
The old casino was replaced by the Palais des Festivals in 1982.

THE CARLTON
This hotel was built in 1911 from plans by Charles Delmas, and has no fewer than 355 rooms and suites. The huge dining room with its colonnades, painted ceiling and carved cornices has remained unchanged. The three façades are articulated with projections including foreparts and balconies, and also have vertical brick facings. The window frames, cornices and attic pediments boast elaborate stucco decoration.

HOLIDAY PALACES
These enormous houses had to be big enough to meet the needs of entire aristocratic families that came to Cannes accompanied by numerous servants.

HUGE BUILDINGS. The first *hôtels* were constructed in the middle of the town, or on the slopes of Californie and Croix-des-Gardes Hills, but houses were subsequently built along the beach. They boast a range of architectural styles, but they all have one thing in common: their colossal size.

THE NOGA HILTON HOTEL AND ITS ILLUSTRIOUS PREDECESSORS. The Noga Hilton Hotel was opened on the Croisette in 1992; with 225 rooms and suites, it certainly conforms to local tradition. The site was previously occupied by two buildings that the people of Cannes hold in particular affection: the Cercle Nautique and the old Palais des Festivals. For over thirty years, the twenty steps leading up from La Croisette to the entrance and to the staircase leading to the balcony, were the most coveted in the whole world by those hungry for fame and glory.

HÔTEL MARTINEZ ★. Although the Martinez was renovated in the 1980's, the Art Deco interior design has remained unchanged. The dining room is noted for its 1930's furniture: this includes black lacquered armchairs covered in pearl-grey and maroon Alcántara (the chairs in the saloon bar were made by the London firm of Waring and Gillow) and prewar silverware and glassware.

CROIX-DES-GARDES HILL

VILLA FIESOLE
This house was the home of the painter Jean-Gabriel Domergue, who also drew up the plans. It was completed in 1936. Domergue specialized in portraits of women, and famous sitters who came to Villa Fiesole included Josephine Baker, Gina Lollobrigida and Brigitte Bardot. The house was bequeathed to the city of Cannes together with some of Domergue's paintings, and the grounds are sometimes used for official functions. Unfortunately, it is not open to the public.

THE FIRST HOLIDAY RESORT. The Croix-des-Gardes, also known as the English Quarter, is the oldest residential area in Cannes. Its prosperity dates from the time when Lord Brougham bought a large property about halfway up the hill and, between 1835 and 1839, had the first holiday residence built. Lord Brougham managed to persuade some of his friends to join him in Cannes, and some time later Sir Thomas Woolfield purchased a few dozen acres around Brougham's land and then resold the land in small plots in 1860. In all, over twenty villas were constructed by his English friends on these sites beside the sea. Woolfield found himself the owner of a considerable amount of land; he had been greatly assisted by his gardener, John Taylor, a man well versed in business affairs who went on to found the town's first firm of real estate agents. The firm still has offices on La Croisette. John Taylor was appointed British Vice-Consul in 1884.

CHÂTEAU DES TOURS, OR THE VILLA STE-URSULE ★ (Parc Vallombrosa, 6 Avenue Jean-de-Noailles). This castle was built between 1852 and 1856 by two English architects for Sir Woolfield; it is made of pink gneiss in the Gothic style, and is an archetype of the contemporary English homes ● *100* with its porch, stained-glass mullioned windows and bays with Gothic arches. It was bought by the Duke of Vallombrosa in 1858, and sold in 1893 to a hotelier who added two wings.

VILLA ÉLÉONORE-LOUISE ★ (24, Avenue du Docteur-Picaud). This Palladian villa is strongly influenced by ancient styles, and was a major precursor of the town's most characteristic designs ● *100*. Lord Brougham commissioned the villa in

1835, and it was completed four years later. The rectangular ground plan, the main façade and the three stories are in perfect symmetry. A terrace supported by a colonnade of porphyry runs the whole length of the building.

THE CALIFORNIA DISTRICT ★

LUXURY, TRANQUILITY AND IMAGINATION. This district in the east of the town derives its name indirectly from the sponge trees cultivated there in the late 19th century: these exotic plants were greatly prized by the perfume makers of Grasse and Cannes, and they made the growers as rich as Californian gold prospectors. Croix-des-Gardes had already been taken over by the English colony, but California was much more popular with the Russians. Eugène Tripet, the French Consul in Moscow, bought a large piece of land there in 1850, and built the Villa Alexandra, a residence in the oriental style which has now disappeared. After marrying a young member of Russian high society, Tripet successfully encouraged numerous members of the Tsarist aristocracy to buy property in Cannes. These luxury fantasy villas boasted an extraordinary range of styles and architecture.

CHÂTEAU SCOTT ★ (151, Avenue du Maréchal-Juin). This castle in the Gothic style was commissioned by a businessman by the name of Hughes Scott, and it was built between 1868 and 1872. It is typical of the "medieval" follies of the period. The Château Scott also fired the imagination of film-makers such as Marcel L'Herbier who made his *Mystery of the Yellow Room* here in 1931.

THE VILLA ROSE-LAWN ★ (42, Avenue du Roi-Albert). When this house was built in 1872, it was known as the Villa des Lotus. This unusual building is made of brick,

stone and wood; its irregular forms and half-timbered façades adorned with bow windows are reminiscent of English cottages.

LE CALIFORNIE ★ (27, Avenue du Roi-Albert). This house was built by the architect Vianey, and is the most typical of the palaces constructed in the neoclassical style.

FIVE TYPES OF VILLA
John Taylor's real estate agency used to provide line drawings and watercolors of the properties on its books. Homes shown to prospective clients in 1864 included Villa Julie-Marie, Villa Desanges, the Château gothique, Château Garibondy and Villa du Château-d'Eau.

VILLA LES MIMOSAS
(10-12, Avenue de la Californie). This house with its irregular ground plan is similar to the villa shown above right. It is one of the biggest English residences in the California district.

Cannes in the Belle Époque by E. Bellini. Bellini was born in 1904, and at different times was a poster artist, caricaturist, the maker of models of carnival floats, book illustrator, theater designer, and maker of jewelry and Murano glass sculptures. His first exhibition as a painter took place in Cannes in 1949. His calashes driving across the Suquet countryside have made him one of the city's permanent ambassadors all over the world.

MASSIF DE L'ESTÉREL

The Estérel Range rises to 2,020 feet at Mount Vinaigre. It is a surprisingly unyielding terrain, although the massif was once covered with forests of mainly holm oaks and corn oaks; they were frequently destroyed by forest fires. The cool temperatures encourage the growth of such tropical plants as palm and eucalyptus trees, American aloe and mimosa; elsewhere, there are wide expanses of trees (locust, pine, chestnut, hornbeam, fig, olive

⊙ One week
🚗 218 miles

and bay) and white briar, cistus and holly (below).

HISTORY. Saint Honorat was born at Trêves in the 5th century, and later withdrew to the Ste-Baume grotto at Cap-Roux in the Estérel Range. Until the 18th century, the massif was an area much frequented by hermits, and was also a bandits' hideout. The rural exodus has left the hills empty, and the old terraced fields are now overgrown with trees.

L'ESTÉREL
The Estérel is a Primary volcanic massif made of porphyry, and is lined throughout its length by layers of sandstone; between them, there are layers of clay from which emerge springs that probably originate in Upper Var.

WALKS AND BICYCLE RIDES. Bicycles are available from Grenouillet Farm near the entrance to Algay on the road from Valescure. The Grenouillet road then climbs up to the forester's lodge at Le Gratadis; shortly afterward, the road to the left goes off to Le Perthus and Le Roussiveau valleys, while the road on the right leads to the Grenouillet Ford where there is an arboretum. At the next crossroads to the south, the left-hand road ascends to the Ste-Baume grotto and Pic d'Aurelle from where there is a spectacular view. The right-hand road goes to Le Trayas via the St-Barthélemy Rock.

VALLON DU PERTHUS ★. A magnificent line of oleander runs alongside the torrent for about 1¼ miles in this state-owned biological reserve.

VALLON DU MAL-INFERNET ★. A road goes to the Belle-Garde Pass from the forester's lodge at Le Gratadis. From there, there is a walk lasting two to four hours to the small Mal-Infernet torrent, a mountain stream hemmed in by steep banks and surrounded by towering peaks. The Mal-Infernet is lined with flora unusual for the Mediterranean area including maple, lime

and ash trees, and holly. The dry slopes facing the sun are carpeted with maquis and dotted with rock rose, heather, apple and mastic trees.

A MODERN SEASIDE RESORT
St-Raphaël was a residential suburb of Fréjus during the Roman Empire; it was called *Epulias* (Banquets) and had a reputation for festivities. The town was first referred to as "St-Raphaël" in the 11th century, but it was not really until the 19th century, and more specifically 1864 when trains began to stop there, that the town was established as a resort. Painters, writers and even royalty have stayed at St-Raphaël.

ST-RAPHAËL

CHURCH OF ST-PIERRE. Work was started on this Romanesque building around 1150 and completed in the 13th century when a tower was added. The tower and church were next to the seigniorial mansion which was rebuilt in the 17th century. As the crenelations indicate, they and the mansion formed a group of fortified buildings.

A STROLL ROUND OLD ST-RAPHAËL. Part of the 14th-century ramparts can be seen in the gardens of the Archeological Museum. Medieval remains include ancient streets, one of the gates of the circuit wall to the east where the road to Fréjus started, and the old bridge over the Pédégal, which is called the Garonne at the river mouth. The seigniorial house

ETÉ · LA CÔTE D'AZUR · HIVER
SAINT-RAPHAËL
VALESCURE · BOULOURIS · AGAY · ANTHEOR · LE TRAYAS

THE PORT AND THE CATHEDRAL IN 1907
Coal and iron extracted from the Estérel Range used to be unloaded here. Bauxite from Var also passed through the port. Maritime links were established between St-Raphaël and Corsica when the island was handed back to France in 1768.

251

Jacques Douza

was rebuilt in 1773, and now houses the LOCAL HISTORY
MUSEUM.

THE ARCHEOLOGICAL MUSEUM. This museum occupies
premises in the former presbytery (1782). It contains objects
from the paleolithic, neolithic and bronze ages, including
trepanned crania and chalcolithic vases; there are also
displays of amphoras and two 13th-century bas-reliefs.

VALESCURE. This district of the town is beyond Old St-
Raphaël and to the north. In the years before World War
One, it was inhabited by artists. The Valescure Golf Club is
one of the oldest in the region, but the Golf Hôtel, which was
opened in 1935, has been converted into apartments.

FRÉJUS

HISTORY. On the fall of *Massilia* in 49, Julius Caesar turned
Fréjus (*Forum Julii*, or Julius' Market) into a military port,
and built a harbor linked to the sea by a canal. The town,
which was the site of a bishopric from 374, was invaded by the
Imperial armies in 1536, the Savoyards in 1707 and the
Austro-Piedmontese in 1746. In 1774, the port, now silted up
and foul-smelling, was filled in. Pope Pius VII passed through
Fréjus in 1809, as did Napoleon Bonaparte on his way back
from Egypt, and later on when he was exiled to the island of
Elba. The armed forces have always played an important part
in the life of the town, from the construction of an air base
(1911) to the inauguration of a
memorial to those who died in
Indochina (1993), but Fréjus is still a
seaside resort first and foremost.

RELIGIOUS BUILDINGS ★. The
complex of episcopal buildings is
located in the center of the
medieval town. It consists of a
baptistery, a cathedral, a canons'
cloister, some outhouses (all
made of reddish-brown
sandstone from the Estérel
Range), and the PALAIS DE
L'ÉVÊQUE (Bishop's
Palace), where the Town
Hall is now situated. The
courtyard of this palace
includes the cathedral's

southern wall and a square, crenelated tower from the 15th century; the latter houses the former CHAPEL OF ST-ANDRÉ, a church with beautiful intersecting ribs. Most of the remaining episcopal buildings were built between the 11th and 14th centuries; an exception is the baptistery which probably dates from the 5th century. The architecture of the PROVOST'S HOUSE is extremely simple, with two bays pierced on the second floor beneath semicircular arches. The BAPTISTERY to the west of the cathedral comprises a single octagonal hall containing eight columns made of black granite that support a cupola separated from the base of the building by a ceiling. The CATHEDRAL has two naves: the main nave has a ribbed vault resting on 13th-century pillars; the stalls in the apse are arranged in two rows on either side of the Bishop's Throne and date from the 15th century. The St Stephen's nave appears to have been rebuilt at the same time as the narthex, which dates from the 12th century and whose regular building stones still bear marks made by workmen. The second floor of the square tower was made in the 12th century, but the octagonal third floor, like the glazed tiles of the spire, dates from the 16th century. The CLOISTER galleries open onto the first floor through Gothic arches. The ceiling of the galleries is decorated with three hundred 15th-century painted panels inspired by the Apocalypse of Saint John.

THE OLD TOWN. The tower in RUE GRISOLLE is one of the few remaining sections of the medieval circuit wall; there are also two more square towers incorporated into more recent buildings to the north and west of the cathedral. Remains of the 16th-century fortifications can be seen to the north of the Old Town just beyond Rue Girardin. The population grew rapidly in the 1700's, and new ramparts were erected, more deterrent than defensive, against the Barbary pirates and other incursions associated with the Wars of Religion.

THE SAINT MARGARET REREDOS
This was painted by the Niçois artist Jacques Rurandi in the 15th century. The crown of pearls worn by Margaret of Antioch, patron saint of women in childbirth, symbolizes her humility and purity.

A DOOR WITH ATLANTES
The private mansion at 53 Rue Sieyès has a magnificent door decorated with 17th-century atlantes.

THE CENTER OF FRÉJUS
The Dominican chapel is a reminder of the religious orders present in Fréjus in the 17th century. The Hôtel des Quatre-Saisons derives its name from the heads of the wall-brackets which symbolize the seasons.

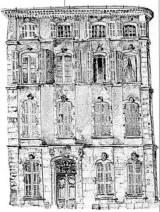

HERMÈS
DICÉPHALE
HAUT-EMPIRE ROMAIN
FRÉJUS
3,70
POSTES 1988
RÉPUBLIQUE
FRANÇAISE

THE AMPHITHEATER
At 374 by 266 feet, the Fréjus amphitheater is only half the size of its counterpart in Nîmes. It could house almost ten thousand spectators who sat in three sections of tiered seats; animals and combatants

appeared out of a cross-shaped ditch in the middle of the theater. After the period of Roman domination, the building became a stone quarry. The only surviving, yet extraordinarily impressive, remains of this amphitheater are the radiating and concentric rubblestone walls which sustained the building and supported the tiered seats. Bullfights, concerts and plays have been put on here since 1907.

THE ROMAN TOWN ★. The PORTE DES GAULES is situated below the esplanade where Chapel of St-François stands; this gate once overlooked the center of the amphitheater, and was defended by two round towers. Two side passageways were allocated for pedestrians while the central route, which was reserved for the chariots, was the beginning of the *decumanus maximus*, a thoroughfare that ran across the town from east to west. The AMPHITHEATER was built around the 1st century of the Christian era, and stood outside the walls. As for the VILLENEUVE THERMAL BATHS, the wine cellar in Rue Jean-Carrara was built over the *caldarium* (hot bath) that heated the water ● *80*. Next to the modern entrance, there is a Roman apse with vaults sprung in the four corners of the hall; the *frigidarium* (cold bath) lies to the west, while structures containing the *tepidarium* (warm room) and the *apodyteria* (changing rooms) are in the east. The town was also surrounded by NECROPOLISES: the oldest, dedicated to Saint Lambert, is on the road heading out of town in the direction of Italy. This road was originally made of compacted gravel, and was once lined with monumental tombs containing funerary urns. Later on, as burial replaced cremation as a Christian rite, these were superseded by lead sarcophagi and wooden coffins.

THE ROMAN PORT. The port was built in a pool situated opposite the town at some distance from the sea, but connected to it by a channel so as to be sheltered from storms. The port was overlooked by enormous structures: the Butte-St-Antoine in the southwest and the Roman Platform in the northeast. AUGUSTUS' LANTERN stands at the eastern end of the road of the same name: this 29-feet-high breakwater marked the end of the channel and the entrance to the outer harbor.

THE TOWN SYMBOL
A two-headed marble herm has been found in
a large building behind the Tourist Office, in
the Tower Enclosure which was once a Roman
district. It represents Bacchus and a faun, and
has become the symbol of Fréjus.

PORT-GRIMAUD

Port-Grimaud was created in 1966, replacing a vast mosquito-infested marshland at the tip of Grimaud Plain. This private joint venture covers an area of 225 acres, of which 203,324 square yards have been built on so far, and is the brainchild of architect and speculator François Spoerry, born in 1912. Entrance to Port-Grimaud is by way of fortified gates, and the tiny islands are linked by Venetian bridges. The town is full of colonnades, 1920's streetlights, trompe l'œil and arches, to which Spoerry added pastiches which have acquired an air of authenticity with the passing of time. The CHURCH OF ST-FRANÇOIS, with its lateral buttresses and square tower, is an imitation fortified church.

GRIMAUD ★

HISTORY. Grimaud lies 3¾ miles inland and is one of the oldest villages in the Maures Massif. In the Middle Ages, it was the fief of Gibelin de Grimaldi who built a *castrum* to defend the Maures Massif and to stop pirate incursions once and for all. From 1119, Grimaud was occupied by Knights Templars, who added fortifications and a network of underground passages.

PLACE NEUVE. This square is decorated with a monumental fountain (1886) and planted with nettle trees; it houses the MUSEUM OF POPULAR ARTS AND TRADITIONS.

THE CASTLE. Documentary references to the castle go back to the 11th century. The main entrance is on Rue du Balladou.

THE VILLAGE. The Renaissance MAISON DES TEMPLIERS (Templars' House) stands opposite the 11th-century ROMANESQUE CHURCH OF ST-MICHEL. GRIMAUD MILL near CHAPEL OF ST-ROCH probably dates from the 12th century; the mill has been very well restored, and its sails have recently been discovered.

IMITATION VENICE
François Spoerry has built a Provençal-style complex where boat owners can tie up their craft next to the quay, just outside their front door or at the bottom of the front garden. The villas, which look a little like fishermen's cottages, are situated beside canals leading down to the sea.

THE RUINS OF GRIMAUD CASTLE
The central block on the summit of the hill is flanked by three thick corner towers. Only a vaulted hall has remained intact.

CHURCH OF ST-MICHEL
In 1964 St-Michel's was restored to its former grandeur and austerity. The square tower is surmounted by a spire; the nave with three bays ends in a half-dome apse, itself crowned by a fresco of Saint Michael Slaying the Dragon in grisaille. In the chapel, there is a 12th-century marble holy-water stoup, probably a gift from King René.

"BRAVADES"
Bravades originated in the 12th century. They are processions in honor of the patron saint of the town ● 67. The St-Tropez *bravades* are particularly spectacular.

"TARTANES BEDECKED WITH FLAGS"
This painting by Paul Signac shows boats of the kind once used for coastal navigation, transporting local products such as cork, oil, wine, chestnuts, sand and wood. There is a reconstruction of one of these boats in the port.

ST-TROPEZ ★

HISTORY. This tiny corsair city had been well known in the 16th century for its sailors and adventurers, but it became an important trading center with fishing and shipbuilding as its main activities. The railways killed off coastal navigation in the 19th century, but the town was revived by tourism; the arrival of the artist Paul Signac in 1894 attracted many artists and writers. The port of St-Tropez was destroyed by the Germans in 1944, but by 1950 Paris's Bohemian district of St-Germain-des-Prés had established its summer quarters here. Soon, writers and actors were haunting the La Ponche Port, and rubbing shoulders with artists like Pablo Picasso.

THE PORT AND THE QUAYS ★. After the war, the old port was rebuilt in its original style by Guy Malenfant. The boathouses disappeared and were replaced by boutiques and cafés on whose terraces the two consummate pleasures of St-Tropez life – seeing and being seen – could be indulged. The CORSAIR'S HOUSE at 11 Quai Suffren has a monumental Renaissance staircase and, further on, an archway gives onto the FISH MARKET. PLACE AUX HERBES plays a key role in the town's morning routine with its fruit, vegetable and flower stalls. The visitor returning to the port and continuing eastward comes to the tower of CHÂTEAU SUFFREN, otherwise known as the Grimaldi Tower. Further on is the 16th-century TOUR DU PORTALET which once formed part of the ancient fortifications.

Paul Signac discovered St
when he sailed into the por
yacht *Olympia*. He decided t
and lived in a small cottag
Graniers Bea

MUSÉE DE L'ANNONCIADE ★. The Museum of
the Annunciation is located in the former
Chapel of Notre-Dame-de-l'Annonciade (1568)
of which only a large, austere outer wall
remains. It was closed down during the
Revolution, then turned into a museum by
Louis Süe (1875–1968) in 1955. The restoration
respected the spirit of the former building: the
spaces and vaults on the first floor ▲ *256*
suggest a religious building, but the hall on the
second floor has been divided up. The initial
collections were put together in 1922, and
largely consisted of gifts from artists working
locally; this was organized by Henri Person. The
painters who came to St-Tropez, inspired by
Paul Signac, may have belonged to a variety of schools (Nabis
and Fauves to Pointillists and Independents), but they all had
in common an interest in color and light, and a commitment
to figurative art that lasted from 1890 to the inter-war years.

ANSE DE LA GLAYE AND PORT DE LA PONCHE. After
the Portalet Tower, the visitor comes to the LA
GLAYE COVE whose restored houses have
preserved all their Italian charm. LA
PONCHE, beyond the 15th-century OLD
TOWER, used to be a fishing port. It is
now a delightful spot for swimming.

THE CITADEL ★. Henry IV authorized the
demolition of the citadel following a
request from the rebellious Tropéziens
who objected to the fortress. It was pulled
down, but then rebuilt in 1652 despite
opposition from the people.

**PAINTERS OF
COLORS AND LIGHT**
The Museum of the
Annunciation has
works by Pierre
Bonnard, André
Derain,

Édouard
Vuillard,
Paul Signac, Georges
Braque, Raoul Dufy,
Henri Matisse,
Georges Seurat,
Maurice Utrillo, Kees
Van Dongen (above:
*Women at the
Railing*), Maurice de
Vlaminck, Georges
Rouault, Albert
Marquet, Henri Cross
and the sculptor
Aristide Maillol.

**"LA PLACE AUX
HERBES"**
This square is still a
lively, central part of
Old St-Tropez. The
painting in the
Museum of the
Annunciation was
done by Charles
Camoin in 1905.

257

> "MY SISTER, MY SWEET, THINK OF THE DELIGHT
> OF JOURNEYING TO LIVE TOGETHER THERE!...
> THERE, ALL IS LOVELINESS AND HARMONY,
> ENCHANTMENT, PLEASURE AND SERENITY"
>
> CHARLES BAUDELAIRE

THE "PROPHETS" AND PROVENÇAL LIGHT

A number of artists including Bonnard, Vuillard, Roussel and Vallotton founded a group called the Nabis (*navi* is Hebrew for "prophet") between 1888 and 1900. They were followers of Paul Gauguin's ideas, and took their inspiration from oriental woodcuts and photography; they also rejected the scientific division of the approach to colors adopted by Paul Signac, and proclaimed the sacred nature of their art. The Musée de l'Annonciade contains Bonnard's *Nude by the Fireplace* of 1919 (below), one of his last Nabi paintings, and Vuillard's *Two Women in the Lamplight* of 1892 (above).

"LUXE, CALME ET VOLUPTÉ"

Matisse (1869–1954) did this painting in St-Tropez in 1904, inspired by Baudelaire's poem "L'Invitation au voyage". This was one of the last Symbolist works that he produced under Signac's influence.

A NEW VISION

Paul Signac (1853–1935) invented Pointillism. This style consisted of juxtaposing pure colors on the surface of the canvas; these are then blended by the eye, and in this way produce more luminous and vibrant colors. Opposite: Signac's *The Storm*.

THE FAUVES

Matisse's *The Gypsy Woman* (above) of 1906 is one of the great Fauvist works. "Fauvism" derives from a comment ("*Donatello parmi les fauves*" – "Donatello among the wild animals") made by an art critic about a Florentine bronze that was next to paintings by Matisse and his friends at the *Salon d'Automne* of 1905. This *Landscape at L'Estaque* by another Fauvist, Georges Braque, was painted in 1906.

Charles Camoin
(1879–1964) was
initially influenced
by Cézanne. He
met Signac in 1905;
he then met
Matisse who urged
him to take up
Fauvism. He
painted this view of
the port of
St-Tropez (above)
in the 1930's.

THE THIRD GENERATION
After the Pointillists and the
Fauvists, Dunoyer de
Segonzac symbolized a return
to a kind of order in which all
excesses were eliminated; he
rallied to the banner of the
so-called "Independent Artists"
who rejected the splendors of
post-Impressionism for more austere
styles inherited from Courbet and
Corot. Below: *St-Tropez Seen from
the Citadel*.

Dunoyer de
Segonzac
(1884–
1974)

PLACE DES LICES
This celebrated square with its plane trees is very popular for relaxation. Sailors, retired folk and show business personalities can all join in games of *pétanque*. Exhibitions are held in the Salle Jean-Desplas and Le Lavoir (1862) on the corner of the square.

"THE TOWER AT ST-TROPEZ" BY PAUL SIGNAC (1896)
This church with its famous tower has a classical pediment. Above the door is a niche containing a statue of St-Tropez.

One of the numerous "beachmen" of "St-Trop"

CHURCH OF ST-TROPEZ ★. This church was built in the 18th century and renovated in the 19th century. It has a light, brightly colored interior, and the pillars in the nave have niches containing busts of saints; Vian's pulpit dates from 1866 and the polychrome marble St-Tropez Altar dates from earlier in the century. The reliquary bust of the saint (to the left of the apse) is carried in procession during *bravades* ; it dates from the 18th century. The *Martyrdom of St-Tropez* and *The Assumption* are listed paintings.

DOWN TO THE BEACH. The chapels and "fantasy castles", built by rich families at the turn of the century, are convenient places to pause on the way down to the beach. CHAPEL OF ST-JOSEPH, a private church in Avenue Augustin-Grangeon, dates from 1650 and was enlarged in 1844; it is dedicated to the patron saint of the carpenters and joiners who have inhabited this area since 1824. The CONVENT CHAPEL on Route de Sainte-Anne was destroyed by the Saracens; the present building, whose foundations, according to legend, contain the remains of the martyr Torpes, dates from the 18th century. The CHAPEL OF STE-ANNE was built in 1627: its walls are covered with ex-votos brought by sailors, and its Provençal porch has inspired the design of many local patios. BORELLI CASTLE was recently restored but is not open to the public. This castle, perched on the hill opposite the citadel, was constructed in the middle of an immense park and combines various architectural styles ● *100* including Russian onion-shaped spires and Moorish influences. The turrets of ST-AMÉ CASTLE may be seen from the path that descends Ste-Anne Hill toward Pampelonne; PAMPELONNE CASTLE is not far from LA MOUTTE CASTLE, bought by Émile Ollivier, Napoleon III's prime minister.

BEACHES. PLAGE DE LA BOUILLABAISSE, on the edge of the town coming in from Ste-Maxime, is a windsurfer's paradise when the mistral is blowing. To the east, beyond PLAGE DES GRANIERS, is PLAGE DES CANEBIERS, which takes its name from the wattle that grows there. The path round Cap St-Pierre is a pleasant alternative to the main road as a way of getting to LES SALINS, where the wild landscape is even reflected in the water. To the north lies PLAGE DE LA MOUTTE , and to the south, the beach at Ramatuelle.

Tropéziennes ● 78, the celebrated local sandals.

RAMATUELLE ★

HISTORY. Until the 18th century, this village, long the property of prosperous local families, suffered frequent pirate raids. During the inter-war years, Ramatuelle benefited from its proximity to St-Tropez, and it was discovered by a number of artists.

TOUR OF THE VILLAGE. In PLACE DE L'ORMEAU (Elm Square), an elm tree was planted during the life of the Duke of Sully (1559–1641) to mark the bringing of peace to the province and the conversion of Henry IV. It used to be part of the town's coat of arms, but has now been replaced by an olive tree. The 16th-

century CHURCH OF NOTRE-DAME, with its 1620 door made of serpentine, once backed onto the former ramparts (the covered way still runs round the roof) and its tower was the watchtower. Built during the reign of Napoleon III in an imitation Arab style, the FORMER PRISONS are situated in the street which starts just beyond the tower and follows a lower route round the old village; the SARRASINE GATE has preserved its original appearance.

GASSIN ★

The peninsula to the south of St-Tropez is dominated by the village of Gassin, 659 feet above the vineyards and forests. This fortified village once served as a look out against pirate raids, warning the more remote areas of imminent dangers.

THE CHURCH ★. This church was mentioned in municipal archives as early as the 16th century; it was restored in 1981. The tower is probably earlier than the rest of the building; it was originally crenelated and subsequently heightened.

THE OLD STREETS. The maze of little streets is connected by means of porticos and stairways. They eventually give way to the fortified TERRASSE DES BARRI from which there is superb view from the Îles d'Hyères to the Alps.

A FORTIFIED VILLAGE
The houses of Ramatuelle follow the pattern of a wall that used to encircle the village. This wall was knocked down at the end of the siege of 1592 during the Wars of Religion by neighboring villages who besieged Ramatuelle to free its inhabitants from

supporters of the League.

FAMOUS NETTLE TREES
The lucky tree in Frédéric Mistral's *Mireille* adorns the Terrasse des Barri. The fruit is a tiny, oval drupe that is green and acid at first, and then reddish-brown and sweet; it is used to make jam.

BORMES AND ITS PIRATES
Bormes was probably founded around 400 BC by the Bormani, a Ligurian tribe that came from Italy and, in the days before Rome brought peace to the region, made a living from piracy. In the 11th century, the inhabitants made their homes on the hill where the village now stands, but this time it was to protect themselves from pirates.

A painting of Bormes by Perzilla (1874–1919).

BORMES-LES-MIMOSAS ★

HISTORY. This village, originally built in a semicircle and boasting a spectacular view of the sea, is dominated by the ruined castle of the lords of Fos. After 1890, the town opened up to tourism and became a seaside resort. Mimosa grows throughout the area, and the name Bormes-les-Mimosas became more common at the turn of the century; it was made the official name in 1968. Bormes has won a prize for the village with the best flower decorations in France; a procession of floral floats takes place every February.

ST FRANCIS OF PAOLA IN BORMES. In 1481, the Calabrian monk Francis of Paola made a brief stop at Bormes at a time when the village was still suffering from the plague, and his prayers are believed to have delivered the village from further misery. In gratitude, the inhabitants built a CHAPEL during the 16th century. Nearby, in PLACE DE LA LIBERTÉ, there is an old mill which was in use as recently as 1914.

BORMES CASTLE. This 13th–14th-century castle was both a peaceful country residence and redoubtable fortress, but only the apartments and the curtain wall remain. It was used as a monastery by the Order of Minims who settled here in 1654, then sold during the Revolution. It is now private property and is not open to the public.

THE STREETS OF BORMES ★. The Montée du Paradis goes from the castle to the CLOCK TOWER (1790). There are numerous *cuberts* (covered ways) underneath the houses which provide shelter from the sun and the wind, and at one time served as meeting places in the evening. The ART AND HISTORY MUSEUM, established at 65 Rue Carnot by the painter Benezit in 1926, contains works from the 19th and 20th centuries, a collection of sacred art and a section on local history. Nearby RUELLE ROMPI-CUOU (Neck-Breaker Street) consists of 492 feet of stairways paved with smooth, round steps; at the bottom there is a central ditch where all used water was once collected.

CHARTREUSE DE LA VERNE ★

HISTORY. The charterhouse, now a monastery, was built in 1170 at the behest of Bishop Pierre Isnard of Toulon, Bishop Fredol of Fréjus, and local lords who handed over their lands and became monks. They followed the Rule of Saint Bruno. The monastery was sacked during the Wars of Religion and was destroyed by forest fires but, thanks to donations and skillful management on the part of the monks, it covered an area of 7,400 acres by the 18th century. The Revolution took place as the monks were in the middle of important building works, and forced them to flee; the charterhouse, which was never really completed, was then sold to the state and the buildings fell into disuse. La Verne was classified as a historic monument in 1921 and is now being restored. The Sisters of Bethlehem have occupied the building since 1982.

TOUR OF LA VERNE. The surviving buildings were constructed between the 12th and the 18th centuries, but the medieval buildings have almost completely disappeared. The charterhouse is built on rows of terraces. The monumental 17th-century entrance leads into the vast Courtyard of Allegiances formed by the first two groups of buildings. These recall the charterhouse's economic independence, with its own stables, forge, bakery, carpenter's shop and olive press. The monastic buildings are opposite the entrance. The main kitchen and annexes are on the first floor, and the empty space behind is the small cloister, the *domus inferior*, which was solely for the use of the dozen or so brothers who served the monks. There were also communal buildings; these include the Romanesque chapel to the north, which is now in ruins, and the refectory to the south, which opened onto the cloister through a bay with six arches; the marvelously restored new chapel is to the west, and the main cloister, the *domus superior* which was reserved for the fathers, is at the far end of the spur. The cells were arranged around the main cloister; each had running water and reproduced the organization of the monastery, serving as oratory, cloister, *scriptorium*, refectory, kitchen, dormitory, workshop and kitchen garden.

WALKING ROUND THE CHARTERHOUSE
The tour begins at Collobrières. Take the D 14, fork onto the little road leading to the charterhouse and leave the car in the Croix-d'Anselme Park. The ONF (Office nationale des forêts) "Feuilles de Chêne" (Oak leaves) path takes four to five hours: after the Boulin Pass, the forest track leads to the charterhouse; from there, the path goes to the right, passes the water tank and climbs up to the peak of L'Ermitage. The return journey takes in Le Bousquet Valley and the peak of La Verne.

WOMEN NOT ADMITTED
Access to the charterhouse is through a monumental doorway made of serpentine, a

dark-green marble extracted from the nearby mountain. The entrance to St-Bruno's Chapel is by way of a porch. The only women allowed to enter the cloisters were princesses of royal blood.

265

HYÈRES

HYÈRES CASTLE ★. The ruins of this fortified castle, pulled down during the Wars of Religion, overlook the north part of the town. Access is by way of a gate, once protected by a portcullis, which stands between two round towers. A narrow path leads to the upper terrace which only has the remains of a water tank. On the north side, there is a postern overlooked by a platform protected by two more round towers. The circuit wall of the upper town once included the more northerly of these towers.

COLLEGIATE CHURCH OF ST PAUL ★. A monumental stairway leads to the entrance which was opened in 1789. The Romanesque narthex contains four hundred ex-votos from the Church of Notre-Dame-de-Consolation which was destroyed in 1944. The Gothic nave dates from the 15th and 16th centuries.

A WALK AROUND THE OLD TOWN ★. The RAMPARTS have survived. The first circuit wall, which dates from the 12th and 13th centuries, once extended for almost ¾ mile, but PORTE ST-PAUL, next to the Collegiate Church, and PORTE BARUC (notable for its dual locking system) are all that remain of the south curtain wall. Three beautiful towers have survived from the north curtain wall. The Bishop's Palace in this first circuit wall had a 13th-century façade; the PORTE FENOUILLET and PORTE DU VERNET are all that remain of the 13th-century second circuit wall which enclosed an extension of the town toward the south. There is a MUSEUM OF RELIGIOUS, MILITARY AND MEDIEVAL ORDERS in the TEMPLARS' TOWER. ST-LOUIS' CHURCH was built during the second half of the 13th century in a square of the same name, and

HYÈRES
ET SES ILES *(PORQUEROLLES ET PORT-GROS)*
La station la plus au sud de la Côte d'Azur

was renovated in 1855; it has a flat chevet, three naves and
six chapels built between the 14th and 17th centuries.
HYÈRES IN THE 19TH CENTURY. Hyères had already been
famous in the 17th century for its microclimate but, from the
19th century onward, it became a well-known resort thanks to
the development of the railways and winter tourism. Hugo,
Michelet, Maupassant, Tolstoy, Queen Victoria and many
members of the British aristocracy were regular visitors to the
superb casino (1854), the enormous hotels and the
astonishing range of villas.

PRESQU'ÎLE DE GIENS ★

A PARADISE OF FLORA AND FAUNA. The former island of Giens,
which once formed part of the Îles d'Hyères, has been
reunited with the mainland by two banks of sand built up by
sea currents and the Rivers Gapeau and Roubaud. This is the
explanation for that rarest of natural phenomena, a double
tombolo. Vast lagoons, known as Étangs de Pesquiers, were
formed there. The salt marshes, established in 1848, have
altered the natural surroundings, but the area's extraordinary
biological resources and 2,650 hours of sunshine every year
provide a wonderful setting for flora and fauna, particularly
sea holly and buck's horn plantain, to continue to flourish.
A PERFECT TRANSITION. Beyond the fine sand beaches of
L'AYGUADE and PORT DES SALINS, there is a marvelous stretch
of land that has not been built on, and which
boasts an uninterrupted succession of natural
environments. These include the sea with a
herbarium of posidonia, a beach where *lys de
mer* grow in July and August, salt marshes,
vineyards and the maquis.
AROUND THE PENINSULA. The poet Saint John
Perse lived and was buried in GIENS. From
the top of the village it is possible to look out
over the entire peninsula. PORT DU NIEL in
the south is quite beautiful. From the tiny
PORT DE LA MADRAGUE northwest of the
village of Giens, there is a track that goes to
Darboussière beach, which is itself the
beginning of a picturesque coastal walk
(round trip: two hours). ALMANARRE BEACH
on the western tombolo is delightful, as is the
CHAPEL OF ST-PIERRE-DE-L'ALMANARRE near the excavations
of the Greek and Roman city of Olbia.

ÎLES D'HYÈRES

A WORLD APART. Thirty to forty million years ago, Corsica and
Sardinia linked the edge of the eastern Pyrenees to the south
of Provence. They then slid into the positions they currently
occupy, thereby leaving the islands of Hyères behind on the
coast. Porquerolles, Port-Cros and Le Levant, and the nearby
uninhabited islands which extend along 14 miles of coastline,
constitute a section of a range of hills that emerged parallel to
the Maures Massif, and which geologically form part of it. A
rise in the sea level following the melting of the glaciers has
gradually edged them further away from the mainland over
the last ten thousand years.

Top: the Tour-
Fondue, a 17th–18th-
century battery.
Above: the port of
Hyères.

Red juniper.

HISTORY. The Îles d'Hyères were well known in prehistory to navigators sailing the Mediterranean, but after the Roman occupation, they became a refuge for hermits. Pirates imposed a rule of permanent insecurity from the 9th to the 16th century. Henry II had the islands

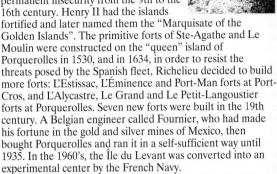

fortified and later named them the "Marquisate of the Golden Islands". The primitive forts of Ste-Agathe and Le Moulin were constructed on the "queen" island of Porquerolles in 1530, and in 1634, in order to resist the threats posed by the Spanish fleet, Richelieu decided to build more forts: L'Estissac, L'Éminence and Port-Man forts at Port-Cros, and L'Alycastre, Le Grand and Le Petit-Langoustier forts at Porquerolles. Seven new forts were built in the 19th century. A Belgian engineer called Fournier, who had made his fortune in the gold and silver mines of Mexico, then bought Porquerolles and ran it in a self-sufficient way until 1935. In the 1960's, the Île du Levant was converted into an experimental center by the French Navy.

PORQUEROLLES ★. FORT STE-AGATHE was built in the 16th century and destroyed in 1793 by the English; it was rebuilt in 1812 and enlarged in 1830. The artillery tower dates from 1531. Beyond the first circuit wall, a passageway leads to the main courtyard situated in the center of the fort, and to the tower and the terrace above it, which commands a view over the whole of the island. During the summer, there is an exhibition that combines the National Park and underwater archeological discoveries. The best way of getting around the island is by bicycle. Porquerolles is famous for its olive and mastic trees and red juniper growing out of the rock, and beaches of fine sand nestling between the turquoise-blue sea and the Aleppo pine forests. The island abounds in rabbits, partridges and pheasants which live side by side with the shy cerfs sikas introduced in the 1970's. In spring, the island resounds to the song of warblers, blackbirds, chaffinches and tits, the most common inhabitants of the woodlands.

Costume worn on the Îles d'Hyères in 1853.

UNDERWATER PATH
A mask and flippers are needed to follow the water-bound signposts. They lead into an underwater forest of posidonia and green, brown and red seaweed sometimes inhabited by groupers.

PORT-CROS ★. The island of Port-Cros was first inhabited by the Count of Noblet during the period 1870–80, and then by the Marquess of Beauregard until 1909, when it was bought by Marceline and Marcel Henry. The Henrys presented Port-Cros to the State in 1963 on condition that a nature reserve was built there. The COASTAL PATH goes to the FORT DE L'ESTISSAC which holds exhibitions every summer. The BOTANY PATH, which starts just below L'Estissac Fort, abounds in euphorbe dendroïde (a strange reddish bush), myrtle with its lingering scent, ciste de Montpellier (a bush with beautiful white flowers which turn yellow in summer), and cat mint. The coastal path finishes at LA PALUD BEACH where an UNDERWATER PATH has been constructed, the bay effectively enclosing a herbarium of posidonia, an essential element in Mediterranean ecosystems; this underwater forest is inhabited by a whole world of sea urchins, fish and crustaceans. The anchorage at BAIE DE PORT-MAN is popular among owners of pleasure craft; it is also one of the island's most attractive places for swimming.

ÎLE DU LEVANT ★. Napoleon had a fort built here in 1812, and in 1892, the State acquired 90 percent of the island. This is now used by a French navy experimental station. The other 10 percent was purchased in 1931 by two doctors, André and Gaston Durville, and includes the naturist village of Héliopolis. The village is perched on the hill and is not visible from the sea. The gardens are full of oleander, mimosa and bamboo, and palm, medlar, lemon and orange trees. Starting from the village, the NATURE PATH descends in the direction of CRIQUE DE LA GALÈRE, from where it is possible to return through the maquis or walk along the beach as far as the port.

TOULON

A LARGE NAVAL PORT. Toulon had its golden age in the 17th century when the French navy increased in size leading to the expansion of the dockyard and of the town itself. A penal colony was established here in 1748. Errors by bourgeois Jacobins enabled Royalists and moderate Republicans to take over the municipality and to free it from English control in 1793. The port was then retaken after fierce struggles which saw Napoleon Bonaparte promoted to general. In 1940, the entire French naval force withdrew to Toulon, and in 1942, despite having given their word to the contrary, the Germans attempted to take command. The ships were scuttled instead, and only four submarines rallied to the call of Free France. The recent transfer of the French navy to Brest has brought major economic problems to the city.

THE QUAYS. QUAI CRONSTADT's cafés and restaurant terraces are ideal spots for lazing in the sun. It is also possible to embark from here for La Seyne, Les Sablettes and the St-Mandrier peninsula, or to go on a tour of the dockyard. The dockyard buildings, destroyed by Allied bombing in 1944, were rebuilt in the early 1950's from plans by the architect Mailly. PUGET'S ATLANTES ★ (1656) on Quai Stalingrad decorate the main entrance to the *Mairie*; during the war, they were kept at Thoronet Abbey.

NATURISM AND NATURE
A nature reserve was created in the 62-acre Arbousiers estate at Héliopolis.

CLIFFS IN THE NORTH
The Île du Levant is 5 miles long and ¾ mile wide. Unlike the other islands, it exposes its steepest side to the mainland.

Toulon in 1850 by Guesdon.

NAVAL MUSEUM
The gate to this museum, with its four columns supporting statues of Mars and Minerva, used to be at the entrance to the dockyard. As master sculptor of Toulon dockyard, Félix Brun collected the most beautiful carvings that decorated ships and galleys, and was involved in the founding of this museum in 1814. Models, explanatory plates and videos present two centuries of French maritime history and the history of Toulon.

Head of a young man in gilt wood, from Pierre Puget's workshops of naval carving.

TOULON ARSENAL. The Old Dock was built during the reign of Henry IV, and new works were undertaken in 1680 from plans revised by Vauban; later, the ramparts were moved westward and the New Dock was constructed. The large supply of workers from the penal colony made it easier to expand the dockyard after 1748. The CLOCK TOWER (Tour de l'Horloge) was built in 1775; this was crowned by a *campanile* and supported the Great Bell (Grosse Cloche) which sounded the starting and finishing times.

Streets and tiny squares with fountains in Toulon.

The surrounding wall was then pushed back even further, and two docks were built, followed by five dry docks. The Milhaud *appartements* (harbors) were constructed at the beginning of the 20th century, and a munitions factory was also built; today, it houses rockets with nuclear warheads. The Mourillon Arsenal in the east of the harbor was built during the reign of Louis-Philippe; it is now an experimental center specializing in the sounds made by submarines. The CORDERIE (Rope Factory) next to the Arsenal in the north was constructed between 1686 and 1701. The rope was laid out on the first floor, and the work of the spinners and hemp dressers was done on the second floor; finished rope was hung from hooks on the north wall. To the east stands the MONUMENTAL GATE OF THE ROYAL SEMINARY (1689), the work of Rombaud Langueneux; the four Doric columns are surmounted by a pediment on which two women symbolize Law and Strength.

THE OLD TOWN ★. When the town was expanded under Vauban's instructions, a new parish was created and, shortly before the Revolution, the CHURCH OF ST-LOUIS was built behind the Sigaud houses in Place d'Armes. It is in the

THE THEATER
The Toulon sculptors Daumas and Montagne executed most of the external carvings; they are dedicated to Art. On the ceiling of the auditorium, the painter Sellier has produced a representation of Hyppolyte Duprat's opera *Farandole de Pétrarque*, of 1824. The theater overlooks the Old Town and parts of the city built in the 19th century.

classical style, and was initially used as a church for the worship of Reason and the Supreme Being. Old Toulon's circuit wall ran between Rue Hoche, Rue d'Alger, Cours Lafayette, Place Puget and Rue Alezard, and formed an extended rectangle. The streets ran north-south and still follow the same direction. The narrow RUE ST-VINCENT, which emerges north of the cathedral, gives an exact picture of what Toulon looked like in those days.

THE CATHEDRAL. Around 1096 a Romanesque cathedral, of which only the first three bays remain, replaced the original 5th-century church. It was enlarged in the 17th century and has three naves: the right-hand nave contains Chapel of St-Joseph and the original church's high altar, while the Chapel of St-Cœur-de-Marie is decorated with Puget's *The Vision of Saint Felix of Cantalice*.

EASTERN TOULON. COURS LAFAYETTE is lined with old plane trees and runs from the area around Place Puget to the port. The new district of La Visitation is above this road and to the east; it has been rebuilt in the Provençal style. PORTE D'ITALIE is the only fortification in the style of Vauban that has survived, while the MOURILLON DISTRICT is one of the liveliest in Toulon with its terraces and small port. FORT ST-LOUIS was designed to defend the entrance to the Grande Rade (outer roadstead) and to hold provisions for a three-month siege. It was protected by the 16th-century TOUR ROYALE, or "Tour-Canon" (Cannon Tower), which was mainly used as a prison.

TOULON IN THE 19TH CENTURY. After visiting Toulon in 1852, Louis-Napoleon authorized the demolition of the old city walls, and decided that the city should expand toward the north. The hospital was built in 1857, the railway station in 1858, the lycée and the theater in 1867, and the Library-Museum (17th–20th century paintings) in 1887. MOUNT FARON corniche overlooks Toulon and its dockyard, and there is a zoo and a memorial to the Normandy landings.

NAVAL CARVING
The building of naval ships was placed under state control in 1631. The same year also saw the emergence in royal dockyards of competent schools of naval sculpture. The first workshop in Toulon was directed by Leray. Projects had to be submitted to the king before they were executed, but under Colbert, creative work was centralized under the direction of Charles Lebrun, first painter to the king. Pierre Puget was appointed to take charge of all the workshops in 1668. This Baroque painter produced many sculptures and paintings in Toulon and the surrounding area. With him, creative naval design returned to Toulon despite the fact that Jean Berain, "designer-in-chief to the King", had been granted sole rights to design the exterior decoration of all ships. Two sculptors from Toulon, Toro and Lange, took over when Puget died in 1694, but new ideas about naval architecture and concerns for economy led to more sober ship decorations.

▲ CANNES
TOWARD BIOT

1 CANNES LE SUQUET 2 CAP DE LA CROISETTE 3 ÎLE STE-MARGUERITE 4 ÎLE ST-HONORAT 5 FORT 6 FORTIFIED MONASTERY 7 ÎLE ST-FÉRÉOL

⏱ One day
🚶 6¼ miles

A FAMOUS PORT
The abundance of archeological material discovered on the Island of Ste-Marguerite bears testimony to the golden age once enjoyed by this port. Ste-Marguerite was situated within striking distance of all the trading-posts of Italy, Gaul, Spain, North Africa and the eastern Mediterranean basin.

EUCALYPTUS TREES
These trees originally came from Australia, and were introduced into France by Labillardière in 1792. The hard, rot-proof wood was used as building material and plywood, in the making of paper, and in the manufacture of industrial and pharmaceutical products.

The Fort on the Island of Ste-Marguerite by Ernest Buttura.

ÎLE STE-MARGUERITE

ROYAL FORT ★. The fortifications in the north of Ste-Marguerite still bear traces of the peoples that have inhabited the island; these have included the Spaniards and the armies of Austria and Piedmont. The original castle, built between 1624 and 1627 by Jean de Bellon, was altered by the Spaniards and became a state prison in 1685. However, it is to Vauban that we owe its latter-day appearance. The main entrance leads to the Bazaine Terrace from which there is a superb view over Cannes Bay. There is also an archeological site where a 1st-century town has been unearthed, together with a huge complex probably linked to the church. The main courtyard is lined with low houses, originally the barracks. The oldest part of the fort houses the MUSEUM OF THE SEA, founded in 1975, and divided a historical section that includes the state prisons, and collections of archeological items exhibited in the old Roman tanks. On the other side of the courtyard, the Spaniards' Well of 1635 leads to the central alley.

AN ISLAND FULL OF ENCHANTMENT ★. A path starts at the exit to the fort and goes all the way round Ste-Marguerite. The island's natural surroundings have been marvelously preserved. A walk through the Botanical Garden and past the cemetery takes the visitor to a beautiful forest of Aleppo pines. A line of giant eucalyptus trees in the center of the island leads to the only private property on Ste-Marguerite: this is the GREAT GARDEN, which is hidden by a wall behind which there is a fortified tower (1637). Just before Batéguier Point, the path forks and runs along the beaches and little creeks.

ÎLE DE ST-HONORAT ★

The Island of St-Honorat is smaller and further away from the coast than Ste-Marguerite and belongs to a monastic community.

ST-HONORAT AND WESTERN SPIRITUALITY.

Saint Honorat settled on this island after living as a hermit in the Estérel Massif for many years. His fame soon attracted numerous disciples, and by the 6th century, Lérins was the most famous monastery in Christianity. In 1791 it was dissolved by Revolutionaries, the community was dispersed and the island sold by auction. In 1869, St-Honorat was once again inhabited by monks, this time Cistercians. Lérins Abbey is now a Benedictine community and continues to attract large numbers of visitors.

ABBAYE DE LÉRINS. Lérins was rebuilt in 1869, and the cloister, the chapter house and the refectory are the only parts that have survived from the Middle Ages. The chapter house, so called because a chapter of the Rule of Saint Benedict is read there every day, is where all the monastic ceremonies take place. Of the various buildings used by the monks, only the fortified monastery, the museum and the church are open to the public. The CHURCH was constructed by Viollet-le-Duc on the site of an ancient shrine, but all that remains is the 10th-century Chapel of the Dead which can still be seen in the left of the church. The steles and pagan sarcophagi in the MUSEUM recall life in the period before Honorat's arrival; the museum also contains remains of stone artefacts and superb polychrome wood statuary from the former abbey.

A FORTIFIED MONASTERY ★. This tower was started by Aldebert II in 1073 and completed in 1215, and was where the monks used to take refuge from the murderous raids that the island was frequently subjected to. The monks came to live here at the beginning of the 15th century when the island was occupied by the Genoese. At that time, the tower contained all the different areas that make up an abbey, except that they were very small and arranged vertically. The first floor had no bays so as to deter attackers from entering. The stairway on the second level which connects the two cloister galleries has sixty-two steps; traditionally, this represents the Sixty-two Articles of the monastic Rule of Saint Benedict. It leads to the Ste-Croix Chapel which still has its original vaulting where the remains of Saint Honorat are kept.

THE CLOISTER
The first floor of the monastery is a central courtyard surrounded by a Gothic cloister on two levels including rooms including the chapter house, the kitchen, the dormitory and the refectory.

273

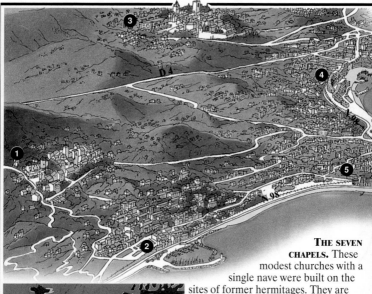

1 VALLAURIS
2 GOLFE-JUAN
3 BIOT
4 MARINA BAIE DES ANGES
5 JUAN-LES-PINS
6 ANTIBES

THE SEVEN CHAPELS. These modest churches with a single nave were built on the sites of former hermitages. They are located in different parts of the island.

VALLAURIS

LINOCUT BY PABLO PICASSO, 1959
This design is cut in relief on linoleum, rubber and plastic; the technique is similar to that employed on wood split with the grain.

A TOWN OF POTTERS
The shops in Rue Hoche are a reminder that it was the excellent quality of the local soil that enabled Vallauris to develop its traditional skills in pottery.

A TOWN RISES FROM THE ASHES. Around 1138, a new village was born in the vicinity of Saint Honorat's retreat, on land which had been the property of Lérins Abbey since 1038. However, it was completely destroyed during the succession of plagues, wars and famines that marked the 14th century, and it was not until 1500 that, at the suggestion of Rainier Lascaris, the area was repopulated by seventy Italian families. The monks then had a village built in the Romanesque style; it was provided with fortifications, but these have now disappeared.

THE CASTLE. This Renaissance structure was built over the ruins of the prior's first house, where he lived until 1787; only the 12th-century Chapel of Ste-Anne survives. The castle became a national museum in 1955 when Picasso presented his composition *War and Peace* to the municipality. This consists of two huge plywood panels in oils executed between

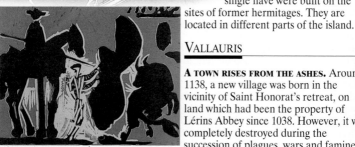

1952 and 1959; they are now in the chapel. The rest of the museum is devoted to pottery. In addition to pieces made by Picasso in the Madoura workshops, there is a rare collection of pottery from the Pre-Colombian era or preceding the arrival of the explorer Hernán Cortés; and a selection of tin-glazed ceramics made in Vallauris and Golfe-Juan between 1870 and 1930. The third floor displays paintings by Alberto Magnelli (1888–1971).

SKILLED POTTERS. The craft of pottery had been encouraged by the Lérins monks since the 11th century, but interest was further stimulated when Italian potters

🕓 Two days
🚐 19 miles

NAPOLEON I AT GOLFE-JUAN
Napoleon abdicated at Fontainebleau on April 6, 1814. The following year, on his return from the island

arrived in 1501. Vallauris production concentrated on kitchen utensils until the end of the 18th century. Picasso produced *The Little Faun* here in 1946 and later invited Cocteau, Miró, Léger and Lurçat to join him. Since 1966, the village has hosted an international biennial exhibition of pottery. The MUSÉE PRIVÉ in Rue Sicard has an exhibition of pottery techniques.

JUAN-LES-PINS

A SEASIDE RESORT IN A PINE FOREST. Juan-les-Pins, the luxury district of Antibes, was given a key role when the municipality decided to build a tourist resort on the site of Le Lauvert (*lac vert* – green lake). It is likely that this vast lagoon, supplied with water by two rivers, was originally an ancient Ligurian port enveloped by swamps in the Middle Ages; that would have been how it acquired its Provençal name of *Gou Jouan Pourri*, which is the origin of its modern name, Juan-les-Pins. There are still pine trees around the casino and the Palais des Congrès, and for centuries there were fishermen's huts clustered round the Pine Fountain (Fontaine du Pin) near the St-Barthélemy Chapel. When the seaside resort opened up in 1882, these memories of the past were rapidly swept aside. The reputation of Juan-les-Pins was made in the years prior to World War Two when the town was written about by Frank Jay Gould and F. Scott Fitzgerald. After that, it continued to expand and the area between it and Antibes was rapidly developed.

INTERNATIONAL JAZZ FESTIVAL. The open-air arena in the Frank-Jay-Gould Pinède (pine forest) is one of the better-known concert venues; every July, jazz lovers converge for a festival founded in 1960 by Jacques Hebey and Jacques Souplet. It was the very first of its kind. Some of the biggest names in jazz, including Armstrong, Hampton, Gillespie, Coltrane and Ray Charles, have performed here. Sydney Bechet, a local by adoption, married Elizabeth Ziegler in Antibes in 1951.

of Elba, he landed at Golfe-Juan and tried to overturn the monarchy of Louis XVIII. So as to evade the troops based in Marseilles, Napoleon decided to reach Grenoble from Grasse by crossing the Alps via Digne and Sisteron.

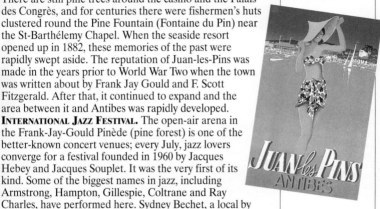

JUAN les PINS
ANTIBES

MUSIC AT JUAN-LES-PINS
The famous tenor sax player Sonny Rollins in concert at the "Pinède de Juan" 1990 as part of the 30th International Jazz Festival at Antibes-Juan-les-Pins. The celebrated "Parade du Jazz" takes place along the ramparts, without doubt the origin of the title of the celebrated "In the Streets of Antibes".

A MEETING PLACE FOR AMERICANS
The Villa Fiamma, which is situated between the roads to Mougins and Nielles, still echoes with the memories of its celebrated guests, the writers of the Lost Generation including Hemingway, F. Scott Fitzgerald, Gertrude Stein and Alice Toklas, Dorothy Parker and John Dos Passos. In 1926, Fitzgerald moved to the Villa St-Louis (now the Hôtel Belles-Rives), a vast mansion with its own private beach near the Juan-les-Pins casino.

A bust of Bechet sculpted by Abel Chrétien is on display in the Pinède.

CAP D'ANTIBES

The Cap was a place of worship for thousands of years, but was also an important military rallying and observation point. A watchtower was built there in the 11th century to match those at Antibes and St-Honorat.

SEASIDE ROUTE. The coast road is one of the most beautiful in the region, whether it is traveled on foot or by car. Juan-les-Pins is sheltered by magnificent parasol pines, but at Cap d'Antibes it is palm trees and Aleppo pines that are most in evidence around the villas and by the sea. A beautiful path has been laid out the length of this wild, storm-lashed coast: this is the Sentier Tirepoil (Tirepoil Path) ★ which is signposted from the back of Michel beach; the walk takes a good half-hour.

EDEN ROC. Cap d'Antibes was made fashionable by Sir James Close, a rich English banker, in November 1861, and others followed him and built themselves beautiful homes there. Later, Hippolyte de Villemessant, the founder and director of *Le Figaro* newspaper, and Adolphe d'Ennery, author of *The Two Orphans*, founded the VILLA SOLEIL as a home for artists in straitened circumstances. Later, it was turned into a luxury hotel, the Eden Roc, which opened in 1870 but was abandoned six months later because of the Franco-Prussian War. In 1889, a young hotelier, Antoine Sella, converted it to the famous

Hôtel du Cap later described by F. Scott Fitzgerald in *Tender Is the Night*.

EILEN ROC. This superb villa, in the Palladian style and commissioned by Charles Garnier, is in Avenue Helen-Beaumont in the middle of a luxurious park. Its name is an anagram of Cornélie, the companion of the owner, a former governor of the Dutch Indies. The park was entirely redesigned in 1927. The last owner, a rich American by the name of Helen Beaumont, presented the villa to the municipality of Antibes which now opens the building to the public on certain days.

NOTRE-DAME-DE-LA-GAROUPE. The two adjoining chapels belonged to a building constructed in the 16th century by Cordeliers. The chapel on the left contains two wooden statues: a black Virgin, Notre-Dame de la Garde, and Our Lady of the Safe Haven (Notre-Dame de Bon-Port), the protector and guide of seafarers. The walls are covered with 16th–20th-century ex-votos, and the church offers a view of the entire coast.

THURET GARDEN. The eminent algologist and botanist Gustave Thuret settled in Cap d'Antibes in 1857 and bought a 10-acre property. Here, he introduced exotic plants which ultimately transformed the landscape of the Côte d'Azur and established the excellence of Mediterranean horticulture. When Thuret died, he left the

The photographer Jacques-Henri Lartigues stayed at the Eden Roc regularly from 1920 onward. Here, he captured a moment of true happiness with his wife, Bibi, on the terrace of the Grand Hôtel.

ROSES BY THE THOUSAND
Certain rose varieties grown by the Meilland company have become famous all over the world; Baccara, Mme Meilland, Carina and Sonia are among the most popular and sought after. Selection is strict: no more than three varieties are chosen for sale because of the exceptional quality of their bloom, their resistance to disease and their capacity to adapt to different climates. Only when they fulfil all these criteria are they put on the market.

This photograph by Lartigue taken in August 1931 is a masterpiece of pure lines and contrasts of light and shade. It expresses with exceptional skill the indolence and elegance of a pre-war social élite.

land to the state so that his acclimatization trials of approximately eighty thousand plants could continue. Management of the garden was handed over to the Ministry of Agriculture and then to the INRA (Institut national de la recherche agronomique – National Institute for Agronomic Research).

MEILLAND CENTERS. Boulevard du Cap has recently changed its name to Boulevard Meilland. This is where the Meilland management and research centers were based until 1993 when they moved to Les Maures (Var). All new rose varieties were produced here by artificial hybridization.

ANTIBES

A GRECO-ROMAN CITY. After founding Massalia (Marseilles) around 600 BC, the Greeks opened up trading posts the length and breadth of the Mediterranean, including one at Antipolis (Antibes). Antipolis was annexed by Rome in 43 BC, a Roman *municipium* was established, and the town was completely transformed. Christianity made its appearance in the 4th century, and a bishop was appointed in 442.

A BISHOPRIC FOR EIGHT HUNDRED YEARS. The Bishops of Antiboul, Antipolis' new name, ruled the city and province throughout the Middle Ages. The time of the Barbarians between the 6th and 10th centuries was dominated by massacres, destruction and pillaging, and the people gradually withdrew into the hinterland; by the 9th century, Antiboul had been totally abandoned. The town was inhabited again in the 10th century as soon as the Sacacens were driven out, and in the 11th century secular and religious powers were formally separated, with the bishop settling in Grasse where he resided until the Revolution.

A BISHOP'S CITY, THEN A ROYAL CITY. Aware that Pope Clement VII coveted Antibes, Mary of Anjou concluded an agreement with the Grimaldi brothers whereby they became the representatives of both the count of Provence and the pope. The Fort Carré (Square Fort), a gem of military architecture, and then the main wall and its bastions (razed to the ground in 1896), were built in the reign of Henry III. Henry IV acquired Antibes from the Grimaldis in 1608, and from that date onward the bishop's city became a royal city and, what is more, a fortified city of great importance.

THE RISE OF ANTIBES
In the 14th century, Antibes was simply a modest town with no more than five hundred inhabitants. From 1482 onward, it benefited from the economic recovery, and a lot of rebuilding was carried out during the reign of Francis I. By 1789, this fortified town had a population of almost five thousand. Thanks to tourism, the small town has now become a large city of 100,000 inhabitants.

Many alluring posters have advertised Antibes (as a summer and winter resort), the Cap and the sandy beach at Juan-les-Pins.

ANTIBES HARBOR
Top of the page: *View of Antibes Harbor* by Janet (1714–89). Below: Antibes' natural harbor and the ramparts of the Old Town by Ernest Buttura.

THE OLD TOWN

The Old Town incorporates both parts of the citadel: the upper town, which stands on the site of ancient Ligurian, Greek and Roman cities, and the lower town, which occupies ground close to the cathedral.

THE CASTLE. The PETITE PLACE (Small Square) opposite the castle was once encircled by

fortified buildings, although the only surviving ones date from the 15th and 16th centuries. The tower, which is 85-foot high, was made in the 11th century; it originally formed part of an observation system to ward off the Saracens. The fortress was abandoned during the Revolution and was later used as a hospital, barracks and museum; the arrival of Pablo Picasso in 1946 brought a change in its fortunes.

PICASSO MUSEUM ★. Picasso often spent time on the Côte d'Azur. He bought a house at Mougins and lived in several houses in Antibes as well as Juan-les-Pins and Cap d'Antibes. In 1946, the curator of Grimaldi Castle invited him to move there, and it was here that he executed twenty-six paintings and forty-three drawings and experimented with a wide range of artistic media. Today, the museum contains works which Picasso did while in Antibes, and others which have been purchased or donated; these include 150 ceramic objects made in the Vallauris kilns between 1947 and 1949, and works such as *Goat, Nude lying on a White Bed, Woman in an Armchair, Man Gobbling Sea Urchins* and *The Antinopolis Suite,* also known as *La Joie de Vivre*. Also included in the exhibition are works by Fernand Léger, Jean-Michel Atlan, Nicolas de Staël ● *106*, Modigliani, Francis Picabia, Alberto Magnelli, Max Ernst and Hans Hartung. The first floor is given over to objects from Antipolis' historic past.

THE CATHEDRAL. The original cathedral was built in the 10th century; it was destroyed in 1124 and rebuilt a year later. The choir and transept date from this period. The façade, presented to Antibes by Louis XV in 1751, has recently been restored. The superb oak doorway (1710) represents Saint

Sebastian, the patron saint of Antibes, and Saint Roch, a noted protector against the plague in those days. The transept contains a beautiful Baroque altar with swathed columns framing a magnificent *Nativity*. Above the altar, in the Corpus Domini Chapel, is one of the last paintings executed by Louis Bréa ★. This is the *Our Lady of the Rosary* (1515), a painting associated with the theme of Our Lady of Mercy: on one side is the Church led by the Pope; on the other are the Christians standing behind the Emperor of Germany. The central panel is surrounded by the fifteen Mysteries of the Rosary. The 18th-century organ case contains a magnificent instrument celebrated for its forty stops spread over three keyboards.

RAMPARTS. The houses in RUE DU BATEAU in the upper town have preserved their Greek and Roman foundations. At one end of this road is a Roman gate, PORTAIL DE L'ORME or ELM GATE, which was restored in the Middle Ages: its internal fortifications, massive walls and portcullis have survived. A tiny MUSEUM OF POPULAR ARTS AND TRADITIONS with

STATUES OF CHRIST IN THE CATHEDRAL
The Corpus Domini Chapel has a 5th-century altar and this superb, lifesize statue of a recumbent Christ made out of the wood of a lime tree.

Hidden during the Revolution and rediscovered in 1938, it has recently been restored. Another Christ of carved wood adorns the choir just above the altar; this statue is 4½ feet tall, and the date 1447 is engraved on one of its feet.

exhibits from the Antibes region has been recently opened in the tower inside the walls. It is in this part of the citadel that the best-preserved Romanesque walls are to be found. The TOURRAQUE is a huge round tower in the southern corner; it supports the ramparts, which are themselves protected by a barbican. There are no openings in the ramparts until PORTE DU RÉVÉLY which towers over PLACE AUDIBERTI, a square built on the site of the ancient port. RAMPE DES SALEURS (Road of the Dry-curers) is a street on an incline that runs round the wall and leads up to the covered way. It was in this district in ancient times that fishermen produced their fish and condiment preserves, a specialty of Antipolis.

THE SEASIDE

A BEACH AND YACHTING HARBOR. La Gravette beach extends as far as the edge of the Old Town. The house where Nicolas de Staël (1914–55) lived and died ★ *106* is on the corner of the sea front and Rampe des Saleurs. Vauban's PORTE MARINE (Sea Gate) is the entrance to the marina which replaced the former commercial port in 1970. Port Vauban has now been altered and enlarged, and is one of the leading boating harbors in the Mediterranean; thanks to the Arcade de la Marine, it is an unusually tranquil spot.

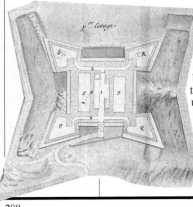

FORT CARRÉ. The Square Fort was built on the rock where the Temple of Mercury stood before being replaced by the Chapel of St-Laurent; the chapel was turned into a defense tower in the 16th century. It is possible to go round the Square Fort along the sea coast. Four

bastions were added to the fort in 1565; they were called Corsica, France, Antibes and Nice after the places they were intended to protect. The square tower was completed fifteen years later. In the 17th century, Vauban planned to turn it into an island and then to extend the fortifications as far as the whole town, but the idea was abandoned because of lack of money. The fort ceased to have any military role in 1870, and it was not restored until 1967.

Antibes. The Artist out Riding With His Son, J. L. E. Messonier, 1868.

TOWN CENTER

PEYNET MUSEUM. Raymond Peynet lived in Antibes from 1978, and left the town a number of his drawings and watercolors. His creation of two lovers sitting in front of a bandstand in Valence dates from 1942.

BASTION ST-ANDRÉ. Built in 1682 by the engineer Niquet, this bastion is near Square Albert-I and is half surrounded by water. It was sufficiently important for a garrison to be permanently based there and a powder magazine built on the hill nearby. The fort's huge stone roof also collected rainwater and poured it into an underground tank. The bakery and a device for heating cannonballs are still in place, and it has housed a small ARCHEOLOGICAL MUSEUM since 1963.

OLD SAFRANIER
The walls of this charming quarter of Old Antibes are covered with geraniums, bougainvillaea and plumbago.

SAFRANIER DISTRICT ★

Near the first bend in the ramparts is an opening that formed a link between the sea and the shallows behind the *gendarmerie* (police station); this pool also served as a small fishing port. It is now dried up and constitutes the center of Safranier, a medieval district approached through the marshes and overlooked by the Rocher du Castelet. Safranier became a free commune in 1966, and now has its own mayor, council and rural police force. Access is along RUE DU BAS-CASTELET, a street consisting of tiny stairways.

BIOT ★

FERNAND-LÉGER NATIONAL MUSEUM. Called the "Cathedral of Modern Art", this museum was designed to exhibit the work of Fernand Léger (1881–1955), and was opened in 1960. In 1967, his wife gave 348 of his original works to the French government, and the museum thereupon became a National Museum. This breathtaking exhibition is dominated by two major works: one is an enormous mosaic on the southern façade covering an area of almost 5,382 square feet and characterized by the vivid coloring which Léger so loved; the other is an exceptionally thick stained-glass window covering 538 square feet. Léger's intellectual journeys are traced in many drawings, studies and oil paintings including *The 14th of July*, *The Acrobats*, *The Cyclists* and *The Building Workers*.
THE CHURCH. This is accessible from Place des Arcades, a

SOPHIA-ANTIPOLIS
Place Sophia-Lafitte is in the center of this 6,000-acre business park, opened in April 1972. The park is host to research bodies, the head offices of companies involved in advanced technology and continuing education institutes. Most of the buildings are located in the commune of Valbonne, and are surrounded by a forest that includes the 1,055-acre Valmasque Park.

▲ CANNES TOWARD BIOT

Fernand-Léger
Museum, in Biot.

The Great Parade
painted in 1953 by
Fernand Léger
(1881–1955).

CRAFT TRADITION
The Briot glassworks
was built in 1956
below the village in
La Brague Valley. It
is possible to visit the
works and watch glass
being worked, blown,
cut and sculpted in
traditional ways.

square notable for its arches and lovely dissimilar ogives dating from the 13th and 14th centuries. The gate (1638) depicts Mary Magdalen, the town's patron saint. This new church was built with materials from the Templars' church pulled down in 1367. It also has two very beautiful late 15th-century reredoses at the end of the nave. The first, by an anonymous artist, is the *Ecce Homo* Reredos, and the predellas have representations of *The Scourging at the Pillar*, *The Crowning with Thorns* and, in the middle, *The Resurrection*. The second is the Virgin of the Rosary Reredos attributed to Louis Bréa whose theme is the Virgin of Mercy.

PLACE DES PÉNITENTS-NOIRS. The tower that belonged to the chapel can still be seen from the square; it is triangular and is covered with glazed tiles. The MUNICIPAL MUSEUM contains pieces of pottery and archeological objects.

POTTERY. The Ligurians who repopulated the village in the 15th century were exceptionally gifted at making objects of glazed terracotta, but Biot's golden age of pottery was during the 18th century when the village had no fewer than thirty-two kilns; at this time, Biot's influence spread as far afield as Genoa. Decline set in shortly before the Revolution and accelerated during the 19th century, and by 1918 there was only one kiln left. The fashion for rustic-style decoration has led to a revival of the industry.

282

NICE

1 IMMEUBLE DE LA COURONNE
2 VILLA HUOVILA
3 PALAIS DE L'AGRICULTURE
4 CHÉRET MUSEUM
5 CENTRE UNIVERSITAIRE MÉDITERRANÉEN
6 IMMEUBLE GLORIA-MANSIONS
7 HÔTEL NEGRESCO
8 MASSÉNA MUSEUM
9 PALAIS DE LA MÉDITERRANÉE
10 PROMENADE DES ANGLAIS

🕐 Three days

A MUCH-COVETED CITY
When the French and Turks laid siege to the city in 1538, a local washerwoman called Catherine Ségurane

distinguished herself by stealing their standard. The enemy laid waste the lower town, but the castle held out. The French returned in 1691 and again in 1706, this time taking the citadel. Louis XIV had the castle pulled down and Nice lost its military role.

HISTORY

ANCIENT NICE. There is evidence in both the encampment at Terra Amata and the Lazaret Grotto of there having been human habitation in these parts as long ago as 400,000 BC. The Ligurians who came much later were themselves colonized in the 5th century BC by the Phocaeans of Marseilles who were in the process of setting up a trading post called Nicaea. The Romans were frequently called upon by Massalia for assistance and finally, around the year 14 BC, they overwhelmed the local populations and settled in Cemenelum (Cimiez). Little is known about the local origins of Christianity, but there were certainly archbishoprics in neighboring Nicaea and Cemelenum.

UNDER CONTINUOUS ATTACK. The city suffered from Saracen raids until William the Liberator, Count of Provence, put a stop to their incursions in 974. By the 12th century, Nice was an autonomous urban republic administered by elected consuls, and had attracted the interest of Genoa and the counts of Provence. When the Provençal Raymond Berenger II conquered Nice in 1229, he initiated an era of peace that was to last a century. This was followed by a period of strife involving political in-fighting, the plague and devastation caused by bands of mercenaries. In 1388 Amedeus II of Savoy persuaded Nice to sign a treaty whereby for five hundred years it would form part of what was to become the Kingdom of Piedmont-Sardinia. Nice provided Savoy with its sole outlet to the sea, and soon became a prosperous fortified town at the very center of transalpine trade. In the 17th century, many Baroque-style religious buildings were built.

IMPACT OF THE REVOLUTION. The town was invaded by French troops in September 1792, and by the following year they had the county under their control. The local bourgeoisie supported the French, but the peasantry were weary of requisitions and conscription and put up a stout resistance. As time went by, the people of Nice became exhausted by the incessant wars,

12 ALBERT I GARDEN
12 OPERA HOUSE
13 QUAI DES ÉTATS-UNIS
14 LES PONCHETTES
15 MISÉRICORDE CHAPEL
16 CATHEDRAL OF STE-RÉPARATE
17 COURS SALEYA
18 CEMETERY
19 PLACE GARIBALDI
20 CASTLE
21 MONUMENT TO THE DEAD
22 CHURCH OF NOTRE-DAME
23 PORT

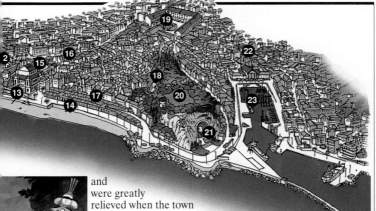

and were greatly relieved when the town was returned to the King of Sardinia in 1814. Around that time tourism was beginning to establish itself as the English took to spending their holidays on the Mediterranean coast. **NICE UNDER FRENCH CONTROL.** Later on, the town of Nice was the subject of an accord whereby the King of Piedmont-Sardinia expressed his gratitude to Napoleon III for the latter's assistance in achieving Italian unity. As many as 84 percent of the people of Nice voted to go over to France. The population grew in the early years of the 19th century, further swollen by Italian immigration. Today, there are major industries established at Sophia-Antipolis, the passenger port is the biggest in France, and the airport is the most important port of entry in southern Europe.

HEROES
The city's heroes include Giuseppe Garibaldi, who fought for France in 1870–1, and André Masséna, Marshal of France and dubbed by Napoleon the "darling child of victory".

COURS SALEYA

The origins of the Cours Saleya go back to the reconstruction of the "Marine Ramparts" in the 16th century. A large amount of urban space was opened up, and it was only toward the end of the 18th century that the area began to look as it does today.
PALAIS DE LA PRÉFECTURE. Completed in 1613, this palace was the property of the dukes of Savoy and the kings of Sardinia, and until the 17th century it was inhabited by the dynasty's sovereigns whenever they were in Nice. Only the main staircase remains of the restoration work carried out by Charles Félix in 1825. The façade was built in 1907 and includes a well-balanced double colonnade, while the décor ranks with the most ostentatious splendors of the Belle Époque.
MISÉRICORDE CHAPEL ★. This church is the work of Bernardo Vittorio Vittone, an 18th-century Italian architect and late exponent of the Piedmontese Baroque. The spectacular

COURS SALEYA
This wide street is a favorite meeting place, and the site of the earliest carnival processions.

The unusual, rectangular nave is similar to th
Roman version built by Da Vignola. It is no
rather outshone by the elaborate decoration (
pillars and walls clad with false marble
medallions, cartouches and cherub

interior architecture includes a central
ellipsoidal section surrounded by circular
apsidioles surmounted by tribunes, and the
imaginative use of curves and space is
enhanced by decoration including gilding,
friezes and polychrome designs. Important
works of art on display in the sacristy
include two representations of the *Virgin
of Mercy*, one signed by Jean Miralhet
(1430), the other attributed to Louis Bréa.

A PROFUSION OF BAROQUE STYLES

There are at least ten religious buildings
dating from the 17th century and hidden
away in the city's maze of stairways and
back streets. They point up the spiritual
revival of the century as did the marked
growth in the number of convents, monasteries and lay
confraternities. Nice benefited from the prodigality of the
dukes of Savoy for many years. Local
architecture was influenced by artistic trends
from the other side of the Alps: these
included Roman, and then Piedmontese,
fashions in religious architecture, and
Genoese styles in civil constructions.
CHURCH OF THE ANNUNCIATION.
This church is better known these
days as the Church of Ste-Rita.
This Benedictine priory is also
one of the oldest churches in
Nice. The Carmelites
acquired the church in 1555
and enlarged the building later.
The chapel has been restored to
its former Baroque glory.
CATHEDRAL OF STE-RÉPARATE ★.
This is one of Nice's finest
examples of early Roman
Baroque of the 17th century.

WONDERFUL DECORATION
The St-Sacrement
Chapel in the north
transept of the
Cathedral of Ste-
Réparate is the
church's crowning
glory. It was
decorated in 1707:
the altar with its large
reredos influenced
by the style of
Bernini is
dominated by
wreathed
columns made
of marble.

PLACE GARIBALDI
This square is lined with houses boasting vaulted porticos, and façades originally adorned by window frames with trompe l'oeil decoration.

St-Réparate is dedicated to a young woman martyr from Palestine whose body is said to have been miraculously transported to Nice by sea; the church once belonged to the Abbaye de St-Pons before it was enlarged and turned into a cathedral five hundred hundred years later. The plans were supplied in 1650 by André Guibert, a local architect, but the clocktower was not built until 1757 and the façade was not completed until the following century. The cathedral has retained most of its original décor including the stucco work on the arches by the Lombard Pietro Riva, the entablature in the nave and the pendentives in the choir and the cupola.

PALAIS LASCARIS ★. This aristocratic residence was built for Jean-Baptiste Lascaris-Vintimille, the duke of Savoy's brigadier, and later inhabited by the counts of Peille; it was

then occupied by the military during the French Revolution before being sold in 1802 as the possession of an emigrant who had fled the Revolution. The building was then turned into a block of flats, and it had fallen into serious disrepair when it was bought by the municipality in 1942. Now restored, it has all the trappings of an affluent residence. The apartments consist of three sitting-rooms with painted ceilings, and the doors are curiously hung on asymmetrical split hinges. The decoration in the ceremonial chamber consists largely of atlantes, caryatids and putti executed around 1700. Three rooms on the second floor are given over to regional ethnography, while the first floor contains an 18th-century pharmacy. Close to the exit, the STE-CROIX CHAPEL has a Baroque façade, and its pediment has a pelican feeding its young; this is the emblem of the White Penitents ● 72.

PLACE ST-FRANÇOIS ★. Although this square is famous for its fish market, it was of little real importance until 1580 when the PALAIS COMMUNAL was built opposite the church. This building's massive yet compact structure is similar to that of Genoese palaces of the 16th century. Only the façade was

redesigned in 1758 by a pupil of Filippo Juvara. **PLACE GARIBALDI.** This royal square, a true masterpiece of urban design, stands at the boundary between the medieval town and the new districts; work was started on it between 1782 and 1784. On the south side, Spinelli's Chapel of St-Sépulchre contains Louis-Michel Van Loo's remarkable painting of *The Assumption of the Virgin*.

ELABORATE FAÇADES
The typically Piedmontese rigor of the façades of the council offices (above) is tempered by emblematic figures and grotesque masks inspired by Ligurian styles. The ground floor is separated from the two other stories by a broad string-course.

The façade of the Palais Lascaris (above) is articulated by projecting balconies supported by carved consoles. The staircase (left) is in a traditional local style and opens onto the courtyard; it is decorated with marble statues in niches adorned with rocaille stucco.

Below: The Hôtel
Atlantique.

MODERN ART

The museum is
devoted to
contemporary art,
and particularly to
the Nice School. The
oldest paintings date
from the 1950's. A

parallel has been
established between
the European New
Realists like Yves
Klein, Martial Raysse
(opposite: *Portrait of
France*), Jean
Tinguely and Niki de
Saint-Phalle, and
American pop art as
represented by Roy
Lichtenstein, Andy
Warhol and George
Segal. The museum
also includes
representatives of
abstract styles like
Morris Louis and
Frank Stella and the
minimalists Sol Le
Witt and Richard
Stella. The local
"Supports-Surfaces"
movement is also
given some
prominence.

THE PAILLON

This coastal river, which at one time used to overflow and
cause widespread destruction, has been made to run
underground in Nice itself and is covered by a large parking
lot and the main bus station, beyond the PALAIS DES
EXPOSITIONS, an enormous edifice built in the 1950's.

NOTRE-DAME-AUXILIATRICE ★. Made entirely of reinforced
concrete, this church is typical of religious art of the 1930's
and was designed by the architects Fèbvre and Deporta. The
interior is frescoed in predominantly blue and yellow tones,
and includes a cruciform ceiling.

ACROPOLIS. This colossal monumental building was
constructed in 1984 in Boulevard Risso, its concrete surface
resting on arches spanning the Paillon. The architects
Georges Buzzi, Pierre Bernasconi and Pierre Baptiste, were
nicknamed "The 3 Bs". The whole building consists of the
PALAIS DES CONGRÈS and the AUDITORIUM, separated by the
AGORA. The floors of the Agora are ornamented by various
works of art: sculptures such as César's *The Thumb* and Paul
Belmondo's *The Conqueror*; paintings by Vasarely (*Gestalt*)
and Lenzi (*Retro-nostalgia*); and tapestries by Raymond
Moretti.

MUSEUM OF MODERN AND CONTEMPORARY ART ★. The four
towers linked by footbridges and the alternating blind and
transparent walls give this museum, which opened in 1990, a
curiously solid yet floating appearance. It is the work of the
architect Yves Bayard. One level is reserved for permanent
collections and another for temporary exhibitions. It also
contains Nice's new theater: like the museum, this octagonal
building is covered with slabs of gray-blue Carrara marble
which get lighter in color nearer the top.

LYCÉE MASSÉNA. This was an Augustinian monastery before
the Revolution, but under the Empire, and with the assistance
of André Masséna, Duke of Rivoli, it was turned into a boys'
school. The Jesuits took over in 1818, but King Charles Albert
removed them in 1848. The building then became the *Collegio
nazionale*, and was described as a "lycée" when the town was
handed over to France. The school's present appearance owes
much to the architect Henri Ebrard, who enlarged it and
restored it in the neoclassical manner. On the left-hand side is
a large sundial surmounted by a belltower with a clock.

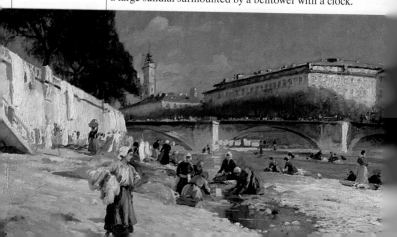

APOLLINAIRE AT THE LYCÉE MASSÉNA
After settling in Monaco with his mother in 1885,
the poet Guillaume Apollinaire was first a pupil at
the Collège St-Charles; he then went to Cannes,
and finally to Nice where he studied rhetoric,
passing the written examination and failing the oral.

ESPACE MASSÉNA. In 1835, the architect Vernie designed this square with porticos and two large buildings decorated with eight pilasters of a composite order. The buildings were eventually constructed in 1852, the year in which the square took the name of Masséna; its tall fountains, added in 1983, give it a very modern appearance. Rue Masséna and Rue de France offer

delightful walks in the midst of this lively pedestrian zone.

AVENUE THIERS

This busy, popular main road is notable for several interesting buildings. The HÔTEL CECIL, built in 1899 by Guiraudon, was the first house in Nice to have a corner rotunda with a cupola; the idea was spectacularly taken up by the Ruhl at the Negresco a few years later.

THE RAILWAY STATION. One of the first demands that the people of Nice made when their city passed over to France was for an extension of the railway line. The station has hardly changed since it was built in 1863 in Louis XIII style from plans by Bouchot.

POST OFFICE ★. The brick Art Deco façade is massive and somber in the manner of buildings in northern France; it took Nice by surprise, particularly in an area that has rather more in common with an operetta set. Three stylized glass designs by Guillaume Tronchet (1931) depict the work of the post office.

THE RUSSIANS IN NICE

THE RUSSIAN CHURCH ★ (6, Rue Longchamp). While the Empress Alexandra Feodorovna, widow of Nicholas I, was in Nice in 1857, she launched a subscription to build an Orthodox church; despite their numbers, the Russians did not have a place of worship in Nice. The original project was drawn up by a Russian architect, and this was reworked by a local artist by the name of Barraya who added a metal dome. The chapel is on the second floor. The first floor is taken up by a Russian bookshop.

CATHEDRAL OF ST-NICOLAS ★. This, the most beautiful Russian Orthodox building outside Russia, was built on the grounds of Villa Bermond, thanks to the generosity of the Empress Maria Feodorovna, the widow of Alexander III. It was in this house Alexander II's eldest son, Nicholas, died in 1863. The cathedral's foundation stone was laid in 1903. The domes, surmounted by crosses, are covered in gold leaf.

CATHEDRAL OF ST-NICOLAS
The materials used in the construction include carefully chosen bricks from the Rhineland, and majolica and tiles from Florence.

THE PALLADIUM
This building (1928) is remarkable for its elegance and sense of grandeur, enhanced by balconies with repetitive rounded forms.

PLACE MASSÉNA
The large fountain with bronze sculptures was transferred in 1976. The statue of Apollo was removed. The restoration program based on a layout provided by Roger Seassel and sculptures by Jeanniot date from 1935. However, the inauguration did not take place until 1956.

THE CLOISTER
Once upon a time, the cloister incorporated
the monastery's kitchen garden and orchard.
Today, its wonderfully balanced design and
atmosphere of tranquility make it ideal for
spiritual retreats.

**"ABRAHAM AND THE
THREE ANGELS"**
This, the most
important collection
of Chagall's works on
permanent display in
a single place,
consists of a series of
seventeen large-
format paintings
inspired by Genesis,
Exodus and the Song
of Solomon. The
architect André
Hermant produced
an extremely
restrained design
using stone from La
Turbie (Alpes-
Maritimes), and the
building stands in a
garden planted with
Mediterranean flora.
Chagall himself did
an illustration of the
creation of the world
for the stained glass
in the concert hall
and the mosaic over
the ornamental pond.

"DEPOSITION"
Around 1515–20,
Louis Bréa adopted
the Renaissance
model of a unified
reredos: the side
bands were replaced
by two pillars, and the
whole retable was
surmounted by a
large entablature.
Here, the artist
expresses with dignity
and restraint the
intensity of the sacred
drama which the
Franciscans held so
dearly.

THE CARABACEL DISTRICT

At the end of the 18th century, what had once been a stone
quarry at the foot of the Cimiez Hill was turned into a
residential area for prominent residents of Nice. The British
followed their example in 1840 and settled there as well, away
from the crowds and the seaside. Magnificent hotels and
apartment blocks recall this golden age; they include the
Second Empire Hôtel Impérial and the Chamber of
Commerce, a neoclassical building whose interior is a fine
example of the virtuosity and eclecticism of local architecture.

BOULEVARD DE CIMIEZ

Nice's most celebrated hill beyond Carabacel derives its name
from Cemenelum, the ancient Roman township dating from
the 1st–5th centuries and the main town in the Augustan
province of Alpes-Maritimes. Until the 19th century, it was a
hill planted with olive trees. Its rapid urbanization typified the
entire Côte d'Azur after Nice passed to France in 1860 and

was the work of Henri Germain who, in
1880, bought some land and built the 65-
foot-wide Boulevard de Cimiez. Once
developed, the plots of land were sold to
companies and private individuals; no fewer
than nine large houses were built on them, an
indication of the affluence that characterized
the Belle Époque. In the years that followed
World War One, when many aristocratic
families lost their fortunes, the houses were
turned into flats.
THE HÔTEL-PALACE. This building is the best
example of the style promoted by Baron
Haussmann. It is also characteristic of
seaside architecture ● *100* with its large
balconies, loggias, and bow windows looking
out over the parks and the sea.

CHAGALL MUSEUM ★. The museum, also used for concerts, contains canvases, drawings and gouaches on religious themes donated by the artist himself.

ANCIENT HISTORY. The 3rd-century ROMAN BATHS are close to the AMPHITHEATER. They were arranged in two rows over 328 feet long, and the hydraulic system relied on impressive technical skills. An early Christian bishop's church consisting of a baptistery and a basilica are housed in the western section of the baths. The ARCHEOLOGICAL MUSEUM contains objects discovered in digs at Cimiez and underwater excavations in Golfe-Juan.

MATISSE MUSEUM ★. This museum is located in the 17th-century Genoese Villa Garin de Coconato, notable for its trompe l'œil façades. The painter's personal collection is now on display in a newly built wing; Matisse settled in Nice in 1917 and died there in 1954. The museum includes works from every period of his life, from his earliest paintings in the 1890's like *Still Life with Books* to gouaches such as *The Wave* and *Flowers and Fruit* which he did toward the end of his career.

CIMIEZ MONASTERY. When the Franciscans arrived in Cimiez in 1546, they built a small cloister and restored the existing church. The highly informative and interesting FRANCISCAN MUSEUM ★ contains an excellent history of Saint Francis, the Franciscans and the monastery. The CHAPEL ★ was originally built by Benedictine monks, and was replaced in 1450 by a church with a single nave; this was acquired by the Franciscans a hundred years later and became an important place of pilgrimage. The interior contains some magnificent reredoses including Louis Bréa's celebrated *Pietà* (1475), the artist's first known work, a *Crucifixion* and a *Deposition* by the same painter, possibly executed with the assistance of his brother, Antoine.

▲ NICE
SEASIDE

BRITISH PATRONAGE
The British were attracted by Nice's mild winters, and started going there as early as 1730. However, the pebble beach was the domain of the local fishermen, and this underlined the need for a promenade along the sea front. Rev. Lewis Way collected money from the English colony and had a 6½-foot-wide road built in 1832; it gave work to local peasants who were reduced to penury during the winter. Local people referred to it as the Camin dei Anglès, but it was officially named "Promenade des Anglais" in 1844.

THE OLD PORT

The construction of the port commenced in 1749 under the direction of Devinanti; three hundred convicts dug up the harbor and built a track to Les Ponchettes and the road to Turin. Shortly before 1880, the port grew to its present size when the last houses separating the port from Place Île-de-Beauté were pulled down. The best spot for a view is the JETTY, much loved by Chekhov who frequently took walks along it. Nearby is the Monument to the Dead (1928) by the local architect Roger Seassol and the sculptor Jeanniot.
TERRA AMATA MUSEUM. This museum in Boulevard Carnot was opened following the unexpected discovery in 1966 of the 400,000-year-old remains of a camp of elephant hunters. This Quaternary-Era fossil beach at Terra Amata was discovered during excavations directed by Henry de Lumley; the museum also contains a reconstruction of the encampment.

AROUND THE CASTLE

The *castrum* was built in the 10th century, and was then fortified by the counts of Provence and later by the dukes of Savoy; in 1520, it was provided with a platform protected by three bastions. However, the north side remained vulnerable due to the hill's gentle incline so a citadel was constructed, but Louis XIV distrusted this redoubtable fortress and had it demolished.
TERRASSE FRÉDÉRIC-NIETZSCHE ★. This terrace has a beautiful view over the town and surrounding area. Excavations have uncovered Greek and Ligurian remains and the ancient foundations of the Cathedral of Ste-Marie.

QUAI DES ÉTATS-UNIS

LES PONCHETTES ★. Les Ponchettes (the word derives from *pounchetta*, pointed rocks of a kind much in evidence locally) is the name given to a section of the coastline that precedes the low houses with flat roofs. A second parallel row of identical houses lies behind them. The latter were built between 1750 and 1790 on the site of the old fortifications, while the sea-front houses date from the 19th century. Stairways lead up to the roofs where local people went for walks in the days before the coast was built up.

SEASIDE MUSEUM-GALLERIES ★. Parts of the old naval dockyard are still visible in the walls of these two galleries which house the paintings of Raoul Dufy (1877–1953) and the work of Gustav-Adolf Mossa (1883–1991), a local artist and curator of the Fine Arts Museum.

THE OPERA HOUSE. Italian opera companies were performing here as early as 1816, but the modern Opera House dates from 1885. It was built from plans by the city architect and subsequently altered by Charles Garnier. The PÂTISSERIE AUER in Rue St-François-de-Paule has been in the same family since 1820; it is worth a visit for its witty Rococo décor and the stained-glass windows in the tea room.

PROMENADE DES ANGLAIS

The Promenade's present appearance, with its dual carriageway and wide southern pavement, goes back to 1931. By contrast with the cramped, brightly colored Old Town, the Promenade represents a new, white town. The first villas, which stood in their own grounds, were replaced from 1840 onward by houses with smaller and smaller gardens. Blocks of flats became the order of the day round 1930.

PALAIS DE LA MÉDITERRANÉE. This magnificent casino has been closed since 1977 and, with finance supplied by the American Frank Jay Gould, is to be replaced by a conference and leisure center; only the officially classified façade will be preserved. The Palais de la Méditerranée was built from plans by Charles and Marcel Delmas and was opened in 1929; it was one of the most important buildings built in the Art Deco style.

CHÉRET MUSEUM ★. This museum occupies a private house in the Second Empire style, and contains works by local artists Van Loo, Fragonard, Van Dongen, Carpeaux and Dalou. Of particular interest are the slender, pastel silhouettes of "young women" by Jules Chéret, a high-spirited artist of the Belle Époque.

THE NEGRESCO
The idea for this hotel grew out of a meeting between Negresco, a Romanian from Bucharest who was to become restaurant manager at Nice's municipal casino, and the motor car manufacturer, Alexandre Darracq. It was Darracq who financed the construction which was carried out in 1913 by an architect who specialized in hotels and restaurants, Édouard Niermans. Niermans provided a colossal façade flanked by two enormous towers.

THE ART AND HISTORY MUSEUM ★ Built between 1898 and 1901, this museum is located inside the Palais Masséna. It houses the Chevalier de Cessole's library and works by pre-Renaissance artists from Nice and Italy.

293

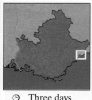

🕐 Three days
🚗 31 miles

HISTORY

Villefranche was handed over to Savoy in 1388. In 1557 Duke Emmanuel Philibert, fully aware of the harbor's strategic importance, undertook the construction of a formidable system of fortifications incorporating a citadel, Mount Alban and the Harbor Basin. The U.S. Mediterranean Fleet had quarters here from 1945 to 1962.

CHAPEL OF ST-PIERRE Cocteau took great pleasure in adding more and more references to the sea. The walls are covered with the mesh-work of a stylized fishing net and the two candelabra adorned with human faces are surmounted by a fork resembling a harpoon.

VILLEFRANCHE-SUR-MER ★

CHAPEL OF ST-PIERRE ★. Dating from the 14th century, this chapel was decorated by Cocteau in 1964 and presented to the Fishermen's Guild.

CITADEL OF ST-ELME. This well-renovated citadel covers an area of about seven acres, and is an excellent example of bastioned fortification of the second half of the 16th century. In order to avoid the damage occasionally caused by cast-iron cannon-balls, the medieval walls were replaced by bastioned fortifications that cushioned the shots. This discovery was completed by the adoption of a geometrical plan that left no blind spots and had curtain walls alternating with bastions, thereby facilitating cross-shooting. Today, the citadel encompasses the Town Hall, a museum and an auditorium, and a 1,200-seater open-air theater; some gardens have been laid out between the curtain walls. The ART AND HISTORY MUSEUM, which occupies several buildings that were once the barracks, has a number of varied collections. The most important of these is the VOLTI FOUNDATION which consists of bronzes, beaten leather, terracotta and original red-chalk drawings which trace the development of Volti himself, a local

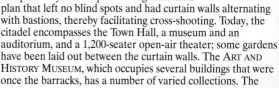

VILLEFRANCHE s MER
PORT DE TOURISME

artist who was a successor to Maillol; then there is the GOETZ-BOUMEESTER COLLECTION which provides an introduction to the work of these two artists, both of them friends of Picasso, Picabia and Miró, and of Hartung who lived at Villefranche; and finally, the ROUX COLLECTION which has a magnificent display of glazed ceramic figurines representing scenes of everyday life from the 11th to the 15th centuries.

MOUNT ALBAN ★. The FOREST on Mount Boron was substantially retimbered from 1860 onward, and is now a favorite area for walks. The elegant FORT is one of the Renaissance's best surviving examples of military architecture; it was turned into a type of fortress known locally as a *bastille* in the 18th century and, for all its shortcomings, maintained its military role until 1914. Around the fort is an unusual form of *garrigue* that consists of bush dotted with carob trees.

THE OLD TOWN
(Below: *View of Villefranche* by Guiaud, 1856.) The tiny squares and open spaces have been

tastefully renovated, and are perfect for gentle strolls; elsewhere, stairways and alleyways tumble down little gaps of light toward the port. The houses with their narrow entrances rest on vaulted cellars where oil and wine were once kept, and goats and sheep were given shelter.

BEAULIEU-SUR-MER ★

After a long wait, Beaulieu was connected to Nice by road in 1862. After that, it became a popular venue for rich winter tourists and numerous members of royal families.

VILLA KERYLOS ★. This old villa ▲ *298*, rebuilt between 1902 and 1908, is in Rue Gustave-Eiffel: Eiffel spent his winters here after 1895, devoting his time to meteorology, one of his favorite hobbies. The extraordinary project to build this house was the fruit of a meeting between a keen Hellenist, Théodore Reinach (1860–1928), and a young architect with experience of archeological digs, Emmanuel Pontremoli (1865–1956). Their aim was a building that combined, on the

OTEL MÉTROPOLE

295

FROM ONE CREEK TO THE NEXT
Unusually for the Côte d'Azur, it is possible to go all the way round the peninsula of Cap-Ferrat on foot (7 miles). The walk round Pointe St-Hospice, a detour lasting some forty-five minutes, starts off in the shade of

some very beautiful and windswept Aleppo pines; another path links Lilong Cove and Pointe de Passable (one hour). The limestone cliffs include sections of lunar landscape, and the small creeks beyond the lighthouse will tempt more experienced swimmers. The best way back to St-Jean is along the Chemin du Roy and past the Villa des Cèdres, a property that once belonged to Leopold II of Belgium; with twelve thousand species of exotic plants, the Villa des Cèdres contains one of the finest private botanical gardens in Europe. The animals in the nearby zoo can shade under the trees. Above: the harbor of St-Jean in the 19th century, before the age of tourism.

one hand, a grand residence incorporating the comforts considered essential in the Belle Époque and, on the other, a house which reflected day-to-day life in Ancient Greece. From the outside, Kerylos presents as an imposing white building surrounded by terraces adorned with colored pergolas; inside, the layout, the décor and the objects that make up the collections (tanagras, vases, oil lamps, bronzes, and red and black figures) recall Classical Greece.

A WALK. The most convenient route to St-Jean is along the coast path, the Promenade Maurice-Rouvier (20 mins).

ST-JEAN-CAP-FERRAT ★

HISTORY. Until 1880, St-Jean was a tiny fishing village. Then, in 1896, two financiers called Bloch and Peretmere developed the first plots of land, and some twenty villas sprang up in 1900. Leopold II of Belgium soon became the Cap's leading landowner, but the interwar period attracted new enthusiasts including the Duke of Connaught and Princess Helen of Serbia. World War Two put a stop to this period of hedonism, and on February 26, 1944 the whole population was evacuated and the peninsula mined by the Germans. The French navy liberated the town in August of the same year.

VILLA EPHRUSSI-ROTHSCHILD ★. Béatrice de Rothschild bought this property ▲ *298* in 1905, Aron Messiah having been responsible for designing this "tiny *palazzo* of Venetian inspiration" which included architectural styles from all over the world. The gardens are as numerous as they are varied; there are French, Spanish, Italian and Japanese gardens, lapidary and exotic gardens, and a newly replanted, semicircular rose garden.

CURIOSITIES OF CAP-FERRAT. Although Cap-Ferrat has magnificent villas that are invisible to the average passerby, the town has four pebble beaches, numerous creeks, a small picturesque harbor, seven miles of coastal paths, a delightful zoo and luxuriant vegetation. The St-Hospice Chapel was restored by the Duke of Savoy in 1655, and enlarged in 1778 and 1826. After the fort was pulled down, the nearby tower (1750) was built as a defense against pirate attacks.

ÈZE★

This village succeeded an earlier Ligurian township built on the Bastide Oppidum. We know from a magnificent silver patera in the British Museum that the inhabitants were trading with the Greeks as early as the 4th century BC. For reasons of security, the people took refuge on the rocky peak in the early Middle Ages, and in the 12th century surrounded themselves with ramparts; these were pulled down in 1706 on the orders of Louis XIV. Until the 1970's, the town grew citrus fruits and carnations; it now lives off tourism.

THE EXOTIC GARDEN. This garden, completed in 1950, contains a large number of rare species and a fine collection of succulents including cacti, aloes, agaves, torch-thistle and opuntia. There is a marvelous view from the castle ruins. More adventurous visitors will climb the steep CHEMIN FRÉDÉRIC-NIETZSCHE (one hour) and drop down toward Èze-sur-Mer on the other side. Climbing the hill by this path was very popular with Nietzsche himself.

HISTORY OF THE PRINCIPALITY OF MONACO

Monaco has been a flashpoint for French and Italian power struggles since antiquity. The Rock (Rocher) was originally part of the Roman Empire and then, during the 10th and

A PERCHED VILLAGE
Èze is like an eyrie suspended 1,280 feet above sea level. The village straddles the three Corniches, and is one of the most popular spots anywhere on the Côte d'Azur. Èze has been scrupulously restored, and has preserved its intersecting medieval alleys and aristocratic turreted houses in Place du Planet. Walkers will enjoy strolling dreamily along the terraces of the restaurants nestling in the ancient ramparts.

Beaulieu and St-Jean-Cap-Ferrat boast two magnificent villas, both of them survivors from a period when rich patrons could let their fantasies run away with them: Kerylos is the fruit of the research carried out by a fervent Hellenist; Villa Ephrussi-Rothschild is the whim of a collector of genius. These two "follies" have been bequeathed to the Institut de France. They are open to the public, and the refinement and splendor of the decorations and the grounds may now be appreciated by all.

THÉODORE REINACH

Reinach came from a banking family that had lived in Mainz. Reinach devoted his life to the study of Ancient Greece. An archeologist, papyrologist, epigraphist, philologist and numismatist, he was a man of many talents.

FRESCOS IN THE ANCIENT STYLE

The owners' rooms, that is to say the bedrooms, bathrooms and resting rooms, are on the first floor. The walls are painted with frescos of mythological subjects including the legend of Pelops, the founder of the Olympic Games, and the expedition of the Argonauts following the quest for the Golden Fleece. They were painted using the ancient processes of shellac and tempera on fresh mortar and on a coating of powdered marble.

During the digs at Delphi in 1893, Reinach deciphered and retranscribed the Hymns to Apollo, and asked the composer Gabriel Fauré to put them to music.

The furniture, which was designed by the cabinet-maker Bettenfeld, includes wonderfully balanced chairs, stools, couches with leather hangings, and three-legged tables. They are all made of the wood of fruit trees, and are pegged and inlaid with ivory, boxwood and ebony.

MEDITERRANEAN LAYOUT

The first floor is organized around an interi[or] courtyard known as the "peristyle", with reception rooms leading off it. These room[s] are the main drawing room (*andron*), the dining room (*triklinos*), a small drawing roo[m] (*oïkos*) and the library.

TOUR DE FORCE

Villa Ephrussi occupies seventeen acres. A large amount of land had to be excavated in the course of the construction. The house is surrounded by seven theme gardens. The parterres in the French style were designed to be an extension of the drawing room, while the gardens in foreign styles offer seclusion.

BÉATRICE EPHRUSSI
Her father, Antoine de Rothschild, was a director of the Bank of France.

A MUSEUM-VILLA

It was Béatrice Ephrussi's wish to bring all her acquisitions together in a museum that felt as if it was lived in. Her ambition was not fulfilled until after her death. She had a great love of 18th-century French art, and put together a magnificent collection of Sèvres and Vincennes porcelain, wainscoting in the Pompei style, and Gobelins tapestry.

AUTHENTIC AND IMITATION

The *triklinos*, where people ate their meals in recumbent positions, has a superb mosaic in polychrome marble. The paving stones and coffered ceilings adorned with gold leaf are copies of works on display on Delos and at Herculaneum.

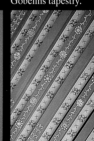

"MONACO TOWN"
This oil painting by Joseph Bressan (1732) used to hang in the Officers' Drawing Room in the Prince's Palace. The palace was first a fortress, then a medieval castle and finally a residence worthy of the Italian Renaissance.

A COUNTRY WITH TWO FACES
Monaco is the world's smallest sovereign state (373 acres), the Vatican City excepted,with the highest concentration of inhabitants to the square yard. It has a dual image; on the one hand, it is the city of gambling, millionaires and luxurious lifestyles, and on the other it is a major financial and industrial metropolis.

11th centuries, the Kingdom of Burgundy-Provence. At the beginning of the 13th century, strategic interest in this long-uninhabited spot eventually attracted the attention of Genoa, and Monaco's fate was thereafter closely linked to Genoese civil wars. In 1342, Charles Grimaldi was made Lord of Monaco, and in 1646 he bought the lordships of Roquebrune and Menton. In the 16th century, Monaco came under the protectorate of the great powers, who recognized her independence and did not impose vassalage: following a period under the protectorate of Spain (1525–1641), Monaco was under French protection from 1641 to 1814, then under Sardinian protection until 1860. Important changes in the life of the city took place with the opening up of facilities for gambling (outlawed in neighboring countries) in 1863,

the abolition of land tax and patents in 1869 and the building of a rail link with Nice in 1868. From 1949 onward, around the beginning of Prince Rainier III's reign, tax advantages proved attractive to foreign business. Since 1962, Monaco has had a hereditary and constitutional, but not parliamentary, monarchy, and although the Principality is a sovereign state, it still has special links with France. For example, French is the official state language, and the Monégasque franc has the same value as its French counterpart.

THE ROCK ★

LE PALAIS PRINCIER. Three crenelated towers remain of the 13th-century fortress. In the 16th century the All Saints Tower (Tour de Tous-les-Saints) and the Bastion de Serravalle were added to strengthen the castle. The Italian Renaissance, too, left its mark on the castle which

became a palace. The southern wing, known as the Wing of the Grand Apartments, was further embellished by the addition of the Hercules Gallery by the Milanese artist Domenico Gallo. A suite of drawing rooms, the Palatine Chapel at the far end of the Main Courtyard and the gate opening onto Place du Palais were built during the reign of Prince Honoré II. Albert I had the Pavillon de l'Horloge rebuilt and the present prince had new private apartments added in the southwest wing which had been destroyed after the 1789 Revolution.

TOUR OF THE CASTLE. The Grand Apartments are open to the public in summer. The first point of call is the superb Main Courtyard and its frescoed galleries. The Hercules Gallery is decorated with frescos attributed to Francesco Mazzuchelli (1573–1626) representing four mythological and legendary characters. The lunettes in the vaulting depict the birth, labors and death of Hercules; this decoration is attributed to a Genoese artist of the 17th century. The small Gallery of Mirrors leads to the Grand Apartments, whose charm is enhanced by extensive wainscoting, painted ceilings, portraits of ancestors and some beautiful pieces of furniture. The Louis XV Chamber, the York Chamber and the Yellow Room form the Royal Quarters built by Honoré II for his guests. The ceiling of the Throne Room, used for the swearing of oaths and the solemnization of marriages, is decorated with frescos by Orazio de Ferrari.

THE NAPOLEONIC MUSEUM. This museum on the first floor of the new wing of the palace houses a collection that includes the hat worn by Napoleon at Marengo. Pictures, maps, engravings and Monégasque stamps provide a quick summary of the Principality's history.

OLD MONACO. Five hundred people lived on the Rock in the Middle Ages, occupying a small area to the east of the square crossed by Rue Basse, Rue du Milieu and Rue des Briques. The houses, some of them adorned with a decorated lintel, followed an early ground plan imported from Genoa of a vaulted ground floor and a straight staircase to one side. The inhabited area ended to the east with the Church of St-Nicolas and cemetery. Beyond that were gardens which were formally laid out from the 16th century onward. The Miséricorde Church, built at the end of Rue Basse in 1646, was owned by the Black Penitents.

THE CATHEDRAL OF THE IMMACULATE CONCEPTION. The architect Lenormand used a layout based on Romanesque and Auvergne styles for this cathedral, and embellished it with characteristics of Provençal churches. All the members of the Monaco royal family are buried here. Particularly remarkable is the collection of reredoses attributed to the School of Bréa and distributed in the transepts and the ambulatory. There are two representations of the *Pietà*: the "White Penitents' Pietà" and the "Pietà of the Curé Teste". Three panels depicting Saint Roch, Saint James the Greater and Saint Lawrence, and three polyptychs are dedicated to Saint Nicholas, Sainte Dévote and Our Lady of the Rosary.

OCEANOGRAPHICAL MUSEUM. The creator of this temple to the sea, built between 1899 and 1910, was Albert I; as soon as it opened, he converted it into an annex of the Oceanographic Institute of Paris, which he had also founded.

Skeleton of a 65½-foot-long whale harpooned by Albert I.

CACTI
These plants often come from desert regions. During the rainy season, they accumulate the reserves of aqueous sap that they need to survive during dry periods. At night-time, the rocks release the heat that has been accumulated during the day.

SAINTE DÉVOTE
Louis Bréa worked in the County of Nice, Monaco and Liguria during the second half of the 15th century. A native of Nice, he shared with Lombard artists a solemn style enhanced by the use of gold, the softness of the relief work, the choice of intense colors and the range of white and grey. He borrowed from Flemish painters a smooth, luminous technique and a penchant for naturalism.

There are temporary exhibitions, permanent displays and film shows to entertain the visitor. The beautiful Hall of Applied Oceanography has maintained its old-fashioned appearance; here, old cases made of glass and glazed wood contain over ten thousand species of shellfish, pearls, mother-of-pearl, shells and coral. There is also a spectacular aquarium with almost five thousand fish in ninety tanks.

SALLE GARNIER
The use of gold and crimson is reminiscent of the Paris Opéra, but the Salle Garnier is much smaller. The Monte-Carlo Opera has been associated with some of the great performances of the 20th century through the involvement of one immensely talented man, Raoul Gunsbourg; after a period as director of the Tsar Nicholas II Theater, he was in charge of the Monte-Carlo Opera from 1892 to 1945. In 1911, he invited Diaghilev's Ballets russes to perform at the Salle Garnier; in 1926, they became the Ballets de Monte-Carlo.

THE CASINO ● 68
This museum to gambling is a magnificent tribute to Belle Époque architecture. It charms visitors and gamblers alike. Nothing has been moved in the Renaissance Room, the Europe Room (still lit by eight huge chandeliers of Bohemian crystal) or the private rooms with their mahogany wainscoting engraved in gold. The gambling still goes on: French, American and English roulette, baccarat, *trente-et-quarante*, blackjack and, since 1991, punto banco and pai gow poker.

THE CONDAMINE

Before 1860, this small, semicircular space occupying the end of the port was nothing but gardens and orchards. The part most appealing to tourists is where it opens onto the harbor at the Quai Albert-I. This is also where spectators congregate to watch the final stages of the Monte Carlo Rally and the entire Monaco Grand Prix.

JARDIN EXOTIQUE ★. This amazing garden of succulent plants ▲ *301* was started in 1913, but it was not opened until 1933. The natural arrangement of the rocks forms a cliff on which the plants are displayed, and the entire rocaille is accessible thanks to a series of ramps, stairways and tunnels. The garden is well protected from the wind by a crag called the Pic de la Tête-du-Chien, and is therefore ideal for cacti.

NICE TOWARD MENTON

THE "HIRONDELLE"
This two-hundred-ton schooner was Prince
Albert I's first study ship.

GROTTE DE L'OBSERVATOIRE ★. This
grotto, situated slightly below the Exotic
Garden, has displays of carved stone
tools, fossils and skeletons of animals
from both glacial and tropical regions. Most impressive are
the fantastic forms, such as concretions, draperies, columns
and stalagmites, that the water has fashioned out of the
limestone.
THE MUSEUM OF PREHISTORIC ANTHROPOLOGY. Founded by
Albert I in 1902, this museum soon became too small to
accommodate the results of research and was transferred to a
modern building near the Exotic Garden. Digs are carried out
in the museum, but the presentation of the exhibits is old-
fashioned and difficult for non-experts to follow.

MONTE CARLO

THE CASINO ★. The Casino, a survivor
from the Belle Époque, belongs to the
Société des bains de mer. This luxurious
building was completed in 1863 and
further decorated by the millionaire
François Blanc who, in 1863, acquired its
exclusive use for fifty years. A theater,
designed by Charles Garnier, the
architect of the Paris Opéra, was added
in 1879.
HÔTEL DE PARIS. Also a product of the
Belle Époque, this hotel was modeled on
the Grand Hôtel on Avenue des
Capucines in Paris and opened in
January 1864. Its huge success prompted
François Blanc to carry out the first of
the hotel's seven enlargements. The
famous cellars, hewn out of the rock,
contained twenty-five thousand bottles
(or ⅔ mile of cases) of vintage wine.

HÔTEL HERMITAGE. This hotel enjoyed
great popularity throughout the 19th century thanks to the
intimate charm of the décor and a rigorous policy of frequent
restoration. It also achieved success despite the oppressive
presence of its elder brother, the Hôtel de Paris. The
decoration of the façade and other parts has been influenced
by the Prince's Palace. This luxury hotel is neoclassical in
style, and has benefited from the attentions of many artists,
including Gustave Eiffel, who designed the glass roof of the
winter garden around a venerable palm tree.
NATIONAL MUSEUM OF MONACO. The collections of
mechanical and other toys belonging to Madeleine de Galéa
(1874–1956) are quite remarkable. One of the outstanding
exhibits, a beautiful crib containing over two hundred *santons*
● 70, is the work of Neapolitan artists of exceptional skill.

ROQUEBRUNE
The Provençal
character of this
village is accentuated
by the red tiles, the
old stones and the
slender cypress trees.
The huge castle and
the church with its
ocher façade are of
considerable
architectural interest.
LA TURBIE'S TROPHY
The "Trophy"
commemorates
Emperor Augustus'
victory over the
Ligurians. It dates
from 6–7 BC, but it
fell into disrepair
toward the end of the
Roman Empire, and
was turned into a
fortress in the Middle
Ages before being
pulled down in 1705.
No restoration work
was undertaken until
1929, when a
monument 105 feet
high was erected on
the original building's
base. The third floor
is set back and
supports a circular
peristyle of twenty-
four Doric columns
topped by a frieze of
metopes.

VILLA CYRNOS
This house was built in 1893 for the Empress Eugénie, a lady with a weakness for historical pastiche. The gallery-loggia is embellished with mosaics and paintings apparently influenced by the Italian Renaissance.

A WALK AROUND OLD MENTON
Menton's sparkling façades are a great attraction for visitors. Moreover, until the 19th century, the houses were neither roughcast nor painted, and it was therefore possible to see the various materials used in their construction – stone, bricks, pebbles, soil and amalgams all bound together by lime mortar. As the walls began to peel, the inhabitants decided to adopt the Italian system of painting their façades every color of the rainbow from pale yellow to deepest ocher.

CAP-MARTIN

Cap-Martin is an affluent area where enormous villas, lost in an oasis of greenery, have managed to escape the frenzy of the real-estate business. It is a place to discover on foot, since cars are forbidden in the vicinity of these luxury homes. During the Ancien Régime, Anthony I Grimaldi sometimes went hunting on the rocky promontory of Cap-Martin. In 1889, a British company laid out three roads and built the Grand Hôtel; affluent people from all over Europe started to come here on holiday. A Danish architect, Hans Georg Tersling, was responsible for most of the villas, largely neoclassical palaces surrounded by luxuriant gardens. A walk round Cap-Martin is a wonderful, peaceful experience and takes less than an hour. It is advisable to leave the car in Avenue Douine. The private villas clustered between Avenue de France and Avenue de l'Impératrice-Eugénie can only be seen from the alleyways.

HISTORY. Menton was founded on land owned by Italian lords living under the suzerainty of the Republic of Genoa. In 1346, Menton became the property of the Grimaldi family and remained so until 1848, the year in which the town rose up against its Monégasque rulers. Napoleon III bought the rights from the Prince on February 2, 1861 and, in a plebiscite, the inhabitants voted to become a part of France.

The first railway line built in 1884 brought many tourists ● 58, mostly English and Russian, who came in search of a cure for their tuberculosis. An earthquake on February 23, 1887, World War One and the Russian Revolution interrupted this period of prosperity. But the English returned and, between the two wars,

formed a large colony. After many years of cultivating olive trees and citrus fruit, Menton now grows flowers which are sold to the perfumeries of Grasse ▲ *228*; the town's true heritage lies in its marvelous gardens which were laid out in the last century and are still famous for their tropical plants.

THE BAROQUE DISTRICT ★

PARVIS ST-MICHEL ★. This square is the setting for the Menton Chamber Music Festival held here every summer. The ground is covered in a mosaic of black and white stones decorated with stylized "H"s and rounded forms; it suggests the Grimaldi coat of arms and the initials of Prince Honoré II, who had the square built in the 17th century.

CHURCH OF ST-MICHEL ★. The church was consecrated in 1675, but the campanile was not built until 1701; the façade was redone in the Baroque style in 1819. The central vault was decorated with trompe l'œil works by Cerruti-Maori after Murillo (*The Immaculate Conception*) and Raphael (*Saint Michael Slaying the Dragon*). At one time, there were hangings emphasizing the Baroque character of this church, but all that remains is some 18th-century amaranthine Genoese damask which is laid out every five years. The ceilings of the side chapels are also painted, while the choir, dominated by the organ case (1666), is noted for the St Michael Reredos (1565) by a local artist named Manchello.

CHAPEL OF THE IMMACULATE CONCEPTION. Built in 1687 by the Battuti Confraternity, the oldest confraternity of penitents in Menton, this church was restored in 1887. Cerruti-Maori did the frescos here as well; the marble mosaic reredos behind the high altar contains a statue of the Virgin.

THE LITTLE PORT DISTRICT

THE BASTION (JEAN COCTEAU MUSEUM) ★. Honoré II had this built in 1636 as part of the town's defenses. It became a granary in the 19th century and a prison during World War Two. It has housed the Jean Cocteau Museum since 1967.
THE MARKET ★. The market hall was built in 1896 on a part of the foreshore which served as the harbor. The décor of grotesques of glazed ceramics and of strange grimacing masks is most bizarre. There is a secondhand market every Friday in the small PLACE AUX HERBES nearby, and RUE ST-MICHEL, the town's main shopping street, is very popular with tourists.
PROMENADE DU SOLEIL. This avenue which runs along the sea front is very evocative of Menton's golden age and winter tourism. The Vendôme, Balmoral and Westminster Hotels are now generally used by members of *mutuelles* (friendly

societies), but they still convey an idea of the enormous palaces that once welcomed royalty and the famous personalities of the day. The Casino du Soleil is newer and is a great favorite with gamblers. It also hosts galas and concerts.

PAINTED FRIEZES
These friezes, which date from the years 1860–1930, illustrate a popular art form that was typical of Menton; they are also examples of a technique that came from Piedmont where zinc and paper stencils were used to reproduce motifs on walls. Most of these friezes were executed with colored pigments diluted in slaked lime; the technique is known as tempera.

Fresco in the Church of St-Michel by Cerruti-Maori.

DESIGNED FOR WAR, BUT NOW DEVOTED TO ART
Although Cocteau never saw his museum completed, everything in it is his, from the form of the stairway to the glass cases with wrought-iron ribs. The entrance is adorned with a mosaic of black and white stones; the floor is decorated with a salamander, the walls with pastels and a tapestry, *Judith and Holofernes* (1948). The *Innamorati* pastels, executed in 1957–8, are displayed on the second floor. In this series, Cocteau used thick chalks on colored paper, a technique much loved by Picasso.

THE CITY CENTER

THE BIOVÈS GARDENS. This delightful area full of palm trees, cycads and flowering parterres separates Avenue Verdun and Avenue Boyer. It is also the venue for the annual Fête du Citron (Lemon Festival) which has been held every February since 1934; this event uses one hundred and twenty tons of citrus fruit (grapefruit, sweet and Seville oranges, lemons and kumquats), and includes a procession of floats covered with fruit.

CERAMICS IN MENTON
Françoise Blanc opened a ceramics factory in Menton around 1870, and attracted the greatest ceramic artists of the day including Pierre Adrien Dalpayrat, the creator of Dalpayrat Red, Félix Tardieu, a specialist in the style of Bernard Palissy, and Léopold Magnat. They came to settle in Menton in 1880. Today, the Perret-Gentil family continues to produce dinner services decorated with oranges, lemons and olives.

LEMON CAPITAL
The micro-climate and the humidity have favored the growing of olive trees and citrus fruit ever since the 15th century. By the beginning of the 19th century, it constituted the town's basic economy. However, it gradually declined, due to bad weather and market conditions. Today, Mazet and Capra are the only two important producers of citrus fruit left.

PALAIS DE L'EUROPE. Built in 1908–9 by the Danish architect Georg Hans Terslin in the style of Charles Garnier, this was the first big casino in Menton. It now houses the tourist office and the library; the theater reopened its doors in 1974.

NEAR THE TOWN HALL

THE COUNCIL OFFICES IN MENTON. These offices were built in the middle of the 19th century by Baron Ardoïno, but were used for gambling. As reminders of the building's frivolous past, the façade is in the Italian manner, and the council chamber is still decorated with the painted and gilt gypsum figures of the former theater. Interestingly, the register office was decorated by Jean Cocteau.

MUSEUM OF REGIONAL PREHISTORY. This thoroughly modern museum focuses on the history of human development in the Mediterranean rim. The basement is devoted to popular arts and traditions.

THE CARNOLES DISTRICT

PALAIS CARNOLES ★. This palace was built in 1771 by Anthony I, Prince of Monaco, and included fifty bedrooms in addition to the servants' quarters. The building was sold in 1863 and used as a casino until 1868. It was then enlarged in 1896, and provided with two small wings and a typical 18th-century façade; the interior was redesigned in the style of the First Empire. The MUSEUM was opened in 1977 and contains works from the Italian schools of the 14th, 15th and 16th centuries. The second floor is devoted to contemporary art (including Saura, Poliakoff, Terechkovitch, Delvaux, Tal Coat and Sutherland); it also hosts temporary exhibitions and has a collection of prints. The PARK (1725) is the oldest garden in Menton, and includes tennis courts as well as a section given over to citrus fruits. Lastly, there is a 17th-century hexagonal tower, a curious fortified survival of a former convent.

SERRE DE LA MADONE ★. This 15-acre garden in the Gorbio Valley is one of the most unexpected pieces of scenery in the entire region. Thanks to the work of Sir Lawrence Johnston, responsible for laying out the garden, the sub-tropical plants have acclimatized very successfully. The garden lies on the

> **"THE ART OF GARDENING IS PROBABLY THE MOST AMBIGUOUS THERE IS – THE MOST DIFFICULT, AND YET THE MOST EASILY ABSORBABLE, OF ALL"**
>
> ROGER CAILLOIS

lower part of the hill, and the entrance gives a wonderful view of the spectacular terracing.

THE GARAVAN DISTRICT

VAL RAHMEH EXOTIC BOTANICAL GARDEN. This garden was designed to be on several levels, and was opened in 1925 by the Governor of Malta, Lord Percy Radcliffe; it only became a botanical garden in the 1950's through the work of its last owner, a Miss Campbell. The number of tropical and sub-tropical plants has been increased, with an emphasis on edible ones. The autumn flowerings, ranging from the orangey-red hibiscus to the pale yellow datura, are quite superb.

VILLA FONTANA ROSA. This house is on Avenue Vicente-Blasco-Ibáñez; it was bought by the well-known Spanish writer Blasco Ibáñez (1867–1928) in the 1920's. The house was in such a poor state of repair that it had to be pulled down in 1985, but the author's life is recalled in the alterations he made to his garden: like some parks in Seville, this garden includes a number of spots especially reserved for reading.

VILLA MARIA SERENA. Built by Charles Garnier in 1880, this villa has many terraces designed to enjoy the wonderful view. The exotic plants include cycads, palm and dragon trees, strelitzia, bougainvillaea, tupidentis, dragos and dorianthes.

DOMAINE DES COLOMBIÈRES ★. This is the greatest achievement of the designer, illustrator and landscape artist Ferdinand Bac (1859–1952), who was also responsible for redesigning the gardens of the Midi. He laid out Les Colombières in 1918–19 for the Ladan-Bockairy family, and continued to work on the interior until 1927. The house is painted red ocher and is delightful, and the materials, the coloring and the Modernist design of the furnishings are fine examples of Bac's artistry. He also drew up an itinerary round the garden, and introduced many fountains, statues, colonnades and ponds.

PALAIS CARNOLES
The decoration on the ceiling of the second-floor drawing room is bordered with a frieze of lions and the 'H' of Prince Honoré V.

INTERIOR ELEGANCE
The walls of Les Colombières are covered with superb neoclassical frescos of mythological themes. The fresco in the dining room shows Peleponesia.
Above: The drawing room with decoration featuring the Muses.

SERRE DE LA MADONE
From the ornamental pond there is a good view of the Italian-style symmetrical staircases which frame the small fountains up to the house.

1 ENTREVAUX 2 ST-PAUL 3 VENCE 4 VILLENEUVE-LOUBET 5 CAGNES-SUR-MER 6 NICE

🕐 Three days
🚗 93 miles

CIBORIUM (detail)
The panels of this portable wooden ciborium (1595) were painted by Antoine de Hondis. They represent biblical scenes.

THE COLOMBE D'OR
This restaurant was built after World War One and was altered in 1949. It rapidly became a favorite haunt of writers and poets, and actors including Simone Signoret, Yves Montand and Gérard Philipe. Chagall, Lurçat, Léger, Braque, Bonnard and Miró all donated works, and the restaurant now looks like an art gallery.

ST-PAUL-DE-VENCE ★

HISTORY. This little town perched on a rocky, fortified spur became an important military stronghold in the 16th century, during the wars between Charles V of Spain and Francis I. St-Paul was the first town prepared to oppose Nice, and it was provided with further fortifications by François de Mandon de St-Rémy, Francis I's military engineer in Provence. The circuit wall, which replaced the 12th-century fortifications, was built between 1537 and 1547, and St-Paul was not downgraded as a military outpost until 1868.

THE CIRCUIT WALL AND THE COVERED WAY. RUE GRANDE links the narrow PORTE DE VENCE (also known as PORTE ROYALE) to the north and PORTE DE NICE to the south. It is possible to walk round the circuit wall by simply following the covered way. The most remarkable remains of the former medieval fortifications are the TOWER, crowned with machicolations, and the central TURRET, where the council offices now are.

COLLEGIATE CHURCH OF THE CONVERSION OF ST-PAUL. The Romanesque choir is the oldest part of this church.

Gothic side aisles added to the single 13th-century nave in the 15th century give the church a substantial, square appearance. St-Paul's is dominated by a tower that was rebuilt in 1740, and its TREASURY is one of the most beautiful in Alpes-Maritimes.

THE MAEGHT FOUNDATION ★. The rooms and gardens of this building are interconnected by means of large bays. Many painters and sculptors were involved in the design through personal contributions. These works include a mural mosaic by Chagall, stained-glass windows by Braque, sculptures by Giacometti, a maze by Miró decorated

with sculptures and ceramics, and "mobiles" and "stabiles" by Alexander Calder. Collections of works by Kandinsky, Matisse, Hartung, Picasso and Klee are exhibited on a rotation basis.

CASTLE OF NOTRE-DAME-DES-FLEURS. The Nahon family, owners of the GALERIE BEAUBOURG in Paris, have followed the Maeght family's lead and converted this 19th-century castle near Vence into a cultural and commercial center. Here, they exhibit the work of artists showing at their Paris gallery. These include Arman, César, Dado, Niki de St-Phalle, Tinguely and Wols.

VENCE ★

CATHEDRAL OF THE NATIVITY OF THE VIRGIN. Built on the site of an earlier church, this Romanesque building has often been altered. The FURNISHINGS are exceptionally beautiful: they include Gothic stalls ★ in the tribunes carved between 1463 and 1467 by the Grasse artist Jacques Ballot. There is also a small museum in the tribunes which contains some very old objects including a 15th-century reliquary presented by Pope Paul III while passing through this former bishopric. In 1979, the baptistery was decorated by Marc Chagall with a mosaic entitled *Moses Saved from the Waters*.

THE CIRCUIT WALL AND THE GATES ★. Here and there, it is still possible to see the crenelations and arrow-slits of the elliptical circuit wall, particularly in the north curtain wall. Of the five gates in the old ramparts, only the 13th-century PORTAIL-LEVIS (Portcullis Gate) and the 14th-century PORTAIL DU SIGNADOUR have survived.

VENCE CATHEDRAL
The Chapel of the Saints and of the Guardian Angel has a magnificent Baroque reredos.

AIMÉ MAEGHT (1906–81) Maeght opened his first gallery of contemporary art in

Cannes in 1937, and another in Paris in 1945. In 1964, he and his wife, Marguerite, decided to establish a center where artists

could meet, that could promote their their works. This took the shape of a foundation located just outside St-Paul, and designed by Catalonian architect Josep Lluis Sert.

▲ NICE TOWARD MOUSTIERS

THE ROSARY CHAPEL (MATISSE CHAPEL).
Matisse settled in Nice in 1917 and then, in 1943, in Vence, where he was cared for by the Dominican Sisters. To show his gratitude, he offered to build a chapel for their new house. The chapel is easily recognizable from the 42-foot wrought-iron cross and the roof of white and blue tiles. The design by Auguste Perret (1874–1954) is entirely subordinated to the needs of the decoration. Cactus with stylized palm leaves was chosen by Matisse to decorate the stained-glass windows; it illustrates the Tree of Life, a theme usually represented by an olive tree, in a most original manner. The decoration, on bricks first painted and then enameled, was done in ink and with a brush. The exterior and interior panels take up the themes of the Virgin and Saint Dominic.

THE CITADEL VILLAGE OF ENTREVAUX
Entrevaux has a magnificent situation, surrounded by mountains and overlooking the Var. It has preserved its old appearance through its convex tiles and a fort which is linked to a winding, crenelated wall, a defense system erected under Vauban's direction between 1693 and 1705.

THE MAIN GATE INTO ENTREVAUX
The bridge, which was built between 1655 and 1658, is original, but the abutment-pier was hollowed out to make way for a moat under the portcullis. The village built two round towers to defend the entrance in 1690.

ENTREVAUX ★

A CITADEL. In Roman times, there was a town situated down in the valley, called Glanate, or Glandèves. This town was laid to waste on many occasions and threatened with flooding by the River Var, and finally it was abandoned. The inhabitants later settled on a rock overlooking the Var where there had been a hamlet called Entrevaux since the 11th century. Entrevaux was attacked and captured by Charles V in 1536, but an uprising by the people forced the occupiers to flee in 1542. The villagers thereupon placed themselves under the protection of the King of France. Entrevaux is still surrounded by a ring of boulders designed by Vauban in 1693.

THE CASTLE ★. Vauban was also responsible for the route which provides direct access to the castle; this consists of a series of sloping paths constructed on the side of the rock. The visitor arrives at the castle by passing through the Orbitelle Wall, which is all that remains of the medieval wall and is level with the powder tower; the main entrance is next to the ninth of the sloping paths. The

PETIT CHÂTELET (1697) has a moat and a portcullis with a single swipe-beam. The first section on the right consists of rooms and cells added between 1914 and 1922, and the tenth and eleventh paths go up as far as the castle proper. The present building was constructed between 1691 and 1724 over the remains of a medieval fort, and the entrance gives onto a hall. The large vaulted rooms to the right and left, the cellar and the powder magazine, are separated by a fine staircase which leads up to the first terreplein. This is where the CHAPLAIN'S BARRACKS, four rooms converted during the Revolution for some twenty men, are located; beyond is the COURTYARD where there is a water tank and cannons pointing towards the mountain. The castle's permanent staff used to live immediately above the vestibule. To one side, an arched gallery leads to the GREAT HALL, originally a medieval room but whose windows and fireplaces date from 1724. A stairway then climbs up to the turret platform and to the COMMANDANT'S HOUSE, which was rebuilt in 1697 on the very highest point of the rock and commands a magnificent view.

THE CATHEDRAL ★. The cathedral forms part of the rampart and was consecrated in 1627. The crenelated tower, completed around 1660, accentuates the church's defensive appearance. The austere exterior is in striking contrast to the sumptuous décor, particularly the reredoses and the 17th-century paintings in the nave and the choir (right). The main entrance (1667) is a magnificent piece of joinery (below). The stalls and the walnut wainscoting (1657) have preserved their elegantly decorated misericords.

A FRONTIER TOWN
When Allos and Barcelonnette surrendered to Savoy in 1388 after the murder of Queen Jeanne, Colmars refused to be subject to the House of Anjou and became a town of considerable strategic importance. The situation remained unchanged until 1713, when the return of Allos and

COLMARS

FORTS DE VAUBAN. When Louis XIV decided to strengthen the town's defenses against a possible invasion from Provence, the old towers were replaced by new ones, and some advance towers were placed in front of the Savoy and France gates to facilitate cross-firing.

FORT DE FRANCE. This fortress at the entrance to the town is today in ruins. The Fort de France had merely a support role: it was a simple, square redoubt with two watchtowers at the corners and four artillery embrasures on each side to cover the bridge, the town and the two sides of the valley.

FORT DE SAVOIE ★. This fortress has a more sophisticated ground plan and is in two parts: a weaker side which is turned toward France, with thinner walls and loopholes for light arms, a brick watchtower and a small covered way; and a strong side facing Savoy and Piedmont.

the River Ubaye to France signaled an end to the town's military interests. Little remains of the town's ramparts (1391); most of the present fortifications date from the 17th century.

311

⏱ Two days

🚗 124 miles

THE OLD TOWN
Whitewashed stone
houses, many of them
narrow buildings with
three or four stories,
are typical of this
Haute Provence
village. At street
level, a large door
opens onto an old
stable or shed, and a
staircase leads up to
the first floor. At one
time, the attic often
contained corn lofts
and drying
rooms
for

prunes
and figs.

**THE EX-VOTOS FROM
NOTRE-DAME-DU-
ROC**
The numerous ex-
votos ● *72* (crowns,
models and ex-votos
expressing gratitude)
covering the walls are
an indication of how
long this church was
popular with pilgrims.
The oldest of the ex-
votos, a vow to Notre-
Dame-de-Grace,
dates from 1757; the
most interesting are
two representations of
processions with
penitents wearing
their distinctive dress.
One of them shows
the White and Blue
Penitents making a
procession from the
town to the Rock in
1835 and praying for
"deliverance from
cholera".

CASTELLANE

HISTORY. The Romans built a
small harbor here on the River Verdon,
and named the town Salinae after the
nearby salty springs. However, when the
Saracens invaded ● *47*, the population took
refuge on the Rock, an escarped hill that provided
more secure shelter. This was the origin of Petra Castellana,
an early medieval village; the ruins of the Church of St-
André-du-Roc are still visible. The Rock soon proved to be
too small, and there was also a shortage of water, and during
the 11th century the inhabitants slowly made their way down
the hill again. Later, the new township grew to such an extent
that they decided to build the Church of St-Victor. After
peace was again threatened in the 14th century the lower
town was fortified in 1359, but when Castellane was handed
over to the French Crown, the Rock fortress was pulled down

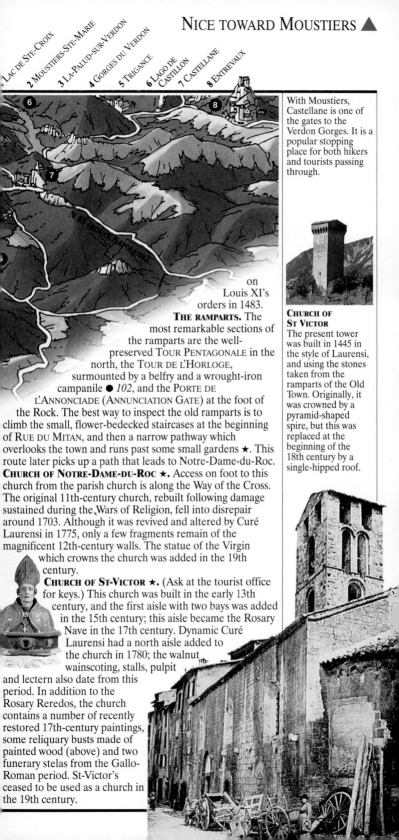

With Moustiers, Castellane is one of the gates to the Verdon Gorges. It is a popular stopping place for both hikers and tourists passing through.

CHURCH OF ST VICTOR
The present tower was built in 1445 in the style of Laurensi, and using the stones taken from the ramparts of the Old Town. Originally, it was crowned by a pyramid-shaped spire, but this was replaced at the beginning of the 18th century by a single-hipped roof.

on Louis XI's orders in 1483.

THE RAMPARTS. The most remarkable sections of the ramparts are the well-preserved TOUR PENTAGONALE in the north, the TOUR DE L'HORLOGE, surmounted by a belfry and a wrought-iron campanile ● *102*, and the PORTE DE L'ANNONCIADE (ANNUNCIATION GATE) at the foot of the Rock. The best way to inspect the old ramparts is to climb the small, flower-bedecked staircases at the beginning of RUE DU MITAN, and then a narrow pathway which overlooks the town and runs past some small gardens ★. This route later picks up a path that leads to Notre-Dame-du-Roc.

CHURCH OF NOTRE-DAME-DU-ROC ★. Access on foot to this church from the parish church is along the Way of the Cross. The original 11th-century church, rebuilt following damage sustained during the Wars of Religion, fell into disrepair around 1703. Although it was revived and altered by Curé Laurensi in 1775, only a few fragments remain of the magnificent 12th-century walls. The statue of the Virgin which crowns the church was added in the 19th century.

CHURCH OF ST-VICTOR ★. (Ask at the tourist office for keys.) This church was built in the early 13th century, and the first aisle with two bays was added in the 15th century; this aisle became the Rosary Nave in the 17th century. Dynamic Curé Laurensi had a north aisle added to the church in 1780; the walnut wainscoting, stalls, pulpit and lectern also date from this period. In addition to the Rosary Reredos, the church contains a number of recently restored 17th-century paintings, some reliquary busts made of painted wood (above) and two funerary stelas from the Gallo-Roman period. St-Victor's ceased to be used as a church in the 19th century.

ÉDOUARD ALFRED MARTEL
(1859–1938)
This French speleologist is famous for his explorations of the Dargilan and Padirac chasms. In three days of exceptional bravery in August 1905, he became the first person to carry out a complete exploration of the 13 miles of the Verdon Gorges. Today, the Martel Trail covers a more remote part of the Gorges from La Maline to Point Sublime.

GORGES DU VERDON ★

EXPLORATION DEFERRED. Until the beginning of the 20th century, the deepest of these gorges were thought to be impenetrable. They were only known to a few woodcutters who ventured down into the depths, on the end of ropes, in search of the stumps of boxwood used in making *boules* equipment. Armand Janet was the first to attempt an exploration in a canoe in 1896, but the violent currents forced him to give up. Before long, the Minister of Agriculture found himself obliged to step up supplies of drinking water to the region, and he began to take an interest in the Verdon. In 1905, he charged Édouard Alfred Martel with the task of carrying out a geological study which was to start with a reconnaissance of the gorges. The first comprehensive exploration took place in the same year.

EXPLORATION À LA CARTE. Many first-time visitors prefer to do a complete tour of the Gorges in a car, driving from one bank to the other. This road trip is about 82 miles long and takes a whole day. Observation platforms offer superb panoramic views of the countryside and of the five sentinel villages perched on the edge of the gorges. However, there are other itineraries open to enthusiasts. Less popular with the majority of tourists, for instance, is the ROUTE DES CRÊTES ★, unquestionably the most beautiful and wildest route, passing fantastic escarpments and exceptional views. This route starts at the village of La Palud, and the round trip takes three hours. A complete exploration along the waterway involves a two-day walk from Rougon, and hikers prepared to forego this can choose from ten SENTIERS DE RANDONNÉE ★ (registered hiking trails) which are all well signposted, take from two to eight hours and are of varying difficulty. Those interested in following these trails should consult the *Guide des sentiers du Verdon*. The Sentier Martel on the right bank, and the Imbut Path on the left, are marked by the Touring Club de France. The length of the RIVER TRIP (six to eight hours), the technical difficulties and the absence of emergency exits mean that only experienced kayakers should try it; furthermore, the level of the water can vary abruptly because of the Chaudanne and Castillon dams upstream. In any event, the journey

commences beyond Caréjuan Bridge and finishes at Aiguines Bridge. Inflatable rafts and hydrofoils are rapidly gaining popularity.

THE PRE-GORGES AND ROUGON. After Castellane, the route runs alongside the Verdon and offers many opportunities for stopping for a swim or going fishing, particularly at the junction with the Taloire Track and in the small harbor at Chasteuil. Near CARÉJUAN BRIDGE, at the point where the river joins the Jabron, there is a considerably narrower, 2½-mile stretch of path which marks the beginning of the Gorges. The GRAND CANYON itself begins at the confluence of the Baou at Tusset Bridge, and continues for 13 miles as far as Le Galetas and the beginning of the Lac de Ste-Croix. As it passes through sheer escarpments and fantastic jagged cliffs, the Verdon descends 502 feet at an average incline of 26 feet and at a speed that never drops below 6½ feet a second. On arriving at Rougon, effectively the gate to the Gorges, the visitor can either climb up to the village, from where there is a fabulous view over the Verdon, or push on to Point Sublime and then as far as the SAMSON CORRIDOR ★ at the far end of the Gorges. The walker has two routes to choose from. One is the SENTIER MARTEL ★ (eight hours to cover the 10 miles); this is the most famous and most spectacular, although it is advisable to do it in the reverse direction, starting from the Chalet de la Maline in La Palud. The other route is the SENTIER ENCASTEL–RANCOUMAS ★ (five hours to cover 8½ miles), which is shaded for much of the way and has panoramic views out over the cliffs at L'Escalès, the Baumes Frères Défilé, the Samson Corridor and the Irouelle Plain.

LA PALUD. Human habitation at La Palud goes back a very considerable period of time; a Gallo-Roman village and a number of tombs have been discovered there by chance. The spread of Christianity was accompanied by the arrival of monks; the chapel made of rock seems to suggest that they settled in the St-Maurin Grottos. Rebuilt in 1870, the CHURCH has preserved its Romanesque tower made of St-Maurin tufa-stone on a square ground plan. Since the 15th century, there has been a castle ★ on the site of the present building, the fief of the powerful

> "THERE IS NOTHING MORE ROMANTIC THAN THE MINGLING OF THESE ROCKS AND ABYSSES, OF THESE GREEN WATERS AND PURPLE SHADOWS, OF A SKY THAT LOOKS LIKE SOME HOMERIC SEA AND A WIND THAT SPEAKS WITH THE VOICE OF DEAD GODS"
>
> JEAN GIONO

AN UNUSUALLY FASCINATING PLACE
The village of Moustiers is built in a semicircle on a tufa-stone mass; it stands by the entrance to a fissure that opens onto a huge, buff, limestone cliff. It is from here that the torrent rushes into the middle of the village in a series of cascades.

AERIAL VIEW OF MOUSTIERS
Energetic walkers will choose the steep path lined by the Way of the Cross up to the shrine overlooking the village.

Demandolx family. This huge building was enlarged after 1744 and has recently been restored; its double-hipped roof gives it a very proud appearance, yet this rectangular castle flanked by turrets dominates the nearby houses in a curiously unostentatious manner. La Palud is the departure point for the ROUTE DES CRÊTES, although walkers should beware that this trail can be dangerous in winter. The large number of observation points dotted along this route give plenty of opportunities for taking in an astonishing variety of vertiginous views. The Mediterranean vegetation strewn with lavender is quite breathtaking, as are the views from the observation points at the BARRE DE L'ESCALES; with luck, there will also be a chance to watch climbers defying gravity as they negotiate its smooth, vertical walls. The LA CARELLE, TRESCAIRE and DENT D'AIRE OBSERVATION POINTS have also become popular for rock climbing: there are facilities for climbers at all levels and for abseiling along the ravines and by the waterfalls. The path between Moustiers and Castellane was no more than an uneven mule track until the end of the 18th century; then, thanks to Pierre Louis de Demandolx, Lord of La Palud, a road was built in 1787 which ran along the right bank of the Verdon. Since the dam was filled with water in 1972, the outlet into the Verdon Gorges has offered a truly fantastic spectacle, with the torrent going all shades from emerald to turquoise as it rushes into the artificial Lac de Ste-Croix.

MOUSTIERS-STE-MARIE ★

CHURCH OF NOTRE-DAME ★. This 12th-century building was originally the priory church. The restrained power of the Romanesque nave, made of calcareous tufa-stone and covered with broken-barrel vaulting, is most impressive. The huge Gothic choir was rebuilt in the 14th century; it has aisles, three bays, is slightly in front of the nave, and ends in a flat wall. Side chapels were almost certainly added during the 17th century. The church at Moustiers is also notable for its FURNISHINGS; they include 16th-century painted panels, and a 5th-century sarcophagus

NOTRE-DAME
The church's beautiful tower has three levels of decreasing height; it is in the Lombard style of the 12th century. The tower houses a clock dating from 1447, one of the oldest in Alpes-de-Haute-Provence.

with a bas-relief representing the Crossing of the Red Sea. The TREASURY contains Moustiers faïence of the 18th century, a processional cross, 16th-century collection plates, and an ex-voto ● 72 from the Church of Notre-Dame-de-Beauvoir.

THE FAÏENCE MUSEUM. This museum has occupied the underground medieval crypt of a former monastery since 1978. It contains characteristic objects from various 17th- and 18th-century workshops including those of Clérissy (plates and dishes in monochrome blue), Olerys and Laugier (mainly designs of polychrome grotesques) and Ferrat (plates, baskets ornamented with openwork); there are also later pieces

"VIEW OF MOUSTIERS"
Watercolor by Paul Martin (1830–1903)

A DEEPLY DEVOUT TOWN
In the 5th century, the Bishop of Riez summoned the monks of Lérins ▲ 272 to his diocese. He installed them near the Verdon Gorges in this village which had come to be known as Monasterium (Moustiers). After being forced to flee by the invading Lombards and Saracens, the monks did not return to Moustiers until the end of the 11th century. Their substantial earnings enabled them to carry out major building programs from the 12th to the 15th centuries.

EX-VOTOS FROM NOTRE-DAME-DE-BEAUVOIR
These ex-votos in the church sacristy show how important Moustiers was for its devotion to the Virgin Mary and as a place of pilgrimage.

including a beautiful representation of Christ on the cross. It is a magnificent achievement on the part of the founder, Marcel Provence; he is also generally credited with the rebirth of Moustiers faïence, having had a kiln built in 1927 and set up the academy and museum in 1929. Further tribute is paid to him in the form of a collection of photographs.

THE VILLAGE CENTER. Moustiers is altogether a delightful village with its alleyways, houses of rubble limestone, door jambs in tufa-stone and light-colored tile roofs. Many of the houses date from the 18th century, but some of the older ones are paneled or corbeled. The most beautiful house, by the north door of the church, has a double-corbeled corner and traces of cruciform mullions.

CHAPEL OF NOTRE-DAME-DE-BEAUVOIR ★. A steep path marked by small shrines of the Way of the Cross leads to this church; the chapel, which was referred to in documents as early as 1052, stands on a narrow shelf between two high rocky walls. The single-nave Notre-Dame-de-Beauvoir has a 12th-century Romanesque part with two bays, slightly broken barrel vaulting and two Gothic bays added in the 16th century. The tufa-stone tower is topped with a pyramid-shaped structure and dates from the same period. The main entrance consists of beautifully carved 16th-century leaves, and the choir is dominated by a large carved and gilt wood reredos of the 17th century.

PEILLON

CHAPEL OF THE WHITE PENITENTS. This small chapel contains superb frescos which recall those painted by Giovanni Canavesio in the Church of Notre-Dame-des-Fontaines at La Brigue. The angular gestures, grimacing faces and bulging eyes are strikingly similar; there are even some identical scenes, including that of the hanging Judas, his soul being torn out of him by a black devil.

CHURCH OF THE TRANSFIGURATION. Standing on the highest point in the village, this church is typical of the 18th-century taste for ancient styles. The façade has a double row of pillars, each supporting a cornice and a triangular pediment. The 17th-century painting adorning the high altar illustrates the Transfiguration. Two walks are signposted near the exit: one is to Peille (one-and-a-half hours); the other leads to the CHAPEL OF ST-MARTIN (one-and-a-half hours) and to La Turbie (two hours).

PEILLE

Peille was first a consulate and then the main town of a medieval bailiwick until, in 1651, it became a county ruled by the famous Nice family of Lascaris-Vintimille. Built in the 13th century for a confraternity of penitents, the CHAPEL OF ST-SÉBASTIEN is now the Town Hall. The tiny Museum of Arts and Traditions is near Place de la Colle-Inférieure.

PALAIS DU JUGE MAGE. This severe edifice, formerly known as the Palais des Consuls, is in Place André-Laugier and was once the law court. The façade suggests that it was constructed between the end of the 13th century and the beginning of the 14th.

COLLEGIATE CHURCH OF STE-MARIE. This building, located on a hillock on the road leading to La Turbie, belonged to the canons of the Order of Saint Ruf from the 12th to the 17th century.

Encircled by penitents' chapels the church at L'Escarène is a Baroque shrine of exceptional beauty.

THE SALT ROUTE In the late 16th century, the road from Nice to Turin passed through L'Escarène, Col de Braus, Sospel, Col de Brouis, Breil-sur-Roya, Saorge, Fontan, Tende and Col de Tende. On the other side of the Alps, the route went through Limone, Vernante and Cuneo. Salt, used to preserve food, serve the needs of cattle and manufacture leather; came from the marshes of Hyères and Toulon, and was unloaded at Nice.

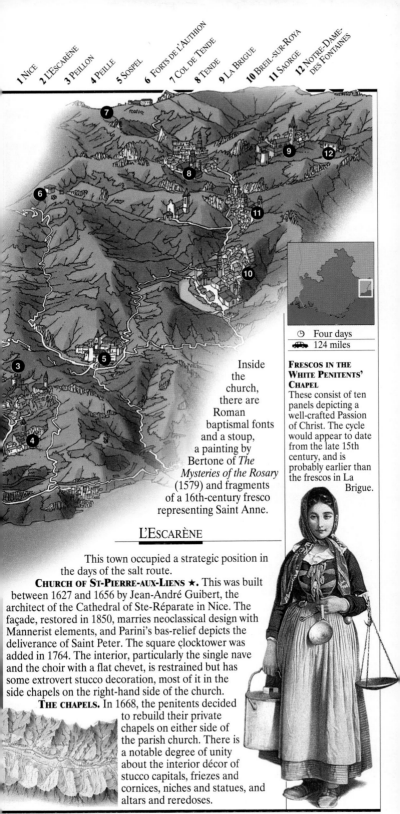

Four days
124 miles

FRESCOS IN THE WHITE PENITENTS' CHAPEL
These consist of ten panels depicting a well-crafted Passion of Christ. The cycle would appear to date from the late 15th century, and is probably earlier than the frescos in La Brigue.

Inside the church, there are Roman baptismal fonts and a stoup, a painting by Bertone of *The Mysteries of the Rosary* (1579) and fragments of a 16th-century fresco representing Saint Anne.

L'ESCARÈNE

This town occupied a strategic position in the days of the salt route.

CHURCH OF ST-PIERRE-AUX-LIENS ★. This was built between 1627 and 1656 by Jean-André Guibert, the architect of the Cathedral of Ste-Réparate in Nice. The façade, restored in 1850, marries neoclassical design with Mannerist elements, and Parini's bas-relief depicts the deliverance of Saint Peter. The square clocktower was added in 1764. The interior, particularly the single nave and the choir with a flat chevet, is restrained but has some extrovert stucco decoration, most of it in the side chapels on the right-hand side of the church.

THE CHAPELS. In 1668, the penitents decided to rebuild their private chapels on either side of the parish church. There is a notable degree of unity about the interior décor of stucco capitals, friezes and cornices, niches and statues, and altars and reredoses.

319

"The Immaculate Virgin"
This reredos in the Church of St-Michel was probably painted around 1530 by François Bréa. The central panel portrays the Blessed Virgin Mary, who is only identifiable from the inscription on the

phylactery as she is not wearing her traditional blue mantle. The Virgin is seen with Saint Susanna and Saint Martha. The cult of the Immaculate Conception came under heavy attack from Protestants, but was frequently represented by artists of the Counter-Reformation long before the Church proclaimed it as dogma.

Sospel

Sospel was the second most important town in the County of Nice, and occupied a strategic position for many years.

The Old Bridge. The familiar outline of this bridge has come to be the town's emblem. As early as the 16th century, it linked the medieval town with a new district under construction, and also served as a tollgate on the salt route. It was fully restored by the École des Beaux-Arts in 1953.

The St-Nicolas district. The 15th-century former Palais Communal is at the far end of the Old Bridge; it stands close to a lovely 18th-century fountain. There are some beautiful doors in Rue de la République, and at no. 14 there is an old capital decorated with a running dog. To the north, the 17th-century Ste-Croix Chapel, where the Confraternity of White Penitents has premises, contains a 17th-century wooden carving of Christ and a 14th-century statue of Saint Nicholas.

Medieval town. One of the façades has a Renaissance window and doors in the form of a Roman arch. The entrance to no. 28 Rue St-Pierre is adorned by a fine lintel. Further on, there is a late medieval house boasting numerous carved stones: this may have been the home of Viguier, the Count of Savoy's representative.

Cathedral of St-Michel. This church's classical façade is superbly set off by the cobbled square and its medieval, arcaded houses. Only the 12th-century Romanesque clocktower remains of the early church. The present cathedral was built in the middle of the 17th century: its dimensions and painted decoration give it considerable Baroque charm, particularly the two 16th-century triptychs which are kept in the marvelous Chevet Chapel. The *Pietà* reredos, whose side panels show Saint Catherine of Alexandria and Saint Nicholas, also includes the donors of the church wearing White Penitents' hoods. The triptych entitled *The Immaculate Virgin* has long been attributed to Louis Bréa but is probably the work of his nephew François.

COLORED MAP OF SOSPEL
These works of 1742–8 were designed to make the town safe.

FORT ST-ROCH. ThThis fort was built between 1930 and 1934 to guard the Grazian railway tunnel which, it was feared, would be taken over by the Italian army. It was designed to enable two hundred and forty men and five officers to survive not seeing the light of day for three months.

WALKS. The tourist office advertises over twenty-five walks around Sospel. The hike round the Castès Fort (two hours, 2 miles) to the east takes in the forest; the walk to Mount Barbonnet (three-and-a-half hours, 5 miles) starts behind the Cathedral of St-Michel and may include a visit to the fort.

A STRATEGIC ROLE
The first fortresses on the Maginot Line, which stretched from the North Sea to the Mediterranean, were built in the Alpes-Maritimes. Four of them, the forts at Agaisen, St-Roch, Castillon and Le Barbonnet, protected Sospel. The St-Roch Fort is still in existence.

BREIL-SUR-ROYA

OLD TOWN. The picturesque streets of the Old Town follow the inclination of the mountain. Place de Brancion, where the CHURCH OF SANCTA-MARIA-IN-ALBIS ★ stands, provides a reminder of Italy with its pink arcades, the trompe l'œil decoration of the windows, and clocktower covered with glazed tiles. This 17th-century Baroque church is in the form of a Greek cross extended at the sides by chapels; the painted ceilings of the interior depict the Assumption of the Blessed Virgin. The rich furnishings

include an exceptionally valuable collection of gold plate, a triptych dedicated to Saint Peter by an anonymous Ligurian artist (c. 1500), a carved group of the Passion and a very beautiful 17th-century organ case. The nearby Mercy and White Penitents' chapels contain painted and carved decoration that is very lovely but in need of restoration.

RIGHT BANK. The Romanesque CLOCHER ST-JEAN behind the railway station is what survives of a church pulled down in 1707. The road running past the tower climbs up to the CHURCH OF NOTRE-DAME-DU-MONT on the former site of the village, which is now an olive grove. The church has been restored on many occasions. It has preserved many vestiges of early Romanesque art, including a chevet depicting Lombard bands of the 11th century and an apsidiole in the south.

BREIL, A TOWN ON BOTH SIDES OF THE ROYA
Breil straddles the River Roya, and is situated at the point where the roads from Nice and Ventimiglia meet. The river is slightly swollen by a small dam and an artificial lake. The town's economy was once based on trade and the growing of olives; today it relies on tourism.

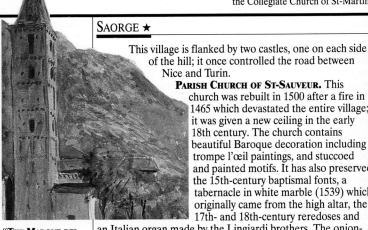

Predella on the Saint Martha reredos in the Collegiate Church of St-Martin.

SAORGE ★

This village is flanked by two castles, one on each side of the hill; it once controlled the road between Nice and Turin.

PARISH CHURCH OF ST-SAUVEUR. This church was rebuilt in 1500 after a fire in 1465 which devastated the entire village; it was given a new ceiling in the early 18th century. The church contains beautiful Baroque decoration including trompe l'œil paintings, and stuccoed and painted motifs. It has also preserved the 15th-century baptismal fonts, a tabernacle in white marble (1539) which originally came from the high altar, the 17th- and 18th-century reredoses and an Italian organ made by the Lingiardi brothers. The onion-shaped bell tower dates from 1812.

THE MADONE-DEL-POGGIO. All that remains of this 11th-century chapel is the chevet with three apses decorated with arcatures. Fragments of a mural painting representing the Coronation of the Virgin Mary are just visible above the porch. There are frescos of scenes from the life of the Virgin Mary in the apse; they are attributed to Baleison (c. 1480).

FRANCISCAN MONASTERY. This 17th-century building is at the end of the village. In the front of the newly restored façade is a covered porch surmounted by balustrades and an onion-shaped bell tower. The church contains a fine reredos in carved wood dating from the 17th century; the cloister is decorated with paintings of the life of Saint Francis, and numerous sundials are attached to the surrounding walls.

WALK ★. A two-hour walk includes the Bendola Canyon, the waterfalls and the Ste-Croix Chapel; it starts behind the Franciscan Monastery.

"THE MADONE DEL POGGIO"
In this work by Mossa, the church is easily identifiable by its lovely Romanesque clock tower in the Lombard style with six stories. It stands alongside the main building.

THE "PERCHED VILLAGE" OF SAORGE
Saorge stands high above the gorges that the River Roya flows through. It is one of the best examples of a "perched village" in the Alpes-Maritimes with its tall, tiered houses. As much as 328 feet separates the top of the highest house from that of the lowest. The old village is a maze of covered alleys, most of them in the form of stairways, lined with innumerable 15th-century houses boasting carved doors and lintels.

LA BRIGUE ★

The magical spectacle of the Bergue and Paganin Gorges hewn out of mauve schist eventually gives way to this town formerly owned by the Lascaris family; a few remnants of the medieval castle have survived.

COLLEGIATE CHURCH OF ST-MARTIN ★. This church was built in the late 15th and early 16th centuries, and is in the Lombard Romanesque style although there are certain unmistakable Gothic influences. The richness of the interior décor consists of numerous early paintings on wood, including a *Crucifixion* (1510), the work of a painter influenced by Bréa, a triptych of *Saint Martha* (1530), a reredos of *Our Lady of the Snows* (1507) by Fuseri, an unusually realistic reredos depicting *The Martyrdom of Saint Erasmus* (c. 1530) by an anonymous Lombard artist and a panel of *The Assumption of the Virgin* by the School of Bréa. The Nativity Reredos is attributed to Louis Bréa: this theme was unusual for Nice but was very common in Liguria.

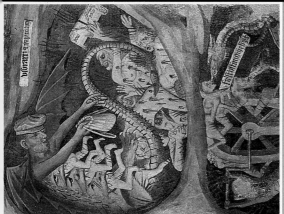

LAST JUDGEMENT
The frescos in the Church of Notre-Dame-des-Fontaines were inspired by the Apocrypha and embody a remarkable amount of religious teaching. The paintings in the nave illustrate Christ's Passion, those on the east wall the Last Judgment, and those in the choir the life of the Virgin Mary. Through its subject matter, conception and style, the cycle denounces the powerful and proclaims Christ's forgiveness. In this way, even the horrific picture of Judas hanging seems to contradict official condemnation: he is hanging from an olive tree, the tree of reconciliation and peace.

THE COL DE TENDE
Six forts were built on this pass (6,135 feet) by the Italians after 1882.

CHAPEL OF THE ANNUNCIATION. This chapel to the left of the church has a surprising ellipsoidal ground plan, and houses a splendid collection of priests' objects and vestments. Its façade is Baroque, while that of the CHAPEL OF THE ASSUMPTION on the right in the main square is decorated in the Renaissance manner.

CHURCH OF NOTRE-DAME-DES-FONTAINES ★. This shrine, which stands close to seven springs famous for their curative powers, contains remarkable frescos dating from the second half of the 15th century; they are the work of Canavesio, a Piedmontese painter whose style gave expression to the violence and anguish that characterized the last few years of the century. Only the paintings in the vault of the choir and the transverse ribs are by his pupil Baleison; these are in a more precious style closer to that of illuminators.

WALK ★. A four-hour, signposted walk through the Mercantour Park goes as far as the Fraches Waterfall and an abandoned hamlet of the same name.

VALLÉE DES MERVEILLES AND VAL DE FONTANALBA ★

Mount Bégo rises to 9,422 feet, forming a massive barrier in the midst of a vast area dotted with thousands of rock engravings. On either side of the *massif* are two enormous stretches of land: the better known is the Vallée des Merveilles which covers an area of 1,480 acres, while the lesser known of the two, the Val de Fontanalba, is explored much less and covers an area of about 160 acres. Both valleys form part of the Parc national du Mercantour, and were declared historic monuments in 1989.

They are visited on foot, independently or in guided tours.

ANCIENT HISTORY. These mountainous valleys were filled with glaciers during the last glaciation of the Alpine Quaternary and it is likely that the river of ice descended as far as

These valleys contain the largest number of lakes in the Alpes-Maritimes.

Painted murals developed as an art form in Alpes-Maritimes between the 13th and 16th centuries. There were two dominant processes: frescos and tempera painting. The artists concerned were itinerants, most of them coming from Piedmont and Liguria. Although the majority remained anonymous, some of the names, including those of Canavesio and, particularly, his pupil Baleison, have come down to us. Many of their works have been identified.

Strictly speaking, frescos are made by applying damp plaster to a wall and painting on it while it is still damp. Tempera painting uses pigments to which gum has been added; they are painted onto a dry surface.

ICONOGRAPHY

These paintings were commissioned by parish churches and confraternities, and were designed to provide religious instruction for illiterate people. Generally speaking, scenes from the Old Testament ceased to be depicted after the 13th century. The most common themes were taken from the New Testament (including the Childhood of Christ, the Passion and the Last Judgment) and the lives of the saints.

The saints were presented as protectors against epidemics and natural catastrophes. Saint Maurus was widely venerated throughout the county of Nice in the early 15th century. (Left: A painting by Andrea de Cella.)

CANAVESIO

From 1480 onward, this Piedmontese priest and painter worked in the county of Nice where he rapidly established himself as the leading artist in the field of murals. Canavesio specialized in tempera painting, a technique which allowed him to make alterations as well as creating most brilliant colors. His highly personal style veered toward realism and the dramatic.

JEAN BALEISON

His style made him the outstanding representative of international Gothic in the Alpes-Maritimes. His technique is fresco, which does not allow the use of all the colors in the coat of plaster.

COLORS

Basic colors were yellow and red ocher (iron oxides), blue-grey (natural schist) and silver-white (lead carbonate). Green (copper acetate) and violet (madder) were then added. Blue (cobalt and lapis lazuli) was a highly prized color, and was used exclusively on refined works of art until 1450, when lazulite began to be imported from Persia. At the time, there were no more than fourteen coloring matters.

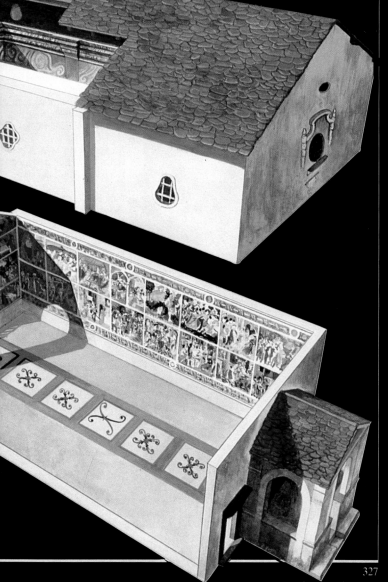

A CONTINUING ENIGMA
Generally speaking, the few archeologists who have interpreted these engravings agree that they are expressions of religious belief. About thirty thousand of them have been listed, and can be grouped under four headings: representations of anthropomorphic and geometric figures, bovids, weapons and tools. These headings sometimes merge to produce more complex compositions.

St-Dalmas-de-Tende. Its slow course eroded huge cliffs, producing pits and hollows and deep stria in the rocks and quarrying of erratic blocks, and overdeepened (at a stage earlier than the constrictions of harder rock) depressions in which there are now lakes and peat bogs. These depressions were formed over thousands of years in a damp, cold climate, and in an extremely wet terrain where moss grew abundantly. About fifteen thousand years ago, the climate began to get warmer, the glacier gradually withdrew and the depression of Lake Long-Supérieur emerged out of the ice. Slowly, the glacier also abandoned the series of terminal moraine which were helping to hold back the waters of the lakes.

A DENUDED LANDSCAPE. Six thousand years ago, when the climate was damper than it is today, there was an enormous forest of firs here; these were later replaced by larches and then by alpine grass. In the early summer after the snow had melted, the uneven grass blended with other plants such as reeds, sedge, epilobes, pansies, saxifrage and *Linaria alpina*. During the glaciations of the Quaternary Era, the hardy, resistant mugho and dwarf pine survived by clinging to the ice-free cliffs.

SIGNPOSTED WALKS. These walks have been designed to enable visitors to view some of the most important engravings in the area without a guide. Each rock on the route is marked by a screen-printed sign tracing the engravings on it and providing an analysis of the motifs. The Vallée des Merveilles path overlaps with GR 52 at the bottom of the valley; it is an easy walk and takes in only five rocks. These days, the Val de Fontanalba is only open to small groups accompanied by an official guide; during the summer period, contact an organization called Destination Merveilles. This walk follows the Way of the Cross and passes the observation table.

Above: *The Sorcerer, The Head of the Tribe* and *Christ*.

THE ROCK ENGRAVINGS. They were produced on large, flat, orange and green stones by small hammer taps which removed the top layer of the rock. Most of these engravings date from the early Bronze Age (1800–1500 BC), although Mount Bégo had been inhabited by humans since the Neolithic Period.

PRACTICAL
INFORMATION

The mild Mediterranean winters have always attracted tourists.

Mountainous inland areas, like the Ubaye Valley, provide a cool refuge in the summer.

The Côte d'Azur is the most important tourist region in France, with up to twenty-four million tourists a year. Its varied scenery ranges from the marshy plains of the Camargue to the alpine hinterland of Nice, and includes the Palace of the Popes and the Verdon canyon.

USEFUL INFORMATION

◆ In Britain:
French Tourist Office,
178 Piccadilly,
London W1V 0AL
Tel. 0891 244123
◆ In the U.S.:
French Tourist Office
– in New York,
444 Madison Av.,
NY 10022
– in Los Angeles
Tel. 310-271-2358
– in Chicago
Tel. 312-751-7800

◆ In France:
Information is available from the two regional tourism committees (Côte d'Azur and Provence) or from one of the five departmental committees and the Monaco tourist authority. About 300 local tourist offices have information on accommodation.

ADDRESSES

COMITÉ RÉGIONAL DE TOURISME
◆ Provence
2, rue Henri-Barbusse
13001 Marseilles
Tel. 04 91 39 38 00
Fax 04 91 56 66 61
◆ Côte d'Azur
55, prom. des Anglais
06000 Nice
Tel. 04 93 37 78 78
Fax 04 93 86 01 06
DIRECTION DU TOURISME ET DES CONGRÈS DE MONACO
2a, bd. des Moulins
98030 Monaco
Cedex
Tel. 04 92 16 61 66
Fax 04 92 16 60 00
COMITÉ DÉPARTEMENTAL DU TOURISME
◆ Alpes-Maritimes
2, rue Gustave-Deloye
06000 Nice
Tel. 04 93 85 26 63
Fax 04 93 62 21 56

◆ Alpes-de-Haute-Provence
19, rue Docteur-Honnorat, BP 170
04005 Digne-les-Bains Cedex
Tel. 04 92 31 57 29
Fax 04 92 32 24 94
◆ Bouches-du-Rhône
13, rue Roux-de-Brignoles
13001 Marseilles
Tel. 04 91 13 84 13
Fax 04 91 33 01 82
◆ Var
Bd du Maréchal-Foch
BP 99
83003 Draguignan Cédex
Tel. 04 94 50 55 50
Fax 04 94 50 55 51
◆ Vaucluse
La Balance –
BP 147
Place Campana
84008 Avignon
Tel. 04 90 86 43 42
Fax 04 90 86 86 08

PETS

Dogs and cats must be over three months old and must be vaccinated against rabies.

DOCUMENTATION

EUROPEAN CITIZENS:
◆ a valid identity card;
◆ no customs formalities.
TOURISTS FROM OTHER COUNTRIES:
◆ a valid passport;

◆ régime des franchises (customs form);
◆ tourist visits are limited to three months, with or without a visa.

THE TOURIST INDUSTRY IN PROVENCE

The Provençal tourist industry represents ten percent of the region's GDP or 55,000 salaried jobs. Forty-seven percent of tourists come in the summer. The low season is the spring. Provence has 2,600 hotels with a total capacity of 150,000 beds. There are six hundred three- and four-star hotels in Provence and the region contains over 30 percent of all France's four-star hotels. There are also 850 campsites, providing 100,000 places (equivalent to 300,000 beds), as well as nearly 55,000 houses and apartments for rent and over a thousand rooms in private homes.

WHEN TO GO

In May and June the days get longer and warmer without becoming stifling and the countryside is full of flowers.

In September the sea is at its warmest and the sun is still very hot. The vendanges (grape harvests) begin.

AVERAGE COSTS FOR A WEEK
These include accommodation, food, local transport and entertainment for a family of four. Travel costs to Provence are not included.

Hotel accommodation	£2,000 / $3,000
Camping	£700 / $1,050
Renting	£1,000 / $1,500

SPRING		March to May	
		MARCH	**MARCH**
		25° / 50°	46° / 57°
April 23	Feast of Saint George, Arles		
April	Monte Carlo Open (tennis)	**APRIL**	**APRIL**
May	Monaco Grand Prix (formula 1)	32° / 57°	50° / 61°
May	Nîmes feria		
May	Cannes International Film Festival	**MAY**	**MAY**
		37° / 66°	55° / 68°
★ Pilgrimage to Saintes-Maries-de-la-Mer			

SUMMER		June to August	
		JUNE	**JUNE**
		43° / 70°	61° / 73°
July	Feast of Sainte Madeleine, Beaucaire		
July	Aix-en-Provence Music Festival	**JULY**	**JULY**
July-August	International Jazz Festival, Antibes, Juan-les-Pins	46° / 79°	66° / 81°
August	"Les Chorégies", Orange	**AUGUST**	**AUGUST**
August	The Nice "Battle of flowers"	46° / 77°	66° / 81°
★ The Avignon festival			

AUTUMN		Sep. to Nov.	
		SEPTEMBER	**SEPTEMBER**
		43° / 70°	63° / 75°
September	Wine harvest, Châteauneuf-du-Pape		
October	Sacred music festival, Abbaye St Victor, Marseilles	**OCTOBER**	**OCTOBER**
		34° / 61°	57° / 68°
November	International Dance Festival, Cannes	**NOVEMBER**	**NOVEMBER**
		27° / 48	50° / 61°
★ The wine harvest at Châteauneuf-du-Pape			

WINTER		Dec. to Feb.	
		DECEMBER	**DECEMBER**
		19° / 43°	46° / 55°
End Nov/Dec	Santons Fair, Marseilles		
February	Mimosa Corsos, Bormes-les-Mimosas	**JANUARY**	**JANUARY**
February	Feast of the Lemons, Menton	18° / 41°	43° / 54°
February	Nice Carnival	**FEBRUARY**	**FEBRUARY**
		19° / 45°	43° / 55°
★ A hike in the Tanneron range			

warm, sunny   variable, cloudy   rain   cold, snowy

Les températures minimales et maximales en degrés Celsius à Barcelonnette et sur la côte.

THE CLIMATE

Provençal weather is usually sunny throughout the year, with heavy rains spread over no more than a hundred days a year, and very high temperatures in the summer. The lower reaches of the Rhône Valley and the neighboring areas are swept by the famous mistral, a strong wind from the north which can blow for up to 120 days a year. In winter, when it is at its strongest and coldest, it can be quite unpleasant. It blows as far east as St-Raphaël in the Var, but gradually weakens as it veers eastward. The Côte d'Azur, which is sheltered from the wind by the Alps, is known for its exceptionally mild weather (the January average in Monaco is 50°F). The Provençal Alps get a lot of sun and little wind and have good snow falls in the winter over the higher ranges. The air is very clear. Beware of changes in temperature; although daytime temperatures are generally mild, even in winter, the nights are chilly all year round.

NATIONAL HOLIDAYS IN FRANCE

◆ Easter Monday
◆ Labor Day: May 1
◆ Ascension: May
◆ Pentecost: June
◆ National "Bastille" Day: July 14
◆ Assumption: August 15
◆ All Saints Day: November 1
◆ Armistice Day: November 11

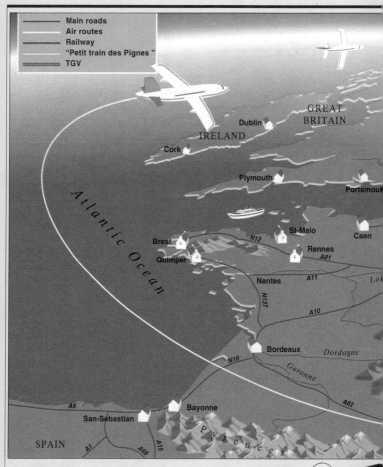

Legend:
- Main roads
- Air routes
- Railway
- "Petit train des Pignes"
- TGV

GREAT BRITAIN

Dublin

IRELAND

Cork

Plymouth

Portsmout

Atlantic Ocean

St-Malo

Caen

Brest

N12

Quimper

Rennes

A81

Nantes

A11

Lo

N137

A10

Bordeaux

Dordogne

N10

Garonne

A62

Bayonne

A8

San-Sebastian

SPAIN

A1

A63

A15

Pyrenees

BY TRAIN

OUTWARD JOURNEY
Trains leave London Victoria in the early afternoon (1.05pm and 1.25pm) for Dover, where a 4pm ferry crossing reaches Calais in time for the overnight train to Provence. During the final five hours the train stops in all the main stations from Avignon to Menton.

THE RETURN TRIP
The train leaves Provence in the evening and arrives at London Victoria early the following afternoon. The journey to Marseilles takes about 17 hours, 21 to Nice. You can go via Paris: London to Paris takes 10 hours via ferry or 7 hours via hovercraft. On arrival in Paris at the Gare du Nord, transfer to the Gare de Lyon to catch a TGV (high-speed train) for Marseilles (5 hours) or Nice (7 hours). Return fare is about £250 to Nice, £200 to Marseilles.

BY AIR

Provence has two international airports.

NICE
Several airlines fly direct from London. Prices from around £200 to £650 return. There are direct flights from Manchester on weekdays and Saturdays, and from Birmingham on Saturdays and Sundays.
Delta Airlines fly from New York to Nice. Prices range from $638 to $1,348 for economy class. Other US airlines offer flights to Provence via Paris; travelers then have to reserve a seat on AirInter to travel to the Provence region.

◆ Avignon-Caumont Airport
Tel. 04 90 81 51 51 (national flights only)

◆ Nice-Côte d'Azur Airport
Tel. 04 93 21 30 12
◆ British Airways, Nice
Tel. 04 93 18 00 19
MARSEILLES
There are up to four flights daily from London. Prices range from £140 to £675.
◆ Marseilles-Marignane Airport
Tel. 04 42 89 09 74
◆ British Airways, Marseilles
Tel. 04 42 78 21 24
The airport is at Marignane, 15 miles north of Marseilles.

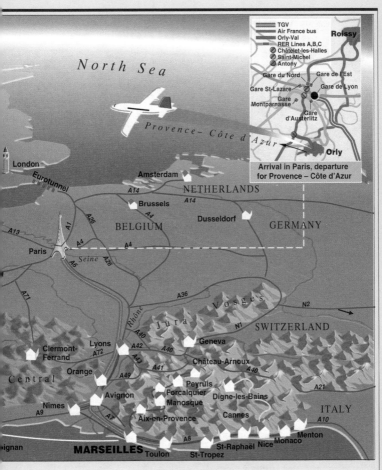

TGV
Air France bus
Orly-Val
RER Lines A,B,C
① Châtelet-les-Halles
② Saint-Michel
③ Antony

Roissy

Gare du Nord
Gare de l'Est
Gare St-Lazare
Gare de Lyon
Gare Montparnasse
Gare d'Austerlitz

Orly

Arrival in Paris, departure for Provence – Côte d'Azur

North Sea

London
Eurotunnel
Amsterdam
Provence – Côte d'Azur

A14
NETHERLANDS
A14
Brussels
A4
Dusseldorf
GERMANY
BELGIUM
A1
A26
A4
A13
Paris
A4
A26
Seine
A6
A36
Rhône
Vosges
N2
Jura
N1
A71
A40
SWITZERLAND
Clermont-Ferrand
Lyons
A72
A42
A40
Geneva
A43
A40
Château-Arnoux
Orange
A41
Peyruls
A40
A21
Central
A49
Forcalquier
Avignon
Manosque
Digne-les-Bains
ITALY
Nîmes
A9
A7
Aix-en-Provence
Cannes
A10
A8
Menton
Monaco
MARSEILLES
Toulon
St-Raphaël
Nice
ignan
St-Tropez

AIRPORT SHUTTLES

◆ The Marseilles shuttle goes to and from the Gare St-Charles every hour. It takes 30 minutes and costs 40F.

◆ A shuttle runs from Aix-en-Provence to Marseilles-Marignane airport every hour, takes about 30 minutes and costs 30F.

◆ The Nice shuttle departs every 20 minutes and provides a 15-minute transfer into town costing 20F.

◆ To get to Cannes from Nice airport, a shuttle leaves every hour. It takes 45 minutes on the highway, at 65F, or

one and a half hours along the coast road at 43F.

◆ There are shuttles from Nice to Monaco every 90 minutes which take an hour and cost 75F.

◆ Up to nine buses go between Nice and Grasse daily. The journey takes an hour and cost 48F.

HELICOPTERS

Nice-Monaco, 7 minutes, 350F. Heli Air Monaco Tel. 04 92 05 00 50. 36 round trips a day.

CROSSING THE CHANNEL

By car with five passengers: Ferries

◆ Dover-Calais. One and a half hours. Prices range from £160 to £245 depending on the season.

◆ Newhaven-Dieppe. 4 hours.

◆ Southampton-Cherbourg, 6 hours by day and 8 hours overnight. Prices range from £160 to £315. Reductions are available in the low season and for day or short-stay returns.

◆ Folkestone-Boulogne hovercraft crossings take 40 minutes and catamaran

crossings take 50 minutes. Prices range from £150 to £350.

◆ Channel tunnel crossings take 35 minutes Folkestone-Calais. Full fares cost £150 to £350.

BY CAR

The London-Marseilles drive, excluding the Channel crossing, is 742 miles, costing 324F in *autoroute* tolls, while the drive to Nice is nearly 840 miles and tolls amount to 388F.

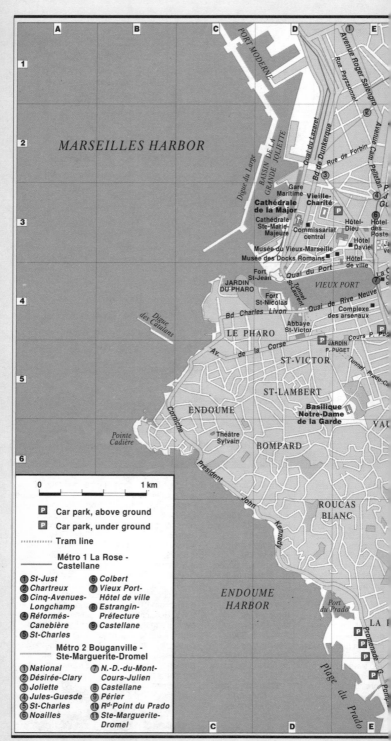

MARSEILLES HARBOR

PORT MODERNE

Digue du Large

Digue des Catalans

BASSIN DE LA GRANDE JOLIETTE

Quai du Lazaret

Bd de Dunkerque

Rue de Forbin

Avenue Roger Salengro

Rue Peyssonnel

Avenue Cam. pelletan

Gare Maritime

Cathédrale de la Major

Cathédrale Ste-Marie-Majeure

Commissariat central

Vieille-Charité

Hôtel-Dieu

Hôtel des Poste

Hôtel Daviel

Musée du Vieux-Marseille

Musée des Docks Romains

Hôtel de ville

Fort St-Jean

Quai du Port

VIEUX PORT

JARDIN DU PHARO

Fort St-Nicolas

Tunnel St-Laurent

Quai de Rive Neuve

Bd Charles Livon

Complexe des arsenaux

LE PHARO

Abbaye St-Victor

JARDIN P. PUGET

Cours P. Pug

Av. de la Corse

ST-VICTOR

Tunnel Prado-Ca

ST-LAMBERT

Basilique Notre-Dame de la Garde

ENDOUME

VAU

Pointe Cadière

Corniche

Théâtre Sylvain

BOMPARD

Président

ROUCAS BLANC

John

Kennedy

ENDOUME HARBOR

Port du Prado

Promenade G.

Plage du Prado

LA

pompi

Legend:

0				1 km

P Car park, above ground

P Car park, under ground

.... Tram line

Métro 1 La Rose - Castellane

① St-Just
② Chartreux
③ Cinq-Avenues-Longchamp
④ Réformés-Canebière
⑤ St-Charles
⑥ Colbert
⑦ Vieux Port-Hôtel de ville
⑧ Estrangin-Préfecture
⑨ Castellane

Métro 2 Bouganville - Ste-Marguerite-Dromel

① National
② Désirée-Clary
③ Joliette
④ Jules-Guesde
⑤ St-Charles
⑥ Noailles
⑦ N.-D.-du-Mont-Cours-Julien
⑧ Castellane
⑨ Périer
⑩ Rd-Point du Prado
⑪ Ste-Marguerite-Dromel

The Marseilles map (▲ 334) and that of Nice (above) provide quick reference to the sites of interest. In Nice, most of these are in the "old town", in the narrow strip along the sea front and can easily be visited on foot. Marseilles, unlike any other Provençal town, has a "métro" (subway or tube) and a tramway, as indicated on the map.

DRIVING IN FRANCE

The speed limit in France is 130 km/h (80 mph) on freeways (*autoroutes*) and 110 km/h (70 mph) on express freeways (*voies express*), 90 km/h (55 mph) on

national trunk roads (*routes nationales*), and 50 km/h (30 mph) in towns and villages. Freeway road-signs are in white letters on a blue background; other roads have signs in black letters on a white background with a small box above indicating whether the road is a D (*départementale*) or N (*nationale*)

followed by the number. Place-name signs in black on a white background with a red frame sometimes give the Provençal version of the name. While the freeway network is extensive, it is prone to traffic jams in the summer. Most towns have pay-and-display parking systems or parking meters. Places are scarce in the high season and public transport or traveling on foot can be the best ways to get around

CAR RENTAL

Car rental facilities are plentiful throughout the Provence region. There are car rental desks in all airports and main town railway stations. You will need a European or international driving license.

AVIGNON
◆ Avis
Tel. 04 90 27 96 10
◆ Hertz
Tel. 04 90 82 37 67
◆ Europcar
Tel. 04 90 82 49 85
DIGNE-LES-BAINS
◆ Avis
Tel. 04 92 32 04 89
MARSEILLES
◆ Avis
Tel. 04 91 64 71 00
◆ Hertz
Tel. 04 91 14 04 24
◆ Europcar
Tel. 04 91 90 11 00
NICE
◆ Avis
Tel. 04 93 87 90 11

◆ Hertz
Tel. 04 93 87 11 87
◆ Europcar
Tel. 04 93 88 64 04
NÎMES
◆ Avis
Tel. 04 66 21 00 29
◆ Hertz
Tel. 04 66 76 25 91
◆ Europcar
Tel. 04 66 21 31 35
TOULON
◆ Avis
Tel. 04 94 89 14 38
◆ Hertz
Tel. 04 94 41 60 53
◆ Europcar
Tel. 04 94 41 09 07

LOCAL EXPRESS TRAINS (TER)

French national railways (SNCF) and bus companies provide regular services under the *Action Région Transport* (ART) programme, organized by the regional authorities. These trains and buses provide an efficient network of public transport throughout Provence. Timetables and routes are available in all SNCF railway stations and also in bus stations.

SNCF STATIONS

All information about timetables, fares, reservations and tickets available from Tel. 08 36 35 35 35

SOS FOR TRAVELERS

◆ Nice-ville station
Tel. 04 93 16 02 61
◆ Marseilles-St-Charles station
Tel. 04 91 62 12 80

TAXIS

Taxi companies in the main towns generally operate a 24-hour service.
◆ Aix-en-Provence
Tel. 04 42 26 29 30

◆ Avignon
(center)
Tel. 04 90 82 20 20
◆ Digne-les-Bains
Tel. 04 92 31 50 50,
04 92 31 66 66
or 04 92 31 26 02
◆ Marseilles
Tel. 04 91 02 20 20,
04 91 49 91 00
or 04 91 03 60 03
◆ Nice
(center)
Tel. 04 93 13 78 78
◆ Toulon
(center)
Tel. 04 94 93 51 51
◆ Nîmes
(center)
Tel. 04 66 29 40 11
or 04 66 29 43 49

THE MÉTRO

Marseilles is the only Provençal town with a subway. Its two lines link the center to the suburbs. Both the métro and the tram operate from 5am to 9pm and use the same tickets (8F for an individual ticket and 42F for a book of six tickets).
Information:
Tel. 04 91 91 92 10.

BUSES

In some towns buses provide a convenient way of getting around during the day and at night. Local information is available at tourist information offices.

Buses operate in Nice from 4am to 9pm and minibuses serve the neighboring hills (8F for an individual ticket, 30F for 5 or 23F for a day pass).
For local information contact:
Tel. 04 93 16 52 10.

BUS STATIONS

◆ Aix-en-Provence
42, rue de la Pierre
Tel. 04 42 27 17 91
◆ Avignon
Av. Monclar
Tel. 04 90 82 07 35
◆ Digne-les-Bains
Rond-point du 11 Novembre
Tel. 04 92 31 50 00
◆ Marseilles
3, pl. Victor-Hugo
Tel. 04 91 08 16 40
◆ Nice
Prom. Paillon
Tel. 04 93 85 61 81
◆ Toulon
Gare SNCF
Tel. 04 94 93 11 39
or 04 94 92 97 41
◆ Nîmes
Rue Ste-Félicité
Tel. 04 66 29 52 00

BOATS

There are many boat companies to help you discover the charms of the islands off the coast of Provence. They run daily trips from all the major ports.

LOCAL BOATING FACILITIES

◆ Bandol–Île de Bendor
Tel. 04 94 29 44 34
◆ Cannes–Île Ste-Marguerite, Île St-Honorat
Tel. 04 93 39 11 82
◆ Six-Fours–Île des Embiez
Tel. 04 94 74 99 00
◆ Îles d'Hyères (Porquerolles, Port-Cros, Île du Levant) – Hyères
Tel. 04 94 58 21 81
or:
– Le Lavandou
Tel. 04 94 71 01 02
or:
– Toulon
Tel. 04 94 62 41 14
◆ Îles de Lérins –Antibes
Tel. 04 93 34 58 21
or:
– Golfe-Juan
Tel. 04 93 63 81 31

or:
– La Napoule
Tel. 04 93 49 15 88
or:
– Théoule-sur-Mer
Tel. 04 93 49 74 33
◆ La Ciotat–Île Verte
Tel. 04 42 08 61 32
◆ Marseilles (Vieux-Port)–Château d'If –Île de Frioul
Tel. 04 91 55 50 09

CORSICA

Corsica is one of the wonders of the Mediterranean. The SNCM and the CMN run ferries all year round from Toulon, Nice and Marseilles to the different ports of the *Île de Beauté* (Ajaccio, Bastia, Calvi, L'Île Rousse, Porto-Vecchio,

Propriano). Prices vary according to the season: from 270F (£34 / $50) to 310F (£39 / $60) for adults. These rates do not include the cost of a cabin. Prices for private vehicles range from 193F to 1,169F (£25 / $40 to £150 / $225) depending on the size and the time of year.
◆ Marseilles
SNCM
Tel. 04 91 56 30 30
CMN
Tel. 04 91 91 91 26
◆ Nice
SNCM
Tel. 04 93 13 66 66
◆ Toulon
SNCM
Tel. 04 94 16 66 60

◆ LIVING IN PROVENCE

Provençal seaside and ski resorts have two distinct rhythms of life: during the season when all their facilities are exploited to the full, and off season when prices tend to drop and many hotels, restaurants and other tourist stores and services close down. Inland towns and villages, on the other hand, including main cities like Marseilles (France's second largest city) and four others which have over 100,000 inhabitants, remain fully operative throughout the year with all the normal services you might expect, such as banks, post and tourist information offices.

MONEY

The franc is divided into *centimes*: 100 c = 1 franc. There are 500, 200, 100, 50 and 20 franc notes; and coins of 20, 10, 5, 2 and 1 franc as well as 50, 20, 10 and 5 centimes.

CREDIT OR BANK CARDS

Throughout France credit cards are accepted by almost all hotels, restaurants and stores. Forty percent of French bank branches have auto-teller machines. You will find at least one in towns of any importance. International credit cards such as Visa, Mastercard or Eurocheque enable you to withdraw up to 2,000F a week from the auto-teller network.

TRAVELERS' CHECKS

Hotel chains, a great many restaurants and most stores will accept payment in French franc travelers' checks. Most organizations that accept travelers checks will have a sticker in the window advertizing the fact. However, it is probably best to ask first. If you carry travelers' checks in your home currency you will need to change them in a bank or bureau de change which usually take a commission at a minimum rate or as a percentage of the amount changed.

EUROCHEQUES

Most European countries issue Eurocheques. These are accompanied by a Eurocard bank guarantee card that may also be used for withdrawals on personal accounts in certain banks. It provides a bank reference for the recipient to verify the validity of personal checks drawn in French francs. The credit ceiling for the use of Eurocheques is 7,000F and no single check can be issued for more than 1,400F. If a store or other business accepts a check above these limits it is not covered if the issuing party becomes insolvent.

BANKS

Banks are generally open from 9 to 12am and 2 to 5pm (some branches in major towns stay open at lunchtime). They are closed Sundays, holidays and usually on Saturdays. Bureaux de change usually have longer hours and are often open on holidays.

LOSS OR THEFT

Contact the closest *gendarmerie* or *commissariat de police* immediately. Tel: 17

CREDIT CARDS

Call the issuing company as soon as possible and send a registered letter to your bank. Expect a replacement card to take about three weeks to be issued.
◆ Visa
Tel: 01 42 77 11 90
◆ Eurocard Mastercard
Tel: 01 45 67 84 84
◆ American Express
Tel: 01 47 77 72 00
◆ Diner's Club
Tel: 01 47 62 75 00

EUROCHEQUES

Inform the issuing bank as soon as possible.

PERSONAL DOCUMENTS

Inform your national consulate immediately of the loss of passports or other national identity documents.

TELEPHONES

CALLING FRANCE

To call France from abroad dial the

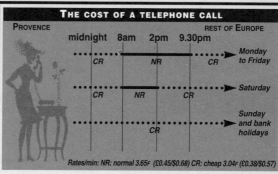

THE COST OF A TELEPHONE CALL

Rates/min: NR: normal 3.65F (£0.45/$0.68) CR: cheap 3.04F (£0.38/$0.57)

international code, then 33, followed by the prefix 1, 2, 3, 4 or 5 (according to the region required) and the eight-figure number.

CALLING ABROAD FROM FRANCE

Dial 00, then the country code, area code and number. A call to the US from Provence by a calling card using AT&T costs $4.27 for the first minute and $1.13 for each additional minute.

CALLS WITHIN FRANCE

For local and inter-regional calls dial the ten-figure number. For calls within the Paris region, dial the ten-digit number. For directory enquiries in France dial 12.

PHONE BOOTHS

These are everywhere, even in the countryside, and are card-operated. Cards are of 50 and 120 units, costing 40F, 60F and 97.50F respectively.

MINITEL

This is a small keyboard and screen linked to the phone network through which information from a "server" may be accessed by means of simple codes. There is one available in all post offices on which you can view the electronic phone directory free by keying 3611.

MAIL

The normal rate for cards or letters up to 20 g (0.7 oz) within Europe and France itself is 3F. A postcard or letter from France to the U.S. costs 4.30F. Stamps can be bought in post offices (there are often automatic machines to avoid delay) and tobacconists (*tabacs*). Main post

offices are open from 8am to 6.30pm; village ones have shorter hours and close for lunch; all are open till noon on Saturdays.

EMERGENCY NUMBERS

MEDICAL EMERGENCIES
SAMU
Tel. 15
◆ Alpes-de-Haute-Provence
Tel. 04 92 30 17 38
◆ Alpes-Maritimes
Tel. 04 93 92 55 55
◆ Bouches-du-Rhône
Tel. 04 91 38 20 00
◆ Var
Tel. 04 94 61 61 15
FIRE
Tel. 18
POLICE
Tel. 17

USEFUL NUMBERS AND ADDRESSES

BRITISH CONSULATES
◆ 24, av. Prado
13006 Marseilles
Tel. 04 91 53 43 32
◆ 11, rue Paradis
06000 Nice
Tel. 04 93 82 32 04
US CONSULATE
◆ 12, boulevard Paul Paytral, 13386 Marseilles CX 06
Tel. 04 91 54 92 00

NEWSPAPERS

Papers and magazines from most countries as well as European editions of American publications are widely available. You can buy them at news stands or in the many newsagents throughout Provence.

POLICE COMMISSARIATS

◆ Caserne de Salles, 84000 Avignon
Tel. 04 90 80 51 00
◆ 2, rue Monges, 04000 Digne-les-Bains
Tel. 04 92 30 86 60
◆ 2, rue Antoine-Becker, 13002 Marseilles
Tel. 04 91 39 80 00
◆ Rue Louis-Notari, 98000 Monaco

Tel. 04 93 15 30 15
◆ 1, av. Maréchal-Foch, 06000 Nice
Tel. 04 92 17 22 22
◆ 16, av. Feuchères, 30000 Nîmes
Tel. 04 66 62 82 82
◆ 1, rue du Commissaire-Morandin, 83000 Toulon
Tel. 04 94 09 80 00

◆ Living in Provence

Hotels

In accordance with French standards there are six grades of hotel: from no star (*sans étoile*) to four star *de luxe*. Rooms should be vacated at 12 noon. Prices are per room, not per person. It is wise to reserve in advance in the holiday seasons (Easter, July-August).

Hotel chains
◆ Baladhotel:
This association of hoteliers caters specifically for walkers, cyclists and horse riders and is coordinated under a national charter.
Maison de la randonnée
4, rue Voltaire
38000 Grenoble
Tel. 04 76 51 76 00.

◆ Relais et châteaux:
A national group of hotels in converted châteaux and manor houses, often in grounds that are game parks or environmentally protected areas.
Relais et Châteaux
15, rue Galvani
75017 Paris
Tel. 01 45 72 90 00

◆ Logis de France:
Provide rural accommodation in accordance with local traditions, particularly as regards food and wine, offering good value for money.
Logis de France
83, av. d'Italie
75013 Paris
Tel. 01 45 84 83 84

Club de vacances

"Villages Vacances Familles", VVF, is an organization specializing in family holidays and European exchanges. Allow 1,500F per person per week to cover full board and lodging. Reservations by phone:
Tel. 01 60 81 60 60 and 04 78 95 76 76
By mail:
VVF-Service réservation
BP 101
91415 Dourdan Cedex
Agence de Marseilles
45, rue Breteuil
13005 Marseilles
Tel. 04 91 55 01 25

Season rentals

Private houses or apartments
Estate agents and private owners, through the local tourist offices (*syndicats d'initiative*), offer weekly, fortnightly or monthly rentals. Allow a minimum of 3,000F a week for a house large enough for four people; there is no legal limit to rates charged.

Gîtes ruraux
A charter of standard services protects both the client and the owner of *gîtes ruraux*. They are often located in traditional country houses. Prices range from 800F to 7,500F a week, for four to six people, depending on the season, location and the classification from one to three "ears of corn" (rural equivalent of stars) as a measure of comfort and facilities.
◆ Gîtes de France
35, rue Godot-de-Mauroy
75009 Paris
Tel. 01 49 70 75 75
or ask at the departmental tourist information office.

Camping

France is one of the best equipped European countries for camping, both in quantity and in quality of facilities. A total of 850 campsites are known to exist in Provence, ranging from one to four star, many of which are by the sea. Prices vary according to the category to which the campsite belongs, the location and services offered, such as water and electricity. The Conseil Régional du Tourisme (CRT) of Provence (PACA) and the CRT Riviera-Côte d'Azur publish free brochures that advertise the local campsites. You can also obtain from any good bookstore:
◆ *Guide de la Fédération française du camping-caravaning*. Lists all the campsites in France; price 50F
◆ *Guide Michelin du camping-caravaning en France*.

EQUIVALENT MEN'S SIZES		EQUIVALENT WOMEN'S SIZES	
FRANCE	US(UK)	FRANCE	US(UK)
JACKETS		SKIRTS AND DRESSES	
44	36	34	4 (8)
46	36/38	36	8 (10)
48	38	38	10 (12)
50	40	40	12 (14)
52	42	42	14 (16)
54	42/44	44	16 (18)
56	44	46	18 (20)
TROUSERS		JACKETS	
44	36	36	6 (8)
46	38	38	10 (12)
48	40	40	12 (14)
50	40/42	42	14 (16)
52	42	44	16 (18)
54	44	46	18
SHOES		48	20
40½	8 (7½)	50	22
41	8½ (8)	WOMEN'S SHOES	
42	9½ (9)	36½	5½ (4)
43	10½ (10)	37	6 (4½)
44	11 (10½)	37½	6½ (5)
45	11½ (11)	38½	7 (5½)
		39	7½ (6)
		39½	8 (6½)
		40½	8½ (7)

WHAT THINGS COST

ONE BOTTLE OF CHÂTEAUNEUF-DU-PAPE: 55–100F

ONE COFFEE: 10F

ONE LITER BOTTLE OF OLIVE OIL (TOP QUALITY): 80F

ONE NIGHT IN A PALACE IN CANNES: 2,000F

ONE BOUILLABAISSE: 30–250F

ONE MUSEUM ENTRANCE TICKET: 20F

ONE HOUR'S WINDSURFING BOARD RENTAL: 60F

ONE DAY ON A PRIVATE BEACH, WITH LUNCH: 300F

CAMPERS

There are about twenty service areas spread throughout Provence which provide electricity, water and waste processing for campers (known in France as *camping-cars*). These are listed in the *Guide officiel des aires de service*, published by Edirégie and available at a cost of 40F from newsagents or by calling 01 45 93 72 72.

RESTAURANTS

Provence has a wide variety of restaurants offering a broad range of prices and types of food. In summer beware of inflated prices and questionable quality. Ask the local people before you choose a restaurant. Restaurants are are generally open between 12.30pm and 3pm at lunchtime and from 8pm to 10pm in the evening. Some restaurants stay open all day. Service is supposed to be included in the menu prices and is therefore added to the bill. While visiting Provence you should be certain to sample the exquisite seafood: fish, shellfish and molluscs, and the celebrated *pissaladière*, a type of onion pie with *pissala* (anchovy paste) and black olives, accompanied by some of the delicious local wines.

MARKETS

Every town or village has an open-air market once or twice a week, usually in the main square. These offer fresh produce at the best prices: fish, meat, local vegetables and fruit that are in season, as well as some traditional dishes, cooked and ready to take away.

"STATIONS VERTES" AND "VILLAGES DE NEIGE"

A number of villages have been brought together under a special charter to provide tourists with reasonably priced nature holidays and entertainments in a restful rural environment, both summer and winter.

The Provence region has seventeen of these "green holiday resorts" and four "snow villages". Information about these special resorts is available from the *Fédération française des stations vertes de vacances et des villages de neige*, BP 598, 21016 Dijon-Cedex.

LIVING IN THE SUN

PROTECTION FROM BURNS AND DEHYDRATION
The sun is very strong in Provence from March to October. It is essential to protect your skin from sunburn and harmful rays by using sun protection creams available in pharmacies and supermarkets. You should wear a hat if you plan to spend a long time on the beach or walking in the hills. Don't forget to drink lots of water and especially to give plenty to children.

KEEPING THE HOUSE COOL
To keep your accommodation cool remember to close the shutters and blinds in the middle of the day, as the Provençaux themselves do.

◆ FESTIVALS AND MARKETS

ARTS FESTIVALS

ALPES-DE-HAUTE-PROVENCE			
"LES RICHES HEURES MUSICALES"	Simiane-la-Rotonde	July-August	04 92 75 90 47
ALPES-MARITIMES			
INTERNATIONAL FILM FESTIVAL	Cannes	May	04 93 39 01 01
INTERNATIONAL JAZZ FESTIVAL	Antibes-Juan-les-Pins	July	04 92 90 53 00
"GRANDE PARADE DU JAZZ"	Nice	July	04 93 71 89 60
MUSIC FESTIVAL	Menton	August	04 93 57 57 00
BOUCHES-DU-RHÔNE			
"AIX EN MUSIQUE"	Aix-en-Provence	June–July	04 42 21 69 69
INTERNATIONAL CONFERENCE ON PHOTOGRAPHY	Arles	July	04 90 93 24 75
FESTIVAL OF MUSIC AND OPERA	Aix-en-Provence	July	04 42 17 34 00
GYPSY MOSAIC	Arles	July	04 90 93 24 75
INTERNATIONAL JAZZ FESTIVAL ALBERT-MAIOLI	Salon-de-Provence	July	04 90 56 49 08
SACRED MUSIC FESTIVAL	Marseilles	end October	04 91 33 33 79
VAR			
EUROPEAN EXHIBITION OF YOUNG STYLISTS	Hyères	end April	04 94 65 22 72
CHÂTEAUVALLON DANCE FESTIVAL	Ollioules	July	04 94 24 11 46
INTERNATIONAL CONFERENCE ON MEDIEVAL MUSIC	Le Thoronet (Abbey)	mid July	04 94 73 85 00
JAZZ IN RAMATUELLE	Ramatuelle	mid July	04 94 79 26 04
THEATER FESTIVAL	Ramatuelle	1st half Aug.	04 94 79 26 04
ORGAN FESTIVAL	Ste-Baume	August	04 94 78 00 09
FESTIVAL OF STRING QUARTETS	Fayence	end October	04 94 68 58 33
VAUCLUSE			
INTERNATIONAL FESTIVAL OF STRING QUARTETS	Fontaine-de-Vaucluse	May–Sep.	04 90 74 48 03
"NUITS D'ÉTÉ DE LOURMARIN" FESTIVAL	Lourmarin	July	04 90 68 15 23
AVIGNON FESTIVAL	Avignon	July	04 90 82 67 08
"OFF" FESTIVAL	Avignon	July	04 48 05 20 97
THE "CHORÉGIES"	Orange	July–August	04 90 51 83 83

MAIN MARKETS

ALPES-DE-HAUTE-PROVENCE			
BARCELONNETTE	all goods	Wednesday and Saturday	Place du Gravier
CASTELLANE	all goods	Wednesday and Saturday	Place Sauvaire
FORCALQUIER	all goods	Monday	town center
MANOSQUE		Saturday morning	Place de la Mairie, Marcel-Pagnol and du Terreau
SISTERON		Wed. and Sat. morning	Place Dr-Robert
ALPES-MARITIMES			
ANTIBES	Provençal	every day exc. Monday	Cours Massena
CANNES	antiques	Saturday	Allée de la Liberté
NICE	flowers	every day exc. Monday	Cours Saleya
	fish	every day	Place Saint-François
VENCE	antiques	Wednesday	old town
VILLEFRANCHE	flea market	Sunday and holidays	port
BOUCHES-DU-RHÔNE			
AIX-EN-PROVENCE	fruit and veg.	Thursday, Saturday	Place Richelme and de la Madeleine
	flowers	Tues., Thurs., Sat.	town hall
MARSEILLES	fish	every day	old port, quai des Belges
	all goods	every day	Velten
	flowers	Tuesday and Saturday	Allée de Meilhan
VAR			
BORMES-LES-MIMOSAS	arts and crafts	Friday eve. (summer) Monday eve. (summer)	in the village La Favière
TOULON	Provençal	every day exc. Monday	Cours Lafayette, Mourillon, Pont-du-Las, St-Jean-du-Var
	old prints	1st Sat. of the month	Place du Théâtre
VAUCLUSE			
AVIGNON	antiques	Saturday	Place Crillon
L'ISLE-SUR-LA-SORGUE	antiques	Sunday	Av. Quatre-Otages
VALRÉAS	truffles	Wednesday (Nov.-March)	town center

MAIN FESTIVALS AND SPORTING EVENTS

ALPES-DE-HAUTE-PROVENCE

"LES ORALIES DE HAUTE PROVENCE"	Valensole, Forcalquier, Castellane, Quinson, Digne, Volx	October
"FESTIVAL DES NUITS DE LA CITADELLE"	Sisteron	mid July–mid August

ALPES-MARITIMES

AUTOMOBILE RALLY	Monte-Carlo	January
CELEBRATION OF THE FEAST OF STE-DÉVOTE	Monaco	January
FEAST OF THE LEMONS	Menton	end February
PILGRIMAGE OF THE MADONNA OF UTELLE	Utelle	Easter Monday
OPEN TENNIS CHAMPIONSHIP	Monte-Carlo	April
GRAND PRIX	Monaco	May
TRADITIONAL MAY FESTIVAL	Nice	May
ROSE FESTIVAL	Grasse	May 15–20
"BRAVADES"	Cannes	May 17–19
"BATTLE OF FLOWERS"	Nice	August
FESTIVAL OF POTTERY	Vallauris	August

BOUCHES-DU-RHÔNE

"LA CHANDELEUR"	Marseilles	February 2
FESTIVAL OF THE "GARDIANS"	Arles	May 1
PILGRIMAGE AND FESTIVAL OF THE GYPSIES	Les-Saintes-Maries-de-la-Mer	May 24–25
FESTIVAL OF TARASQUE	Tarascon	June 26–25
NAUTICAL CONTESTS	Martigues, Istres Port-Saint-Louis, Port-de-Bouc, Fos-sur-Mer	every weekend in July and August
VOTIVE FESTIVAL WITH RELEASE OF BULLS IN THE TOWN	St-Rémy-de-Provence	October 1
PILGRIMAGE AND DEVOTION TO STE-MARIE SALOMÉ	Les Saintes-Maries-de-la-Mer	3rd Sunday in October
"PASTRAGES" (OFFERING OF LAMB BY SHEPHERDS)	Aureille, Eygalières, Les Baux-de-Provence, St-Rémy-de-Provence, Fontvieille	Dec. 24 or 25

VAR

The "TRIPETTES" OF ST-MARCEL	Barjols	mid January
MIMOSA AND FLOWER PARADES	Ste-Maxime, Bormes, St-Raphaël, Hyères, Ollioules, Le Lavandou, Draguignan	from Feb. to May
"COUPE DU MONDE" OF FUNBOARD	Hyères	2nd week of March
"TOUR DE FRANCE" OF CLASSIC CARS	Le Castellet	April 16
FRENCH OLYMPIC WEEK OF 1000 SAILS	Hyères	April 23–30
"BRAVADE"	Fréjus	4th week of April
SPANISH "BRAVADES" AND FESTIVALS	St-Tropez	May
FESTIVAL OF STE-MARIE MADELEINE	La Ste-Baume	July 22

VAUCLUSE

CYCLE TOUR OF VAUCLUSE		April
PARADE	Cavaillon	May
ANNOUNCEMENT OF THE GRAPE HARVEST	Châteauneuf-du-Pape	September

MAIN FAIRS

BOUCHES-DU-RHÔNE

GARLIC & HERB FAIR	Marseilles	mid-June–end July
"SANTONS" (ORNAMENTAL CHRISTMAS FIGURES)	Marseilles	end November –end December

GARD

FAIR OF STE-MADELEINE	Beaucaire	July

VAR

FAIR OF CRAFTS AND REGIONAL PRODUCTS	Plan-d'Aups	mid May
"FLORALIES"	Sanary-sur-Mer	mid May
CRAFT AND WINE-MAKING FAIR	Vidauban	1st w/e in Aug.
POTTERY FAIR	Fayence-Tourettes	mid September
CHESTNUT FAIR	La Garde-Freinet	November

VAUCLUSE

HORSE PASSION	Avignon	January
TRUFFLE FAIR	Carpentras	July
POTTERY MARKET	Apt	August
FAIR OF ST-SIFFREIN	Carpentras	November
CRAFT AND "SANTONS" FAIR	Sorgues	December

343

"So schnell" by Dominique Bagouet at the 1993 Avignon Festival.

Theater productions in the Cour d'honneur of the Palace of the Popes.

In a region where more than four hundred festivals take place each year and with nearly as many theater companies as the Paris region, it seems natural for Avignon to host a festival of world theater and for the whole region to be a center for major musical events. There are a number of entertaining ancient Provençal traditions, one of which is bullfighting.

THE AVIGNON FESTIVAL ▲ 138

This annual festival is in two parts: the "in" festival and the "off" festival. The first is the official part of the festival. All the performances, including theater, readings, dance and modern music are specially created for the event and are produced according to a carefully prepared artistic program. Each year it focuses on the creativity of a different country. The second part of the festival is made up of a program sampling the numerous current trends in the world of entertainment, as represented by the young authors and artistes who participate.

THE "IN" FESTIVAL
Performances take place throughout July in historic sites such as the Cour d'honneur of the Palace of the Popes or the Carrières de Boulbon, among others. A copy of the program is available in Paris by telephoning 01 44 61 84 84 or from the Festival d'Avignon, St-Louis d'Avignon, Rue Portail-Bocquier, 84000 Avignon Tel. 04 90 14 14 14, 10am to 6pm from the beginning of June. Reservations can be made by mail, telephone or from the festival office at the above address address. Seat prices range from 70F to 270F.

THE "OFF" FESTIVAL
This takes place in a wide variety of unusual locations, including over-heated rooms, gymnasiums and circus tents. The streets and squares are alive with busking actors, musicians, dancers and parades.

Avignon turns into a performing town. Tickets and programs can be reserved and bought from "Avignon Public Off", Place du Palais, 84000 Avignon Tel. 04 90 85 79 62 or BP 5, 75521 Paris Tel. 01 48 05 20 97.

Tickets costing 60F to 100F are available at a 30 percent discount to members of the "Avignon Public Off" association. Membership for the season costs 65F. For information call 01 48 05 20 97.

FACILITIES FOR FESTIVAL-GOERS

◆ Festigarde (when available): child-minding Tel. 04 90 86 12 91
◆ Certain centers are available for budget travelers. The "centre jeune" is for young people aged sixteen to twenty-five and includes a series of encounters and activities. For over eighteens the "centre séjour" offers basic accommodation. CEMEA, 76, bd de la Villette, 75940 Paris Cedex 19, Tel. 01 40 40 43 43 or 8, rue Mistral, 84000 Avignon, Tel. 04 90 27 09 98.

TRANSPORTATION
◆ BUSES
Avignon runs an extra bus service for the duration of the festival. A special card for people attending the "off " festival is available at a cost of 30F, and buys unlimited bus travel for seven days.
◆ PARKING
Parking lots at the station and under the Palace of the Popes are open throughout the festival to keep traffic away from the old town center.

Paco Ojeda at the spring corrida.

Richard Milian at St-Laurent-d'Aigouze.

BULLFIGHTING EVENTS

As the Bouches-du-Rhône and the Gard are the natural habitat of wild bulls, these *départements* have a traditional season of taurine events from March to November. Local arts and crafts and traditional dress are on display and the *ferias* are celebrated with ancient rituals.

THE SPANISH "CORRIDA"

Three *toreros* take turn, in order of seniority, at fighting and killing two bulls each. This meeting of man and beast takes place under the expert eye of the president of the fight and an audience of critical *aficionados*. The *torero* must seek their approval to kill the bull with the sword; if he is not worthy or the bull is especially "*bravo*" this may be denied.

♦ Nîmes has two *ferias*: one at Pentecost, in spring, and the other during the grape harvest at the end of summer, Tel. 04 66 67 28 02. Arles has an Easter *feria* and another on the feast of the Assumption (August 15). Tel. 04 90 96 03 70.

THE "NOVILLADE"

These have the same rules as *corridas* and provide young *toreros* with the chance to fight bulls under four years old.

♦ Saintes-Maries-de-la-Mer has a *feria* known as *Printemps des novillades* at the beginning of March, Tel. 04 90 97 82 55.

PORTUGUESE "CORRIDAS"

These bull fights are on horseback and do not end in a kill.

♦ Spanish and Portuguese *corridas* and *novillades* form part of the program of the *Feria du cheval* (mid July) at Saintes-Maries-de-la-Mer.

THE "COURSE CAMARGUAISE"

In these arena games teams of professional players compete to seize rosettes from the horns of bulls. Each rosette is worth a prize. They are held in many Provençal towns: Tarascon, end of June (Tel. 04 90 91 03 52), St-Martin-de-Craux, May and October (Tel. 04 90 47 38 88), Saintes-Maries-de-la-Mer, Easter to October, Châteaurenard, May to October (Tel. 04 90 94 23 27).

ENCIERO

Young "*vachettes*" are run through the streets of the town. Mid July, during the *nuit taurine* at St-Rémy-de-Provence.

ANTIBES JAZZ FESTIVAL ▲ 275

Concerts take place throughout July at La Pinède, Square Gould, 06160 Juan-les-Pins. The Maison du Tourisme issues programs from the end of May and reservations should be made in June. 11, pl. de Gaulle, 06160 Antibes,

Tel. 04 92 90 53 00 51, bd Guillaumont, 06160 Juan-les-Pins, Tel. 04 92 90 53 05. Tickets cost around 200F. If you are traveling by car be sure to allow plenty of time to park in town when the concerts are on.

AIX-EN-PROVENCE MUSIC FESTIVAL ▲ 215

In the Palais de l'Ancien Archevêché there are operas and concerts throughout the month of July. They take place in the afternoon and evening. Programs and reservations can be obtained from the beginning of the year from:

♦ Festival d'art lyrique, Palais de l'Ancien Archevêché, 13100 Aix-en-Provence, Tel. 04 42 17 34 00. Allow 250F to 700F per ticket. No problem parking; there are numerous parking lots all over town.

"CHORÉGIES D'ORANGE" ▲ 182

In this choral music season you must reserve a long time in advance for the highly sought-after Saturday night operas. Programs are available locally or by mail, as of January. Chorégies d'Orange BP 205 84107 Orange Cedex

Tel. 04 90 34 24 24 or 04 90 34 15 52 Reservations can be made at the same address using the tear-out coupons from the programs. Any remaining places are sold on the night. Prices depend on the quality of the performance, ranging from 70 to 850F. Be sure to reserve your accommodation in advance because this is a major attraction. It can be just as nice to stay in a neighboring town.

◆ Beaches

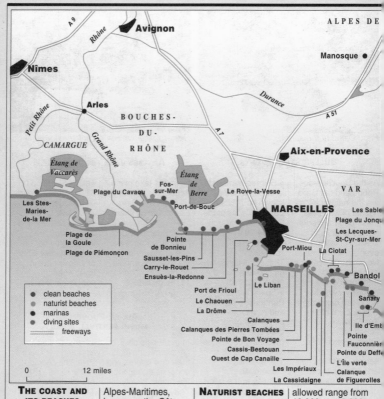

THE COAST AND ITS BEACHES

Bouches-du-Rhône has over 45 miles of fine sandy beaches (Camargue), over 70 miles of rocky coast (*Côte bleue*, the *calanques*, the Soubeyranes cliffs), and wide bays facing east (Cassis, La Ciotat). The most popular part of Provence is the Var coast – 180 miles of rocky creeks and about 20 miles of sandy beaches, some of which nestle in beautiful bays (Bormes-les-Mimosas, Cavalaire, Fréjus-plage, St-Tropez, Pampelonne, Port-Grimaud). Most of this coast is dotted with cliffs, coves, *calanques*, capes and promontories. Ninety-six percent of the coast of the Alpes-Maritimes, known as the Côte d'Azur, is now built up. It has about 17 miles of sand and pebble beaches sheltered by sheer rock promontories forming gulfs and bays (golfe de la Napoule, golfe Juan, baie des Anges), or lining the 55 miles of waterfronts of its coastal towns.

PRIVATE BEACHES

These are most common in the Var and along the Côte d'Azur. They offer facilities such as deck chairs, umbrellas and water sports and charge an entrance fee plus supplements for facilities and activities. Prices vary according to their reputation and official rating (one to four umbrellas).

NATURIST BEACHES

The Île du Levant, in the Var, harbors *Héliopolis*, a renowned naturist or nudist center. Some other beaches in Provence have the official *sans maillot* (no bathing clothes) classification and topless bathing for women is accepted everywhere. However it is worth checking with the local authorities or the French Naturist Federation (Tel. 01 47 64 32 82) before indulging in total nudity; fines for nudity where it is not allowed range from 10,000F to 15,000F.

WATER QUALITY

All municipal authorities (*mairies*) are required by law to publish regular water quality reports for their beaches.

THE BLUE FLAG
A blue flag is awarded each year to beach resorts that participate in a clean environment operation and meet the standards set by the European Environmental Education Foundation for beach quality.

SEA WATER TEMPERATURES ON THE MEDITERRANEAN COAST (IN °F)												
J	F	M	A	M	J	J	A	S	O	N	D	
56	54	56	59	65	68	72	72	69	65	62	58	

Note: these are averages. July and August water temperatures can actually range from 59° to 86°F

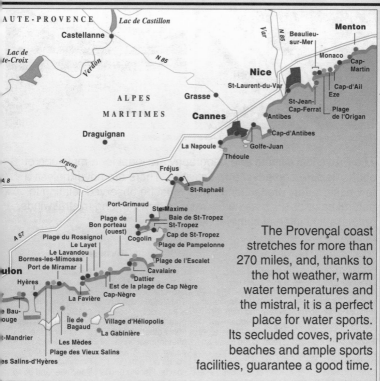

The Provençal coast stretches for more than 270 miles, and, thanks to the hot weather, warm water temperatures and the mistral, it is a perfect place for water sports. Its secluded coves, private beaches and ample sports facilities, guarantee a good time.

SCUBA AND DEEP-SEA DIVING

The French Federation for Underwater Research and Sport offers guided underwater "tours" along pre-established routes for beginners, as well as exploration tours of shipwrecks for more experienced divers.
◆ Marseilles
Tel. 04 91 33 99 31

MOTOR BOATS

Motor boats, launches and yachts are extremely popular on the coast of Provence. Local tourist offices can provide information about hiring or chartering *véhicules nautiques à moteur* (nautical motor vehicles) and water-skiing equipment.

WINDSURFING

The Provençal beaches are considered to be among the world's best windsurfing spots.
◆ BOUCHES-DU-RHÔNE:
Stes-Maries-de-la-Mer, Port-St-Louis-du-Rhône, Carro, Marseilles (plage du Prado and Pointe-Rouge) and La Ciotat.
◆ VAR:
Les Lecques, Six-Fours, Giens.
◆ ALPES-MARITIMES: Antibes.
◆ Several inland lakes, such as Ste-Croix in the Var and Serre-Ponçon in the Bouches-du-Rhône, offer sailing and windsurfing and provide safer conditions than the open sea when the wind is strong.

YACHTING

Provence has many excellent and well-equipped ports for yachts and sailing vessels of all descriptions.

LEARNING TO SAIL

Qualified instructors of the *Fédération française de voile*, with offices in most ports, provide courses for beginners and more experienced sailors as well as for windsurf and funboard fanatics.
◆ Fédération de voile Ligue Provence-Alpes Tel. 04 91 77 19 38 (Alpes-de-Haute-Provence, Bouches-du-Rhône, Vaucluse)
◆ Ligue Côte d'Azur Tel. 04 93 74 77 05 (Alpes-Maritimes, Var)

"SÉCURITÉ OBLIGE"

All forms of boating and nautical sports are governed by strict laws in France. These regulate equipment standards, traffic rules (speed limits, priorities, etc.), safety rules and compulsory "driving" or sailing licenses. The various federations, sailing clubs, boat rental companies, port authorities and instructors will give you all the necessary information.

WEATHER CONDITIONS

Beware of the strength of the sun and the wind, which can change direction very suddenly.

Rock climbing
in the Bouches-du-Rhône.

Mison Lake in the
Alpes-de-Haute-Provence.

The Provençal climate and geography are ideal for a multitude of sports, leisure and adventure activities. There are nevertheless a few basic safety precautions which must be observed relating to natural hazards such as heavy rains, storms, strong mistral winds, fire risks and intense summer heat.

IN THE AIR

Provence's natural conditions as well as a network of sports clubs cater for a number of air-borne sports.

FLYING
A number of small airports and flying clubs provide facilities and lessons.
◆ Fédération nationale d'aéronautique
Tel. 01 53 67 83 20
◆ Fédération française de planeur ultraléger motorisé
Tel. 01 49 81 74 43

DELTA-PLANING AND GLIDING
These free-flight sports involve certain risks and require special equipment. You should therefore refer to the clubs and federations and practice them only on one of approved sites of which there are plenty, particularly in the Alpine parts of Provence.
◆ Fédération française de vol libre
Tel. 04 93 88 62 89
◆ Fédération française de vol à voile
Tel. 01 45 44 04 78

ROCK SPORTS

ROCK CLIMBING
Provence offers ample opportunities for climbing at all levels: sea cliffs, deep canyons, highly contrasted limestone mountain faces and Alpine ranges up to ten thousand feet. Local clubs manage the circuits and provide training and guiding facilities.
◆ Fédération française de la montagne et de l'escalade16, rue Louis-Dardenne 92170 Vanves
Tel. 01 41 08 00 00

◆ Club alpin français
Tel. 01 42 02 68 64
Rules the shelters.

SPELEOLOGY (CAVING)
There are magnificent pot-holes, crevasses and limestone caves in the Bouches-du-Rhône.
◆ Fédération française de spéléologie
Tel. 01 43 57 56 54
◆ École française de spéléologie
Tel. 04 78 39 43 30

RIVER SPORTS

CANOEING, RAFTING AND CANYONING
The Verdon canyon is a canoeing paradise for experts. Many other places offer interesting easier runs. These sports do require special training and general fitness. Canoes and kayaks can also be used at sea.
◆ Fédération française de canoë-kayak
Tel. 01 45 11 08 50
Also manages rafting activities. The canyoning programs are run by the *guides de haute montagne* ▲ *350*.

FISHING
Sea, river, mountain torrent and lake fishing are all available in Provence. The best trout river is the Sorgue, which springs from the Fontaine-de-Vaucluse, and good fishing is to be had in the Alpine torrents. Check with local organizations for licenses, permits and seasons.
◆ Alpes-de-Haute-Provence
Tel. 04 92 32 25 40
◆ Alpes-Maritimes
Tel. 04 93 72 06 04
◆ Bouches-du-Rhône
Tel. 04 42 26 59 15
◆ Var
Tel. 04 94 69 05 56
◆ Vaucluse
Tel. 04 90 86 62 68

ARTIFICIAL LAKES

A number of artificial lakes are equipped and managed specifically for bathing, sailing and fishing. This applies to such lakes as Sainte-Croix in the Var and the Alpes-de-Haute-Provence and Serre-Ponçon in the Alpes-de-Haute-Provence.

An image of the regional sport of "pétanque" in a painting by C. Camoin.

Postcard from a Provençal golf club, beginning of the 20th century.

ON LAND

GOLF

With its forty-three golf courses and twenty-four schools with practise and compact courses, Provence is a dreamland for golf lovers. Each club sets its own membership fees and conditions. The best equipped *départements* are the Alpes-Maritimes with twelve eighteen-hole courses, the Bouches-du-Rhône with ten, seven of which are eighteen-hole and the Var with thirteen courses, ten of which are eighteen-hole.
◆ Ligue Provence-Alpes-Côte d'Azur
Domaine Riquetti
13290 Les Milles
Tel. 04 42 39 86 83

"PÉTANQUE" ● 65

This sport, the symbol of Provence, can be played by all. The rules are simple: two players or two teams of two (*doublette*) or three (*triplette*) oppose each other. Playing singly or in *doublette* each player has three *boules*, in *triplette* they have two. The aim of the game is to get the most boules as close as possible to the *cochonnet*, a small wooden target ball thrown 20–35 feet away. Players must stand behind the playing line drawn in the sand, feet together or *pieds-tanqués*. A game is played for a total of thirteen points.
◆ Fédération française de pétanque et de jeu provençal
Tel. 04 91 50 53 58.

REGIONAL NATURE RESERVES

The creation and management of these nature reserves (*parcs naturels*) are part of the regional program for the conservation and protection of the local natural and cultural heritage.

CAMARGUE

Centre d'information de Ginès
Pont-de-Gau
13460 Les Saintes-Maries-de-la-Mer
Tel. 04 90 97 86 32

LUBÉRON

Maison du parc
60, pl. Jean-Jaurès
84404 Apt-Cedex
Tel. 04 90 04 42 00

BEWARE

Access to Provençal rivers is forbidden when water is being released from the hydroelectric dams and after heavy storms or rainfall which in this region can cause sudden spates.

FIRE RISK

Due to the hot sun, strong winds and the lack of rain, there are frequent forest fires in Provence. Thousands of acres of pine forests are destroyed each year. A number of safety rules have to be complied with:
◆ never throw away unextinguished cigarettes or matches
◆ never light camp fires
◆ never leave glass objects in the *pinèdes* (pine forests)

NATIONAL PARKS

These state-run parks are designed for the conservation of nature in uninhabited areas.

ÎLE DE PORT-CROS

◆ Direction du parc
50, av. Gambetta
83400 Hyères
Tel. 04 94 12 82 30
◆ Centre d'accueil
Pointe Nord
(on the port)
83400 Port-Cros
Tel. 04 94 05 90 17
◆ Bureau d'information
(on the port)
BP 15
83400 Porquerolles
Tel. 04 94 58 33 76

LE MERCANTOUR

◆ Centre d'information
23, rue d'Italie
06000 Nice
Tel. 04 93 16 78 88
◆ Maison du parc
Quartier de l'Andon
06660 St-Étienne-de-Tinée
Tel. 04 93 02 42 27
La Sapinière
04400 Barcelonnette
Tel. 04 92 81 21 31

PROTECTED AREAS

Certain areas and natural landscapes are considered part of France's national heritage and are protected and administered by joint public and private associations which also involve the local municipalities. The Réserve Géologique de Haute-Provence is an "open-air museum" includes eighteen sites spread over 375,000 acres and illustrates the earth's evolution over three hundred million years.
◆ Centre de géologie
Quartier St-Benoît
04000 Digne-les-Bains
Tel. 04 92 31 51 31

◆ TREKKING

A trek on horseback in the Camargue.

Discovering the Bouches-du-Rhône on foot.

The Provençal countryside, in some places hilly, in others mountainous, has many shady trekking routes for hikers, horseback riders and cyclists. These are best explored in the summer when the sun and heat attract crowds to the beaches and you can discover the varied landscapes of the Provence heartland in peace. In winter the southern Alps can be explored on skis (cross-country, piste and ski-trekking) or through other winter sports.

TREKKING

Information on trekking routes and places to stay is provided by the different *départements* and in the *Topo-guides* booklets, available in most bookshops, which list the established circuits, providing maps and practical information. Local or thematic circuits are offered by

The "G.R." (*Grandes Randonnées*) are well signposted trekking trails.

SIGNS

 Trail continues

 Secondary trail

 Right turn

 Left turn

✕ Wrong way

SENTIER G.R.6 Identification panel

G.R 38 ▷ Distance arrow

many tourist offices and by trekking associations. Some walks are closed from July 1 to September 15 due to fire risks.

◆ **ALPES-DE-HAUTE-PROVENCE**
The ADRI-CIMES Association publishes brochures for walking, riding and cycling treks. It also provides a guide to accommodation: *gîtes*, shelters and hostels. Maison des Alpes-de-Haute-Provence, 19, rue Honnorat, 04000 Digne-les-Bains, Tel. 04 92 31 07 01 Verdon Accueil provides information on trekking in the Verdon canyon. Tel. 04 94 70 21 64

◆ **VAR**
The open-air activities section of the Var tourist authority has an information center for all forms of trekking in the *département*. 1, bd. de Strasbourg, 83000 Toulon. Tel. 04 94 18 59 77

◆ **ALPES-MARITIMES**
Full information is available from the departmental tourist authority in the form of brochures in the series *Randoxygène*.

It also provides a list of *gîtes* and mountain refuges. Special committees cater for horseback trekkers (Tel. 04 93 42 62 98) and walkers (Tel. 04 93 09 91 27), offering suggested routes throughout the area.

◆ **VAUCLUSE**
The *Maison des pays* has a wealth of information. Place Puits-des-Boeufs, 84000 Avignon, Tel. 04 90 85 55 24. The list of *gîtes* in the Vaucluse is published by the *Association départementale des gîtes du Vaucluse*. Tel. 04 90 85 45 00.

◆ **BOUCHES-DU-RHÔNE**
The Bouches-du-Rhône has fewer trekking trails and less information to offer. Contact the *Comité de cyclotourisme et VTT* (mountain-biking) Tel. 04 42 81 59 05, the *Comité de randonnée pédestre* Tel. 04 91 98 08 71, the *Association camarguaise de tourisme équestre* Tel. 04 90 97 83 23; the departmental

tourist authority and the different local tourist offices.

"ACCOMPAGNATEURS DE MOYENNE MONTAGNE"
These guides, who have a state diploma, are specially trained to guide you on mountain treks with snowshoes or on mountain bikes. They can be contacted through:
◆ Alpes-de-Haute-Provence M. Raoust Tel. 04 92 89 04 19
◆ Alpes-Maritimes M. Bousquet Tel. 04 93 89 88 98
◆ Maison du parc du Mercantour Parc de la Sapinière 04400 Barcelonnette Tel. 04 92 81 21 31

GUIDES DE HAUTE MONTAGNE
These skilled guides can take groups skiing, abseiling and mountaineering.
◆ Bureau des guides du Mercantour Tel. 04 92 09 27 16
◆ Guides de Valberg Tel. 04 93 02 52 77
◆ Guides de l'Ubaye, office de tourisme Tel. 04 92 81 04 71 (Barcelonnette).

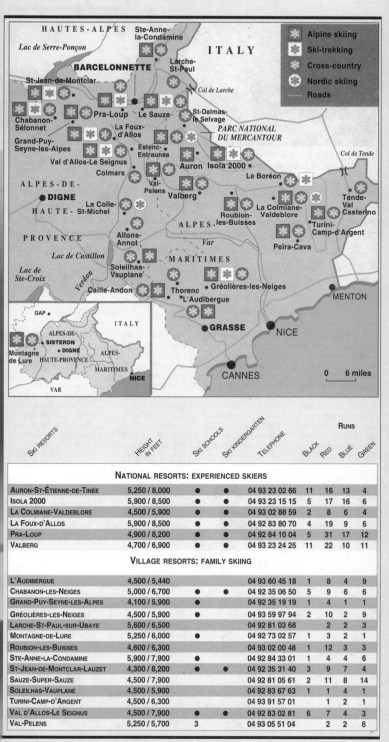

SKI RESORTS	HEIGHT IN FEET	SKI SCHOOLS	SKI KINDERGARTEN	TELEPHONE	RUNS			
					BLACK	RED	BLUE	GREEN
NATIONAL RESORTS: EXPERIENCED SKIERS								
AURON-ST-ÉTIENNE-DE-TINÉE	5,250 / 8,000	●	●	04 93 23 02 66	11	16	13	4
ISOLA 2000	5,900 / 8,500	●	●	04 93 23 15 15	5	17	16	6
LA COLMIANE-VALDEBLORE	4,500 / 5,900	●	●	04 93 02 88 59	2	8	6	4
LA FOUX-D'ALLOS	5,900 / 8,500	●	●	04 92 83 80 70	4	19	9	6
PRA-LOUP	4,900 / 8,200	●	●	04 92 84 10 04	5	31	17	12
VALBERG	4,700 / 6,900	●	●	04 93 23 24 25	11	22	10	11
VILLAGE RESORTS: FAMILY SKIING								
L'AUDIBERGUE	4,500 / 5,440			04 93 60 45 18	1	8	4	9
CHABANON-LES-NEIGES	5,000 / 6,700	●	●	04 92 35 06 50	5	9	6	6
GRAND-PUY-SEYNE-LES-ALPES	4,100 / 5,900	●		04 92 35 19 19	1	4	1	1
GRÉOLIÈRES-LES-NEIGES	4,500 / 5,900	●		04 93 59 97 94	2	10	2	9
LARCHE-ST-PAUL-SUR-UBAYE	5,600 / 6,500			04 92 81 03 68		2	2	3
MONTAGNE-DE-LURE	5,250 / 6,000	●		04 92 73 02 57	1	3	2	1
ROUBION-LES-BUISSES	4,600 / 6,300			04 93 02 00 48	1	12	3	3
STE-ANNE-LA-CONDAMINE	5,900 / 7,900	●		04 92 84 33 01	1	4	4	6
ST-JEAN-DE-MONTCLAR-LAUZET	4,300 / 8,200	●	●	04 92 35 31 40	3	9	7	4
SAUZE-SUPER-SAUZE	4,500 / 7,900			04 92 81 05 61	2	11	8	14
SOLEILHAS-VAUPLANE	4,500 / 5,900			04 92 83 67 63	1	1	4	1
TURINI-CAMP-D'ARGENT	4,500 / 6,300			04 93 91 57 01		1	2	1
VAL D'ALLOS-LE SEIGNUS	4,500 / 7,900	●	●	04 92 83 02 81	6	7	4	3
VAL-PELENS	5,250 / 5,700	3		04 93 05 51 04		2	2	6

◆ "Green" Walks

In February the Tanneron hills are filled with the delicate smell of flowering mimosa.

Le Sauze, one of the pretty villages of the Ubaye Valley.

Provence is not just a coastal region. Much of its territory is mountainous and hilly with spectacular enclosed valleys. The variety of its landscapes is stunningly beautiful. The abundance of flora and fauna to be seen on these three amazing inland itineraries in the Alpes-Maritimes and the Alpes-de-Haute-Provence will satisfy the most demanding visitor.

THE UBAYE VALLEY

The Ubaye river has carved a 50-mile valley, running from east to west, in the southern French Alps. It springs from the high peaks on the border with Italy and joins the Durance at the Serre-Ponçon lake after flowing through Barcelonnette. The complex geology of this valley produces a fascinating variety of landscapes. The vegetation consists of Alpine pastures where local and migratory sheep and cattle have grazed for centuries among arnicas, gentians and edelweiss, *arménies des Alpes*, bright pink campions, forget-me-nots, the queen of Alpine flowers – the legendary *génépis* – and artemesias. With a little patience, you can see over 120 species of birds between the Serre-Ponçon Lake and the more remote peaks of the Ubaye

Valley; these include woodcocks, hazel hens and golden eagles. Ibex, chamois, moufflons, deer, roe deer, wild boar and wolves also live in this area. The recent return of the wolves illustrates the ecological equilibrium of this valley.

THE SASSE VALLEY

The Sasse runs to the northeast of Sisteron. From the high peaks of Bayons it channels the raging waters of torrents and cascades and then flows into the Durance beyond Valerne. Its flora includes bindweed, velvety edelweiss and sweet-smelling thyme and lavender. It is a paradise for rock and fossil enthusiasts, where skilled geologists can observe no less than ten layers of the earth's crust. Hills that were

once barren have been successfully re-forested and turned into green landscapes populated with wildlife. The infinite variety of soil colors in conjunction with the purity of the sky produce constantly changing views throughout the day from dawn to dusk. The contrast between two environments as different as the Alps and the Mediterranean can be both restful and stimulating.

MIMOSA COUNTRY

To the south of Grasse, near Mandelieu, are the Tanneron hills. This area with clear skies and fertile topsoil contrasts through its vegetation with the mostly calcareous hills of the rest of Provence. Alongside the cork oaks are wild and planted mimosa

forests, interspersed with eucalyptus. In January and February, the flowering season for mimosa, the Tanneron hills become sweet-smelling mountains of gold. A magnificent view of the whole range is to be had from the summit.

This tour can be extended as far as the St-Cassien Lake in the Var.

352

◆ USEFUL WORDS ◆

BONJOUR, *Good morning*
AU REVOIR, *Goodbye*
OUI, *Yes*
NON, *No*
S'IL VOUS PLAÎT, *Please*
MERCI, *Thank you*
PARDON, *Sorry*
JE NE COMPRENDS PAS, *I don't understand*
QU'EST-CE QUE C'EST?, *What is it?*
COMBIEN?, *How much/many?*
QUAND?, *When?*
COMMENT?, *How?*
OÙ?, *Where?*
QUI?, *Who?*
QUOI?, *What?*
JE VOUDRAIS, *I would like*
AIDEZ-MOI, *Help me*
GENDARMERIE, *Police station*
POLICE, *Police*
CONSULAT, *Consulate*

◆ CALENDAR ◆

LUNDI, *Monday*
MARDI, *Tuesday*
MERCREDI, *Wednesday*
JEUDI, *Thursday*
VENDREDI, *Friday*
SAMEDI, *Saturday*
DIMANCHE, *Sunday*
WEEK-END, *Weekend*
JOUR FÉRIÉ, *Public holiday*
JANVIER, *January*
FÉVRIER, *February*
MARS, *March*
AVRIL, *April*
MAI, *May*
JUIN, *June*
JUILLET, *July*
AOÛT, *August*
SEPTEMBRE, *September*
OCTOBRE, *October*
NOVEMBRE, *November*
DÉCEMBRE, *December*

◆ NUMBERS ◆

UN, *One*
DEUX, *Two*
TROIS, *Three*
QUATRE, *Four*
CINQ, *Five*
SIX, *Six*
SEPT, *Seven*
HUIT, *Eight*
NEUF, *Nine*
DIX, *Ten*
CINQUANTE, *Fifty*
CENT, *Hundred*
MILLE, *Thousand*

◆ ACCOMMODATION ◆

HÔTEL, *Hotel*
GÎTE, *Rural inn or shelter*
LOCATION SAISONNIÈRE, *Season's rental*
CAMPING, *Camp site*
AUBERGE DE JEUNESSE, *Youth hostel*
SALLE DE BAINS, *Bathroom*
TOILETTES, *Toilet*
CHAMBRE SIMPLE, *Single room*
CHAMBRE DOUBLE, *Double room*
NOTE, *Bill/check*
RÉSERVER, *Reserve*

◆ MONEY ◆

ARGENT, *Money*
ESPÈCES; *Cash*
MONNAIE, *Change*
BILLET, *Bank note*
PIÈCE, *Coin*
BANQUE, *Bank*
CARTE DE CRÉDIT, *Credit card*
CHÈQUE DE VOYAGE, *Traveler's check*
DISTRIBUTEUR DE BILLETS, *Auto-teller*
COMMISSION, *Commission*

◆ MAIL ◆

TÉLÉPHONE, *Telephone*
CABINE TÉLÉPHONIQUE, *Phone booth*
TÉLÉCARTE, *Phonecard*
BUREAU DE POSTE, *Post office*
TÉLÉGRAMME, *Telegramme*
CARTE POSTALE, *Postcard*
MANDAT-POSTE, *Postal order*
LETTRE, *Letter*
COLIS, *Parcel*
ADRESSE, *Address*
ANNUAIRE, *Directory*

◆ HEALTH ◆

URGENCE, *Emergency*
PHARMACIE, *Pharmacy*
HÔPITAL, *Hospital*
MÉDECIN, *Doctor*
DENTISTE, *Dentist*
INFIRMIÈRE, *Nurse*
ASPIRINE, *Aspirin*
RENDEZ-VOUS, *Appointment*

◆ TRANSPORT ◆

VOITURE, *Car*
BUS, *Bus*
TRAIN, *Train*
AVION, *Plane*
BATEAU, *Boat, ship*
VÉLO, *Bicycle*
AUTOCAR, *Coach/bus*
CARNET DE TICKETS, *Book of tickets*
COMPOSTER, *Date stamp*
RÉDUCTION, *Reduction*
CORRESPONDANCE, *Connection*
ARRÊT, *Stop*
STATION, *Metro station*
GARE, *Railway station*
TERMINUS, *Terminal*
ESSENCE, *Petrol/gas*
GASOIL, *Diesel fuel*
ESSENCE SANS PLOMB, *Unleaded petrol/gasoline*
LOCATION DE VOITURES, *Car rental*
PANNE, *Breakdown*
PRIORITÉ, *Priority*
HUILE, *Oil*

◆ FINDING YOUR WAY ◆

PLAN, *Map*
MAISON, *House*
RUE, *Street*
AVENUE, *Avenue*
CHEMIN, *Path*
PLACE, *Square*
QUAI, *Platform (station)*
PONT, *Bridge*
ÎLE, *Island*
À DROITE, *To the right*
À GAUCHE, *To the left*
CARREFOUR, *Crossroads*
ROUTE, *Road*
AUTOROUTE, *Freeway*
VILLE, *Town*

◆ FOOD ◆

RESTAURANT, *Restaurant*
CAFÉ/BAR, *Café/bar*
MANGER, *To eat*
BOIRE, *To drink*
CARTE, *Menu*
MENU, *Fixed menu*
FROID, *Cold*
CHAUD, *Hot*
SEL, *Salt*
SUCRE, *Sugar*
POIVRE, *Pepper*
PETIT DÉJEUNER, *Breakfast*
DÉJEUNER, *Lunch*
DINER, *Dinner*
VIANDE, *Meat*
BŒUF, *Beef*
PORC, *Pork*
POULET, *Chicken*
MOUTON, *Lamb*
POISSON, *Fish*
CRUSTACÉS, *Crabs/lobsters etc.*
COQUILLAGES, *Shellfish*
LÉGUMES, *Vegetables*
FRUITS, *Fruit*
FROMAGE, *Cheese*
DESSERT, *Dessert*
GLACE, *Ice cream*
PÂTISSERIE, *Pastry*
PLAT, *Dish*
VERRE, *Glass*
ASSIETTE, *Plate*
PAIN, *Bread*
EAU, *Water*
VIN BLANC, *White wine*
VIN ROUGE, *Red wine*
VIN ROSÉ, *Rosé wine*
BIÈRE, *Beer*
CAFÉ, *Coffee*
HUILE D'OLIVE, *Olive oil*

◆ STORES ◆

OUVERT, *Open*
FERMÉ, *Closed*
ENTRÉE, *entrance*
SORTIE, *Exit*
LIBRAIRIE, *Bookstore*
GRANDE SURFACE, *Supermarket*
ÉPICERIE, *Grocery*
BOULANGERIE, *Bakery*
BOUCHERIE, *Butcher's store*
BUREAU DE TABAC, *Tobacconist*
MAISON DE LA PRESSE, *Newsagent*
MARCHÉ, *Market*
ACHETER, *To buy*
VENDRE, *To sell*
PRIX, *Price*

◆ ENTERTAINMENT ◆

CINÉMA, *Movie theater*
FILM, *Movie*
CONCERT, *Concert*
DISQUE, *Record*
MUSIQUE, *Music*
THÉÂTRE, *Theater*
PIECE DE THÉÂTRE, *Play*
BILLET, *Ticket*
DANSE, *Dance*
FESTIVAL, *Festival*
BOÎTE DE NUIT, *Night club*
SPECTACLE, *Show*
ENTRACTE, *Interval*
PROGRAMME, *Program*
PLAGE, *Beach*
MER, *Sea*
SKI, *Skiing*
SKI NAUTIQUE, *Water skiing*
MONTAGNE, *Mountain*
RIVIÈRE, *River*
PÊCHE, *Fishing*
ÉQUITATION, *Riding*
NATATION, *Swimming*
RANDONNÉE, *Trekking*
PLANCHE À VOILE, *Windsurfing*
CRÈME SOLAIRE, *Suntan lotion*
GOLF, *Golf*
CLUB SPORTIF, *Sports club*
STADE, *Stadium*

◆ CULTURE ◆

GUIDE, *Guide/guidebook*
VISITE LIBRE, *Unaccompanied visit*
VISITE GUIDÉE, *Guided tour*
MONUMENT, *Monument*
ÉGLISE, *Church*
MONASTÈRE, *Monastery*
MUSÉE, *Museum*
JARDIN, *Garden*
CHAPELLE, *Chapel*
CATHÉDRALE, *Cathedral*
CHÂTEAU, *castle*
PARC NATUREL, *Nature reserve*
SITE PROTÉGÉ, *Protected area*
BIBLIOTHÈQUE, *Library*
FONTAINE, *Fountain*
LIEU DE VISITE, *Place of interest*
LIVRE, *Book*
HORAIRE, *Timetable*

FABRIQUE

Ets. AUX GOURMETS
Marché Remel Kebira

Assorted "berlingots".

Old fashioned truffle packaging.

Thoughts of Provence evoke images of a special way of life, with all sorts of delicious regional cuisine made with aromatic herbs and olive oil, as well as excellent wines, delicious sweetmeats, fabrics that inspire the Paris *couturiers*, sun-soaked perfumes and much more.

THE BOUILLABAISSE

This typical Provençal dish, the "soup that's not a soup", containing all the rock fish from the coast, olive oil, onions, tender leeks, garlic, and *rouille* sauce made of cayenne pepper,

peeled tomatoes, herbs and spices from the *garrigue*.

AROMATIC HERBS

Provençal cuisine depends entirely on aromatic herbs. They can be found in all the markets that regularly animate the main square of most towns and villages.

TRUFFLES

This rare and highly prized tuber is found mainly in the Comtat Venaissin and the Tricastin areas.

From November to March truffle markets are held in Richerenches on Saturdays and Valréas on Wednesdays.

SAULT NOUGAT

There are two sorts of nougat, the white creamy kind that is honey-flavored and sticks to your teeth and the dark, hard, nutty caramel-flavored kind that cracks between your teeth. Eat with care.

◆ André Boyer
84390 Sault-en-Vaucluse
Tel. 04 90 64 00 23

"BERLINGOTS"

These hard-boiled candies are still made in the traditional way.
◆ Confiserie Villeneuve-Hardy
288, rue Notre-Dame
84200 Carpentras
Tel. 04 90 63 05 25

CANDIED FRUIT

◆ Auer ▲ *293*, one of the best *confiseurs* (candy makers) in Nice is famous for candied fruit in the Italian tradition. 7, rue St-François-de-Paule, 06000 Nice
Tel. 04 93 85 77 98
◆ The fruit of the Vaucluse is used by the master sweet-makers of Apt and Carpentras to make delicious sweets. Maison Bono, 280, allée Jean-Jaurès, 84200 Carpentras
Tel. 04 90 63 04 99

HONEY

The great abundance of flowers which flourish in Provence provides a wide variety of honeys. Try lavender and thyme honey.
◆ Jean Cartoux, Av. de l'Oratoire, 84390 Sault-en-Vaucluse
Tel. 04 90 64 02 32

OLIVE OIL

The best "vintages" come from the foot of the Alpilles (near les Baux-de-Provence in the Bouches-du-Rhône). Always buy "*huile d'olive vierge première pression à froid*".
◆ Le Moulin de Maître Cornille, coopérative oléicole de la vallée des Baux
13520 Maussane-les-Alpilles
Tel. 04 90 54 32 37
◆ Union du groupement des oléiculteurs
22, av. Henri-Pontier
13100 Aix-en-Provence
Tel. 04 42 27 15 02

FOUGASSE

A flat bread made with yeast and olive oil. Provençal bakeries offer this traditional bread flavored with olives or orange flowers, according to season.

In the "vendange" (grape harvest) nothing has changed.

A vineyard near Aix-en-Provence.

CÔTES DE PROVENCE

Since 1977 these wines have gradually acquired their *appellation d'origine controllée* (A.O.C. quality label) and include the major production of French rosé. Rosé is best drunk at a temperature of 42˚F to 45˚F, like white wine. It is an ideal table wine for white meats and grilled fish, as well as a perfect match for *bouillabaisse*. The whites are dry, perfect as an apéritif and well suited to shellfish, fish and first courses. Reds should be drunk coolish at about 54˚F with game, red meat and cheeses. Unlike the rosés and whites, best savored in the year of production, reds should be kept for three to four years before being opened. The top of the range receives the label *vin enchantelé*. Most wineries open their *cave* (cellar) for wine tasting and direct sales.
◆ The Comité interprofessionnel Côtes de Provence, 83460 Les Arcs provides all the necessary information,
Tel. 04 94 73 33 38

MAISON DES VINS DES ARCS

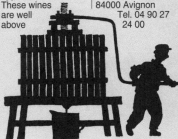

Open to visitors on the N7 road at Les Arcs, on the banks of the Argens. Set lunches are served costing 130–190f per person or *à la carte* (closed Monday).
Tel. 04 94 47 48 47.
The Maison des Vins also organizes introductory courses in *dégustation* (wine tasting)
Tel. 04 94 47 47 70.

BANDOL

This high quality, limited local production gained its A.O.C. label in 1941. The reds are spicy and rich in red berry flavors with blackberry or "hedge-row" after-tastes. The rosés are fine and delicate with a hint of peach. White Bandol is like the flowers of Provence with a honeyed bouquet.
◆ Wine tasting and direct sales in all wineries and Maison des Vins de Bandol, Allée Vivien, 83150 Bandol, Tel. 04 94 29 45 03.

CÔTES-DU-RHÔNE

Côtes-du-Rhône wine is produced on the 125-mile stretch of land flanking the river from Vienne to Avignon and from Donzère to the valleys of Eygues and Ouvèze. Very strict criteria determine the *cru* appellation. These wines are well above the average regional standard. Sweeter wines are produced in the Beaumes-de-Venise and Rasteau areas.
◆ Comité interprofessionnel des vin d'A.O.C. Côtes-du-rhône 6, rue des Trois-Faucons 84000 Avignon
Tel. 04 90 27 24 00

CHÂTEAUNEUF-DU-PAPE

This wine, which is known to have graced the table of the 16th-century Pope Innocent VI, has achieved world fame: 50 percent of production is exported. The wine's exceptional quality is due to its thirteen *cépages* (varieties) and to the traditional skills of the different producers. The reds reach a balanced maturity after a few years, offering fruity and spicy aromas. Their full flavor is a reward that is best accompanied by red meat, game and cheeses. Whites should be tasted young, as an apéritif or with cold meats, paté, fish or cheese. There is a yearly wine festival in August at Châteauneuf-du-Pape.
◆ Fédération des syndicats de producteurs de Châteauneuf-du-Pape
Tel. 04 90 83 72 21.

The "lavandières" (washer-women).

Santons factory.

PERFUME

The many species of flowers growing in the vicinity of Grasse gave rise to a flourishing and world-famous perfume and soap industry.
◆ Parfumeries Galimard
Tel. 04 93 09 20 00
◆ Parfumeries Fragonard
Tel. 04 93 36 44 65
◆ Parfumeries Molinard
Tel. 04 93 36 01 62

PROVENÇAL FASHION

The import of Indian silks in the 17th century inspired the traditional design of Provençal cottons with "paisley" type patterns. They are a main feature in the regional costumes.
◆ Souleïado
39, rue Proudhon
13150 Tarascon
Tel. 04 90 91 08 80
Souleïado cottons have found export markets due to their simple beauty and traditional designs. The Souleïado museum provides an interesting historical view of Provençal fabrics.
◆ Les Olivades
Chemin des Indienneurs
13103 St-Étienne-
du-Grès
Tel. 04 90 49 19 19

LAVENDER

Fields of flowering lavender, cultivated for the production of essential oils, offer a beautiful spectacle and a delicious smell. On August 15 each year the town of Sault-en-Vaucluse celebrates the lavender festival with village balls and processions of horse-drawn carts.
◆ Musée de la Lavande
Route de Gordes
84220 Coustellet
Tel. 04 90 76 91 23
◆ Maison des producteurs
Rue de la République
84390 Sault-en-Vaucluse
Tel. 04 90 64 08 98
Open Easter to November 11.

FURNITURE

Arles furniture is traditionally both functional and stylish. It is elegant and discreet, often adorned with wood carvings. In the many antique stores you can find rush-covered chairs, *boutis*, Apt earthenware or 17th- to 19th-century garden furniture.
◆ Ferdinand Dervieux
11, rue Félix-Gras
84000 Avignon
Tel. 04 90 82 14 37
◆ Hervé Baume
19, rue Petite-Fusterie
84000 Avignon
Tel. 04 90 86 37 66

THE "VILLAGE WITH 100 POTTERS"

Vallauris is to some extent the traditional craft capital of Provence. Many potters have made it their home. Every two years it holds a "Biennale" of ceramics which attracts potters and ceramic artists from all over the world.
◆ The "Syndicat des potiers" has made Vallauris its headquarters and provides a list of ceramics workshops that are open to visitors.
Tel. 04 93 63 82 58.

FAIRS

Many Provençal specialty arts and crafts have their own regular celebrations and market fairs. Departmental tourist authorities can provide detailed information on when and where these events are held.

SANTONS ● 70

These small clay nativity figures traditionally portray the trades and personalities of Provençal villages.
◆ The Champtercier *santon* fair is one of the best.
◆ Pierre Graille
Rue J.-de-Fontvierano
84240 Grambois
Tel. 04 90 77 90 45
This *santon* maker's unique pieces represent the inhabitants of the village. They can be seen each year in the Church of Grambois between Christmas and Candlemas (Feb. 2).

SANDALS

The "tropézienne" sandals (spartan type with leather straps) produced by the K. Jacques family are exported all over the world. Purses and shopping bags are also made by them.
K. Jacques
25, rue Allard
83990 St-Tropez.
Tel. 04 94 97 41 50.

THE PAGE NUMBERS IN ITALIC REFER TO THE ITINERARY SECTION.

◆ CHOOSING A RESTAURANT

◆ Less than 150F
◆◆ From 150 to 400F
◆◆◆ From 400 to 600F
◆◆◆◆ More than 600F

	PAGE	PRICE PER PERSON	GOURMET CUISINE	TERRACE	PROVENÇAL CUISINE	SETTING
AVIGNON						
AUBERTIN (VILLENEUVE-LÈS-AVIGNON)	365	◆◆	●	●		
LE BAIN-MARIE (AVIGNON)	364	◆		●		
LE CAFÉ DES ARTISTES (AVIGNON)	364	◆		●	●	
CHRISTIAN ÉTIENNE (AVIGNON)	364	◆◆	●	●		
LES DOMAINES (AVIGNON)	364	◆		●		
LE GRANGOUSIER (AVIGNON)	364	◆◆	●		●	
TAPALOCAS (AVIGNON)	364	◆				
LA TREILLE (AVIGNON)	364	◆		●		
LE VERNET (AVIGNON)	364	◆	●			
LA VIEILLE FONTAINE-HÔTEL DE L'EUROPE (AVIGNON)	364	◆◆	●	●	●	
LE WOOLLOMOOLOO (AVIGNON)	364	◆		●		
AVIGNON TO NÎMES						
LES ARCADES (AIGUES-MORTES)	368	◆◆		●		
BÉRANGÈRE (LES BAUX-DE-PROVENCE)	366	◆◆				
BISTROT DU CHAPON FIN (NÎMES)	368	◆		●	●	
LE DELTA (STES-MARIES-DE-LA-MER)	368	◆		●		
DOMAINE DE VALMOURIANE (ST-RÉMY-DE-PROVENCE)	366	◆◆		●		
L'ENCLOS DE LA FONTAINE (NÎMES)	368	◆◆		●		
LE JARDIN DE FRÉDÉRIC (ST-RÉMY-DE-PROVENCE)	366	◆◆		●		●
LOU MAS DU JUGE (STES-MARIES-DE-LA-MER)	368	◆◆				
LE MAGISTER (NÎMES)	368	◆◆			●	
LOU MARQUES (ARLES)	367	◆		●		●
LE MÉDIÉVAL (ARLES)	367	◆◆		●		●
LES MILLE PÂTES (TARASCON)	365	◆				
L'OUSTAU DE BAUMANIÈRE (LES BAUX-DE-PROVENCE)	366	◆◆◆	●	●		
LE POISSON BANANE (ARLES)	367	◆◆		●		
LE RÉGALIDO (FONTVIEILLE)	367	◆◆		●		
LA RIBOTO DE TAVEN (LES BAUX-DE-PROVENCE)	366	◆◆		●		
LE ROBINSON (BEAUCAIRE)	365	◆		●		
LE ST-JEAN (TARASCON)	366	◆◆				●
LE SALON PROVENÇAL (ARLES)	367	◆		●		
LE VALLON DE VALRUGUES (ST-RÉMY-DE-PROVENCE)	366	◆◆		●		
ORANGE						
LE PARVIS (ORANGE)	369	◆◆		●	●	●
LE TRIMALCION (ORANGE)	369	◆		●	●	●
LE YACA (ORANGE)	369	◆		●	●	
ORANGE TO LOURMARIN						
L'AGNEAU GOURMAND (LOURMARIN)	371	◆◆		●		
CHEZ SERGE (CARPENTRAS)	370	◆		●		●
COMPTOIR DU VICTUAILLER (GORDES)	370	◆		●		
L'ÉTRIER (VALRÉAS)	369	◆		●		
LA FENIÈRE (LOURMARIN)	371	◆◆	●	●		
LA FÊTE EN PROVENCE (VAISON-LA-ROMAINE)	369	◆◆	●	●		
LA GLORIETTE ET POMPONETTE (VAISON-LA-ROMAINE)	369	◆		●		●
MAS DE TOURTERON (GORDES)	371	◆◆	●	●		
L'OUSTALLET DE GEORGES (LOURMARIN)	371	◆		●	●	
RESTAURANT BERNARD MATHYS (APT)	371	◆◆	●	●		
RESTAURANT DU CHÂTEAU (FONTAINE-DE-VAUCLUSE)	370	◆		●		
RIVES DE L'AUZON (CARPENTRAS)	370	◆◆		●	●	
MARSEILLES						
L'ATELIER DU CHOCOLAT (MARSEILLES)	372	◆		●		●
LA BAIE DES SINGES (MARSEILLES)	372	◆		●		●
LE CARRÉ D'HONORÉ (MARSEILLES)	372	◆◆		●		
CHEZ FONFON (MARSEILLES)	372	◆◆◆				
LE CLOS DES ARÔMES (CASSIS)	373	◆		●		
LA COUPOLE (MARSEILLES)	373	◆				●
LA GROTTE (MARSEILLES)	373	◆		●		●
LE LUNCH (MARSEILLES)	373	◆◆		●		
MIRAMAR (MARSEILLES)	373	◆◆◆	●		●	
MONSIEUR BRUN (CASSIS)	373	◆		●		●
LE PANIER DES ARTS (MARSEILLES)	373	◆				●
PATALAIN (MARSEILLES)	373	◆◆◆	●			
AIX-EN-PROVENCE						
ÉTAPE LANI (AIX-EN-PROVENCE)	374	◆◆	●		●	●
LE PAGOPON (AIX-EN-PROVENCE)	374	◆				

	PAGE	PRICE PER PERSON	GOURMET CUISINE	TERRACE	PROVENÇAL CUISINE	SETTING
LE PIGONNET (AIX-EN-PROVENCE)	374	◆◆		●		
LA TABLE DU ROI (AIX-EN-PROVENCE)	374	◆◆		●		
TRATTORIA CHEZ ANTOINE (AIX-EN-PROVENCE)	374	◆◆				●
AIX-EN-PROVENCE TO GRASSE						
CHEZ BRUNO (LORGUES)	375	◆◆		●	●	
CHEZ NOUS (ST-MAXIMIN)	375	◆◆		●	●	
DOMAINE DE CHÂTEAUNEUF (NANS-LES-PINS)	375	◆◆	●	●	●	
DOMAINE ESPAGNE (RIANS)	375	◆		●		
MAÎTRE BOSCQ (GRASSE)	376	◆◆				
LE MOULIN DE LA FOUX (DRAGUIGNAN)	375	◆◆				
MANOSQUE TO DIGNE-LES-BAINS						
BECS FINS (SISTERON)	376	◆◆		●	●	
FERME-AUBERGE LES BAS CHALLUS (FORCALQUIER)	376	◆		●	●	
LE GRAND PARIS (DIGNE-LES-BAINS)	377	◆◆	●	●	●	
HOSTELLERIE DES DEUX-LIONS (FORCALQUIER)	376	◆◆			●	
LA SOURCE (MANOSQUE)	376	◆◆		●		●
CANNES						
MAÎTRE PIERRE (CANNES)	377	◆◆	●			
L'ONDINE (CANNES)	377	◆◆	●			
RESTAURANT ARMÉNIEN (CANNES)	377	◆◆	●			
CANNES TO TOULON						
AU SOURD (TOULON)	380	◆◆		●		
LE BISTROT DES LICES (ST-TROPEZ)	378	◆◆		●		
LA BOULANGERIE (GRIMAUD)	378	◆◆◆		●		
LE CELLIER (TOULON)	380	◆			●	
LES JARDINS DE BACCHUS (HYÈRES)	379	◆◆				
LES JARDINS DE SAN PEDRO (ST-RAPHAËL)	378	◆◆				
LE LIDO (TOULON)	380	◆◆		●		
L'OLIVIER (ST-TROPEZ)	378	◆◆		●		
PASTOREL (ST-RAPHAËL)	378	◆◆			●	
LES POTIERS (FRÉJUS)	378	◆◆				
LA TOQUE BLANCHE (FRÉJUS)	378	◆◆				
CANNES TO BIOT						
AUBERGE DU JARRIER (BIOT)	381	◆◆		●		
L'AVION BLEU (NICE)	382	◆				
BACON (ANTIBES)	381	◆◆	●	●		
BOCCACCIO (NICE)	382	◆◆				
LA GOUSSE D'AIL (VALLAURIS)	380	◆◆	●			
GRAND CAFÉ DE TURIN (NICE)	382	◆		●		
MAS DE LA PAGANE (ANTIBES)	381	◆◆		●		
LA MERENDA (NICE)	382	◆◆				
LE POT D'ÉTAIN (NICE)	382	◆◆		●		
LE RESTAURANT DES ARCADES (BIOT)	381	◆◆		●	●	●
LES TERRAILLIERS (BIOT)	381	◆◆◆		●		
LE VENDÔME (NICE)	382	◆	●			
NICE TO MENTON						
AUBERGE DU TROUBADOUR (ÈZE)	383	◆◆		●		
LA CIGALE (LA CONDAMINE)	383	◆				
LA CIGALE (MONTE-CARLO)	383	◆				
LA GRIGNOTIÈRE (VILLEFRANCHE-SUR-MER)	382	◆◆				
LE MÉTROPOLE (BEAULIEU-SUR-MER)	383	◆◆◆		●		
AU NID D'AIGLE (ÈZE)	383	◆		●		
LA PIGNATELLE (BEAULIEU-SUR-MER)	383	◆◆		●		
LE PINOCCHIO (MONACO)	383	◆◆				
POLPETTA (MONTE-CARLO)	383	◆◆				
LE PROVENÇAL (ST-JEAN-CAP-FERRAT)	383	◆◆	●			
LE ST-BENOÎT (MONTE-CARLO)	383	◆◆				
LE SLOOP (ST-JEAN-CAP-FERRAT)	383	◆◆		●		
LA VÉRANDA (MENTON)	384	◆◆	●	●		
NICE TO MOUSTIERS-STE-MARIE						
AUBERGE DES TEMPLIERS (VENCE)	385	◆◆		●		
LA BROUETTE (ST-PAUL-DE-VENCE)	384	◆◆		●		
LE ST-PAUL (ST-PAUL-DE-VENCE)	384	◆◆◆				●
LES SANTONS (MOUSTIERS-STE-MARIE)	386	◆◆		●	●	●

◆ Choosing a Hotel

♦ Less than 150F ♦♦ From 150F to 400F ♦♦♦ From 400F to 600F ♦♦♦♦ More than 600F	PAGE	PRICE	HOTEL RESTAURANT	QUIET	SETTING	SWIMMING POOL	GARAGE, CAR PARK	NO. OF
AVIGNON								
L'Anasthasy (Avignon)	365	♦♦	●	●	●			4
Auberge de la Cassagne **** (Avignon)	365	♦♦♦	●	●	●			21
Hôtel Cloître St-Louis**** (Avignon)	365	♦♦♦	●	●	●	●	●	80
Hôtel de l'Europe **** (Avignon)	365	♦♦♦♦	●			●	●	47
Hôtel de la Mirande **** (Avignon)	365	♦♦♦♦	●		●		●	19
Le Prieuré **** (Villeneuve-lès-Avignon)	365	♦♦♦♦	●	●	●	●	●	26
AVIGNON TO NÎMES					●			
La Cabro d'Or *** (Baux-de-Provence)	366	♦♦♦♦	●				●	24
Château des Alpilles **** (St-Rémy-de-Provence)	366	♦♦	●			●	●	18
Hostellerie de Cacharel *** (Les Saintes-Maries-de-la-Mer)	367	♦♦♦	●	●	●			11
Hostellerie de la Reine Jeanne ** (Baux-de-Prov.)	366	♦♦	●					9
Hôtel Plazza (Nîmes)	368	♦♦	●				●	28
Hôtel St-Jean ** (Tarascon)	366	♦♦	●		●	●		12
Hôtellerie des Remparts *** (Aigues-Mortes)	368	♦♦			●			16
Imperator Concorde **** (Nîmes)	368	♦♦♦♦	●			●	●	59
Jules César **** (Arles)	366	♦♦♦♦	●				●	55
Mas d'Aigret *** (Baux-de-Provence)	366	♦♦♦	●		●	●		15
Mas de la Chapelle **** (Arles)	366	♦♦♦	●		●		●	15
Mas de la Fouque *** (Les Stes-Maries-de-la-Mer)	367	♦♦♦	●	●	●	●		14
Mas du Clarousset *** (Les Stes-Maries-de-la-Mer)	367	♦♦♦	●	●	●			10
Mas du Tadorne *** (Les Stes-Maries-de-la-Mer)	367	♦♦♦♦	●		●	●		15
Les Mazets des Roches *** (Tarascon)	366	♦♦♦			●		●	24
Nord Pinus **** (Arles)	366	♦♦♦♦	●		●		●	23
Le Robinson (Beaucaire)	365	♦♦	●	●	●	●		30
La Régalido **** (Fontvieille)	366	♦♦♦♦	●		●		●	14
St-Victor *** (Fontvieille)	366	♦♦♦♦				●	●	11
Les Templiers *** (Aigues-Mortes)	368	♦♦♦			●			9
Val Majour ** (Fontvieille)	366	♦♦♦	●			●	●	32
Hostellerie du Vallon de Valrugues **** (St-Rémy-de-Provence)	366	♦♦♦♦				●	●	41
Villa Glanum ** (St-Rémy-de-Provence)	366	♦♦			●		●	23
ORANGE					●			
Hôtel Arène *** (Orange)	369	♦♦	●		●		●	30
Mas des Aigras (Orange)	369	♦♦			●		●	11
ORANGE TO LOUMARDIN					●			
Auberge du Lubéron *** (Apt)	371	♦♦	●		●		●	15
Le Beffroi *** (Vaison-la-Romaine)	369	♦♦♦	●		●		●	22
Les Bories **** (Gordes)	371	♦♦♦♦	●	●	●	●		17
Ferme de la Huppe (Gordes)	371	♦♦♦	●		●			6
Le Fiacre ** (Carpentras)	370	♦♦			●		●	20
La Gacholle *** (Gordes)	371	♦♦♦	●		●			12
Le Grand Hôtel ** (Valréas)	369	♦♦	●		●			15
Hôtel Forum ** (Carpentras)	370	♦♦	●		●		●	28
Hôtel de Guilles *** (Lourmarin)	371	♦♦♦	●		●			28
Hôtel des Lices Burrhus ** (Vaison-la-Romaine)	369	♦♦			●	●		22
Hôtel du Parc ** (Fontaine-de-Vaucluse)	370	♦♦			●			12
Le Moulin de Lourmarin (Lourmarin)	371	♦♦♦♦	●	●	●			20
MARSEILLES					●			
Le Bestouan ** (Cassis)	373	♦♦♦	●		●			30
Capitainerie des Galères ** (Marseilles)	373	♦♦♦	●		●	●	●	141
Concorde Palm Beach **** (Marseilles)	373	♦♦♦	●		●	●	●	145
Mercure *** (Marseilles)	373	♦♦♦	●			●	●	199
New Hôtel Bompard *** (Marseilles)	373	♦♦			●		●	46
Petit Nice **** (Marseilles)	373	♦♦♦♦	●		●		●	15
Roches Blanches *** (Cassis)	373	♦♦♦	●			●	●	28

	PAGE	PRICE	HOTEL RESTAURANT	QUIET	SETTING	SWIMMING POOL	GARAGE, CAR PARK	NO. OF ROOMS
ST-FERRÉOL ** (MARSEILLES)	373	◆◆						19
AIX-EN-PROVENCE								
LES AUGUSTINS * (AIX-EN-PROVENCE)**	374	◆◆◆						30
CHÂTEAU DE LA PIOLINE (AIX-EN-PROVENCE)	374	◆◆◆◆	●	●			●	21
HOSTELLERIE LA BASTIDE (AIX-EN-PROVENCE)	374	◆◆	●	●			●	16
LES INFIRMERIES DU ROI RENÉ * (AIX-EN-PROVENCE)**	374	◆◆◆			●	●	●	66
MAS DES ÉCUREUILS * (AIX-EN-PROVENCE)**	374	◆◆◆					●	23
MAS D'ENTREMONT (AIX-EN-PROVENCE)	374	◆◆◆◆	●	●			●	18
NÈGRE COSTE * (AIX-EN-PROVENCE)**	37	◆◆◆			●	●	●	37
VILLA GALICI * (AIX-EN-PROVENCE)**	374	◆◆◆◆			●	●	●	
AIX-EN-PROVENCE TO GRASSE								
DOMAINE DE CHÂTEAUNEUF (NANS-LES-PINS)	375	◆◆◆◆	●	●	●			95
DOMAINE ESPAGNE (RIANS)	375	◆◆	●	●			●	4
LES ÉTOILES DE L'ANGE * (DRAGUIGNAN)**	375	◆◆	●				●	29
HOSTELLERIE DU MOULIN DE LA FOUX ** (DRAGUIGNAN)	375	◆◆	●		●	●	●	28
HÔTEL DE FRANCE (ST-MAXIMIN-LA-STE-BAUME)	375	◆◆◆	●				●	26
HÔTEL DU PATTI * (GRASSE)**	376	◆◆	●				●	50
VICTORIA * (DRAGUIGNAN)**	375	◆◆◆					●	22
MANOSQUE TO DIGNES-LES-BAINS								
AUBERGE DE CHAREMBEAU ** (FORCALQUIER)	376	◆◆		●	●		●	12
GRAND HÔTEL DU COURS * (SISTERON)**	376	◆◆	●				●	50
HÔTELLERIE LE COLOMBIER (FORCALQUIER)	376	◆◆				●	●	15
LE PROVENCE ** (MANOSQUE)	376	◆◆	●				●	14
VILLA GAÏA (DIGNE-LES-BAINS)	377	◆◆◆		●	●		●	12
CANNES								
LE CARLTON ** (CANNES)**	377	◆◆◆◆	●				●	
CHANTECLAIR ** (CANNES)	377	◆◆			●			15
CRISTAL ** (CANNES)**	377	◆◆◆◆	●				●	51
LE MAJESTIC ** (CANNES)**	377	◆◆◆◆	●				●	287
LE MARTINEZ ** (CANNES)**	377	◆◆◆◆	●	●			●	430
MOLIÈRE * (CANNES)**	377	◆◆◆			●	●		45
CANNES TO TOULON								
BYBLOS ** (ST-TROPEZ)**	379	◆◆◆◆				●	●	107
BELLO VISTO * (GASSIN)	379	◆◆					●	9
LE COLOMBIER * (FRÉJUS)**	378	◆◆	●				●	72
LA FERME D'AUGUSTIN * (RAMATUELLE)**	379	◆◆◆◆						
LA FIGUIÈRE * (RAMATUELLE)**	379	◆◆◆				●	●	
HOSTELLERIE PROVENÇALE "LA QUÉBÉCOISE" ** (HYÈRES)	379	◆◆◆◆		●	●		●	12
HÔTEL ARÉNA * (FRÉJUS)**	378	◆◆					●	22
LE MANOIR ** (ÎLE DE PORT-CROS)	380	◆◆◆◆	●	●	●			25
LE MIRAGE * (BORMES-LES-MIMOSAS)**	379	◆◆◆◆	●			●	●	45
PALMIERS * (BORMES-LES-MIMOSAS)**	379	◆◆					●	
LA POTINIÈRE * (ST-RAPHAËL)**	378	◆◆◆	●				●	
LE PRÉ DE LA MER * (ST-TROPEZ)**	379	◆◆◆◆		●	●		●	
LA RÉSIDENCE DU CAP-BRUN * (TOULON)**	380	◆◆◆			●		●	20
RÉSIDENCE DE LA PINÈDE ** (ST-TROPEZ)**	379	◆◆◆◆					●	50
SOL E MAR * (ST-RAPHAËL)**	378	◆◆◆	●			●		
CANNES TO BIOT								
LES ARCADES ** (BIOT)	381	◆◆◆	●					12
AUBERGE DE LA VALLÉE VERTE ** (BIOT)	381	◆◆	●			●	●	14
BEAU SOLEIL * (VALLAURIS)**	380	◆◆					●	30
BEACHÔTEL * (ANTIBES)**	381	◆◆◆◆	●				●	43
LES BELLES RIVES ** (ANTIBES)**	381	◆◆◆◆					●	45
CALIFORNIA * (VALLAURIS)	380	◆◆					●	14
CASTEL GAROUPE AXA * (ANTIBES)**	381	◆◆◆◆				●	●	27
HÔTEL DU GOLFE ** (VALLAURIS)	380	◆◆◆				●	●	19
MAS DE LA PAGANE ** (ANTIBES)	381	◆◆◆	●				●	

◆ CHOOSING A HOTEL

◆ Less than 150F
◆◆ From 150F to 400F
◆◆◆ From 400F to 600F
◆◆◆◆ More than 600F

	PAGE	PRICE	HOTEL RESTAURANT	QUIET	SETTING	SWIMMING POOL	GARAGE, CAR PARK	NO. OF R.
NICE								
ATLANTIC ** (NICE)**	382	◆◆◆◆				●	●	123
BEAU RIVAGE ** (NICE)**	382	◆◆◆◆						118
FLORIDE ** (NICE)**	382	◆◆					●	20
LA PÉROUSE ** (NICE)**	382	◆◆◆◆	●	●				65
LE NEGRESCO ** (NICE)**	382	◆◆◆◆	●				●	150
WINDSOR * (NICE)**	382	◆◆◆◆	●				●	60
NICE TO MENTON								
ABELA HÔTEL (MONACO)	383	◆◆◆◆	●		●		●	210
L'AIGLON * (MENTON)**	384	◆◆◆◆	●			●	●	32
BEACH PLAZA (MONTE-CARLO)	383	◆◆◆◆	●			●		300
CAP ESTEL ** (ÈZE)**	383	◆◆◆◆	●				●	40
LA FLORE ** (VILLEFRANCHE-SUR-MER)	382	◆◆◆				●	●	31
LA FRÉGATE ** (ST-JEAN-CAP-FERRAT)	383	◆◆	●					10
GRAND HÔT. DU CAP-FERRAT ** (ST-JEAN-CAP-FERRAT)**	383	◆◆◆◆	●			●	●	59
LE HAVRE BLEU ** (BEAULIEU-SUR-MER)	383	◆◆					●	22
HÔTEL DES AMBASSADEURS ** (MENTON)**	384	◆◆◆◆	●				●	50
HÔTEL BALMORAL (MONACO)	383	◆◆◆◆				●		85
HÔTEL DE FRANCE (MONACO)	383	◆◆	●					26
HÔTEL HERMITAGE (MONACO)	383	◆◆◆◆	●		●	●	●	220
HÔTEL LOEWS (MONACO)	384	◆◆◆◆	●			●	●	635
HÔTEL TERMINUS (MONACO)	384	◆◆◆	●					54
HÔTEL DE PARIS (MONACO)	384	◆◆◆◆	●		●		●	129
MAGALI ** (MENTON)	384	◆◆◆				●		40
MÉTROPOLE ** (BEAULIEU-SUR-MER)**	383	◆◆◆	●		●	●		
LA RÉSERVE DE BEAULIEU ** (BEAULIEU-SUR-MER)**	383	◆◆◆◆	●			●		
ROYAL RIVIERA ** (ST-JEAN-CAP-FERRAT)**	383	◆◆◆◆	●			●	●	70
LES TERRASSES D'ÈZE ** (ÈZE)**	383	◆◆◆◆	●			●	●	
VIKING * (MENTON)**	384	◆◆◆	●					34
WELCOME * (VILLEFRANCHE-SUR-MER)**	382	◆◆◆◆	●					32
NICE TO MOUSTIERS-STE-MARIE								
AUBERGE DES CRÊTES * (LA PALUD-SUR-VERDON)	385	◆◆	●				●	12
LA BONNE AUBERGE ** (MOUSTIERS-STE-MARIE)	386	◆◆	●				●	16
LE CHAMOIS ** (COLMARS-LES-ALPES)	385	◆◆	●			●	●	26
CLOSERIE DES GENÊTS * (VENCE)	385	◆◆						8
LA COLOMBE D'OR ** (ST-PAUL-DE-VENCE)**	384	◆◆◆◆	●			●	●	26
LE COLOMBIER ** (MOUSTIERS-STE-MARIE)	386	◆◆	●				●	22
LA FERME ROSE (MOUSTIERS-STE-MARIE)	386	◆◆	●		●		●	7
HÔTEL DU LEVANT ** (CASTELANE)	385	◆◆	●				●	27
LE MAS D'ARTIGNY ** (ST-PAUL-DE-VENCE)**	384	◆◆◆◆	●			●	●	82
LES ORANGERS * (ST-PAUL-DE-VENCE)**	385	◆◆◆◆			●		●	8
PROVENCE ** (LA PALUD-SUR-VERDON)	385	◆◆	●				●	20
RÉSIDENCE-CLUB LES COUGNAS (ENTREVAUX)	385	◆◆◆	●				●	10
LA ROSERAIE * (VENCE)**	385	◆◆◆	●			●	●	12
VAUBAN (ENTREVAUX)	385	◆◆	●					10
NICE TO LA VALLÉE DES MERVEILLES								
AUBERGE DE LA MADONE * (PEILLON)**	386	◆◆◆	●				●	20
AUBERGE PROVENÇALE ** (SOSPEL)	386	◆◆	●					
AUBERGE ST-MARTIN * (LA BRIGUE)	386	◆◆	●			●	●	
CASTEL-DU-ROY * (BREIL-SUR-ROYA)**	386	◆◆	●				●	
LE ROYA ** (BREIL-SUR-ROYA)	386	◆◆	●	●				14
MIRVAL ** (LA BRIGUE)	386	◆◆	●	●			●	18

USEFUL ADDRESSES

☀ BEAUTIFUL VIEW
C CENTRAL LOCATION
⊡ ISOLATED
◑ TYPICAL RESTAURANT
🏛 LUXURY HOTEL
P PARKING LOT
🚗 SUPERVISED CAR PARK
☐ TELEVISION
⌂ QUIET
⌇ SWIMMING POOL
✶ REDUCTIONS FOR CHILDREN
✗ NO PETS
⊤ MEALS SERVED OUTSIDE
♣ PARK OR GARDEN

GENERAL INFORMATION

◆ "In season" indicates certain places of interest whose opening times or timetables are only valid during the tourist season: April to October.

BOAT
▲ 336-337

BUS STATION
▲ 336-337

CAR RENTAL
▲ 336-337

RAILWAY STATION
▲ 336-337

AVIGNON

84000   ▲ 136-49

USEFUL ADDRESSES

COMITÉ DÉPARTEMENTAL DE TOURISME DU VAUCLUSE
La Balance
Pl. Campana, BP 147
Tel. 04 90 86 43 42
Fax. 04 90 86 86 08

COMMISSARIAT CENTRAL
(Central police station)
Caserne de Salle
Tel. 04 90 80 51 00

HOSPITAL
CH d'Avignon
305, rue Raoul-Follereau
Tel. 04 90 80 33 33

MAIRIE
(Town hall)
Pl. de l'Horloge
Tel. 04 90 80 80 00
Open daily 7.45am–7pm

TOURIST OFFICE
41, cours Jean-Jaurès
Tel. 04 90 82 65 11
Fax. 04 90 82 95 03

CULTURE

ANCIEN COUVENT DES CARMES
Pl. des Carmes
Open Mon.–Fri.

7.45–9am and
6.30–7.30pm. Sat.
5–7pm, Sun.
9.30am–12 noon
Only the church is open to visitors.

CATHEDRAL OF NOTRE-DAME-DES-DOMS
Pl. des Palais
In season: Open
7am–7pm, Apr.–Sep.

CHAPEL OF THE PÉNITENTS NOIRS
Rue Banasterie
Under restoration.

CHÂTELET
Pont Bénezet
Annex of the Tourist office
In season: Open
9am–6.30pm, Apr.–Sep.

CONVENT OF THE CÉLESTINS
Pl. des Corps-Saints
Tel. 04 90 82 67 08
Open during the festival.

CHURCH OF ST-AGRICOL
Rue Petite-Fusterie
Open half an hour before services:
Sat. 5pm and Sun. 9am

CHURCH OF ST-DIDIER
Pl. St-Didier
Open daily 9am–noon
and 2–7pm

CHURCH OF ST-PIERRE
Pl. St-Pierre
Open Fri. 2–5pm and
Sat. 9–11am. Closed
July–August

HÔTEL DES MONNAIES
Pl. du Palais-des-Papes
Closed to the public.

MAISON JEAN-VILAR
8, rue Mons
Tel. 04 90 86 59 64
Open Tue.–Fri.
9am–noon and 2–6pm,
Sat. 10am–5pm

MUSÉE AUBANEL
7, pl. St-Pierre
Tel. 04 90 82 95 54
Visits on request.

MUSÉE CALVET
65, av. Joseph-Calvet
Tel. 04 90 86 33 84
Under restoration.

MUSÉE DU MONT-DE-PIÉTÉ
6, rue Saluces
Tel. 04 90 86 53 12
8.30–11.30am and
1.30–5.30pm
Free entrance.

MUSÉE DU PETIT-PALAIS
Pl. du Palais
Tel. 04 90 86 44 58
In season: Open
Sun.–Mon.
10.30am–6.30pm,
May–Sep.

MUSÉE LAPIDAIRE
27, rue de la République
Tel. 04 90 85 75 38
Open Sun.–Mon.
10am–noon and 2–6pm

MUSÉE REQUIEN
67, rue Joseph-Vernet
Tel. 04 90 82 43 51
Open Mon.–Fri.
9am–noon and 2–6pm

MUSÉE VOULAND
17, rue Victor-Hugo
Tel. 04 90 86 03 79
In season: Open
Tue.–Sat. 10am–noon
and 2–6pm, June–Sep.

PALAIS DES PAPES
Pl. du Palais-des-Papes
Tel. 04 90 27 50 73
Open 9am–6.15pm
Closed May 1

PALAIS DU ROURE
3, rue du Collège-du-Roure
Tel. 04 90 80 80 88
Open from 3pm by
arrangement

ROCHER DES DOMS
Tel. 04 90 86 45 57
In season: garden open
7.30am–7.30pm

SYNAGOGUE
Pl. Jérusalem
Tel. 04 90 85 21 24
Open Mon.–Fri.
10am–noon and 3–5pm

THEATER
Pl. de l'Horloge
Tel. 04 90 82 23 44

RESTAURANTS

★ **LE BAIN-MARIE**
5, rue Pétramale
Tel. 04 90 85 21 37
Light dishes,
extensive menu.
〒

★ **LE CAFÉ DES ARTISTES**
Pl. Crillon
Tel. 04 90 82 63 16
Closed Sun. and Jan.
Attractive menu and
good Provençal cooking.
🅒 🕴 〒 ◐

★ **CHRISTIAN ÉTIENNE**
10–12, rue de Mons
Tel. 04 90 86 16 50
Closed Sat. lunch and
Sun.
Near the Palace of the
Popes. Excellent
cuisine, balcony terrace.
🅒 🕴 🅟 〒

★ **LES DOMAINES**
28, pl. de l'Horloge
Tel. 04 90 82 58 86
Vast choice of classic
dishes. Impressive wine
list.
🅒 🕴 〒

LE GRANGOUSIER
17, rue Galante
Tel. 04 90 82 96 60
Closed Sun., Mon. lunch
and Aug. 15–31
🅒

TAPALOCAS
10, rue Galante
Tel. 04 90 82 56 84
Open noon–1pm
Closed Dec. 25 and Jan.
Spanish food and
atmosphere.

LA TREILLE
Chemin de l'Île-Piot
Tel. 04 90 85 31 22
Gourmet cuisine served
on the banks of the
Rhône.
🕴 🅟 〒

LE VERNET
58, rue Joseph-Vernet
Tel. 04 90 86 64 53
Closed Sun., Mon. lunch
in low season
🅒 🕴

LA VIEILLE FONTAINE-HÔTEL DE L'EUROPE
12, pl. Crillon
Tel. 04 90 14 76 76
Closed Sun.
Gourmet cuisine, local
specialties.
🅒 🕴 🅟 🚗 〒 ◐

★ **LE WOOLLOMOOLOO**
16, rue des Teinturiers
Tel. 04 90 85 28 44
Closed Sun.–Mon.
Fast food eating,
meeting and fun place.
Cakes, salads and
exotic cooking.
🕴 〒

ACCOMMODATION

L'ANASTHASY
Île de la Barthelasse
Tel. 04 90 85 55 94
Fax 04 90 82 94 49
Open all year.
Bed and breakfast.

**AUBERGE
DE LA CASSAGNE ★★★★**
450, allée de Cassagne
Tel. 04 90 31 04 18
Fax 04 90 32 25 09
*Very comfortable in a
magnificent park.
Good food. Tennis.*

CAMPING MUNICIPAL
Île de la Barthelasse
Tel. 04 90 82 63 50
Closed Nov.–Feb.
Central. Tennis.

**HÔTEL CLOÎTRE
ST-LOUIS ★★★★**
20, rue du Portail-
Boquier
Tel. 04 90 27 55 55
Fax 04 90 82 24 01
*Situated in superbly
renovated 17th-century
Jesuit monastery. Roof-
top swimming pool.*

★ **HÔTEL
DE L'EUROPE ★★★★**
12, pl. Crillon
Tel. 04 90 82 66 92
Fax 04 90 85 43 66
*Great comfort in the
heart of town.*

★ **HÔTEL
DE LA MIRANDE ★★★★**
4, pl. de l'Amirande
Tel. 04 90 85 93 93
Fax 04 90 86 26 85
*The best hotel in town;
by Palace of the Popes.*

SPECIALTY FOODS

**COMITÉ
INTERPROFESSIONNEL
DES VINS D'A.O.C.
CÔTES-DU-RHÔNE**
6, rue des Trois-Faucons
Tel. 04 90 27 24 00

SHOPPING

FURNITURE
Ferdinand Dervieux
11, rue Félix-Gras
Tel. 90 82 14 37
Hervé Baume
19, rue Petite-
Fusterie
Tel. 04 90 86 37 66

VILLENEUVE-LES-AVIGNON

30400   ▲ 149

USEFUL ADDRESSES

TOURIST OFFICE
Pl. Charles-David
Tel. 04 90 25 61 55
Fax 04 90 25 91 55

CULTURE

**CHARTREUSE DU
VAL-DE-BÉNÉDICTION**
Rue de la République
Open Apr.–Sep.
9am–6.30pm, Oct.–Mar.
9.30am–5.30pm.
Closed Jan. 1, May 1,
Nov. 1, Nov. 11, Dec 25

**COLLEGIATE
CHURCH OF
NOTRE-DAME**
Rue de la République
In season: Open Apr.–
Sep.10am–12.30pm and
3–7pm. Closed Tue.,
Jan. 1, Feb., May 1,
Nov.1 , Nov. 11, Dec. 25.

**GARDENS OF
ABBAYE ST-ANDRÉ**
Tel. 04 90 25 55 95
Open Apr.–Sep.
10am–12.30pm and
2.30–6pm; Oct.–Mar.
10am–12.30pm and
2–5pm. Closed Mon.

**MUSÉE PIERRE-
DE-LUXEMBOURG**
Rue de la République
In season: Open Apr.–
Sep.10am–12.30pm and
3–7pm. Closed Tue.,
Jan. 1, Feb., May 1,
Nov.1 , Nov. 11,
Dec. 25.
Entrance 20F;
children 12F.

TOURS JUMELLES
La Montée du Fort
Free access.

**TOUR PHILIPPE-
LE-BEL**
Rue Montée-de-la-Tour
Tel. 04 90 27 49 68
*Same opening times as
Collegiate Church of
Notre-Dame.*

RESTAURANTS

AUBERTIN
1, rue de l'Hôpital
Tel. 04 90 25 94 84
Closed Sun. eve. and
Mon. out of season.
Gourmet cuisine.

ACCOMMODATION

CAMPING DE LA LAUNE
Chemin St-Honoré
Tel. 04 90 25 76 06
Open Apr.–Sep.
Sports facilities.

LE PRIEURÉ ★★★★
7, pl. du Chapitre
Te. 04 90 25 18 20
Fax 04 90 25 45 39
Closed Nov. 2–Mar. 5
Beautiful garden. Tennis.

BEAUCAIRE

30300   ▲ 150

USEFUL ADDRESSES

TOURIST OFFICE
24, cours Gambetta
Tel. 04 66 59 26 57

CULTURE

CHÂTEAU MÉDIÉVAL
Pl. du Château
Tel. 04 66 59 47 61
In season: Open
Apr.–Sep. 10am–noon
and 2.15–6.45pm.
Closed Tue. and
public hols.
*Falconry displays 3pm,
4pm, 5pm Apr. –Nov.*

**COLLEGIATE CHURCH
OF NOTRE-DAME-DES-
POMMIERS**
Rue Ledru-Rollin
Open 9am–noon

**MUSÉE MUNICIPAL
AUGUSTE-JACQUET**
Pl. du Château
Tel. 04 66 59 47 61
In season: Open
Apr.–Sep. 10am–noon
and 2.15–6.45pm.
Closed Tue. and public
hols. In the medieval
castle. Entrance 11F;
children 2.50F.

RESTAURANTS

★ **LE ROBINSON**
Rte de Remoulin
(Pont du Gard)
1 mile north of
Beaucaire on the D 986
Tel. 04 66 59 21 32

Closed Feb.
*Traditional cuisine.
Disabled access.*

ACCOMMODATION

★ **LE ROBINSON**
Rte de Remoulin
(Pont du Gard)
1 mile north of
Beaucaire on the D 986
Tel. 04 66 59 21 32
Fax 04 66 59 00 03
Closed Feb.
Logis de-France.

TARASCON

13150   ▲ 151

USEFUL ADDRESSES

TOURIST OFFICE
59, rue des Halles
Tel. 04 90 91 03 52
Fax 04 90 91 22 96

CULTURE

CHÂTEAU
Bd du Roi-René
Tel. 04 90 91 01 93
In season: Open Apr.–
Sep.9am–7pm.
Closed May 1, All Saints,
Nov. 11, Dec. 25, Jan 1.

**COLLEGIATE CHURCH
OF STE-MARTHE**
Pl. de la Concorde
Open daily 9am–noon
and 2–5pm

**MAISON DE
TARTARIN**
55 *bis*, bd Itam
Tel. 04 90 91 05 08
In season: Open 10am–
noon and 2.30–7pm,
Apr.–Sep. Closed Sun.
and Dec. 15–Mar. 15
Open till 5pm, closed Sun
Entrance 6F;
children 6F.

MUSÉE SOULEÏADO
39, rue Prud'hon
Tel. 04 90 91 08 80
Open Mon.–Fri. by
appointment.
Entrance 30F.
Textile museum.

RESTAURANTS

LES MILLE PÂTES
4, rue Eugène-Pelletan
Tel. 04 90 43 51 77
Closed Wed. evening,
Sat. midday and Sun.
midday.
*Local specialties and
pasta.*

Le St-Jean
24, bd Victor-Hugo
Tel. 04 90 91 13 87
Closed Fri. evening, Sat.
midday and
Dec. 15–Jan. 15
Local specialties.
🚶 🅿 🚫 ◑

ACCOMMODATION

Hôtel St-Jean ★★
24, bd Victor-Hugo
Tel. 04 90 91 13 87
Closed Dec. 15–Jan. 15
*Rooms decorated by
Souleïado.*

**Les Mazets
des Roches ★★★**
Rte de Fontvieille
Tel. 04 90 91 34 89
Fax 04 90 43 53 29
🚶 🛏 🅿 🚻

Youth hostel
31, bd Gambetta
Tel. 04 90 91 04 08
Ckosed Dec. 15–
Jan. 15

ST-ÉTIENNE-DU-GRÈS

13103

SHOPPING

Les Olivades
Chemin des Indienneurs
Tel. 04 90 49 19 19
Provençal fashions.

ST-RÉMY-DE-PROVENCE

13210   ▲ 152

USEFUL
ADDRESSES

Tourist office
Place Jean-Jaurès
Tel. 04 90 92 05 22
Fax 04 90 92 38 52

CULTURE

**Centre d'Art
Présence Van Gogh**
8, rue Estrine
Tel. 04 90 92 34 72
Open Apr.–Oct.
10.30am–12.30pm and
2.30–6.30pm. Closed
Mon.

**Dépôt
Archéologique
de Glanum**
Place Flavier
Tel. 04 90 92 64 04
Open Apr.–Dec.
10am–6pm. Closed
Christmas, Jan.–Mar.
and May 1.

**Glanum
archeological site**
Route des Baux-
de-Provence
Tel. 04 90 92 23 79
Open Apr.–Sep.
9am–7pm, Oct.–Mar.
9.30am–12.30pm,
2–5pm

Musée des Alpilles
Pl. Favier
Tel. 04 90 92 08 10
Open Apr.–Jun.,
Sep.–Oct. 10am–noon
and 2–6pm; Jul.–Aug.
10am–noon and 3–8pm;
Nov.–Dec. 10am–noon
and 2–5pm

RESTAURANTS

**Domaine
de Valmouriane**
Petite route des Baux,
2½ miles on the N 99
and D 27 roads
Tel. 04 90 92 44 62
🚶 🛏 🚗 🚻

**★ Le Jardin
de Frédéric**
8 *bis*, bd Gambetta
Tel. 04 90 92 27 76
Closed Wed.
🚶 🚻

**Le Vallon
de Valrugues**
Chem. Canto-Cigalo
Tel. 04 90 92 04 40
🚶 🅿 🚻

ACCOMMODATION

**★ Château
des Alpilles ★★★★**
Rte du Rougadou (D 31)
Tel. 04 90 92 03 33
Fax 04 90 92 45 17
Closed Jan.–mid Mar.
🏠 🚶 🅿 🚻

**Hostellerie
du Vallon de
Valrugues ★★★★**
Chemin Canto-Cigalo
Tel. 04 90 92 04 40
Fax 04 90 92 44 01
🚶 🛏 🚗 🚻 ♟

★ Villa Glanum ★★
46, av. Vincent-Van-Gogh
Tel. 04 90 92 03 59
Fax 04 90 92 00 08
Closed Nov.–Feb.
🏠 🚶 🛏 🅿 🚻

NIGHTLIFE

Le Café des Arts
30, bd Victor-Hugo
Tel. 04 90 92 13 41
Open until 12.30am.
Closed Nov. 2–17 and
Feb.

LES BAUX-DE-PROVENCE

13520   ▲ 153

USEFUL ADDRESSES

Tourist office
Îlot "Post Tenebras Lux"
Tel. 04 90 54 34 39

CULTURE

Citadel
Grand-Rue
Tel. 04 90 54 55 56
Open Mar.–May and
Oct. 9am–6.30pm;
Nov.–Feb. 9am–5pm

**Church of
St-Vincent**
Pl. de l'Église
Open 9am–8pm

**Montmajour
Abbey**
Rte de Fontvieille
Tel. 04 90 54 64 17
In season: Open
9am–5pm, Apr.–Sep.

**Musée d'Art
contemporain
Hôtel de Manville**
Mairie, Grand-Rue
Tel. 04 90 54 34 03
In season: open
9am–8pm

**Musée d'Histoire
de Baux**
Hôtel de la Tour-de-Brau
Tel. 04 90 54 55 36
Open daily Mar.–May
8.30am–7pm; Jun.–Aug.
8.30am–9pm; Sep.–Oct.
9am–6pm; Nov.–Feb.
9am–5pm

**Musée
Yves-Brayer**
Hôtel des Porcelets
Tel. 04 90 54 36 99
Open Easter to All
Saints (Nov. 1)
10am–noon and
2–6.30pm. Closed Jan.
1– Feb. 20

**Pavillon de
la Reine Jeanne**
Vallon de la Fontaine
*Not open to
visitors.*

RESTAURANTS

Bérangère
Rue Treincat
Tel. 04 90 54 35 63
Closed Tue. evening
and Wed.

**★ L'Oustau
de Baumanière**
Val d'Enfer
Tel. 04 90 54 33 07
Closed Wed.–Thur.
lunchtime out of season
and Jan. 16–Mar. 4
🛏 🚗 🚻

**La Riboto de
Taven**
Val d'Enfer
Tel. 04 90 54 34 23
Closed Tue. evening
out of season and Wed.
all year around
*Two "troglodyte" dining
rooms.*
🚶 🅿 🚻

ACCOMMODATION

La Cabro d'Or ★★★
Rte d'Arles
Tel. 04 90 54 33 21
Fax 04 90 54 45 98
Closed Nov. 12–Dec. 21
🚶 🛏 🅿 🚻

**Hôstellerie de
la Reine Jeanne ★★**
Grand-Rue
Tel. 04 90 54 32 06
Fax 04 90 54 32 33
Closed Nov. 15–
Feb. 15
🚶 🚻

Mas d'Aigret ★★★
D 27 A road
Tel. 04 90 54 33 54
Fax 04 90 54 41 37
Closed Jan.–Feb.
🚶 🛏 🅿 🚻

SPORT

**Golf des Baux-
de-Provence**
Domaine de Manville
Tel. 04 90 54 37 02

FONTVIEILLE

13990

RESTAURANT

LE RÉGALIDO
Rue Frédéric-Mistral
Tel. 04 90 54
60 22
Closed Dec.–Jan.
P ⌘ ⚥

ACCOMMODATION

LA RÉGALIDO ★★★★
Rue Frédéric-
Mistral
Tel. 04 90 54 60 22
Fax 04 90 54 64 29
Closed Jan.
P ⌘

ST-VICTOR ★★★
Chemin des
Fourques
Tel. 04 90 54 66 00
Fax 04 90 54 67 88
⌓ P ⌘ ⚥

VAL MAJOUR ★★
22, rte d'Arles
Tel. 04 90 54 62 33
Fax 04 90 54 61 67
Closed Oct. 16–Mar. 20
Tennis.
⌓ P ⌘ ⚥

ARLES

13200   ▲ *154–63*

USEFUL ADDRESSES

TOURIST OFFICE
Esplanade
Charles-de-Gaulle
Bd des Lices
Tel. 04 90 18 41 20

CULTURE

LES ALYSCAMPS
Av. des Alyscamps
*Same opening times as
the Cryptoporticus.*

AMPHITHEATER
Rond-point des Arènes
Tel. 04 90 49 36 86
Open Apr.–Sep. 10am–
6.40pm, Oct.–Mar.
10am–4.40pm

**CHURCH OF NOTRE-
DAME-DE-LA-MAJOR**
Pl. de la Major
Tel. 04 90 96 07 38
Open 9am–6pm
Visit the crib in winter.

**CHURCH OF
ST-HONORAT**
Les Alyscamps
*Same opening times as
the Cryptoporticus.*

**CHURCH OF
ST-TROPHIME**
Pl. de la République
In season: Open Apr.–
Sep. 9am–12.30pm and
2–7pm. Closed Jan. 1,
Nov. 1 and Dec. 25

**COMMANDERIE
STE-LUCE**
Rue du Grand-Prieuré
Tel. 04 90 49 37 58
*Open for exhibitions.
Check times at the
Musée Réattu opposite.*

CRYPTOPORTICUS
Rue Balze
Tel. 04 90 49 36 36
Open May–Sep. 9am–
12.30pm and 2–7pm ;
Oct.–Mar. 10am–
4.30pm. Closed Jan. 1,
Nov. 1 and Dec. 25

**ÉCOLE NATIONALE
DE PHOTOGRAPHIE**
Galerie Aréna
16, rue des Arènes
Tel. 04 90 99 33 33
Exhibitions.

ESPACE VAN-GOGH
Rue Félix-Rey
Tel. 04 90 49 39 39
*Visits to the courtyard
and the Media-library.*

**FONDATION VINCENT-
VAN-GOGH**
Palais de Luppée
26, rond-point
des Arènes
Tel. 04 90 49 94 04
Open 9.30am–12.30pm
and 2–7pm. Closed
Mon. and Sat. (morning
Oct.–Mar.)

**MUSÉE
CAMARGUAIS**
Mas du Pont-de-Rousty
Tel. 04 90 97 10 82
In season: Open
Apr.–Sep. Wed.–Mon.
9.15am–6.45pm

MUSÉE RÉATTU
Rue du Grand-Prieuré
Tel. 04 90 96 37 68
Open daily Apr.–Sep.
9am–12.15pm and
2–7pm; Oct.–Mar.
10am–12.15pm and
2–5.30pm

**MUSEON
ARLATEN**
29, rue de la République
Tel. 04 90 96 08 23
Open Apr.–Sep.
9am–noon
and 2–6.30pm;
Oct.–Mar. 9am–noon
and 2–5pm. Closed
Mon. Oct.–June

**PALAIS DE
L'ARCHEVÊCHÉ**
35, pl. de la République
Tel. 04 90 18 41 20
*University. Closed to the
public.*

**RENCONTRES
INTERNATIONALES
DE LA PHOTOGRAPHIE**
10, rond-point des
Arènes
Tel. 04 90 96 76 06
Early July.

**RÉSERVE NATIONALE
DE CAMARGUE
LA CAPELIÈRE**
D 36 b road
Tel. 04 90 97 00 97
Open Mon.–Sat.
9am–noon and 2–5pm

ROMAN THEATER
Rue de la Calade
In season: Open
9am–12.15pm and
2–6.45pm, Apr.–Sep.

**THERMES DE
CONSTANTIN**
(Constantine's Baths)
Rue Dominique-Maisto
*Same opening times as
the Cryptoporticus.*

RESTAURANTS

LOU MARQUES
Bd des Lices
Hotel Jules-César
Tel. 04 90 93 43 20
Closed Nov.– Dec. 23
⚥ ⌓ 🚗 ⌘ ♨ P

★ LE MÉDIÉVAL
9, rue Truchet
Tel. 04 90 96 65 77
Closed Tue.
⌓

**★ LE POISSON
BANANE**
6, rue du Forum
Tel. 04 90 96 02 58
Open eves. Closed Wed.
⌘ ⌓ ⚥

LE SALON PROVENÇAL
65, rue Amédée-Pichot
Tel. 04 90 96 13 32
Closed Mon.
⚥ ⌘ ⌓

ACCOMMODATION

JULES CÉSAR ★★★★
Bd des Lices / BP 116
Tel. 04 90 93 43 20
Fax 04 90
93 33 47

Closed 1st weekend
Nov.–Dec. 22
⚥ ⌓ P ⌘

**MAS DE LA
CHAPELLE ★★★★**
Petite rte de Tarascon
Tel. 04 90 93 23 15
Fax 04 90 96 53 74
Closed Feb.
Tennis.
⌓ P ⌘

★ NORD PINUS ★★★★
14, pl. du Forum
Tel. 04 90 93 44 44
Fax 04 90 93 34 00
⚥ ⌘ P

YOUTH HOSTEL
20, av. Foch
Tel. 04 90 96 18 25
Closed Dec. 23–31

LES SAINTES-MARIES-DE-LA-MER

13460   ▲ *169*

USEFUL ADDRESSES

TOURIST OFFICE
5, avenue Van-Gogh
BP 34
Tel. 04 90 97 82 55

CULTURE

AVIGNON CASTLE
Parc naturel régional
de Camargue
Tel. 04 90 97 58 58
Open Apr.–Oct. 10am–
noon and 1.30–4.30pm

**CENTRE
D'INFORMATION
GINÈS**
Parc naturel régional
de Camargue
Pont-de-Gau
Tel. 04 90 97 86 32
In season: Open
Apr.–Sep. 9am–6pm.
Closed Fri. and
public hols.

CHURCH
Pl. de l'Église
Tel. 04 90 97 80 25
In season: Open
8am–noon and
2–6pm

MUSÉE BARONCELLI
Rue Victor-Hugo
Tel. 04 90 97 87 60

In season: Open
10am–noon and
2–6pm

**PONT-DE-GAU BIRD
SANCTUARY**
Pont-de-Gau
Tel. 04 90 97 82 62
Open 9am–end of the
day. Closed Dec. 25 and
Jan. 1.

RESTAURANTS

LE DELTA
Pl. Mireille
Tel. 04 90 97 81 12
Closed Jan. 10–Feb. 10
☆ ☂ ⌣

LOU MAS DU JUGE
Quartier Pin-Fourcat
Rte d'Aigues-Mortes
Tel. 04 66 73 51 45
*Booking compulsory.
Choice of menus, no
"carte".*
🅿 ⌘ ☆

MAS DE LA FOUQUE
Rte du Petit-Rhône,
2 miles (D 38)
Tel. 04 90 97 81 02
Closed Tue. midday and
Nov.–Mar. 15
🚗 ☂ ⌣ 🅿

ACCOMMODATION

★ **HOSTELLERIE
DE CACHAREL** ***
Rte de Cacharel
Tel. 04 90 97 95 44
Fax 04 90 97 87 97
*Pleasant setting for
horseback riding.
Country food.*
⌂ ⌣ ☂

★ **MAS DU
CLAROUSSET** ***
Rte de Cacharel
Tel. 04 90 97 81 66
Fax 04 90 97 88 59
Pleasant setting.
⌂ ☆ ⌣ 🅿 ☂

★ **MAS DE
LA FOUQUE** ***
Rte du Petit Rhône
Tel. 04 90 97 81 02
Fax 04 90 97 96 84
Open Apr.–Nov.
Tennis.
⌂ ☆ ⌣ 🅿 ☂

MAS DU TADORNE ***
Chem. Bas-des-Launes
Tel. 04 90 97 93 11
Fax 04 90 97 71 04
☆ ⌣ 🅿 ☂

YOUTH HOSTEL
École communale
Lieu-dit de Pioch Badet
Tel. 04 90 97 51 72

AIGUES-MORTES

30220 ▲ 170

CULTURE

FORTIFICATIONS
Tel. 04 66 53 61 55
In season: Open
June–Sep. 5 9am–7pm;
Sep. 6–30, 9.30am–
6pm; and Apr.–May
9am–noon and
2–5.30pm. Closed May
1, Nov. 1 and 11, Dec. 31
and Jan. 1.

RESTAURANT

★ **LES ARCADES** ***
23, bd Gambetta
Tel. 04 66 53 81 13
Closed Mon.
*Traditional cuisine.
Disabled access.*
⌘ ☂ 🄲

ACCOMMODATION

★ **HÔTELLERIE
DES REMPARTS** ***
6, pl. Anatole-France
Tel. 04 66 53 82 77
Fax 04 66 53 73 77
Disabled access.
🄲 ☐

★ **LES TEMPLIERS** ***
23, av. de la République
Tel. 04 66 53 66 56
Fax 04 66 53 69 61
Disabled access.
🄲 🚗 ⌘ ☐

NÎMES

30000 ▲ 172–8

USEFUL ADDRESSES

TOURIST OFFICE
6, rue Auguste
Tel. 04 66 67 29 11
Fax 04 66 21 81 04

CULTURE

AMPHITHEATER
*See Tourist office for
visits.*

**ARCHEOLOGICAL
MUSEUM**
Bd Amiral-Courbet
Tel. 04 66 67 25 57

Open 11am–6pm
Closed Mon.

CARRÉ D'ART
Pl. de la Maison-Carrée
Tel. 04 66 76 35 35
Open 11am–6pm.
Closed Mon.
Modern art museum.

CATHEDRAL
Pl. aux Herbes
Open Mon.–Fri.
8.30am–6pm

**LYCÉE
ALPHONSE-DAUDET**
Bd Victor-Hugo
Closed to the public.

MAGNE TOWER
Jardin de la Fontaine
In season: Open
May–Sep. 9am–7pm

MAISON CARRÉE
Pl. de la Maison-Carrée
In season: Open
9am–7pm May–Sep.

**MUSÉE DES
BEAUX ARTS**
Rue Cité-Foulc
Tel. 04 66 67 38 21
Open 11am–6pm.
Closed Mon.

**MUSÉE D'HISTOIRE
NATURELLE ET DE
PRÉHISTOIRE**
Bd Amiral-Courbet
Tel. 04 66 67 39 14
Open 11am–6pm.
Closed Mon.

**MUSÉE DU
VIEUX NÎMES**
Palais de l'Ancien-
Évêché, Pl. aux
Herbes
Tel. 04 66 36 00 64
Open 11am–6pm.
Closed Mon.

ST PAUL'S CHURCH
Bd Victor-Hugo
Open 8am–6.30pm

TEMPLE OF DIANA
Jardin de la Fontaine
Open: Apr.–May 7am–
10pm; June–Sep. 15
7am–11pm; Sep. 16–
Oct. 8am–9pm and
Nov.–Dec. 8am–8pm

RESTAURANTS

**BISTROT DU
CHAPON FIN**
3, rue Château-Fadaise
Tel. 04 66 67 34 73
Closed Sat. midday, Sun.
and Aug. 14–Sep. 5
Disabled access.
⌘ ☂ 🄲 ◑

**L'ENCLOS
DE LA FONTAINE**
Quai de la Fontaine
Tel. 04 66 21 90 30
Disabled access.
⌘ ☂ 🅿 🄲 ◑

LE MAGISTER
5, rue Nationale
Tel. 04 66 76 11 00
Closed Sat. midday,
Sun. and Aug. 1–15
*Local and traditional
cuisine.*
🄲

ACCOMMODATION

HÔTEL PLAZZA
10, rue Roussy
Tel. 04 66 76 16 20
Fax 04 66 67 65 99
*Air conditioning;
elevator.*
🄲 🚗 ☐

**IMPERATOR
CONCORDE** ****
Quai de la Fontaine
Tel. 04 66 21 90 30
Fax 04 66 67 70 25
🄲 🅿 ⌘ ☐

◆

ORANGE

84100 ▲ 180–3

USEFUL ADDRESSES

TOURIST OFFICE
5, cours Aristide-Briand
Tel. 04 90 34 70 88
Fax 04 90 34 99 62

CULTURE

**CATHEDRAL
OF NOTRE-DAME-DE-
NAZARETH**
Pl. de l'Hôtel-de-Ville
Open 8am–5pm

FORMER TOWN HALL
Rue de l'Ancien-Hôtel-
de-ville
Closed to the public.

MUNICIPAL MUSEUM
Rue M.-Roch
Tel. 04 90 51 18 24
In season: Open
Apr.–Sep. Mon.–Sat.
9am–7pm, and Sun.
9am–noon and
1.30–7pm.

Closed Dec. 25, Jan. 1.
and May 1.
Entrance 25F;
children 20F.
*Same ticket gives
access to the Théâtre
Antique.*

RESTAURANTS

LE PARVIS
3, cours Pourtoule
Tel. 04 90 34 82 00
Fax 04 90 51 18 19
Closed Nov. 15–30.
*Local specialties. Near
the Théâtre Antique.*
☆ ✝ ◑

LE TRIMALCION
12, rue Petite-
Fusterie
Tel. 04 90 34
09 96
*Traditional
local cuisine.*
☆ 🅿 ✝

LE YACA
24, pl. Sylvain
Tel. 04 90 34
70 03
In season: Closed Wed.
*Family food. Near the
Théâtre Antique.*
⌿ 🅿 ✝ ◑

ACCOMMODATION

HÔTEL ARÈNE *
Pl. de Langes
Tel. 04 90 34 10 95
Fax 04 90 34 91 62
Closed Nov. –15 Dec.
*In a shady square near
the Théâtre Antique.
Supervised car park.*
☆ 🅿 🚗 ✝

MAS DES AIGRAS
Chemin des Aigras
Tel. 04 90 34 81 01
☆ 🔄 🅿 🚗 ✝

CHÂTEAUNEUF-DU-PAPE

84230

USEFUL ADDRESSES

TOURIST OFFICE
Place du Portail
Tel. 04 90 83 71 08
Fax 04 90 83 50 34

SPECIALTY FOODS

**FÉDÉRATION DES
SYNDICATS DE
PROMOTEURS DE
CHÂTEAUNEUF-DU-
PAPE**
Tel. 04 90 83 72 21
Six miles from Orange.

VALRÉAS

84600　　▲ 184

USEFUL ADDRESSES

TOURIST OFFICE
Place Aristide-Briand
Tel. 04 90 35 04 71

CULTURE

**CHAPEL OF THE
PÉNITENTS BLANCS**
Pl. Pie
*Collect key from the
presbytery, 8, pl. Pie.*

**CHURCH OF NOTRE-
DAME-DE-NAZARETH**
Pl. Pie
In season: Open
9am–7pm, May–Sep.

CLOCK TOWER
Rue Château-Robert
*Guided tours in July
and August organized
by the Tourist office.*

HÔTEL DE SIMIANE
Pl. Aristide-Briand
Open Mon.–Sat. 3–5pm
Now the Town Hall.

**MUSÉE DU
CARTONNAGE ET DE
L'IMPRIMERIE**
(Museum of Cardboard
and Printing)
3, rue du Mal-Foch
Tel. 04 90 35 58 75
In season: Open Apr.–
Sep. 10am–noon and
3–6pm. Closed public
hols. July 14, and
Aug 15.
Entrance 10F;
children 5F.

RESTAURANT

L'ÉTRIER
2, cours Tivoli
Tel. 04 90 35 05 94
Closed Nov. 1–15, Tue.,
Wed. out of season.
Traditional cuisine.
☆ 🅿 ✝

ACCOMMODATION

LE GRAND HÔTEL *
28, av. du G.-de-Gaulle
Tel. 04 90 35 00 26

Closed Dec. 25–Jan. 30,
Sat., Sun. out of season.
Traditional cuisine.
☆ 🔄 🅿 ✝

VAISON-LA-ROMAINE

84110　　▲ 185

USEFUL ADDRESSES

TOURIST OFFICE
Pl. du Chanoine-Sautel
Tel. 04 90 36 02 11

CULTURE

CASTLE
Signposted itinerary from
the upper town.
Closed to the public.

**CATHEDRAL OF NOTRE-
DAME-DE-NAZARETH**
Av. Jules-Ferry
In season: Open 9am–
12.30pm and 2–6.45pm,
June–Aug. Closes at
5.45pm Mar.–May and
Sep.–Oct.

CLOISTER
Av. Jules-Ferry
Entrance ticket to all
sites for 5 days 34F;
children 12F.
*Same opening times as
the cathedral.*

MAISON DES MESSII
Site de Puymin
Pl. de l'Abbé-Sautel
*Same opening times as
the cathedral.*

**MAISON DU BUSTE
EN ARGENT**
Site de Villasse
Pl. de l'Abbé-Sautel
*Same opening times as
the cathedral.*

**MUSÉE THÉO-
DESPLANS**
Site de Puymin
Pl. de l'Abbé-Sautel
In season: Open June–
Aug. 10am–1pm and
2.30–7.30pm; Mar.–May
and Sep.–Oct. 10am–
1pm and 2.30–6.15pm
Entrance for all sites for
five days 34F, children
12F.

**OLD BISHOPRIC
OR CHAPEL OF
STE-CONSTANCE**
Rue des Fours
Closed to the public.

PALAIS ÉPISCOPAL
Rue de l'Évêché
*Open during
exhibitions.*

PORTE VIEILLE
Haute ville
Pl. Poids

ST-QUÉNIN CHAPEL
Av. St-Quénin
*Key from the Tourist
office.*

VILLA DU PAON
Quartier Thès
Closed to the public.

RESTAURANTS

LA FÊTE EN PROVENCE
Pl. du Marché
Tel. 04 90 36 36 43
Fax 04 90 36 36 32
*Regional cooking; open
late during the Festival.*
☆ 🅿 ✝

**LA GLORIETTE
ET POMPONETTE**
22, Grand-Rue
Tel. 04 90 28 77 74
Closed Sun., Jan. and
Thur. out of season.
*Old-fashioned bread
and fine tarts.*
☆ ✝

ACCOMMODATION

LE BEFFROI *
Rue de l'Évêché
Tel. 04 90 36 04 71
Fax 04 90 36 24 78
Closed Nov. 15–
Dec. 15 and Feb.
15–Mar. 15
🅲 ⌿ ☆ 🅿 🚗

**HÔTEL DES LICES
BURRHUS ***
Pl. Montfort
Tel. 04 90 36 00 11
Fax 04 90 36 39 05
Closed Nov. 15–
Dec. 15
☆ ✝

CARPENTRAS

84200　　▲ 188

USEFUL ADDRESSES

TOURIST OFFICE
170, allée Jean-Jaurès
Tel. 04 90 63 57 88
or 04 90 63 00 78
Fax 04 90 60 41 02

CULTURE

BELFRY
Pl. de
l'Horloge
*Closed
to the
public.*

369

BIBLIOTHÈQUE INGUIMBERTINE ET MUSÉE DUPLESSIS-COMTADIN
234, bd Albin-Durand
Tel. 04 90 65 04 92
In season: Open Mon. 2–6.30pm, Tue.–Fri. 9.30am–6.30pm, Sat. 9.30am–noon

CATHEDRAL OF ST-SIFFREIN
Pl. du Gen.-de-Gaulle
Tel. 04 90 63 08 33
Open 8am–7pm
Closed Sun. and public hols.

LA CHARITÉ
Rue Cottier
Tel. 04 90 63 46 35
Open 9am–noon, 2–6pm

CHURCH OF NOTRE-DAME-DE-L'OBSERVANCE
Pl. de l'Observance
Tel. 04 90 63 27 15
Closed noon–2pm

ÉVÊCHÉ
In the law courts.
Pl. du Gen.-de-Gaulle
Visits arranged through the tourist office.

HÔTEL-DIEU
Av. Victor-Hugo
Tel. 04 90 63 80 00
Open Mon., Wed. and Thur. 9–11.30am
Entrance 20F; children 10F.
Visits arranged through the tourist office.

MUSÉE LAPIDAIRE
Rue des Saintes-Maries
Tel. 04 90 63 04 92
Closed for restoration.

MUSÉE SOBIRATS
112, rue du Collège
Tel. 04 90 63 04 92
Open daily except Tue. 10am–noon and 2–6pm

ROMAN ARCH
Pl. d'Inguimbert

SYNAGOGUE
Pl. Maurice-Charetier
Tel. 04 90 63 39 97
Open 10am– noon and 3–5pm. Closed Fri. afternoon, Sat., Sun. and public hols.

RESTAURANTS

CHEZ SERGE
90, rue Cottier
Tel. 04 90 63 21 24
Armenian specialties, pasta, pizza.

Reservations recommended.
☆ 🄿 ⛨

RIVES DE L'AUZON
47, bd du Nord
Tel. 04 90 60 62 62
Fax 04 90 60 49 73
Closed Sun. eve, Mon.
Covered terrace on the banks of the Auzon.
☄ ☆ 🄿 ⛨ ◑

ACCOMMODATION

LE FIACRE ★★
153, rue Vigne
Tel. 04 90 63 03 15
Fax 04 90 60 49 73
Former "hôtel particulier".
🄲 ☆ 🄿 🚗 ⛨

HÔTEL FORUM ★★
24, rue du Forum
Tel. 04 90 60 57 00
Fax 04 90 63 52 65
🄿 🚗 ⛨

SPECIALTY FOODS

CONFECTIONERS
MAISON BONO
280, allée Jean-Jaurès
Tel. 04 90 63 04 99
VILLENEUVE-HARDY
288, rue Notre-Dame-de-Santé
Tel. 04 90 63 05 25

SAULT-EN-VAUCLUSE
84390

SPECIALTY FOODS

ANDRÉ BOYER
Tel. 04 90 64 00 23
Fax 04 90 64 08 99
Sault nougat specialist.

JEAN CARTOUX
Av. de l'Oratoire
Tel. 04 90 64 02 32
Honey producer.

SHOPPING

MAISON DES PRODUCTEURS DE LAVANDE
Rue de la République
Tel. 04 90 64 08 98
Open Easter–Nov. 11

FONTAINE-DE-VAUCLUSE
84800　　▲ 190

USEFUL ADDRESSES

TOURIST OFFICE
Chemin de la Fontaine
Tel. 04 90 20 32 22
Fax 04 90 20 21 37

CULTURE

CHÂTEAU DES ÉVÊQUES DE CAVAILLON
50 yards past bridge toward Cavaillon, opposite Hôtel des Sources.
Ruins.

CHURCH OF ST-VÉRAN
Av. Robert-Garcin
Open daily.

MUSÉE DE L'APPEL DE LA LIBERTÉ
Chemin du Gouffre
Tel. 04 90 20 24 00
Open daily except Tue. Jul.–Aug. 10am–7pm; Mar.–June and Sep.–Oct. 15 10am– noon and 2–6pm. Entrance 10F; children free.

MUSÉE-BIBLIOTHÈQUE FRANÇOIS-PÉTRARQUE
Left bank of the river Sorgue
Tel. 04 90 20 37 20
Irregular opening times. Closed Tue. Entrance 10F; children free.

MUSÉE DE LA SPÉLÉOLOGIE LE MONDE SOUTERRAIN DE NORBERT CASTERET
Chemin du Gouffre
Tel. 04 90 20 34 13
In season: Open May–Aug. 10am–noon and 2–6.30pm, Closed Nov. 11–Jan. Entrance 27F; children 17F.

VALLIS CLAUSA CRAFT CENTER
Chemin de la Fontaine
Tel. 04 90 20 34 14
Open 9am–12.30pm and 2–6.30pm. Closed Dec. 25 and Jan. 1.

RESTAURANT

RESTAURANT DU CHÂTEAU
Tel. 04 90 20 31 54
Closed Jan.–Feb.
Traditional cuisine. Fine veranda on the river.
☆ 🄿 ⛨

ACCOMMODATION

HÔTEL DU PARC ★★
Les Bourgades
Tel. 04 90 20 31 57
Fax 04 90 20 27 03
Closed Wed. and Jan. 2–Feb. 15
On the banks of the river Sorgue.
☆ 🄿 🛏 ⛨

GORDES
84220　　▲ 190

USEFUL ADDRESSES

TOURIST OFFICE
Le Château
Tel. 04 90 72 02 75
Fax 04 90 72 04 39

CULTURE

AUMÔNERIE ST-JACQUES
Behind the church.
Open May–Sep. 20 10.30–12.30pm and 2.30-6pm. Free entrance.
Exhibition of painting and sculpture.

CHURCH OF NOTRE-DAME-DE-L'ASSOMPTION ET ST-ÉTIENNE
Pl. du Château
Open 9am–6pm

MAISON LHOTE
Rue André Lhote
Closed to the public.

MUSÉE VICTOR-VASARELY
Pl. du Château
Tel. 04 90 72 02 89
Open 10am–noon and 2–6pm. Closed Tue., July–Aug. Entrance 25F; children 15F.

SÉNANQUE ABBEY
Rte de Cavaillon then rte de Venasque, 1½ miles from town center.
Tel. 04 90 72 05 72
Open Mar.–Oct. Mon.–Fri. 10am–noon and 2–6pm; weekends, public hols, religious days, school vacations 2–6pm. Entrance 18F, children 8F.

RESTAURANTS

COMPTOIR DU VICTUAILLER
Pl. du Château
Tel. 04 90 72 01 31
Closed Tue., Nov. 15–Dec. 15, Jan. 15–Mar. 15
Reservation advised for lunch, essential for dinner. Good wine list.
☆ 🄿 ⛨

★ MAS DE TOURTERON
Les Imberts
Tel. 04 90 72 00 16
Closed Mon. and
Nov. 15–Dec. 27 and
Jan. 10–Feb. 10
*Outstanding restaurant,
lovely garden. Reserve.*
P 🚗 ╤ ◐

ACCOMMODATION

LES BORIES ★★★★
Rte de l'Abbaye-
de-Sénanque
Tel. 04 90 72 00 51
Fax 04 90 72 01 22
Closed Jan.–Feb.
Tennis.
⚊ ➘ **P**

FERME DE LA HUPPE
D 156 road
Les Pourquiers
Tel. 04 90 72 12 25
Fax 04 90 72 01 83
Closed Nov.–Mar.
⌂ ⚘ ➘ **P** ✗

LA GALOCHE ★★★
Rte de Murs
Tel. 04 90 72 01 36
Fax 04 90 72 01 81
Closed Nov. 15–Mar. 15
Tennis.
⚊ ➘ **P** ╤

COUSTELLET
84220

CULTURE

**MUSÉE DE LA
LAVANDE**
Rte de Gordes
Tel. 04 90 76 91 23

APT
84400　　▲ 193

USEFUL ADDRESSES

TOURIST OFFICE
4, av. Philippe-de-Girard
Tel. 04 90 74 03 18
Fax 04 90 04 64 30

CULTURE

ANCIEN ÉVÊCHÉ
Pl. de la Mairie
Closed to the public.

**ANCIEN HÔPITAL
DE LA CHARITÉ**
Av. Philippe-de-Girard
Closed to the public.

**CATHEDRAL OF
STE-ANNE**
Rue des Marchands
In season: Open
9.30am–noon and
3–7pm, May–Sep.

CHAPEL
OF STE-CATHERINE
Rue Scudéry
*Services 1st and
3rd Sun. in the month,
11am.*

CLOCK TOWER
Rue des Marchands
Closed to the public.

**MUSÉE D'ARCHÉOLOGIE
ET D'HISTOIRE**
7, rue de l'Amphithéâtre
Tel. 04 90 74 00 34
In season: Open June–
Sep. 10am–noon and
2–5.30pm. Closed Tue.
and Sun. Entrance 10F;
children 5F.

**MUSÉE DE
PALÉONTOLOGIE
MAISON DU PARC
DU LUBÉRON**
60, pl. Jean-Jaurès
Tel. 04 90 04 42 00
In season: Open
June–Sep. 8.30am–
noon and 1.30–7pm.
Closed Sat. afternoon,
Sun. and public hols.

PORTE DE SAIGNON
Rue St-Pierre

RESTAURANT

**RESTAURANT
BERNARD MATHYS**
Le Chêne-Route 100
Tel. 04 90 04 86 64
Closed Tue.–Wed.
and Jan.
Gourmet cuisine.
⚘ **P** 🍴 ╤

ACCOMMODATION

**AUBERGE
DU LUBÉRON ★★★**
17, quai Léon-Sagy
Tel. 04 90 74 12 50
Fax 04 90 04 79 49
Closed Jan. 1–15
On the bank of the river.
C **P** 🚗 ╤

SPECIALTY FOODS

APTUNION
Route d'Avignon
Tel. 04 90 76 31 31
*Candy factory, just over
a mile from Apt.*

SHOPPING

DOMINIQUE BOUGINEAU
30, av. Victor-Hugo
Tel. 04 90 74 52 22
Earthenware.

BONNIEUX
84480　　▲ 194

USEFUL ADDRESSES

TOURIST OFFICE
7, place Carnot
Tel. 04 90 75 91 90
Fax 04 90 75 92 94

CULTURE

CASTLE
On the road out of the
village toward Lourmarin
Closed to the public.

**MUSÉE DE LA
BOULANGERIE**
Rue de la République
Tel. 04 90 75 88 34
In season: Open June–
Sep. daily except Tue.
10am– 12.15pm and
3–6.15pm

NEW CHURCH
Allée des Tilleuls
Opening times vary.

OLD CHURCH
Opening times vary.

LOURMARIN
84160　　▲ 195

USEFUL ADDRESSES

TOURIST OFFICE
9, av. Philippe-de-Girard
Tel. 04 90 68 10 77

CULTURE

BELFRY
Pl. du Castellas
Closed to the public.

CASTLE
Av. Raoul-Dautry
Tel. 04 90 68 15 23
Open July–Sep. 10.30–
noon and 2.30–6.30pm.
Entrance 30F; children
18F.

CHURCH OF
ST-ANDRÉ
Pl. de l'Église
Open Sun. 9.30am.

PROTESTANT TEMPLE
Av. Raoul-Dautry
Closed to the public.

RESTAURANTS

**L'AGNEAU
GOURMAND**
Rte de Vaugines
Tel. 04 90 68 21 04
Closed Wed.–Thur.
midday (except July)
and Nov.–Feb. 15
(except Christmas and
Jan. 1.)
Old farm.
⚊ ⚘ ➘ **P** ╤

LA FENIÈRE
9, rue Grand-Pré
Tel. 04 90 68 11 79
Fax 04 90 68 18 60
Closed last week June,
first week Oct.,
Christmas week and
first 2 weeks Jan.
*This restaurant is
famous for its gourmet
food. Outstanding
wine list.*
⚘ **P** ╤

**L'OUSTALET DE
GEORGES**
Av. Philippe-de-Girard
Tel. 04 90 68 07 33
Open noon–2pm and
7–10.30pm. Closed
Feb.–Mar. 15
*Art gallery. Disabled
access.*
╤ **P** **C** ◐

ACCOMMODATION

HÔTEL DE GUILLES ★★★
Rte de Vaugines
Tel. 04 90 68 30 55
Fax 04 90 68 37 41
Closed Nov.–Dec. 10
and Jan.
Tennis.
⚘ ➘ **P** ╤

**LE MOULIN
DE LOURMARIN**
Rue Temple
Tel. 04 90 68 06 69
Fax 04 90 68 91 76
Closed Jan. 15–Feb. 15
Old oil mill.
C ⚘ **P** ╤

**CAMPING
DES HAUTES-
PRAIRIES**
Rte de Vaugines
Tel. 04 90 68 02 89
Closed Dec.–Mar.
Sports facilities.
⊡⋅ ➘

LE LUBÉRON

CULTURE

ABBAYE DE SILVACANE
Rte de Cadenet and
La Roque-d'Anthéron
(D 561 road)
Open 9am–7pm

MARSEILLES

13001–13016
▲ 198–205
Roman numerals in
brackets indicate the
arrondissements of
Marseilles.

USEFUL ADDRESSES

CENTRAL POST OFFICE
Pl. de l'Hôtel-des-
Postes (I)
Tel. 04 91 95 47 32

**COMITÉ RÉGIONAL DE
TOURISME DE
PROVENCE**
2, rue Henri-Barbusse
Tel. 04 91 39 38 00
Fax 04 91 56 66 61

**COMITÉ
DÉPARTEMENTAL
DE TOURISME DES
BOUCHES-DU-RHÔNE**
13, rue Roux-de-Brignoles
Tel. 04 91 13 84 13
Fax 04 91 33 01 82

**COMMISSARIAT
CENTRAL**
(Central police station),
Rue du Commissaire-
Becker (II)
Tel. 04 91 39 80 00
at night: 04 91 39 83 84

MAIRIE
(Town Hall)
Quai du Port (II)
Tel. 04 91 55 11 11
Open Mon.–Fri.
8.30am– noon and
2.30–6.30pm

CULTURE

ABBAYE ST-VICTOR
Pl. St-Victor (VII)
Tel. 04 91 33 25 86
Open 8.30am–6.30pm
Music and theater.

ARCHIPEL DU FRIOUL
Tel. 04 91 55 50 09
or 91 54 91 11
Access by boat.

BASTIDE MAGALONE
Cité de la Musique
245, bd Michelet (VIII)
Tel. 04 91 55 14 68
Visits by written request.

**CATHEDRAL OF LA
VIEILLE-MAJOR**
Port de la Joliette (II)
Open 9am–noon and
2.30–5.30pm.
Closed Mon.

**CATHEDRAL OF
STE-MARIE-MAJEURE
(NOUVELLE-MAJOR)**
Pl. de la Major (II)
Open Tue.–Sat. 9am–
noon and 2–5pm, Sun.
8.30am–noon and 2.30–
5.30pm

CHÂTEAU D'IF
Îlot d'If (VII)
Tel. 04 91 59 02 30
Access by boat.

**CHURCH OF THE
RÉFORMÉS-ST-
VINCENT-DE-PAUL**
Square de Verdun (I)
Tel. 04 91 42 35 52
Open Tue.–Sat. 9am–
noon and 2.30-6.30pm,
Mon. 2.30–6.30pm

**"CITÉ RADIEUSE"
LE CORBUSIER**
280, bd Michelet (VIII)
Residents give tours.

**COMPLEXE DES
ARSENAUX**
25, cours d'Estienne-
d'Orves (I)
Closed to the public.

DANAÏDES FOUNTAIN
Cours Joseph-Thierry (I)

FORT ST-JEAN
Quai du Port (II)
Tel. 04 91 54 44 75

FORT ST-NICOLAS
Bd Charles-Livon (VII)

**HOSPICE DE LA
VIEILLE CHARITÉ**
Rue de la Charité (II)
Tel. 04 91 56 28 38
Open 10am–5pm.
Closed Mon.
*Guided tours Sat. and
Sun. 2 and 4pm.*

HÔTEL DAVIEL
2, place du Mazeaud (II)
Tel. 04 91 55 11 11
*Visits arranged by the
tourist office.*

**JARDIN DES VESTIGES
OR "FOUILLES DE LA
BOURSE"**
Rue Henri-Barbusse (I)
In season: Open
10am–8pm

MUSÉE CANTINI
19, rue Grignan (VI)
Tel. 04 91 54 77 75
In season: Open
11am–6pm. Closed
Mon. and public hols.

**MUSÉE D'ARCHÉOLOGIE
MÉDITERRANÉENNE**
Centre de la Vieille-
Charité (II)
2, rue de la Charité
Tel. 04 91 56 28 38
Open June–Sep.
11am–6pm, Oct.–May
10am–5pm. Closed
Mon.

**MUSÉE DES ARTS
AFRICAINS,
OCÉANIENS,
AMÉRINDIENS**
Centre de la Vieille-
Charité (II)
2, rue de la Charité
Tel. 04 91 56 28 38
Open Tue.–Fri.
10am–5pm, Sat.–Sun.
noon–7pm.

**MUSÉE DES
BEAUX-ARTS**
Palais Longchamp
Bd Philippon (IV)
Tel. 04 91 62 21 17
In season: Open
June–Sep. Tue.–Sun.
11am–6pm.

**MUSÉE DES
DOCKS ROMAINS**
Pl. Vivaux (I)
Tel. 04 91 91 24 62
In season: Open 10am–
6pm. Closed Mon.

**MUSÉE GROBET-
LABADIÉ**
140, bd Longchamp (IV)
Tel. 04 91 62 21 82
In season: Open June–
Sep. 11am–6pm.
Closed Mon. and public
hols.

**MUSÉE D'HISTOIRE
DE MARSEILLE**
Centre Bourse (I)
Tel. 04 91 90 42 22
Open noon–7pm.
Closed Sun.

**MUSÉE D'HISTOIRE
NATURELLE**
Palais Longchamp
Bd Philippon (IV)
Tel. 04 91 62 30 78
In season: Open
June–Sep. 11am–6pm.

Closed Mon. and public
hols.

**MUSÉE DE LA MARINE
ET DE L'ÉCONOMIE
DE MARSEILLE**
Hall of the Palais
de la Bourse (I)
Tel. 04 91 39 33 33
Open Wed.–Mon.,
10am–noon and 2–6pm

**MUSÉE DU
VIEUX-MARSEILLE**
Maison
Diamantée
2, rue de la
Prison (II)
Tel. 04 91 56
28 28
In season:
Open Tue.–Sun.
11am–6pm

**NOTRE-DAME
DE LA GARDE**
Pl. du Colonel-Edon
(VII)
In season: Visits to the
crypts 7am–7.30pm,
June–Sep. 20

OPÉRA
Pl. Rever (I)

**PARC ET CHÂTEAU
PASTRÉ**
150, av. Montredon (VIII)
Tel. 04 91 73 26 27
*Free access to garden.
Faïence Museum in the
château.*

RESTAURANTS

★ **L'ATELIER
DU CHOCOLAT**
18, pl. aux
Huiles (I)
Tel. 04 91 33 55 00
Closed Sun., Mon. eve,
Sat. eve and Aug.
🐕 🍴

★ **LA BAIE
DES SINGES**
Cap Croisette (VIII)
Tel. 04 91 73 68 87
Open Apr.–Sep.
*Typically Marseillaise
open-air restaurant.*

**LE CARRÉ
D'HONORÉ**
34, pl. aux Huiles (I)
Tel. 04 91 33 16 80
Closed Sat. midday,
Sun. and Aug. 15–31
🐕

CHEZ FONFON
140, vallon des Auffes
(VII)
Tel. 04 91 52 14 38
Closed Sun., Mon.
and Dec.23–Jan. 2

★ La Coupole
5, rue Haxo (I)
Tel. 04 91 54 88 57
Closed Sun. and end Aug.
⚡

★ La Grotte
Rue Callelongue (VIII)
Tel. 04 91 73 17 79
⚡ ⼲

Le Lunch
Calanque de Sormiou (X)
Tel. 04 91 25 05 37
Open Apr.–Sep.
Beautiful sunsets over the sea.
☄ ⼲

Miramar
12, quai du Port (II)
Tel. 04 91 91 10 40
Closed Sun., 3 weeks in Aug. and Dec. 23–Jan. 6
Excellent bouillabaisse.
⚡ ⼲

★ Le Panier des Arts
3, rue du Petit-Puits (II)
Tel. 04 91 56 02 32
Closed Sat. lunchtime and Sun.
⚡

Patalain
49, rue Sainte (I)
Tel. 04 91 55 02 78
Closed Sat. midday, Sun. and July 14–Aug.
Very good food.
⚡ 🅿

Accommodation

★ Capitainerie des Galères **
46, rue Sainte (I)
Vieux-Port
Tel. 04 91 54 73 73
Fax 04 91 54 77 77
⌂ ⚡ 🅿 ⼲

Concorde Palm Beach ****
2, prom. de la Plage (VIII)
Tel. 04 91 16 19 00
Fax 04 91 16 19 39
⚡ ☄ 🅿 ⼲

Mercure ***
Centre Bourse (I)
Rue Neuve-St-Martin
Tel. 04 91 39 20 00
Fax 04 91 56 24 57
⚡ 🅿 ⼲ ✕ ☎

★ New Hôtel Bompard ***
2, rue des Flots-Bleus
Corniche Kennedy (VII)
Tel. 04 91 52 10 93
Fax 04 91 31 02 14
⚡ 🅿 ⼲ ☄

Petit Nice ****
Corniche Kennedy (VII)
Anse de Maldormé
Tel. 04 91 59 25 92
Fax 04 91 59 28 08
☄ 🚗 ⼲ ⚡

★ St-Ferréol **
19, rue Pisançon (I)
Tel. 04 91 33 12 21
Fax 04 91 54 29 97
Closed Aug. 1–21
Jacuzzi.
⚡

Youth hostel
Château de Bois-Luzy
Allée des Primevères (XII)
Tel. 04 91 49 06 18

Sports

Golf club de La Salette
Imp. des Vaudrans
La Valentine (XI)
Tel. 04 91 27 12 16

Golf St-Ange
45, chemin des Anémones
Les Caillols (XII)
Tel. 04 91 89 91 88

Nightlife

Au Son des Guitares
18, rue Corneille (I)
Tel. 04 91 33 11 47
Open from 11pm. Closed Sun. and Sep. 1–15
Nightclub. Thematic evenings; traditional Corsican guitar music.

Bar de la Marine
15, quai de Rive-Neuve (VIIᵉ)
Tel. 04 91 54 95 47
Open Mon.–Sat.
7am–2am
Late-night bar.

La Cave à Jazz
4, rue Bernard-du-Bois (I)
Tel. 04 91 39 28 00
Closed school vacations.
Student music bar.

La Maison Hantée
10, rue Vian (VI)
Tel. 04 91 92 09 40
Open 7pm–2am
Closed Thur. and Sun.
Late-night bar.

Le Marseillois
Quai du Port (II)
Tel. 04 91 91 61 44
Open Mon.–Sat.
10am–2pm and 8–10pm
Restaurant; musical evenings twice a month.

★ Le Pêle-Mêle
45, rue du Fort Notre-Dame (I)
Tel. 04 91 54 85 26
Open Mon.–Sat.
5pm–2am
Jazz bar.

St-James Club
7, rue Ventura (I)
Tel. 04 91 33 10 63
Open Fri.–Sat.
1970's-style nightclub. Does not accept credit cards.

L'X
30, rue St-Saëns (I)
Tel. 04 91 54 95 55
Open 4.30pm–2am.
Closed Sun.
Music bar.

CASSIS

13260 ▲ 210

Useful Addresses

Tourist office
Place Baragnon
Tel. 04 42 01 71 17
Fax 04 90 42 01 28 31

Restaurants

Le Clos des Arômes
10, rue Paul-Mouton
Tel. 04 42 01 71 84
Closed Nov.–Feb.
Open throughout the Christmas period.
🅿 ⼲

★ Monsieur Brun
2, quai Calendal
Tel. 04 42 01 82 66
Closed Dec. 10–mid Jan.
Open-air restaurant. Sea food specialties in summer.
⼲

Accommodation

★ Le Bestouan **
Plage du Bestouan
Tel. 04 42 01 05 70
Fax 04 42 01 34 82
Open Mar.–Oct.
Tennis.
⚡ ✕ ⼲

★ Roches Blanches ***
Rte des Calanques
Tel. 04 42 01 09 30
Fax 04 42 01 94 23
⚡ ☄ 🅿 ⼲

Youth hostel
Les Calanques
La Fontasse
Tel. 04 42 01 02 72

AIX-EN-PROVENCE

13100 ▲ 212–9

Useful Addresses

Central post office
2, rue Lapierre
Tel. 04 42 16 01 50

Commissariat Central
(Central police station)
10, pl. Jeanne-d'Arc
Tel. 04 42 93 97 00

Mairie
(Town Hall)
Pl. de l'Hotel-de-Ville
Tel. 04 42 25 95 95

Tourist office
2, pl. du Gen.-de-Gaulle
Tel. 04 42 16 11 61
Fax 04 42 16 11 62

Culture

Bibliothèque Méjanes
8-10, rue des Allumettes
Tel. 04 42 25 98 89
Open Tue.–Fri. noon–6pm, Sat. 10am–6pm

Cathedral of St-Sauveur
34, pl. des Martyrs-de-la-Résistance
Tel. 04 42 21 10 51
Open 7.30am–noon and 2–6pm
Triptych can be viewed 10–11.30am and 2–4.30pm, except Sun. Worth a visit.

Château de la Gaude
Rte des Pinchinats
Tel. 04 42 96 93 73
Open Mon.–Thur. 10am–noon and 3–6pm, June–Sep. Closed public hols. and Oct.–May.
Only the garden is open to visitors; entrance 5F.

Church of Ste-Marie-Madeleine
Pl. des Prêcheurs
Tel. 04 42 38 02 81

In season: Open
3–6.45pm, July–Aug.

CHURCH OF ST-JEAN-DE-MALTE
Pl. St-Jean-de-Malte
Tel. 04 42 38 25 70
Open 9am–noon and
3–7pm
*To visit collect the key
from the presbytery, 24,
rue d'Italie.*

CLOCK TOWER
Adjoining Town Hall.

CLOISTER
Pl. de l'Archevêché

FONDATION ST-JOHN-PERSE
Bibliothèque Méjanes
8–10, rue des
Allumettes
Tel. 04 42 25 98 85
Open 9am–noon and
2–6pm. Closed Mon.,
Sat. pm and public hols.
Free entrance.

FONDATION VASARELY
1, av. Marcel-Pagnol
Tel. 04 42 20 01 09
Open daily Jul.–Sep.
10am–1pm and 2–7pm,
Oct.–June (except May)
10am–1pm and 2–6pm.
Entrance 35F.

HALLE AUX GRAINS
Pl. de l'Hôtel-de-Ville
Tel. 04 42 23 44 17
Post office.

LA MIGNARDE
Route des Pinchinats
Tel. 04 42 96 41 86
*Visits by appointment
or through the tourist
office.*

MUSÉE GRANET
Pl. St-Jean-de-Malte
Tel. 04 42 38 14 70
Open 10am–noon and
2–6pm. Closed Tue.,
public hols., Dec. 26
and Jan. 2

MUSÉE D'HISTOIRE NATURELLE
6, rue Espariat
Tel. 04 42 26 23 67
Open 10am–noon and
2–6pm. Closed Sun.
am, public hols.,
Dec. 26 and Jan. 2

MUSÉE PAUL-ARBAUD
2A, rue du 4-Septembre
Tel. 04 42 38 38 95
Open 2–5pm.
Closed Sun. and
Sep. 15–Oct. 15

MUSÉE DES TAPISSERIES D'AMEUBLEMENT ANCIEN
Archevêché
Pl. des Martyrs-de-la-Résistance
Tel. 04 42 23 09 91
Open 10.30am–6pm.
Closed Tue.

MUSÉE DU VIEIL-AIX
17, rue Gaston-de-Saporta
Tel. 04 42 21 43 55
In season: Open
10am–noon and
2.30–6pm, Apr.–Oct.
Closed Mon. and public
hols.

OPPIDUM D'ENTREMONT
7, bd Jean-Jaurès
Tel. 04 42 26 61 87
Open 9am–noon and
2–6pm. Closed Tue.

PALAIS DE JUSTICE
Pl. de Verdun
Tel. 04 42 33 83 00
Open Mon.–Fri.
9am–noon and 2–5pm
*Visit the "salle des
Pas Perdus".*

PAVILLON DE VENDÔME
32, rue Célony
Tel. 04 42 21 05 78
In season: Open
8.30am–noon and
2–6pm. Closed Tue.

PAVILLON LENFANT
346, rte des Alpes
Les Pinchinats
Tel. 04 42 23 48 80
Open Mon.–Fri.
8.30am–5pm
Garden open on request.

RESTAURANTS

★ ÉTAPE LANI
22, rue Victor-Leydet
Tel. 04 42 27 76 16
Closed Mon. midday
and Sun., 3 weeks in
Aug. and 1 week in Jan.
♀ P ⏝ 🚗

★ LE PAGOPON
25, rue Lisse-des-Cordeliers
Tel. 04 42 26 47 88
Closed Sun. evening
and Mon. lunchtime
Asian restaurant.

LE PIGONNET
5, av. Pigonnet
Tel. 04 42 59 02 90
Closed Sat. and Sun.
lunchtime
♀ ⏝ P 🍴

LA TABLE DU ROI
24, bd du Roi-René
Tel. 04 42 37 61 00
⏝ 🍴 ♨

★ TRATTORIA CHEZ ANTOINE
3, rue Clemenceau
Tel. 04 42 38 27 10
Closed Sun., Jan. 1–15
and Aug. 1–15
Food served until
12.30am.

🍴 P ⏝

ACCOMMODATION

LES AUGUSTINS ★★★
3, rue Masse
Tel. 04 42 27 28 59
Fax 04 42 26 74 87
♀ ⚸

CHÂTEAU DE LA PIOLINE
Les Milles
Tel. 04 42 20 07 81
Fax 04 42 59 96 12
Closed Feb.
Formal French garden.
🏠 P ⏝ 🍴 ♨

HÔSTELLERIE LA BASTIDE
Rte de Luynes (D 7)
Tel. 04 42 24 48 50
Fax 04 42 60 01 36
♨ ⛷ P ⏝ 🍴

★ LES INFIRMERIES DU ROI RENÉ ★★★
Chemin des Infirmeries
Tel. 04 42 37 83 00
Fax 04 42 27 54 40
⏝ P ⚸ ♀

MAS D'ENTREMONT ★★★★
Montée d'Avignon
Tel. 04 42 23 45 32
Fax 04 42 21 15 83
Closed Mar. 15–Nov. 1
🏛 ⛷ 🏠 ⏝ P
🍴 ♨

MAS DES ÉCUREUILS ★★★
Chemin du Castel-Blanc
Petite route des Milles
Tel. 04 42 24 40 48
Fax 04 42 39 24 57
♀ ⏝ P ⚸ 🍴

★ NÈGRE COSTE ★★★
33, cours Mirabeau
Tel. 04 42 27 74 22
Fax 04 42 26 80 93
♀ P ☎

★ VILLA GALLICI ★★★
18 *bis*, av. Violette
Tel. 04 42 23 29 23
Fax 04 42 96 30 45
♀ ⏝ P 🍴

YOUTH HOSTEL
3, av. Marcel-Pagnol
Tel. 04 42 20 15 99
Closed Dec. 21–31

SPORT

SET GOLF CLUB
Le Pey Blanc
Chemin Granet
Tel. 04 42 64 11 82

NIGHTLIFE

LES DEUX GARÇONS
53, cours Mirabeau
Tel. 04 42 26 00 51
In season: Open 6pm–4.30am, June–Aug.

SPECIALTY FOODS

CALISSONS D'AIX
CONFISERIE D'ENTRECASTEAUX
2, rue d'Entrecasteaux
Tel. 04 42 27 15 02
LES CALISSONS DU ROY RENÉ
7, rue Papassandi
Tel. 04 42 26 67 86
*Also offers a mail-order
service.*

PÂTISSERIE RIEDERER
6, rue Thiers
Tel. 04 42 38 19 69
*Famous for its delicious
pastries, particularly its
"tarte Émilie" and
"merveilles de
Provence".*

LES ARCS
83460

SPECIALTY FOODS

MAISON DES VINS CÔTES-DE-PROVENCE
N 7 road
Tel. 04 94 47 48 47
◆

LE PLAN-D'AUPS-STE-BAUME
83640

USEFUL ADDRESSES

TOURIST OFFICE
Mairie (Town Hall),
Pl. de la Mairie
Tel. 04 42 04 51 17

CULTURE

GROTTE DE MARIE-MADELEINE
Tel. 04 42 04 50 21
In season: Open
8am–6pm, May–Oct.

HÔTELLERIE DE LA STE-BAUME
Tel. 04 42 04 54 84

MONASTERY
Closed to the public.

MONTAGNE STE-BAUME

CULTURE

PARC ST-PONS
D 42 road 11 miles from Plan-d'Aups.

ST-MAXIMIN-LA-STE-BAUME

83470 ▲ 221

USEFUL ADDRESSES

TOURIST OFFICE
Mairie (Town Hall),
Pl. Jean-Salusse
Tel. 04 94 59 84 59

CULTURE

BASILIQUE ROYALE DE ST-MAXIMIN
Pl. de l'Hôtel-de-Ville
Open 8am–7pm
*Enquire at the town hall
for information on
guided tours*

COUVENT ROYAL
Pl. Jean-Salusse
Tel. 04 94 59 86 12
Open Apr.–Oct.
9am–6.30pm

RESTAURANT

CHEZ NOUS
35, bd Jean-Jaurès
Tel. 04 94 78 02 57
Disabled access.
✶ ⬛ ⌖

ACCOMMODATION

HÔTEL DE FRANCE
5, av. Albert Ier
Tel. 04 94 78 00 14
Fax 04 94 59 83 80
✶ ⬛ ▣ ☐ ⌑

NANS-LES-PINS

83860

RESTAURANT

DOMAINE DE CHÂTEAUNEUF
On the N 560 road
Tel. 04 94 78 90 06
✶ ◑ ⌖

ACCOMMODATION

DOMAINE DE CHÂTEAUNEUF
On the N 560 road
Tel. 04 94 78 90 06
Fax 04 94 78 63 30
Closed Dec.–Feb.
*Garden, tennis, bicycles
for rental, golf.*
🏛 ⌑

RIANS

83560

RESTAURANT

DOMAINE ESPAGNE
Take the D 23 toward
Ginasservis, then the
D 30 toward La Verdière
for 2 miles; it is 500
yards past the grain silo.
Tel. 04 94 80 11 03,
✶ ⌖ ☐··

ACCOMMODATION

DOMAINE ESPAGNE
Directions as above
Tel. 04 94 80 11 03
Disabled access.
☐·· ▣

BRIGNOLES

83170 ▲ 224

USEFUL ADDRESSES

TOURIST OFFICE
Parking des Augustins
Tel. 04 94 69 01 78

CULTURE

CHÂTEAU COMTAL
Pl. du Palais-des-
Comtes-de-Provence
Tel. 04 94 69 45 18
In season: Open
Wed.–Sat. 10am–noon
and 2.30–6pm, Sun.
and public hols.;
   Apr.–Sep. 9am–noon
and 3–6pm

CHURCH OF ST-SAUVEUR
Pl. de la
Paroisse
Tel. 04 94 69 10 69
Open 8am–8pm

HÔTEL DE CLAVIER
Rue du Palais
Tel. 04 94 59 10 72
Open Mon.–Fri.
9am–noon and 1–5pm.

LE THORONET

83340

USEFUL ADDRESSES

TOURIST OFFICE
10, place des Ormeaux
Tel. 04 94 60 10 94

CULTURE

ABBAYE DU THORONET
2 miles from town on
the road to Cabasse
and Carces
Tel. 04 94 60 43 90
Open 9am–7pm,
Apr.–Sep.
*Exhibitions and
festivals.*

LORGUES

83510

RESTAURANTS

CHEZ BRUNO
Campagne Mariette
Route de Vidauban
Quartier le Plan
Tel. 04 94 73 92 19
Closed Sun. eve, Mon.,
and Sep. 16–June 4
*Known for its local
specialties.*
✶ ▣ ⌖ ☐

DRAGUIGNAN

83300 ▲ 226

USEFUL ADDRESSES

TOURIST OFFICE
9, bd Clemenceau
Tel. 04 94 68 63 30

CULTURE

CHAPEL OF THE MINIME CONVENT
Rue des Minimes
Tel. 04 94 68 09 76
Open Sun. 9am–noon

CHURCH OF ST-HERMENTAIRE
St-Hermentaire area

CLOCK TOWER
Îlot de l'Horloge, old
town
Tel. 04 94 68 63 30
*Visits arranged by the
tourist office.*

MUNICIPAL MUSEUM
9, rue de la République
Tel. 04 94 47 28 80
Open Mon.–Sat.
9am–noon and 2–6pm

RESTAURANTS

★ LE MOULIN DE LA FOUX
Hostellerie du Moulin
de la Foux, Chemin
St-Jean
Tel. 04 94 68 55 33
✶

ACCOMMODATION

LES ÉTOILES DE L'ANGE *
Av. Tuttluigen
Col de l'Ange
Tel. 04 94 68 23 01
Fax 04 94 68 13 30
✶ ⌑ ▣

★ HOSTELLERIE DU MOULIN DE LA FOUX *
Chemin St-Jean
Tel. 04 94 68 55 33
Fax 04 94 68 70 10
✶ ▣

VICTORIA *
52, av. Lazare-Carnot
Tel. 04 94 47 24 12
Fax 04 94 68 31 69
✶ ▣ 🚗 ⌖

GRASSE

06130 ▲ 227

USEFUL ADDRESSES

TOURIST OFFICE
Palais des Congrès
Place du Cours
Tel. 04 93 36 03 56

CULTURE

CATHEDRAL OF NOTRE-DAME-DU-PUY
Pl. du Petit-Puy
Tel. 04 93 36 11 03
In season: Open
9.30–11.45am and
2.30–7.45pm

MUSÉE D'ART ET D'HISTOIRE DE LA PROVENCE
2, rue Mirabeau
Tel. 04 93 36 01 61
Open Apr.–Sep.
Wed.–Sun. 10am–noon
and 2–5pm

MUSÉE INTERNATIONAL DE LA PARFUMERIE
8, pl. du Cours
Tel. 04 93 36 80 20
Open June–Sep.
10am–7pm.

Closed public hols. and
Nov. 7–Dec. 7.
Entrance 13F.

MUSÉE DE LA MARINE
2, bd du Jeu-de-Ballon
Tel. 04 93 09 10 71
Open 10am–noon and
2–6pm. Closed Sun.
and Nov. Entrance 15F.

PALAIS ÉPISCOPAL
Town Hall
*Tours for five or more
through Tourist office.*

**VILLA-MUSÉE
FRAGONARD**
23, bd Fragonard
Tel. 04 93 36 01 61
Fax 04 93 36 02 71
*In season: Open June–
Sep. 10am–1pm and
2–7pm,Closed public
hols. and Nov.–Dec. 7.
Entrance 7F.*

RESTAURANTS

MAÎTRE BOSCQ
13, rue de la Fonette
Tel. 04 93 36 45 76
Closed Sun.
♀

ACCOMMODATION

HÔTEL DU PATTI ★★★
Pl. Patti
Tel. 04 93 36 01 00
Fax 04 93 36 36 40
*Restaurant closed Sun.
and eve. in winter.*
♀ ♠ ℗

SHOPPING

**PARFUMERIE
FRAGONARD**
20, bd Fragonard
Tel. 04 93 36 44 65

**PARFUMERIE
GALIMARD**
73, rte de Cannes
Tel. 04 93 09 20 00

**PARFUMERIE
MOLINARD**
60, bd Victor-Hugo
Tel. 04 93 36 01 62

◆

MANOSQUE
04100   ▲ 230

USEFUL ADDRESSES

MAIRIE
(Town Hall)
Pl. de l'Hôtel-de-Ville
Tel. 04 92 70 34 56

TOURIST OFFICE
Pl. du Docteur-Joubert
Tel. 04 92 72 16 00
Fax 04 92 72 58 98

CULTURE

CENTRE JEAN-GIONO
Bd Élémir-Bourges
Open Tue.–Sat.
9am–noon and 2–6pm

**CHURCH OF NOTRE-
DAME-DE-ROMIGIER**
Pl. de l'Hôtel-de-Ville
*Information is available
from the tourist office.*

**CHURCH OF
ST-SAUVEUR**
Pl. St-Sauveur
Open Mon.–Sat.
8.30am–noon and
1.30–5.30pm. Sun.
8.30am–noon

FONDATION CARZOU
Bd Élémir-Bourges
*In season: Open 10am–
12.30pm and 3–7pm,
May–Sep. Closed Tue.*

HÔTEL D'HERBÈS
Rue Voltaire
Pl. de l'Hôtel-d'Herbès
Open Mon., Tue., Thur.
2–6pm, Wed. 10am–
noon and 2–6pm, Fri.
3–7pm, Sat. 9am–noon

LOU PARAÏS
Montée des Vraies-
Richesses
Open Fri. 2.30–5pm
House of Jean Giono.

PORTE SOUBEYRAN
Bd des Tilleuls

RESTAURANT

LA SOURCE
Rte de Dauphin
Tel. 04 92 72 12 79

Closed Mon. and Sat.
midday
℗

ACCOMMODATION

LE PROVENCE ★★
Rte de la Durance
Tel. 04 92 72 39 38
Fax 04 92 87 55 13
℗

**LA ROCHETTE
YOUTH HOSTEL**
Av. Argile
Tel. 04 92 87 57 44
⊇ ⊜ ✗

FORCALQUIER
04300   ▲ 232

USEFUL ADDRESSES

TOURIST OFFICE
8, pl. du Bourguet
Tel. 04 92 75 10 02
Fax 04 92 75 26 76

CULTURE

**CATHEDRAL OF NOTRE-
DAME-DU-BOURGUET**
Pl. du Bourguet
Open 9am–noon, 2–7pm

**CHURCH OF NOTRE-
DAME-DE-PROVENCE**
In the citadel
*See Tourist office for
opening times.*

**COUVENT DES
CORDELIERS**
Bd des Martyrs
Open Sun. and public
hols., May–June and
Sep. 15–Oct. 31
2.30–4pm; Jul.–Sep. 15
Wed.–Mon 11am–
6.30pm
*Guided tours 11am, 2.30,
3.30, 4,30 and 5.30pm.*

**COUVENT DES
RÉCOLLETS**
Rue St-Pierre
Closed to the public.

**COUVENT DES
VISITANDINES**
Pl. du Bourguet
Open 10am– noon and
3–6pm, July–Sep.

PORTE SAUNERIE
1, bd de la Plaine

RESTAURANTS

★ **FERME-AUBERGE
LES BAS CHALUS**
Tel. 04 92 75 05 67
*Meals based on
regional cheeses.*
♀ ⊇ ℗

★ **HOSTELLERIE
DES DEUX LIONS**
11, pl. du Bourguet
Tel. 04 92 75 25 30
Closed Jan.–Feb.
Local country cooking.

ACCOMMODATION

★ **AUBERGE
DE CHAREMBEAU ★★**
Rte de Niozelles
Tel. 04 92 75 05 69
Fax 04 92 75 24 37
Closed Dec.–Jan.
*Surrounded by 17 acres
of meadows and hills.*
⊇ ℗ ✝

**CAMPING MUNICIPAL
ST-PROMASSE**
Rte de Sigonce
Tel. 04 92 75 27 94
Closed Nov.–Apr.

**HÔTELLERIE
LE COLOMBIER**
Mas des Dragons
Tel. 04 92 75 03 71
Fax 04 92 75 14 30
⊇ ℗ ✝

GANAGOBIE

PRIORY
Open Tue.–Sun 3–5pm

SISTERON
04200   ▲ 236

USEFUL ADDRESSES

TOURIST OFFICE
BP 42, Hôtel de ville
Pl. de la République
Tel. 04 92 61 36 50
Fax 04 92 61 19 57

CULTURE

**CATHEDRAL OF
NOTRE-DAME-DES-
POMMIERS**
Pl. du Gen.-de-Gaulle
Open Mon.–Sat.
2.30–5.30pm

CITADEL
Montée de la Citadelle
Tel. 04 92 61 27 57
Open Mar. 15– Nov. 15
9am–6pm

**MUSÉE DU VIEUX-
SISTERON**
Av. des Arcades
Contact M. Colomb
Tel. 04 92 61 12 27.

RESTAURANT

BECS FINS
16, rue Saunerie
Tel. 04 92 61 12 04
Closed Wed., Sep.–June

ACCOMMODATION

GRAND HÔTEL DU COURS ★★★
Pl. de l'Église
Tel. 04 92 61 04 51
Fax 04 92 61 41 73
Open Mar.–Nov. 15

DIGNE-LES-BAINS

04000　▲ 240

USEFUL ADDRESSES

CENTRAL POST OFFICE
4, rue André-Honnorat
Tel. 04 92 30 30 81

COMITÉ DÉPARTEMENTAL DE TOURISME DES ALPES-DE-HAUTE-PROVENCE
19, rue Docteur-Honnorat, BP 170
Tel. 04 92 31 57 29
Fax 04 92 32 24 94

COMMISSARIAT
(Police station)
2, rue Monge
Tel. 04 92 30 86 60

MAIRIE
(Town Hall)
Bd Martin-Bret
Tel. 04 92 30 52 00

CULTURE

CATHEDRAL OF NOTRE-DAME-DU-BOURG
Quartier du Bourg
To arrange visits:
Tel. 04 92 32 06 48.

CATHEDRAL OF ST-JÉRÔME
Rue Tour-de-l'Église
Open all year Sun.
10.30am–noon, and
June 15–Oct. Tue.–
Thur. and Sat. 3–6pm

FONDATION ALEXANDRA-DAVID-NEEL
27, av. du Maréchal-Juin
Rte de Nice
Tel. 04 92 31 32 38
In season: Jul.–Sep.
Guided tours only (45 min.) at 10.30am, 2pm, 3.30 and 5pm.
Free entrance.

MUSÉE DÉPARTEMENTAL D'ART RELIGIEUX
Chapelle des Pénitents
Pl. des Récollets
Tel. 04 92 32 35 37
Open 9am–1pm and
3–7pm, June–Sep.
Free entrance.
From Sep.–June
Tel. 04 92 31 34 61.

MUSÉE DE DIGNE
64, bd Gassendi
Tel. 04 92 31 45 29
In season: Open
10.30–noon and
1.30–6.30pm, July–Aug.
Closed Mon. and public
hols. Entrance 15F;
children under 12 free.

RESTAURANT

★ LE GRAND PARIS
19, bd Thiers
Tel. 04 92 31 11 15
Fax 04 92 32 32 82
Closed Dec. 20–Feb.
Very good food

ACCOMMODATION

CAMPING LES EAUX CHAUDES
Rte des Thermes
Tel. 04 92 32 31 04
Supervised.

★ VILLA GAÏA
Le Péage, Rte de Nice
Tel. 04 92 31 21 60
Fax 04 92 31 20 12
Closed Dec.–Feb.
Lounges and library,
tennis. Natural-food. No
credit cards.

SPORT

BICYCLE RENTAL
GALLARDO
8, cours des Arès
Tel. 04 92 31 05 29
LE VALLON DES SOURCES
Route des Thermes
Tel. 04 92 30 47 00

CANNES

06400　▲ 244–9

USEFUL ADDRESSES

CENTRAL POST OFFICE
22, rue du Bivouac-Napoléon
Tel. 04 93 39 13 16

COMMISSARIAT CENTRAL
(Central police station)
15, av. de Grasse
Tel. 04 93 39 10 78

MAIRIE
(Town Hall)
Rue Félix-Faure
Tel. 04 93 68 91 92

TOURIST INFORMATION
Palais des Festivals
1, la Croisette
Tel. 04 93 39 24 53
Gare SNCF
(railway station)
Tel. 04 93 99 19 77

TRANSPORT

BUS STATION
Pl. de l'Hôtel-de-Ville
Tel. 04 93 39 18 11

CAR RENTAL
AVIS–RAILWAY STATION
Tel. 04 93 39 26 38
EUROPCAR
59, la Croisette
Tel. 04 93 94 20 00
HERTZ
147, rue d'Antibes
Tel. 04 93 99 04 20

RAILWAY STATION
Pl. de la Gare
Tel. 04 93 39 31 37

CULTURE

MUSÉE DE LA CASTRE
Château de la Castre
Le Suquet
Tel. 04 93 38 55 26
Open Apr.–Jun.
10am–noon and 2–6pm;
Jul.–Sep. 10am–noon
and 3–7pm. Closed Tue.,
public hols. and Jan.

NOTRE-DAME-DE-L'ESPÉRANCE
Pl. de Castre
Tel. 04 93 39 17 49
In season: Open
9am–noon and 2–7pm

PALAIS DES FESTIVALS ET DES CONGRÈS
Esplanade Georges-Pompidou
Tel. 04 93 39 01 01
Visits Wed. 2–5pm

VILLA FIESOLE
Avenue Fiesole
Closed to the public.

RESTAURANTS

★ MAÎTRE PIERRE
6, rue du Maréchal-Joffre
Tel. 04 93 99 36 30
Closed Mon.

★ L'ONDINE
La Croisette (beach)
Tel. 04 93 94 23 15
Open noon–4pm
Closed Nov.–Dec. 20

★ RESTAURANT ARMÉNIEN
82, la Croisette
Tel. 04 93 94 00 58

ACCOMMODATION

LE CARLTON ★★★★
58, la Croisette, BP 155
Cannes Cedex
Tel. 04 93 68 91 68
Fax 04 93 38 20 90
Health center, Turkish
bath.

★ CHANTECLAIR ★★
12, rue Fortville
Tel. 04 93 39 68 88
Closed Nov. 8–Nov. 30
Romantic hotel.

★ CRISTAL ★★★★
13–15, rond-point
Duboys-d'Angers
Tel. 04 93 39 45 45
Fax 04 93 38 64 66
Restaurant closed
Mon.

LE MAJESTIC ★★★★
14, bd de la Croisette
Tel. 04 92 98 77 00
Fax 04 92 98 97 90
Closed Nov. 7–Dec. 17
Private beach, tennis,
golf, casino and
nightclub.

★ LE MARTINEZ ★★★★
75, la Croisette
Tel. 04 92 98 74 14
Closed mid Nov.–Jan.
One of the quietest
luxury "palaces". Tennis
and private beach.

★ MOLIÈRE ★★★
5–7, rue Molière
Tel. 04 96 38 16 16
Fax 04 93 68 29 57
Closed Nov. 15–Dec. 20
Romantic hotel in a
lovely setting.

NIGHTLIFE

DISCOTHÈQUE CARLTON CASINO CLUB
58, la Croisette
Tel. 04 93 68 00 33

DISCOTHÈQUE DU CASINO CROISETTE
Jetée Albert-Édouard
Tel. 04 93 38 12 11

ST-RAPHAËL

83700 ▲ *251*

USEFUL ADDRESSES

TOURIST OFFICE
Rue Waldeck-Rousseau,
Immeuble *Le Stanislas*
BP 210
Tel. 04 94 19 52 52

CULTURE

CHURCH OF ST-PIERRE OR DES TEMPLIERS
Rue de la Vieille-Église
Contact Tourist office.

MUSÉE ARCHÉOLOGIQUE
Pl. de la Vieille-Église
Tel. 04 94 52 22 74
In season: Open
June 15–Sept. 14
10am–noon and 3–6pm.
Closed Tue., public hols.

MUSÉE D'HISTOIRE LOCALE
Pl. de la Vieille-Église
Tel. 04 94 52 22 74
In season: Open
June 15–Sept. 14
10am–noon and 3–6pm.
Closed Tue., public hols.

RESTAURANTS

LES JARDINS DU SAN-PEDRO
Avenue Brooke
Tel. 04 94 83 65 69
Fax 04 94 40 57 20
Closed Sun. eve.
and Mon.

★ **PASTOREL**
54, rue Liberté
Tel. 04 94 95 02 36
Fax 04 94 95 64 07
Closed Sun. eve
and Mon.
Traditional cooking.

ACCOMMODATION

LA POTINIÈRE ★★★
Bd Plaines
Tel. 04 94 95 21 43
Fax 04 94 95 29 10

SOL E MAR ★★★
N 98 road, Le Dramont
Tel. 04 94 95 25 60
Fax 04 94 83 83 61
Closed Oct. 15–Apr. 1

SPORTS

BICYCLE RENTAL
PATRICK MOTOS
Rue du Gen.-Leclerc
Tel. 04 94 53 87 11

GOLF AND TENNIS-CLUB OF VALESCURE
Route du Golf
Tel. 04 94 82 40 46
In season: Open 8am–8pm

GOLF DE L'ESTÉREL, LATITUDE VALESCURE
134, av. du Golf
Tel. 04 94 82 47 88
In season: Open
7.30am–7.30pm

FRÉJUS

83600 ▲ *252*

USEFUL ADDRESSES

TOURIST OFFICE
325, rue Jean-Jaurès
Tel. 04 94 17 19 19

CULTURE

AMPHITHEATER
N 7 coming from Puget-
sur-Argens
Tel. 04 94 17 05 60
(Town Hall)
Open Apr.– Sep. 9.30am–
noon and 2–6.30pm.
Closed Tue.

ARCHEOLOGICAL SITE OF CLOS DE LA TOUR
Behind the tourist office
For visits contact the tourist office.

GROUPE ÉPISCOPAL
Place Formigé
Tel. 04 94 51 26 30
Cathedral open daily
8am–noon and 4–7pm
Cloister and baptistry
In season: Open daily
Apr.–Sep. 9am–7pm.

RESTAURANTS

LES POTIERS
135, rue des Potiers
Tel. 04 94 51 33 74

LA TOQUE BLANCHE
385, av. Victor-Hugo
Tel. 04 94 52 06 14
Closed Mon. and July 1–15

ACCOMMODATION

LE COLOMBIER ★★★
139, rte de Bagnols
Tel. 04 94 51 45 92
Fax 04 94 53 82 85
Closed Nov. 20–Dec. 20
and Jan. 2–early Feb.

HÔTEL ARÉNA ★★★
139, rue du Gen.-de-
Gaulle
Tel. 04 94 17 09 40
Fax 04 94 52 01 52

YOUTH HOSTEL
Chemin du Counillier
Tel. 04 94 53 18 75
Closes at 10pm

SPORTS

BICYCLE RENTAL
HOLIDAYS BIKES
943, av. Provence
Tel. 04 94 52 30 65

CENTRE DE LOISIRS DES JEUNES
(Youth leisure center)
Plage de Veillat, BP 302
Open July–Aug.

PORT-GRIMAUD

83310 ▲ *255*

CULTURE

CHURCH OF ST-FRANÇOIS
Pl. de l'Église
In season: Open
May–Sep.10am– 8pm.

GRIMAUD

83310 ▲ *255*

USEFUL ADDRESSES

TOURIST OFFICE
Bd des Aliziers
Tel. 04 94 43 26 98

CULTURE

CASTLE
Av. de la Cabro-d'Or
toward St-Roch
Ruins.

CHAPEL OF ST-ROCH
Av. de la Cabro-d'Or
toward St-Roch
Closed to the public.

MAISON DES TEMPLIERS
Rue des Templiers
Closed to the public.

MOULIN DE GRIMAUD
Av. de la Cabro-d'Or,
toward St-Roch
Closed to the public.

MUSÉE DES ARTS ET TRADITIONS POPULAIRES
Le Pierredon
Montée Hospice
Tel. 04 94 43 39 29
Open in season

ROMANESQUE CHURCH OF ST-MICHEL
Pl. de l'Église
Open Mon.–Sat. 9am–
7pm, Sun. 10am–7pm

RESTAURANTS

LA BOULANGERIE
Route de Collobrières
Tel. 04 94 43 23 16
Open Easter–Oct. 10
No credit cards.

ST-TROPEZ

83990 ▲ *256–62*

USEFUL ADDRESSES

TOURIST OFFICE
Quai Jean-Jaurès
Tel. 04 94 97 45 21

CULTURE

CHÂTEAU DE PAMPELONNE
Rte des plages
toward Ramatuelle
Closed to the public.

CHÂTEAU DE SUFFREN
Pl. Garrezio
To visit contact the tourist office.

CHURCH
Rue de l'Église
Open 9am–noon and
2–6pm

CITADEL
Montée de la Citadelle
Tel. 04 94 97 59 43
Open June 16–Sep. 14
Sun.–Mon. 2–6pm,
Closed Nov. 15–Dec. 15

MAISON DU CORSAIRE
11, quai de Suffren
Closed to the public.

MUSÉE DE L'ANNONCIADE
Pl. Grammont
Tel. 04 94 97 04 01

In season: Open
Sun.–Mon. 10am–noon
and 3–7pm

TOUR DU PORTALET
At the end of the harbor
Frédéric-Mistral
Closed to the public.

TOUR-VIEILLE
Old town near the
Port des Pêcheurs
Closed to the public.

RESTAURANTS

★ **LE BISTROT
DES LICES**
3, pl. des Lices
Tel. 04 94 97 29 00
Closes at midnight
June–Sep.
☂

★ **L'ESCALIER**
5, rue des Féniers
Tel. 04 94 54 85 85
☂

**L'OLIVIER, BASTIDE
DE ST-TROPEZ**
Route des Carles
Tel. 04 94 97 58 16
Closed Tue., Jan.–Feb. 3
☂ ⌿ 🚗 ✄ ☂

ACCOMMODATION

BYBLOS ★★★★
Av. P.-Signac
Tel. 04 94 56 68 00
Fax 04 94 56 68 01
☂ ⌿ 🚗 ☂

★ **LE PRÉ DE
LA MER ★★★**
Route de Salins
Tel. 04 94 97 12 23
Fax 04 94 97 43 91
🅿

**RÉSIDENCE
DE LA PINÈDE ★★★★**
Plage de la Bouillabaisse
Tel. 04 94 97 66 51
Fax 04 94 97 73 64
Closed Oct. 15–Mar.
☂ ⌿ 🚗 ☂

RAMATUELLE

83350   ▲ 263

USEFUL ADDRESSES

TOURIST OFFICE
1, rue Georges-
Clemenceau
Tel. 04 94 79 26 04
Fax 04 94 79 12 66

CULTURE

OLD PRISON
Rue du Clocher
Closed to the public.

**CHURCH OF
NOTRE-DAME**
Pl. de l'Ormeau
In season: Open
May–Sep. 8am–7pm

PORTE SARRAZINE
Rue Victor-Léon

ACCOMMODATION

**LA FERME
D'AUGUSTIN ★★★**
Route Tahiti
Tel. 04 94 97 23 83
Fax 04 94 97 40 30
⌿ 🅿 ☐ 🛀

LA FIGUIÈRE ★★★
Route Tahiti
Tel. 04 94 97 18 21
Fax 04 94 97 68 48
Closed Oct. 10–Mar.
⌿ 🅿 ☂

GASSIN

83580   ▲ 263

USEFUL ADDRESSES

**TOURIST OFFICE
OF LA FOUX**
Carrefour de La Foux
Tel. 04 94 43 42 10

CULTURE

CHURCH
Pl. de l'Église
Tel. 04 94 56 14 56

ACCOMMODATION

BELLO VISTO ★
Pl. Barrys
Tel. 04 94 56 17 30
Fax 04 94 43 45 36
☂ ☂

BORMES-
LES-MIMOSAS

83230   ▲ 264

USEFUL ADDRESSES

TOURIST OFFICE
1, pl. Gambetta
Tel. 04 94 71 15 17

CULTURE

**CHAPEL OF ST-
FRANÇOIS-DE-PAULE**
Pl. St-François
Open dawn–dusk

**CHARTREUSE DE
LA VERNE**
On the D 214 road,
eleven miles from
Bormes-les-Mimosas
In season: Open 11am–
6pm, Apr.–Sep. Closed
Nov.

**MUSÉE D'ART
ET D'HISTOIRE**
103, rue Carnot
Tel. 04 94 71 56 60
Open Wed. 10am–noon
and 3–5pm and Sun.
10am–noon

ACCOMMODATION

LE MIRAGE ★★★
38, rue Vue-des-Îles
Tel. 04 94 05 32 60
Fax 04 94 64 93 03
Closed Oct.–Mar.
☂ ⌿ 🚗 ☂

PALMIERS ★★★
Hameau de Cabasson
240, chemin Petit-Font
Tel. 04 94 64 81 94
Fax 04 94 64 93 61
☂ 🅿

SPORT

BICYCLE RENTAL
HOLIDAY BIKES
Résidence du Levant
288, bd Front-de-Mer
Tel. 04 94 15 06 51

HYÈRES

83400   ▲ 266

USEFUL ADDRESSES

TOURIST OFFICE
Rotonde Jean-Salusse
Av. de Belgique
Tel. 04 94 65 18 55

CULTURE

CASINO DES PALMIERS
1, av. Ambroise-Thomas
Tel. 04 94 12 80 80
Open midnight–6am

CHURCH OF ST-LOUIS
Pl. de la République
Tel. 04 94 65 20 82
Open. 7am–7pm
No visits during services.

**COLLEGIATE CHURCH
OF ST-PAUL**
Pl. Saint-Paul
Tel. 04 94 65 34 94
Open 2.30–5pm

**MUSÉE DES ORDRES
RELIGIEUX, MILITAIRES
ET MÉDIÉVAUX**
Pl. Massillon
Tel. 04 94 35 22 36
Open Wed.–Mon.
9am–noon and 3–6pm

RESTAURANT

**LES JARDINS
DE BACCHUS**
32, av. Gambetta
Tel. 04 94 65 77 63

Closed first week Jan.,
second two weeks June;
Mon., Sat. lunchtime
July–Aug., and Mon.,
Sun. eve, Sep.–June

ACCOMMODATION

**HOSTELLERIE
PROVENÇALE
"LA QUÉBÉCOISE" ★★**
20, av. Costebelle
Tel. 04 94 57 69 24
Fax 04 94 38 78 27
*Half-board only July
and Aug.*
☂ ⌿ 🛀

SPORT

BICYCLE RENTAL
HOLIDAY BIKES
4, ave. Docteur-Robin
Tel. 04 94 38 79 45
Open 9am–12.30pm
and 3–7pm, Apr.–Sep.

GIENS

83400   ▲ 267

CULTURE

**CHAPEL OF
ST-PIERRE-DE-
L'ALMANARRE**
Lieu-dit L'Almanarre
Fouilles d'Olbia

ÎLE DE
PORQUEROLLES

83400

USEFUL ADDRESSES

TOURIST OFFICE
Carré du Port
Tel. 04 94 58 33 76

CULTURE

**FORT DU GRAND-
LANGOUSTIER**
Pointe du Grand-
Langoustier
Closed to the public.

**FORT DU PETIT-
LANGOUSTIER**
Presqu'île du Petit-
Langoustier
Closed to the public.

FORT STE-AGATHE
Open 10am–5.30pm
May–Oct.
*Information: Parc
national de Port-Cros*
Tel. 04 94 12 82 30

**FORTIN DE
L'ALYCASTRE**
Pointe de l'Alycastre
Closed to the public.

ACCOMMODATION

★ **L'OUSTAU ★★★**
Pl. d'Armes
Tel. 04 94 58 30 13
Fax 04 94 58 34 93
Bicycle and windsurfer rentals.
★ 予

★ **LES GLYCINES ★★★**
Pl. d'Armes
Tel. 04 94 58 30 36
Fax 04 94 58 35 22
Open Apr.–Sep.
Half-board only.
★ 予

ÎLE DE PORT-CROS

83400 ▲ 269

CULTURE

FORT DE L'ESTISSAC
Tel. 04 94 05 90 17
Open 10am–5pm,
June–Sep.

ACCOMMODATION

LE MANOIR ★★
Tel. 04 94 05 90 52
Fax 04 94 05 90 89
Open May 15–Sep.
Half-board only.
★ ♣ 予

TOULON

83000

USEFUL ADDRESSES

COMMISSARIAT CENTRAL
(Central police station)
Rue du Cdt-Morandin
Tel. 04 94 09 80 00

MAIRIE
(Town Hall)
BP 1407, Av. de la République
Tel. 04 94 36 30 00

POST OFFICE
Rue Jean-Bartolini
Tel. 04 94 46 00 22

TOURIST OFFICE
8, av. Colbert
Tel. 04 94 22 08 22

CULTURE

CATHEDRAL OF STE-MARIE-MAJEURE
Notre-Dame-de-la-Seds
Pl. de la Cathédrale
Tel. 04 94 92 28 91
Open 7am–noon and 3–7pm

CHURCH OF ST-LOUIS
Rue Louis-Jourdan
Tel. 04 94 92 82 19
Open 8.30–11.30am and 2.30–6.30pm.
Closed Sun. pm

FORT ST-LOUIS
Corniche Frédéric-Mistral, Le Mourillon
Closed to the public.

MUSÉE D'ART
113, bd Maréchal-Leclerc
Tel. 04 94 93 15 54
Open 1–7pm
Closed public hols.

MUSÉE DE LA MARINE
Pl. Monsénergue
Tel. 04 94 02 02 01
Open July– Aug.
10am–noon and 2.30–7pm. Closed public hols.
Guided tours on request.

PORTE D'ITALIE
Pl. Armand-Vallé

THEATER
Pl. Victor-Hugo
Visits by arrangement.
Tel. 04 94 93 03 76.

TOUR ROYALE OR GROSSE TOUR
Pointe de la Mître
Le Mourillon

RESTAURANTS

AU SOURD
10, rue Molière
Tel. 04 94 92 28 52
Closed July, Sun.
⊞ 予

LE CELLIER
52, rue Jean-Jaurès
Tel. 04 94 92 64 35
Closed Sat., Sun.
◐

LE LIDO
Av. Frédéric-Mistral
Le Mourillon
Tel. 04 94 03 38 18
★ 予

ACCOMMODATION

LA RÉSIDENCE DU CAP-BRUN ★★★
Chem. de l'Aviateur-Gayraud
Tel. 04 94 41 29 46
Fax 04 94 42 24 46
★ ⊇ ⊞

BANDOL

83150

SPECIALTY FOODS

MAISON DES VINS DE BANDOL
22, allée Vivien
Tel. 04 94 29 45 03

ÎLES DE LÉRINS

CULTURE

FORT ROYAL
Île Ste-Marguerite
Tel. 04 93 20 61 64
Open 10am–noon and 2–5pm. Closed Tue. and public hols.

MONASTERY OF ST-HONORAT
Île St-Honorat
Abbaye Notre-Dame-d'Honorat
Tel. 04 93 48 68 68

MUSÉE DE LA MER
Île Ste-Marguerite
Tel. 04 93 43 18 17
Same opening hours as the Royal fort.

VALLAURIS

06220 ▲ 274

USEFUL ADDRESSES

TOURIST OFFICE
Sq du 8-Mai-45
BP 155
Tel. 04 93 63 82 58

CULTURE

CHÂTEAU-MUSÉE DE VALLAURIS
Pl. de la Libération
Tel. 04 93 64 16 05
Open Wed.–Mon.
10am–noon and 2–6pm

MUSÉE NATIONAL PICASSO
Pl. de la Libération
Tel. 04 93 64 16 05
Open 10am–noon and 2–6pm. Closed Tue. and public hols.

MUSÉE DE LA POTERIE
Rue Sicard
Tel. 04 93 64 66 51
In season: Open 9am–7pm. Closed Sat.–Sun. am

RESTAURANT

★ **LA GOUSSE D'AIL**
224, chemin Lintier
Tel. 04 93 64 10 71
Closed Nov. 11–Dec. 20
♣♣

ACCOMMODATION

BEAU SOLEIL ★★★
Imp. Beausoleil via N 7
Tel. 04 93 63 63 63
Fax 04 93 63 02 89
Closed Oct. 15–Mar. 24
Air-conditioned.
★ ⊇ 🚗 ⌖ ☎ 予

CALIFORNIA ★
222, av. de la Liberté
Tel. 04 93 63 78 63

HÔTEL DU GOLFE ★★
Bd de la Plage
Tel. 04 93 63 71 22
Fax 04 93 63 24 71
Open Feb.–Oct. or on request
🚗 予

ANTIBES JUAN-LES-PINS

Antibes 06600 ▲ 278
Juan-les-Pins 06160
▲ 275

USEFUL ADDRESSES

TOURIST OFFICE
11, place du Gen.-de-Gaulle (Antibes)
Tel. 04 92 90 53 00
51, bd Guillaumont (Juan-les-Pins)
Tel. 04 92 90 53 05

CULTURE

ANTIBES CATHEDRAL
Rue St-Esprit
Tel. 04 93 34 06 29
Open 8am–noon and 3–6.30pm
Guided tours by appointment.

FORT CARRÉ
N 98 road
Route du Bord-de-Mer
Past the port
approaching Vallauris
Closed to the public.

GARDENS OF THE VILLA THURET
62, bd du Cap
Chemin Raymond
Tel. 04 93 67 88 00

Open 8am–6pm
Closed Sat.-Sun. and
public hols.
Free entrance.

**MUSÉE DES ARTS ET
TRADITIONS
POPULAIRES**
Cours Masséna
Tel. 04 93 34 50 91
In season: Open Wed.,
Thur. and Sat. 4–7pm

**MUSÉE D'HISTOIRE
ET D'ARCHÉOLOGIE**
Bastion St-André
Av. Maizières
Tel. 04 92 90 54 35
In season: Open 9–
11.45am and 2–6.45pm.
Entrance 6F.

MUSÉE PEYNET
23, pl. Nationale
Tel. 04 92 90 54 30
In season: Open
10am–noon and 3–7pm,
Closed Tue., public hols.
and Nov.

**MUSÉE
PICASSO**
Château Grimaldi
Pl. Mariejol
Tel. 04 92 90 54 20
Open July–Sep.
10am–noon and 3–7pm.
Closed public hols., Tue.
and Nov.
Entrance 20F.

**PHARE DE
LA GAROUPE**
Cap d'Antibes
Tel. 04 93 61 57 63
In season: Open
2.30–6pm

**VILLA AND GARDEN
EILEN-ROC**
Bd du Cap
Tel. 04 93 67 74 33
Open Wed.
1.30–5.30pm, except
school vacations.

RESTAURANTS

**AUBERGE
PROVENÇALE**
61, pl. Nationale
06600 Antibes
Tel. 04 93 34 13 24

★ **BACON**
Bd Bacon
Tel. 04 93 61 50 02

**MAS DE LA
PAGANE**
15, av. du Mas-
Ensoleillé
Tel. 04 93 33 33 78
Service until 1am.
Closed Sun.
🏨 ♣ ⚓ 🅿 ✝

ACCOMMODATION

BEACHÔTEL ★★★
1, av. Alexandre-III
Tel. 04 93 61 81 85
Fax 04 93 61 51 97
Closed Nov.–Dec. 22
and Jan. 2–Mar. 18
🧍 ⚓ ☎

**LES BELLES
RIVES★★★★**
Bd du Littoral
Tel. 04 93 61 02 79
Fax 04 93 67 43 51
Open Apr.–Sep.
Private beach and pier.
♣ ✝

**CASTEL
GAROUPE AXA ★★★**
959, bd Garoupe
Tel. 04 93 61 36 51
Fax 04 93 67 74 88
Closed Nov 15–Mar. 15
🧍 ⚓ ☎ ⚓
🏊 ✝

★ **MAS DE
LA PAGANE ★★**
15, av. du Mas-
Ensoleillé
Tel. 04 93 33 33 78
Fax 04 93 75 55 37
⚓

BIOT
06410   ▲ 281

USEFUL ADDRESSES

TOURIST OFFICE
Pl. de la Chapelle
Tel. 04 93 65 05 85

CULTURE

CHURCH
Pl. de l'Église
*Information from the
Tourist office.*

**MUSÉE NATIONAL
FERNAND-LÉGER**
Chemin du Val-de-Pôme
Tel. 04 93 65 63 61
In season: Open
Wed.–Mon.
10am–noon, 2–6pm.
Entrance 30F.

RESTAURANTS

AUBERGE DU JARRIER
30, passe de la
Bourgade
Tel. 04 93 65 11 68
Closed Jan. 9–Feb. 14
🧍 ✝

**LE RESTAURANT
DES ARCADES**
16, pl. des Arcades
Tel. 04 93 65 01 04
Closed Mon. July–Aug.
🌓 ♣ ✝

LES TERRAILLIERS
11, rte du Chemin-Neuf
Tel. 04 93 65 01 59
Closed Wed., Thur.
midday (July–Aug.) and
Nov.
♣ 🅿 ✝

ACCOMMODATION

LES ARCADES ★★
16, pl. des Arcades
Tel. 04 93 65 01 04
Fax 04 93 65 01 05
*Restaurant closed Sun.
eve–Mon.*
✝

**AUBERGE DE LA
VALLÉE VERTE ★★**
3400, route de Valbonne
Tel. 04 93 65 10 93
Fax 04 92 94 04 91
Closed Dec.
🧍 ⚓ ⚓ ☎ ✝

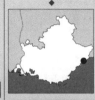

NICE
06000   ▲ 284–93

USEFUL ADDRESSES

**CENTRAL
POST OFFICE**
21, av. Thiers
Tel. 04 93 82 65 00

**COMMISSARIAT
CENTRAL**
(Central police station)
1, av. du Maréchal-
Foch
Tel. 04 92 17 22 22

MAIRIE
(Town Hall)
5, rue de l'Hôtel-de-Ville
Tel. 04 93 13 20 00

TOURIST OFFICE
Av. Thiers (railway
station)
Tel. 04 93 87 07 07
5, promenade des
Anglais
Tel. 04 93 87 60 60
Nice-Ferber (near
airport)
Tel. 04 93 83 32 64

CULTURE

ACROPOLIS
1, esplanade Kennedy
Tel. 04 93 92 83 00

AMPHITHEATER
Parc de Cimiez
Av. de Cimiez
Open all year.

**CATHEDRAL OF
STE-RÉPARATE**
Pl. Rossetti
Tel. 04 93 62 34 40
In season: Open daily
7.30–11.45am and
2.30–7pm

**CHAMBRE DE
COMMERCE**
20, bd Carabassel
Closed to the public.

**CHAPEL OF THE
MISÉRICORDE**
7, cours Saleya
Visits Tue. and Sun. at
3pm from the Palais
Lascaris.

**CHAPEL OF
STE-CROIX**
Rue de la Croix
Renovated in May 1994.

**CHURCH OF THE
ANNUNCIATION OR
STE-RITA**
1, rue de la
Poissonnerie
Tel. 04 93 62 13 62
Open 7.30am–noon
and 2.30–6.30pm

**CHURCH OF GESÙ
OR ST-JACQUES**
12, rue Droite
Tel. 04 93 62 35 20
Open 8am–noon
and 2–6.30pm.

LYCÉE MASSÉNA
2, av. Félix-Faure

**MUSÉE
ARCHÉOLOGIQUE**
Av. Monte-Croce
Colline de Cimiez
Tel. 04 93 81 59 57
Open May–Sep. 10am–
noon, 2–6pm. Closed
Sun. am, Mon., public
hols. and Nov.
Entrance 6F.

**MUSÉE D'ART
MODERNE ET
CONTEMPORAIN**
Prom. des Arts
Tel. 04 93 62 61 62
Open 11am–6pm,
Fri. 11am–10pm.
Closed Tue.
Free entrance.

**MUSÉE DE
PALÉONTOLOGIE
HUMAINE TERRA
AMATA**
25, bd. Carnot
Tel. 04 93 55 59 93

Open Tue.–Sun.
9am–noon and 2–6pm.
Free entrance.

MUSÉE DUFY
77, quai des États-Unis
Tel. 04 93 62 31 24
Open Tue.–Sun. 10am–
noon, 2–6pm. Closed
Sun. am and public hols.
*Also houses the Galerie
de Bord de Mer and
Galerie des Ponchettes.
Entrance free.*

**MUSÉE FRANCISCAIN,
CHURCH AND
MONASTÈRE DE CIMIEZ**
Pl. du Monastère
Tel. 04 93 81 00 04
Open 10am–noon and
3–6pm. Closed Sun.,
public hols. Free entry.

MUSÉE MATISSE
164, av. des Arènes-
de-Cimiez
Tel. 04 93 81 08 08
In season: Open 11am–
7pm, Apr.–Sep. Closed
Tue. and public hols.
Free entrance.

**MUSÉE NATIONAL
DU MESSAGE BIBLIQUE
MARC-CHAGALL**
Av. du Docteur-Ménard
Tel. 04 93 81 75 75
In season: Open July–
Sep. Wed.–Mon. 10am–
7pm. Entrance 27F.

**NOTRE-DAME-
AUXILIATRICE**
17, pl. Dom-Bosco
Tel. 04 93 85 94 60
Open 8.30am–noon
and 2.30–6pm

OPÉRA DE NICE
4-6, rue St-François-
de-Paule
Tel. 04 92 17 40 40

**PALAIS DE LA
PRÉFECTURE**
Pl. Pierre-Gautier
Closed to the public.

PALAIS LASCARIS
15, rue Droite
Tel. 04 93 62 05 54
Open Tue.–Sun. 9.30am–
noon and 2.30– 6pm.
Free entrance.

**PALAIS MASSÉNA,
MUSÉE D'ART
ET D'HISTOIRE**
65, rue de France
35, prom. des Anglais
Tel. 04 93 88 11 34
In season: Open 10am–
noon and 3–6pm.
Closed Mon. and public
hols. Free entrance.

**RUSSIAN ORTHODOX
CATHEDRAL OF
ST-NICOLAS**
Av. Nicolas-II
Tel. 04 93 96 88 02
In season: Open daily
9.30am–noon, 2.30–6pm

**RUSSIAN ORTHODOX
CHURCH**
6, rue Longchamp
Tel. 04 93 87 97 04
Closed to the public.

**TERRASSE FRÉDÉRIC-
NIETZSCHE**
Colline du Château
*Situated above the
waterfall. Accessible from
the eastern end of the
Promenade des Anglais
by stairs or
elevator.*

RESTAURANTS

L'AVION BLEU
10, rue A.-Karr
Tel. 04 93 87 77 47
Open til midnight
☆

BOCCACCIO
7, rue Masséna
Tel. 04 93 87 71 76
☆

**GRAND CAFÉ DE
TURIN**
5, pl. Garibaldi
Tel. 04 93 62 29 52
Closed in June
☆ ☥

★ **LA MERENDA**
4, rue Terrasse
*No credit cards, no
phone.*

LE POT D'ÉTAIN
12, rue Meyerbeer
Tel. 04 93 88 25 95
Closed Sun. midday
☆ ☥

★ **LE VENDÔME**
1, pl. Grimaldi
Tel. 04 93 16 18 28
Closed Sun.
♣ ☥

ACCOMMODATION

ATLANTIC ★★★★
12, bd Victor-Hugo
Tel. 04 93 88 40 15
Fax 04 93 88 68 60
☆ 🚗 ☥

BEAU RIVAGE ★★★★
24, rue St-François-
de-Paule
Tel. 04 93 80 80 70
Fax 04 93 80 55 77
Private beach.
☆

★ **FLORIDE ★★★★**
52, bd Cimiez
Tel. 04 93 53 11 02
*Good view and value for
money.*
⚊ ♣ 🅿

★ **LA PÉROUSE ★★★★**
11, quai Rauba-Capeu
Tel. 04 93 62 34 63
Fax 04 93 62 59 41
*Luxurious and romantic
hotel. Sauna and
jacuzzi.*
☥

LE NEGRESCO ★★★★
37, promenade des
Anglais
Tel. 04 93 16 64 00
Fax 04 93 88 35 68
Private beach.
🅿 ☥

WINDSOR ★★★
11, rue Dalpozzo
Tel. 04 93 88 59 35
Fax 04 93 88 94 57
🏠 ♣ 🛆 🅿 ☥

YOUTH HOSTEL
Route forestière du
Mont-Alban
Tel. 04 93 89 23 64

NIGHTLIFE

CHEZ PAULINE TAPAS
14, rue Tiranty
Tel. 04 93 80 12 44
Open 6.30pm–12.30am

CHEZ WAYNE PUB
15, rue de la Préfecture
Tel. 04 93 13 46 99
Open 9am–midnight

**DISCOTHÈQUE
DU CASINO RUHL**
1, promenade des
Anglais
Tel. 04 93 87 95 87

SPECIALTY FOODS

AUER
7, rue St-François-de-
Paule
Tel. 04 93 85 77 98
Nice's best confectioner.

◆

**VILLEFRANCHE
SUR-MER**

06230   ▲ *294*

USEFUL ADDRESSES

TOURIST OFFICE
Jardin François-Binon
Tel. 04 93 01 73 68

CULTURE

CHAPEL OF ST-PIERRE
Quai Courbet
Port de la Santé
In season: Open 9am–
noon and 3–7pm.
Entrance 12F.
*Chapel decorated by
Jean Cocteau.*

MUSÉE VOLTI
Citadelle de Villefranche
Tel. 04 93 76 33 27
Open July–Aug.
Wed.–Mon. 10am–noon
and 3–7pm; June and
Sep. Wed.–Mon.
9am–noon and 3–7pm.
Closed Sun. am and
Nov. Free entrance

RESTAURANT

LA GRIGNOTIÈRE
3, rue du Poilu
Tel. 04 93 76 79 83
Open Mon.–Sat.

ACCOMMODATION

LA FLORE ★★
100, rue Princesse-
Grace-de-Monaco
Tel. 04 93 76 99 99
☆ 🛆 🚗 ☥

WELCOME ★★★
Quai Courbet
Tel. 04 93 76 76 93
Fax 04 93 01 88 81
Closed Nov.
☥

**BEAULIEU-
SUR-MER**

06310   ▲ *295*

USEFUL ADDRESSES

**TOURIST
INFORMATION**
Place Clemenceau
Tel. 04 93 01 02 21

CULTURE

**VILLA KERYLOS-
FONDATION
THÉODORE
REINACH**
Rue Gustave-Eiffel
Tel. 04 93 01 01 44
Open Mar. 15–June
10.30–12.30pm and
2–7pm, and July–Aug.
and Sep.–Oct 10am–
7pm. Closed Nov.
Entrance 35F.

RESTAURANTS

LE MÉTROPOLE
15, bd Leclerc
Tel. 04 93 01 00 08
Closed end Oct.–Dec. 20
🅿 ⴲ

LA PIGNATELLE
10, rue Quincenet
Tel. 04 93 01 03 37
Closed Wed.
♠♠ ⴲ

ACCOMMODATION

LE HAVRE BLEU **
29, bd Joffre
Tel. 04 93 01 01 40
Fax 04 93 01 29 92
🅿 ⴲ

MÉTROPOLE ****
15, bd Leclerc
Tel. 04 93 01 00 08
Fax 04 93 01 18 51
Closed Oct. 20–Dec. 20
♠ ⌲ 🚗 ⴲ

**LA RÉSERVE
DE BEAULIEU ******
5, bd Leclerc
Tel. 04 93 01 00 01
Fax 04 93 01 28 99
Closed Nov.–Mar.
♠ ⌲ 🚗 ⴲ

ST-JEAN-
CAP-FERRAT

06230   ▲ 296

USEFUL ADDRESSES

TOURIST OFFICE
59, av. Denis-Seméria
Tel. 04 93 76 08 90

CULTURE

**CHAPEL OF
ST-HOSPICE**
Chem. de St-Hospice
Open 9am–6pm

TOWER
Chemin St-Hospice
Closed to the public.

**VILLA EPHRUSSI-
ROTHSCHILD**
Route du Cap
Tel. 04 93 01 33 09
or 04 93 01 33 10
Open 10am–6pm,
Feb. 15–June and
Sep.–Oct.; 10am–7pm,
Jul.–Aug. Closed Dec. 25
Entrance to villa and
gardens 38F.

RESTAURANTS

★ **LE PROVENÇAL**
2, av. Denis-Seméria
Tel. 04 93 79 03 97

Fax 04 93 76 05 39
Closed Feb.
♠♠

LE SLOOP
Port de Plaisance
Tel. 04 93 01 48 63
Closed Wed. midday in
season, and Nov. 15–
Dec. 20
🏛 ♠♠ ⴲ

ACCOMMODATION

LA FRÉGATE **
Av. Denis-Seméria
Tel. 04 93 73 04 51
Closed Dec.–Jan.
ⴲ

**GRAND HÔTEL
DU CAP-FERRAT ******
Bd du Gen.-de-Gaulle
Tel. 04 93 76 50 50
Fax 04 93 76 04 52
*Heated Olympic sea-
water pool, tennis
gymnasium, bicycles.*
♠ ⌲ 🅿 ⴲ

ROYAL-RIVIERA ****
3, av. Jean-Monnet
Tel. 04 93 01 20 20
Fax 04 93 01 23 07
Open Mar.–Oct.
and Dec. 26–Jan. 6
♠ ♠♠ ⌲ 🚗 ⴲ

ÈZE

06360   ▲ 297

USEFUL ADDRESSES

TOURIST OFFICE
Pl. du Gen.-De-Gaulle
Tel. 04 93 41 26 00

CULTURE

JARDIN EXOTIQUE
Rue du Château
Tel. 04 93 41 10 30
Open Mar. 9am–noon
and 2–6.30pm; Apr.–
May 9am–7pm; June
and Sep. 9am– 7.30pm;
and Jul.–Aug. 9am–8pm.
Entrance 12F.

RESTAURANTS

AU NID D'AIGLE
1, rue du Château
Tel. 04 93 41 19 08
Closed Wed.
ⴲ

**AUBERGE DU
TROUBADOUR**
4, rue du Brec
Tel. 04 93 41 19 03
Closed one week in July
and Feb., Nov. 20–Dec.
20 and Sun.–Mon. lunch.
♠♠ ⴲ

CHÂTEAU ÈZA
In the village
Tel. 04 93 41 12 24
Closed Jan.–Apr.
🚗 ⴲ

ACCOMMODATION

CAP ESTEL ****
Beside the Èze
Tel. 04 93 01 50 44
Fax 04 93 01 55 20
Open Apr.–Oct.
Sauna.
⌲ 🅿 ⴲ

**LES TERRASSES
D'ÈZE ******
1138, av. de La Turbie
Tel. 04 93 41 24 64
Fax 04 93 41 13 25
Closed Dec. 20–Jan.
♠ ⌲ 🅿 ⴲ

MONACO
LA CONDAMINE
MONTE-CARLO

98000   ▲ 297

USEFUL ADDRESSES

**DIRECTION DU
TOURISME ET DES
CONGRÈS DE MONACO**
9, rue de la Paix
75002 Paris
Tel. 04 42 96 12 23
Open 9.30am–1pm
and 2–6pm

CULTURE

CATHEDRAL
4, rue Colonel-
Bellando-de-Castro
Tel. 04 93 30 87 70
Open 7am–6pm
Closed Sun. am

**JARDIN EXOTIQUE-
GROTTE DE
L'OBSERVATOIRE**
Bd du Jardin-Exotique
Tel. 04 93 30 33 65
Open 9am–5pm
Closed for Christmas

**MUSÉE
D'ANTHROPOLOGIE
PRÉHISTORIQUE**
In the tropical gardens.

**MUSÉE
OCÉANOGRAPHIQUE**
Av. St-Martin
Tel. 04 93 15 36 00
Open 9.30am–7pm,
Mar.–Oct.

**MUSÉE DES SOUVENIRS
NAPOLÉONIENS**
Place du Palais
Tel. 04 93 25 18 31
Open 10am–5pm
Closed Sat. and Nov.

**MUSÉE NATIONAL
DE MONACO**
17, av. Princesse-Grace
Tel. 04 93 30 91 26
Open 10am–12.15pm
and 2.30–6.30pm
Closed public hols.

PALAIS PRINCIER
Grands Appartements
Tel. 04 93 25 18 31
Open June–Oct.
9.30am–6.30pm

RESTAURANTS

LA CIGALE
18, rue de Millo
Tel. 04 93 30 16 14
"Canteen", fresh fish.

LE LOUIS XV
(Restaurant of Hôtel de
Paris), Place du Casino
Tel. 04 04 92 16 36 36
Last orders 10pm
*Very successful due to
chef Alain Ducasse.*

LE PINOCCHIO
30, rue Comte-Gastaldi
Tel. 04 93 30 96 20
Open until midnight
Italian specialties.

POLPETTA
2, rue Paradis
Tel. 04 93 50 67 84
Open till 11pm
Italian specialties.

LE ST-BENOÎT
10 ter, av. de la Costa
Tel. 04 93 25 02 34
Open till 10.30pm
Fish specialties.

ACCOMMODATION

ABELA HÔTEL
23, av. des Papalins
Tel. 04 92 05 90 00
⌲ ⴲ 🚗

BEACH PLAZA
22, av. Princesse-Grace
Monte-Carlo
Tel. 04 93 30 98 80
*"La Terrasse" restaurant,
private beach, 3 pools,
conference rooms.*
🚗

HÔTEL BALMORAL
12, av. de la Costa
Tel. 04 93 50 62 37

HÔTEL DE FRANCE
6, rue de La Turbie
Tel. 04 93 30 24 64

**HÔTEL
HERMITAGE**
Square Beaumarchais
Tel. 04 92 16 40 00
🚗 ⌲ ⴲ

HÔTEL LOEWS
12, av. des Spélugues
Tel. 04 93 50 65 00
*Casino, cabaret, bar,
five restaurants, ten
conference rooms (for
50 to 1,400 people),
business center.*

HÔTEL DE PARIS
Place du Casino
Tel. 04 92 16 30 00

HÔTEL TERMINUS
9, av. Prince-Pierre
Tel. 04 92 05 63 00
*Restaurant closed
Oct.–Nov.*

NIGHTLIFE

CASINO DE MONTE-CARLO
Place du Casino
Tel. 04 92 16 21 21
*Over 21's only. Opens
from noon.*

SALLE GARNIER
Place du Casino
Tel. 04 92 16 22 29

ROQUEBRUNE CAP-MARTIN
06190 ▲ 304

CULTURE

VILLA CYRNOS
Av. Douine
Closed to the public.

MENTON
06500 ▲ 304

USEFUL ADDRESSES

TOURIST OFFICE
8, av. Boyer, BP 239,
06506 Menton Cedex
Tel. 04 93 57 57 00

CULTURE

CHAPEL OF THE IMMACULATE CONCEPTION
Parvis St-Michel
Tel. 04 93 35 81 63
*Key available from the
Church of St-Michel.*

CHURCH OF ST-MICHEL
Parvis St-Michel
Tel. 04 93 35 81 63
Open Sun.–Fri.
10am–noon and
3–5pm; Sat.
3–5pm

DOMAINE DES COLOMBIÈRES
Bd Garavan
Tel. 04 93 35 71 90
In season: Open 9am–
noon and 3–7pm
*Garden designed by
Ferdinand Bac.*

JARDIN BIOVÈS
Av. Boyer
Open all year.

JARDIN BOTANIQUE DU VAL RAMEH
Av. St-Jacques
Tel. 04 93 35 86 72
In season: Open May–
Sep.10am–noon and
3–6pm. Entrance 20F.

JARDINS SERRE DE LA MADONE
*Private. Visits on the
"Journée du Patrimoine"
Tel. 04 92 10 33 66.*

JARDINS VILLA FONTANA ROSA
6, av. Blasco-Ibanez
Tel. 04 92 10 33 66
Entrance 30F.
*Visits on the third Sun.
of the month at 10am,
or by appointment.*

JARDINS DE LA VILLA MARIA SERENA
21, prom. de la
Reine-Astrid
Entrance 30F.
*Guided tours 10am.
Groups apply to
"Service du Patrimoine"
(Tel. 04 92 10 33 66).*

MUSÉE JEAN-COCTEAU
"Bastion" du Vieux Port
Tel. 04 93 57 72 30
Same opening times
as Musée du Palais
Carnoles.
Free entrance.

MUSÉE DU PALAIS CARNOLES
3, av. de la Madone
Tel. 04 93 35 49 71
In season: Open
June 15– Sep. 15.
10am– noon and
3–7pm. Closed Tue. and
public hols.
Free entrance.
Famous garden.

MUSÉE DE LA PRÉHISTOIRE RÉGIONALE
Rue Loredan-
Larchey
Tel. 04 93 35 49 71
In season: Open
June 15–Sep. 15.
10am–noon and

3–7pm, Closed Tue. and
public hols.
Free entrance.

PALAIS DE L'EUROPE
Av. Boyer
Tel. 04 93 57 57 00
Shows and lectures.

SALLE DES MARIAGES DE LA MAIRIE
Town Hall
17, rue de la
République
Tel. 04 93 57 87 87
Open 8.30am–12.30pm
and 1.30–5pm.
Closed Sat., Sun. and
public hols.
Entrance 5F.
*Room decorated by
Jean Cocteau.*

RESTAURANT

★ LA VÉRANDA
Hotel des
Ambassadeurs
2, rue du Louvre
Tel. 04 93 28 75 75

ACCOMMODATION

HÔTEL DES AMBASSADEURS ★★★★
3, rue Partouneaux
Tel. 04 93 28 75 75
Fax 04 93 35 62 32

L'AIGLON ★★★
7, av. de la Madone
Tel. 04 93 57 55 55
Fax 04 93 35 92 39
Closed Nov.–
mid Dec.

★ MAGALI ★★
10, rue Villarey
Tel. 04 93 35 73 78
Fax 04 93 57 05 04
Closed Nov.

VIKING ★★★
2, av. du G.ˡ-de-Gaulle
Tel. 04 93 57 95 85
Closed Nov. 15–Dec. 15

YOUTH HOSTEL
Plateau
St-Michel
Tel. 04 93 35 93 14
Fax 04 93 35 93 07
Closed Dec. 15– Jan. 31

NIGHTLIFE

DISCOTHÈQUE DU CASINO LUCIEN-BARRIÈRE
2 bis, av. Félix-Faure
Tel. 04 92 10 16 16

ST-PAUL-DE-VENCE
06570 ▲ 308

USEFUL ADDRESSES

TOURIST OFFICE
Maison de la Tour
Rue Grande
Tel. 04 93 32 86 95

CULTURE

COLLEGIATE CHURCH OF THE CONVERSION OF ST-PAUL
Place de l'Église
Open 10am–6pm

FONDATION MAEGHT
Tel. 04 93 32 81 63
In season: Open July-
Sep. 10am–7pm.
Entrance 40F.

RESTAURANTS

LE ST-PAUL
86, rue Grande
Tel. 04 93 22 65 25
Closed Wed. in season,
second weekend in
Jan.–last week in Feb.
16th-century building.

LA BROUETTE
830, rte de Cagnes
Tel. 04 93 58 67 16
Closed Feb., Mon.
Dinner only; until 11pm.

ACCOMMODATION

LA COLOMBE D'OR ★★★★
Pl. du Gen.-de-Gaulle
Tel. 04 93 32 80 02
Fax 04 93 32 77 78
Closed Nov.–Dec. 20

LE MAS D'ARTIGNY★★★★
Rte de la Colle
Tel. 04 93 32 84 34
Fax 04 93 32
95 36
*Tennis,
golf.*

★ **LES ORANGERS** ★★★
Chemin des Fumerates
Tel. 04 93 32 80 95
Fax 04 93 32 00 32

VENCE

06140   ▲ *309*

USEFUL ADDRESSES

TOURIST OFFICE
Pl. du Grand-Jardin
BP 131
Tel. 04 93 58 06 38

CULTURE

**CATHEDRAL OF THE
NATIVITÉ-DE-LA-
VIERGE**
Pl. Clemenceau
Tel. 04 93 58 06 01
In season: Open
9am–6.30pm

**CHAPEL OF THE
ROSARY**
Rte de St-Jeannet
Tel. 04 93 58 03 26
In season: Open
Tue.–Fri. 10–11.30am
and 2.30–5.30pm
Decorated by Matisse.

**CHÂTEAU NOTRE-
DAME-DES-FLEURS**
Galerie Beaubourg
2058, route de Grasse
Tel. 04 93 24 52 00
Open 11am–7pm
Closed Sun.

RESTAURANTS

**AUBERGE
DES TEMPLIERS**
39, av. Joffre
Tel. 04 93 58 06 05
Closed Dec. 20–Jan. 10

ACCOMMODATION

**CLOSERIE DES
GENÊTS** ★
4, impasse Marcellin-
Mauvel
Tel. 04 93 58 33 25

LA ROSERAIE ★★★
91, av. Henri-Girand
Tel. 04 93 58 02 20
Fax 04 93 58 99 31

ENTREVAUX

04320   ▲ *310*

USEFUL ADDRESSES

TOURIST OFFICE
Porte Royale
Tel. 04 93 05 46 73
Fax 04 93 05 43 91

CULTURE

CATHEDRAL
Pl. de l'Église
*For visits, ring at the
presbytery opposite the
cathedral on the right.*

CITADEL
Rue Orbitelle
Entrance 10F.

ACCOMMODATION

**RÉSIDENCE-CLUB
LES COUGNAS**
Mton Blanc,
Val de Chalvagne
Tel. 04 93 05 46 34
Fax 04 93 05 41 71
Open June–Dec.

VAUBAN
4, pl. Moreau
Tel. 04 93 05 42 40
Fax 04 93 05 48 38
Closed Dec.

COLMARS-
LES-ALPES

04370

USEFUL ADDRESSES

TOURIST OFFICE
Hôtel des Postes
Pl. Joseph-Girieud
Tel. 04 92 83 41 92

CULTURE

FORT DE FRANCE
RD 908, Rue Principale
across from the police
station (*gendarmerie*)
Closed to the public.

FORT DE SAVOIE
Entrance of the village
Open July–Aug. 10am–
noon and 2–6.30pm,
*Apply at Tourist office
Sep.–June. Open all
day July–Aug.*

ACCOMMODATION

LE CHAMOIS ★★
In center of village
Tel. 04 92 83 43 29
Closed Nov. 11–Christmas

CASTELLANE

04120

USEFUL ADDRESSES

TOURIST OFFICE
Rue Nationale
Tel. 04 92 83 61 14

CULTURE

**CHURCH OF NOTRE-
DAME-DU-ROC**
Footpath at 35, rue de la
Mérey
*Keys in the presbytery
mailbox (35, rue de
la Mérey).*

CHURCH OF ST-VICTOR
Rue St-Victor
Open July 14–Aug. 15
Tue., Thur.–Sat.
2.30–6pm.
*Aug. 16–July 13 keys
at the Tourist office.*

ACCOMMODATION

**CAMPING CHASTEUIL-
PROVENCE**
Rte des Gorges-du-
Verdon
Tel. 04 92 83 61 21
Fax 04 92 83 75 62
Open Apr.–Sep.

**CAMPING
FRÉDÉRIC-MISTRAL**
Rte de Moustiers
Tel. 04 92 83 62 27
Supervised.

CAMPING DU VERDON
Domaine de la Salaou
Rte des Gorges-du-
Verdon
Tel. 04 92 83 61 29
Fax 04 92 03 69 37
Open May 15–Sep. 15
Supervised.

**GÎTE D'ÉTAPE
AU SOLEIL LEVANT**
La Baume
Tel. 04 92 83 70 82
Open Feb.–Dec.

**GÎTE D'ÉTAPE
L'OUSTAOU**
Chemin des
Listes
Tel. 04 92 83 77
27
Fax 04 92 83 65
67

**HÔTEL DU
LEVANT** ★★
Pl. Marcel-Sauvaire
Tel. 04 92 83 60 05
Fax 04 92 83 72 14

LA PALUD-SUR-
VERDON

04120   ▲ *315*

USEFUL ADDRESSES

TOURIST OFFICE
Château
Tel. 04 92 77 32 02

CULTURE

CHURCH
Place de l'Église
Closed to the public.

ACCOMMODATION

**AUBERGE
DES CRÊTES** ★
Rte de Castellane
Tel. 04 92 77 38 47
Fax 04 92 77 30 40
Open Apr.–Oct. 10

**GÎTE D'ÉTAPE
L'ARC-EN-CIEL**
Place de l'Église
Tel. 04 92 77 37 40

PROVENCE ★★
Rte de la Maline
Tel. 04 92 77 36 50
Fax 04 92 77 31 05
Open Easter–Oct.

MOUSTIERS-
STE-MARIE

04360   ▲ *316*

USEFUL ADDRESSES

TOURIST OFFICE
Rue de la Bourgade
Tel. 04 92 74 67 84
Fax 04 92 74 60 65

CULTURE

**CHAPEL OF NOTRE-
DAME-DE-BEAUVOIR**
Perched above the
village. Access along
path from parking lot at
the top of the village.

**CHURCH OF
NOTRE-DAME**
In season: Open
8.30am–7pm,
Easter–
All Saints

**MUSÉE DE
LA FAÏENCE**
Pl. du
Presbytère
Tel. 04 92 74
61 61
*Currently closed
for restoration
works.*

RESTAURANTS

★ **LES SANTONS**
Pl. de l'Église
Tel. 04 92 74 66 48
Closed Mon. eve and
Tue.
*Terrace overlooking the
Moustiers spring. Fine
cellar of wines from the
South of France.*
🅿 ⴕ

ACCOMMODATION

LA BONNE AUBERGE ★★
Quartier St-Michel
Tel. 04 92 74 66 18
Fax 04 92 74 65 11
Closed Nov. 16–Feb. 15
🚗

LA FERME ROSE
Near Ste-Croix-de-
Verdon
Tel. 04 92 74 69 47
Fax 04 92 74 60 76
⤳

LE COLOMBIER ★★
Quartier St-Michel
Tel. 04 92 74 66 02
Fax 04 92 74 66 70
Closed Dec. 15–Jan. 15
⤳ 🅿 ⴕ

PEILLON
06440 ▲ 318

USEFUL ADDRESSES

TOURIST OFFICE
Mairie (Town Hall)
Tel. 04 93 79 91 04

CULTURE

**CHAPEL OF THE
PÉNITENTS BLANCS**
In the old village
Tel. 04 93 02 59 89
*Group tours on
request at the Mairie
(Tel. 04 93 79 91 04).*

**CHURCH OF THE
TRANSFIGURATION**
Pl. de l'Église, Peillon
*The Mairie arranges
group tours.*

ACCOMMODATION

**AUBERGE
DE LA MADONE ★★★**
Pl. Auguste-Arnulf
Tel. 04 93 79 91 17
Fax 04 93 79 99 36
Closed Oct. 20–Dec. 20
and Jan. 9–Jan. 24
🎎 🅿 ⊘ ⴕ

PEILLE
06440 ▲ 318

USEFUL ADDRESSES

TOURIST OFFICE
Mairie (Town Hall)
Tel. 04 93 91 71 17
Fax 04 93 91 71 79

CULTURE

**CHAPEL OF
ST-SÉBASTIEN**
Pl. Carnot
Open 9am–noon and
2–5pm. Closed Wed.
pm and Sun. pm.

**COLLEGIATE CHURCH
OF STE-MARIE**
Bd Aristide-Briand
*Key available from the
pensioners' home.
(Tel. 04 93 79 90 38).*

**MUSÉE DES ARTS
ET DES TRADITIONS
POPULAIRES
OU MUSÉE DU TERROIR**
Pl. de L'Arna
Tel. 04 93 91 90 54
Open Wed., Sat.-Sun.
and public hols. 2–6pm

**PALAIS DU JUGE-
MAGE**
Pl. André-Laugier
Not open to the public.

L'ESCARÈNE
06440 ▲ 319

USEFUL ADDRESSES

TOURIST OFFICE
Mairie (Town Hall)
Tel. 04 93 79 50 04
Fax 04 93 79 66 28

CULTURE

**CHAPEL OF THE
PÉNITENTS**
Pl. Carnot
*For visits contact the
town hall.*

**CHURCH OF
ST-PIERRE-AUX-LIENS**
Pl. Carnot
Open 9am–6pm

SOSPEL
06380 ▲ 320

USEFUL ADDRESSES

TOURIST OFFICE
Le Vieux Pont
Tel. 04 93 04 15 80

CULTURE

**CATHEDRAL OF
ST-MICHEL**
*Contact Mme Gouveita
at the Tourist office from
10am to noon.*

CHAPEL OF STE-CROIX
Pl. Ste-Croix
*Collect the key from the
tourist office.*

FORT DU BARBONNET
Col St-Jean
Rte de Nice
Guided tours 3pm Sat.
and Sun., July–Aug.
*Information from the
Tourist office.*

FORT ST-ROCH
Open Sat.–Sun. and
public hols. Open
Apr.–May, Sep. and
June–Aug. 2–6pm.
Closed Mon. June–Aug.
and Oct.–Apr.

ACCOMMODATION

**AUBERGE
PROVENÇALE ★★**
Route de Menton
Tel. 04 93 04 00 31
Closed Nov. 11–Dec. 11
🅿 ⴕ

BREIL-SUR-ROYA
06540 ▲ 321

USEFUL ADDRESSES

TOURIST OFFICE
Place Brancheri
Tel. 04 93 04 99 76

CULTURE

**CHURCH OF SANTA-
MARIA-IN-ALBIS**
Pl. Brancion
Open 9am–noon
and 2–6pm

ACCOMMODATION

CASTEL-DU-ROY ★★★
Route de Tende
Tel. 04 93 04 43 66

Fax 04 93 04 91 83
Closed Nov.–Mar.
🎎 ⤳ 🅿 ⴕ

LE ROYA ★★
Pl. Brancheri
Tel. 04 93 04 48 10
Closed Feb. vacation
🎎 🅿 ⴕ

SAORGE
06540

CULTURE

**CHURCH OF THE
MADONE-DEL-POGGIO**
Route de la Madone
Closed to the public.

**FRANCISCAN
MONASTERY**
Tel. 04 93 04 51 23
Open Sun. and public
hols. 10am–noon and
2–4.30pm. Sat. 2–4.30pm

**PARISH CHURCH OF
ST-SAUVEUR**
Place de l'Église
Open 9am–5pm

LA BRIGUE
06430

USEFUL
ADDRESSES

TOURIST OFFICE
Mairie (Town Hall)
Tel. 04 93 04 61 01

CULTURE

**CHAPEL OF THE
ANNUNCIATION**
In season: Open 3–7pm

**COLLEGIATE CHURCH
OF ST-MARTIN**
Pl. St-Martin
Open 8am–6pm

**NOTRE-DAME-
DES-FONTAINES**
*Keys can be collected
from the Café de
la Place.*

ACCOMMODATION

**AUBERGE
ST-MARTIN ★**
Pl. St-Martin
Tel. 04 93 04 62 17
🎎 ⴕ

MIRVAL ★★
3, rue Vincent-Ferrier
Tel. 04 93 04 63 71
Fax 04 93 04 79 21
Closed Nov.–Apr.
*Special prices for
children, parking.*

387

APPENDICES

◆ BIBLIOGRAPHY

◆ GENERAL ◆

◆ BENTLEY (J.): *Provence and the Côte d'Azur* (Aurum, 1992)
◆ BLUME (M.): *Côte d'Azur, Inventing the French Riviera* (Thames & Hudson, London, 1992)
◆ DUBY (G.), HIDELSHEIMER (E.) and BARATIER (E.): *Atlas historique de Provence – Comtat-Venaissin, Orange, Nice, Monaco* (Librairie Armand Colin, Paris, 1969)
◆ DURRELL (L.): *Caesar's Vast Ghosts: Aspects of Provence* (Faber, London, 1990)
◆ GIRARD (J.): *Évocations du Vieil Avignon* (éditions de Minuit, Paris, 1958)
◆ MEHLING (M.): *Provence and the Côte d'Azur* (Phaidon, Oxford, 1986)
◆ POPE-HENNESSY (J.): *Aspects of Provence* (Penguin, Hardmondsworth, 1988)

NATURAL
◆ HISTORY◆

◆ BARAL (R.) and TROADEC (Y.): *Vignes et vins en Provence ; les appellations d'origine de la Provence et de la vallée du Rhône* (Collection de l'université du vin, Suze-la-Rousse, 1989)
◆ BOUGIS (P.) and DEJEAN-ARREGOS (J.): *Guide nature. Mer Méditerranée.* (éditions édimo, Monaco, 1991)
◆ *Connaître les plantes protégées. Région Méditerranée* (Delachaux & Niestlé, Neuchâtel, 1988)
◆ DEJEAN-ARRECGOS (J.): *Guide d'observation de la nature* (Masson, Paris, 1986)
◆ HARANT (g.) and JARRY (D.): *Guide du naturaliste dans le midi de la France* (Delachaus & Niestlé, Neuchâtel, 1987)
◆ LARTIGUES (C. de): *Les plus belles ballades autour d'Aix et de Marseille* (Le Pélican, Montpellier, 1992)
◆ *Walks in Provence* (Footpaths of Europe) (Robertson McCarta, 1989)
◆ RACINE (M.) et al.: *The Gardens of Provence and the French Riviera* (MIT Press, Boston, 1987)
◆ VOLOT (R.) and DÉJEAN-ARRECGROS (J.): *Guide du promeneur Côte d'Azur–Alpes du Sud* (Réalisations éditoriales pédagogiques, Paris, 1982)

◆ FOOD ◆

◆ BAKER (J.): *Simple French Cuisine from Provence and Languedoc* (Faber, London, 1992)
◆ HOLLIGUE (D.): *Classic Cuisine of Provence: The Top 100 Dishes of Provence* (Merehurst, London, 1993)

◆ HISTORY ◆

◆ BARRAL (L.) and SIMONE (S.): *Préhistoire de la Côte d'Azur orientale* (Imprimerie nationale, Monaco, 1968)
◆ BENOIT (F.): *La Provence et le Comtat-Venaissin : arts et traditions populaires* (Aubanel, Avignon, 1989)
◆ BIANCHI (B.): *Histoire de Cannes* (Xavier Richier, Cannes, 1977)
◆ BORDES (M.): *Histoire de Nice et du pays niçois (Privat, Toulouse, 1976)*
◆ BRANCH-JOHNSON (W.): *Folk Tales of Provence* (Chapman & Hall, 1927)
◆ BRANGHAM (A.N.): *History, People and Places in Provence* (Spurbooks, 1976)
◆ BRUNI (R.): *Villages du Lubéron ; Auribeau, Bonnieux, Buoux, Castellet, Saignon, Sivergues* (éditions Équinoxe, Marguerites, 1992)
◆ COSQUER (H.): *La Grotte Cosquer, plongée dans la préhistoire* (Solar, Paris, 1992)
◆ DUCHÊNE (R.): *Histoire de Provence-Alpes-Côte d'Azur. Naissance d'une région, 1945-1985* (Fayard, Paris, 1986)
◆ GAGNIÈRE (S.): *Le Palais des Papes d'Avignon* (Les Amis du palais du Roure, Avignon, 1985)
◆ GONNET (P.), ed.: *Histoire du pays de Grasse et sa région* (Horvath, Roanne, 1984)
◆ LUMLEY (H. de): *Le mont Bégo, vallée des Merveilles et de Fontanalba* (Imprimerie nationale, Paris, 1992)
◆ MALAUSSENA (P.-L.): *La vie en Provence orientale aux XIV et XV siècles* (Paris, 1969)
◆ MONESTIER (M.): *Petit guide de poche des casinos* (éditions Sand, Paris, 1987)
◆ MUHEIM (E.) and REVAULT (E.): *L'abbaye du Thoronet* (éditions CNMHS, 1990)
◆ PREUSSOURE (L.): *Le rêve cistercien* (Découvertes Gallimard,

Paris, 1990)
◆ ROBERT (J.-B.): *Histoire de Monaco* (PUF, Paris, 1973)

◆ RELIGION ◆

◆ FROESCHULE-CHOPARD (M.-H.): *La Religion populaire en Provence orientale au XVIIIe siècle* (Beauchesne, Paris, 1980)
◆ FROESCHULE-CHOPARD (M.-H.): *Les confréries, l'Église et la Cité. Cartographie des confréries du Sud-Est* (Grenoble, centre alpin et rhodanien d'ethnologie, 1988)
◆ VOVELLE (M.): *Piété baroque et déchristianisation en Provence au XVIIIe siècle* (Point Seuil Histoire, abridged edition, 1978)

◆ ARCHITECTURE ◆

◆ BARRUOL (G.) and ROUQUETTE (J.-M.): *Itinéraires romans en Provence* (Zodiaque, La Pierre-qui-Vire, Saint-Léger-Vauban, 1978)
◆ BEAUCHAMP (Philippe de): *L'Architecture rurale des Alpes-Maritimes* (édisud, La Calade, Aix-en-Provence, 1992)
◆ BORNECQUE (R.): *La France de Vauban* (Arthaud, Paris, 1984)
◆ BROMBERGER (C.), LACROIX (J.) and RAULIN (H.): *L'architecture rurale française, Provence* (Berger Levrault -Musée des Arts et Traditions populaires, Paris, 1980)
◆ COLLIER (R.): *La Haute-Provence monumentale et artistique* (Digne, 1986)
◆ COSTE (P.) and MARTEL (P.): *Pierre sèche en Provence* (Les Alpes de lumière, Mane, 1986)
◆ FOUSSARD (D.) and BARBIER (G.): *Baroque niçois et monégasque* (éditions Picart, Paris, 1988)
◆ FUSTER-DAUTIER (N.): *Les Bastides de Provence et leurs jardins* (SERG, Aix-en-Provence, 1977)
◆ JEAN-NEMY (dom Claude): *Les sœurs provençales; Silvacane, Sénanque, Le Thoronet* (Zodiaque, Yonne, 1991)
◆ KUBACH (H.-E.): *Architecture romane* (Gallimard, Paris, 1992)
◆ MASSOT (J.): *Maisons rurales et vie paysanne en Provence* (SERG-Berger Levrault, Paris, 1990)
◆ NORBERG (SCHULZ (C.): *Architecture baroque*

(Histoire de l'architecture, Gallimard/Electa, Milan, 1992)
◆ RAYBAUT (P.) and STEVE (M.): *Hans-Georg Tesling, architecte de la Côte d'Azur* (éditions Serre, Nice, 1990)
◆ THIRION (J.): *Alpes romanes* (Zodiaque, Coll. "La Nuit des temps", La Pierre-qui-Vire, Saint-Léger-Vauban, 1980)
◆ VÉSIAN (H.): *Châteaux et bastides en Haute-Provence* (Aubanel, Avignon, 1991)

◆ ART ◆

◆ APPROUE (J.): *La Provence de Cézanne* (édisud, Aix-en-Provence, 1982)
◆ ASTRO (C.) and THÉVENON (L.): *La peinture au XVIIe siècle dans les Alpes-Maritimes* (éditions Serre, Nice, 1985)
◆ BEAUCHAMP (P. de): *L'art religieux dans les Alpes-Maritimes* (édisud, Aix-en-Provence, 1990)
◆ BERNADAC (M.-L.): *Picasso, le Sage et le Fou* (Gallimard, Paris, 1986)
◆ CACHIN (F.): *Gauguin: "ce malgré moi de sauvage "* (Gallimard, Paris, 1989)
◆ DUMUR (G.): *Nicolas de Staël* (Flammarion, Paris, 1989)
◆ GIRARD (X.): *Matisse, une splendeur inouïe* (Gallimard, Paris, 1993)
◆ JONES (J.R.): *The Man who Loved the Sun: The Life of Vincent van Gogh* (Evans, London, 1966)
◆ LUBIN (A.J.): *Stranger on the Earth* [Van Gogh] (Paladin, London, 1975)
◆ MCLEAVE (H.): *The Man and his Mountain: The Life of Cézanne* (W.H. Allen, London, 1977)
◆ PARMELIN (H.): *Intimate Secrets of a Studio at Notre Dame de Vie* [Picasso] (Abrams, New York, 1966)
◆ ROQUES (M.): *Les peintures murales du sud-est de la France, XIIIe–XVIe siècle* (éditions Serre, Nice, 1989)
◆ TERRASSE (M.): *Bonnard at Le Cannet* (Thames & Hudson, London, 1988)
◆ THÉVENON (L.): *L'art du Moyen Âge dans les Alpes méridionales* (éditions Serre, Nice, 1983)
◆ VAN GOGH (V.): *Letters from Provence* (selected by M. Bailey) (Collins & Brown, London, 1992)
◆ VAN GOGH (V.): *Further letters of Vincent van

Gogh to his brother –
1886–1889 (Houghton
Mifflin & Co., 1929)

◆ LITERATURE ◆

◆ ANOUILH (J.): Point of
Departure
◆ ANTIER (J.-J.): La Côte
d'Azur, ombres et
lumières (France Empire,
Paris, 1972)
◆ ARBAUD (J. d'): La bête
du Vaccarès (Grasset,
Paris, 1985)
◆ BOSCO (H.): Malicroix
(Gallimard, Paris, 1948)
◆ BURRA (E.): Well
Dearie!, The Letters of
Edward Burra, (ed.
William Chappell,
Gordon Fraser, 1985)
◆ COLETTE: Collected
Stories
◆ COLETTE: Earthly
Paradise (trans. Enid
McLeod, Secker &
Warburg, 1966)
◆ DAUDET (A.): Letters
from my Windmill
◆ DAUDET (A.): Tartarin of
the Alps
◆ DICKENS (C): Pictures
from Italy (Chapman &
Hall, 1844)
◆ DUMAS (A.): The Count
of Monte Cristo
◆ DURRELL (L.): Spirit of
Place (Faber & Faber,
1969)
◆ DURRELL (L.): The
Avignon Quartet
◆ FISHER (M.F.K.): Two
Towns in Provence
(Random House, New
York, 1983; Hogarth
Press, London, 1985)
◆ FORTESCUE (Winifred,
Lady): Perfume from
Provence (1935;
reprinted Black Swan,
London, 1992)
◆ FREGNI (R.): Les nuits
d'Alice (Denoël, Paris,
1992)
◆ GIONO (J.): Provence
(Gallimard, Paris,
1993)
◆ GREENE (G.): Loser
Takes All
◆ HEMINGWAY (E.): The
First Forty-nine Stories
(Jonathan Cape, 1944)
◆ HIGHSMITH, (P.): The
Talented Mr Ripley
(Vintage, 1992)
◆ HOPKINSON, (H.) Roast
Chicken and Other
Stories (with Lindsey
Bareham, Ebury Press,
1994)
◆ JAMES (H.): A Little Tour
in France (Tauchnitz,
1954, first pub. 1884)
◆ LEE (V.): The Golden
Keys (Bodley Head,
1925)
◆ MADOX FORD (F.):
Provence – From
Minstrels to the Machine
(George Allen & Unwin
Ltd, 1938)
◆ MAGNAN (P.): Le Poivre
d'Âne (Denoël, Paris,
1988)

◆ MANSFIELD (K.):
Selected Short Stories
◆ MANSFIELD (K.): Letters
of Katherine Mansfield to
John Middleton Murry
(Constable & Co. Ltd,
1951)
◆ MILLER (H.): Letters to
Anaïs Nin (Edited and
introduced by Gunter
Stuhlmann. Peter Owen
1965)
◆ MAYLE (P.): A Year in
Provence (Pan, London,
1992)
◆ MAYLE (P.): Toujours
Provence (Pan, London,
1993)
◆ MAYLE (P.): Hôtel Pastis
(Pan, London, 1994)
◆ MICHELET (J.): La mer
(Gallimard, Paris, 1083)
◆ NUCÉRA (L.): Le ruban
rouge (Grasset, Paris,
1991)
◆ PAGNOL (M.): Jean de
Florette and Manon des
Sources (trans. by W.E.
van Heyningen, André
Deutsch Ltd, 1990)
◆ PETRARCA (F.) Letters
on Familiar Matters
(trans. Aldo S. Bernardo,
Johns Hopkins University
Press, 1982)
◆ PROAL (J.): Les Arnaud
(Terradou, 1991)
◆ RENOIR (J.): Pierre-
Auguste Renoir, mon
père (Gallimard, Paris,
1981)
◆ RUSKIN (J.): Praeterita
(Rupert Hart-Davis,
1949)
◆ SAGAN (F.): Bonjour
Tristresse
◆ SCOTT FITZGERALD (F.):
Tender is the Night (The
Grey Walls Press, 1953,
first pub. 1934)
◆ SÉVIGNÉ (MADAME DE):
Complete Letters
◆ STEVENSON (R.L.):
Travels with a Donkey
◆ STEVENSON (R.L.): The
Cévennes Journal
◆ STEVENSON (R.L): The
Letters of Robert Louis
Stevenson, Vol. II, (ed.
Sydney Colvin, Methuen
& Co. Ltd, 1921)
◆ SÜSKIND (P.): Perfume
(Tr. John E. Woods,
Hamish Hamilton, 1986)
◆ TWAIN (M.): The
Innocents Abroad
(American Publishing
Co., 1875)
◆ WOOLF (V.): The Diary of
Virginia Woolf (ed.
Anne Olivier Bell,
Harcourt Brace
Jovanovich, 1982)
◆ YOUNG (A.): Travels in
France During the Years
1787, 1788 & 1789 (ed.
Constantia Maxwell,
Cambridge University
Press, 1950)
◆ ZOLA (E.): Fortune of
the Rougons

ACKNOWLEDGMENTS

Grateful
acknowledgment is
made to the following for
permission to reprint
previously published
material:

◆ JANICE BIALA: Excerpt
from Provence – From
Minstrels to the Machine
by Ford Maddox Ford
(George Allen & Unwin
Ltd, UK, 1938), copyright
renewed 1962 by Janice
Biala. Reprinted by
permission of Janice
Biala.

◆ ANDRÉ DEUTSCH LTD:
Excerpt from Manon of
the Springs by Marcel
Pagnol, translated by
W.E. van Heyningen,
published by André
Deutsch in 1990.
Reprinted by permission.

◆ CAMBRIDGE UNIVERSITY
PRESS: Excerpt from
Travels in France During
the Years 1787–1789, by
Arthur Young, edited by
Constantia Maxwell,
published in 1950.
Reprinted by permission
of Cambridge University
Press.

◆ DAVID HIGHAM
ASSOCIATES: Excerpt from
Roast Chicken and Other
Stories by Simon
Hopkinson and Lindsey
Bareham, published by
Ebury Press in 1994.
Reprinted by permission.

◆ FABER AND FABER LTD:
Excerpt from The Spirit
of Place: Mediterranean
Writings by Lawrence
Durrell, published by
Faber and Faber, London
in 1969. Reprinted
permission of Faber and
Faber Ltd, London.

◆ FARRAR, STRAUS &
GIROUX, INC.: Excerpt
from Manon of the
Springs by Marcel
Pagnol and translated by
W.E. van Heyningen,
English translation
copyright © 1988 by
W.E. Heyningen.
Reprinted by permission
of North Point Press, a
division of Farrar, Straus
& Giroux, Inc.

◆ HARCOURT BRACE &
COMPANY and THE
HOGARTH PRESS: Excerpt
from The Diary of Virginia
Woolf, Volume 4:
1931–1935 by Virginia
Woolf, copyright © 1982
by Quentin Bell and
Angelica Garnett. Rights
in Canada administered
on behalf of the estate by
The Hogarth Press,

London. Reprinted by
permission of Harcourt
Brace & Company and
The Hogarth Press.

◆ JOHN HOPKINS
UNIVERSITY PRESS: Excerpt
from Letters on Familiar
Matters by Francesco
Petrarca, translated by
Aldo S. Bernardo (John
Hopkins University Press,
1982). Reprinted by
permission.

◆ PETERS FRASER &
DUNLOP GROUP LTD:
Excerpt from "The Light"
by Sir Dirk Bogarde
(European Travel & Life,
Dec., 1988). Reprinted
by permission.

◆ REED CONSUMER BOOKS:
Excerpt from The Letters
of Robert Louis
Stevenson, Vol. II, edited
by Sydney Colvin
(Methuen & Co. Ltd,
1921). Reprinted by
permission.

◆ CHARLES SCRIBNER'S
SONS: Excerpt from "A
Canary for One" by
Ernest Hemingway from
the Complete Short
Stories of Ernest
Hemingway, © 1927 by
Charles Scribner's Sons,
copyright renewed 1955
by Ernest Hemingway.
Reprinted by permission
of Scribner's, an imprint
of Simon & Schuster.

◆ THE SOCIETY OF
AUTHORS: Excerpt from
letter of April 12, 1920,
from Catherine Mansfield
to John Middleton Murry
(Constable & Company
Limited, London, 1951).
Reprinted by permission
of The Society of Authors
as the literary
representative of the
Estate of Katherine
Mansfield.

◆ GUNTHER STUHLMANN,
Author's Representative:
Excerpt from Henry
Miller: Letters to Anais
Nin, edited and with an
Introduction by Gunther
Stuhlmann, copyright ©
1965 by Anais Nin,
copyright © 1988 by The
Anais Nin Trust. All rights
reserved. Reprinted by
permission of the
Author's Representative,
Gunther Stuhlmann.

◆ LIST OF ILLUSTRATIONS

◆ LIST OF ILLUSTRATIONS

postcard. Private collection. Santons, the Carbonel workshop. © L. Giraudou/Gallimard.

List of illustrators:

Nature:
16-17: F. Stephan.
18-19 and 20-21: B. Pearson, P. Robin, .
22-23: P. Place, P. Robin.
24-25: J. Chevallier, C. Felloni.
26-27: J. Chevallier.
28-29: C. Felloni. F. Desbordes.
30-31: C. Felloni, F. Desbordes.
32-33: A. Bobin, A. Larousse.
34-35: J. Chevallier, B. Duhem, C. Felloni, C. Lachaud.
36-37: J. Chevallier, . F. Desbordes, B. Duhem ; A. Larousse.
38-39: J. Chevallier, F. Desbordes, C. Felloni.
40-41: F. Place, P. Robin.
42-43: G. Curiace, C. Felloni, F. Place.
44: C. Felloni, R. Metler.

Architecture:
79: T. Hill.
80-81: C. Faweey, R. Hutchins, Ph. Lhez, Ch. Rivière.
82-83: Ph. Candé, J.-M. Kacedan.
84-85: A. Philipps, G. Szyttia.
86-87: Ch. Rivière, T. Hill.
88-89: x, J.-M. Kacedan, R. Lindsay, M. Sinier, G. Szyttia.
90-91: M. Pommier. .
92-93: D. Brumaud, F. Cusson, M. Sinier.
94-95: S. Doyle. J.-B. Héron, T. Townsend .
96-97: Ph. Candé, F. Cusson, R. Lindsay.
98-99: P. Kostel.
100-101: O. Hubert, C. Rose.
102: E. Gillion, M. Sinier.

Itineraries:
151: T. Hill.
153: N. Castle, C. Felloni.
162: D. Brumaud.
164 and 165: J. Chevallier.
166: C. Felloni.
174-175: P. Poirier.
204: P. Kostel.
210: J. Chevallier.
217: J.-B. Héron.
218-219: J.-B. Héron.
224-225: M. Sinier.
238-239: J.-M. Lanusse.
194-195: M. Sinier.
267: J. Chevallier, C. Felloni.
287: T. Townsend.
310 and 311: J.-M. Kacedan.

314: C. Felloni.

Travel notebook:
M. Pommier.

Maps:
V. Brunot, J.-Y. Duhoo, M. Duplantier, E. Gillion, S. Girrel; F. Liéval, S. Serprix.

Coloring:
I.-A. Chatellard

Computer graphics:
E. Calamy, P. Coulbois, A. Leray, K. Chemineau, C. Mallié, P. Merienne.

We would like to thank the following persons and institutions for their help:
Archives départementales des Alpes-de-Haute-Provence, Digne-les-Bains (Mme Hautefeuille conservateur, et M. Magasson), Archives départementales du Var (Mme Martella, conservateur), Archives départementales de Vaucluse, Archives du Palais princier de Monaco (M. R. Boyer, conservateur), Archives de la S.B.M., Monaco, Association des Amis du Vieux Toulon (M. Fontaine, president), M. Alex Baussy (commissaire priseur, Le Cannet), Mme Lucette Bellini, Cannes, M. P. Bennaroche (expert, Aix-en-Provence), Bibliothèque du chevalier de Cessole, Nice (M. J.-P. Potron, bibliothécaire), Bibliothèque Inguimbertine, Carpentras, Bibliothèque municipale, Marseilles (Mme Jacobi, conservateur fonds ancien), Bibliothèque Méjanes, Aix-en-Provence (Mme D. Oppedit, conservateur, M. P. Ferrand), M. P. Bonnet (Dauphin), M. Ch. Bonnin (expert, Béziers), Daniel Brentchaloff (Conservateur du Patrimoine et président de S.E.S.E.V., Fréjus), M. J.-C. Castex, Paris (collectionneur), Musée Calvet, Avignon, Musée de Carpentras, M. Choll (expert Aix-en-Provence), M. Creusveaux (collectionneur, Aix-en-Provence), M. Maryan Daspet, Musée

municipal, Digne-les-Bains (Mme N. Gomez, conservateur et Mme J. Richaud, documentaliste), Mme S. Durbet-Giono, Galerie Gérard-Guerre, Hôtel Belles-Rives, Golfe-Juan (Mme Estène Chauvin), Hôtel Métropole, Beaulieu-sur-Mer, Hôtel Negresco, Nice (M. M. Palmer, directeur), Hôtel Westminster, Nice (M. P. Gouirand directeur), M. Fabrice Lepeltier, Galerie Martin-Caille, Paris, M. P. Martin-Charpenel, (collectionneur Barcelonnette), M. Ch. Martini de Châteauneuf, Menton (collectionneur), Mme Mattio, Médiathèque Ceccano, Avignon, M. J.-C. Monotolli (collectionneur, Paris), Mme A. de Montry (expert), M. Mme Montagu (agence Taylor, Cannes), Musée du Veil Aix, Aix-en-Provence (Mme N. Martin-Vignes, conservateur), Musée de l'Annonciade, St-Tropez (M. Monery, conservateur), Musée P.-Arbaud, Aix-en-Provence (Mme M.- C. Rémy, conservateur), Muséon Arlaten (Mme D. Serena conservateur), Musée d'art et d'histoire de Provence, Grasse (Mme J. Desjardins, documentaliste), Musée d'art moderne et contemporain, Nice (Mme M. Anssens, photographe and M. P. Chaigneau, conservateur), Musée des Arts et Tradtions populaires, Draguignan (M. Fattori, conservateur), Musée national biblique Marc Chagall, Nice (Mme S. Forestier, conservateur), Musée camarguais, Arles (Mme M.-H. Sibille, conservateur), Musée de Hyères (Mme Nicolaï conservateur), Musée Cantini, Marseilles (M. Cousinou, conservateur, Musée de la Castre, Cannes (Mme M. Wallet, conservateur), Musée Granet, Aix-en-Provence (M. B. Telay), Musée Grobet-Labadié, Marseilles (Mme D. Maternati, conservateur), Musée d'histoire de Marseilles (Mme M. Morel, conservateur), Musée Fernand Léger, Biot (M. R. Bauquier,

conservateur), Musée Masséna, Nice (M. de Lorenzo, photographe), Avignon, Musée municipal d'Orange, Musée Requien, Orange, Musée Picasso, Antibes, Musée du Vieux Marseille, Marseilles (Mme Sportiello, conservateur), Fondation Théodore Reinach, Beaulieu-sur-Mer, Galerie Schmit, Paris, SOCRA (Périgueux), Mme Elia Surtel, M. Traverso, Cannes, Galerie Varine Gincourt, Paris, Centre Jean Giono, Manosque (Mme A. Vigier, conservateur), M. R. Rocca, Palais du Roure, Avignon, Musée de la Vallée, Barcelonnette (M. P. Coste, Mme H. Homps, conservateurs).

PLM posters were reproduced with the kind permission of ACCOR.

Despite our efforts to trace the original publishers or holders of copyright for all the documents used in the guide we are aware of certain gaps. We apologize for any oversight in this respect and would be pleased to settle any outstanding payments due in the case of rights we were unable to identify.

postcard. Private collection. Santons, the Carbonel workshop. © L. Giraudou/Gallimard.

List of illustrators:

Nature:
16-17: F. Stephan.
18-19 and 20-21: B. Pearson, P. Robin, .
22-23: F. Place, P. Robin.
24-25: J. Chevallier, C. Felloni.
26-27: J. Chevallier.
28-29: C. Felloni. F. Desbordes.
30-31: C. Felloni, F. Desbordes.
32-33: A. Bobin, A. Larousse.
34-35: J. Chevallier, B. Duhem, C. Felloni, C. Lachaud.
36-37: J. Chevallier, . F. Desbordes, B. Duhem ; A. Larousse.
38-39: J. Chevallier, F. Desbordes, C. Felloni.
40-41: F. Place, P. Robin.
42-43: G. Curiace, C. Felloni, F. Place.
44: C. Felloni, R. Metler.

Architecture:
79: T. Hill.
80-81: C. Faweey, R. Hutchins, Ph. Lhez, Ch. Rivière.
82-83: Ph. Candé, J.-M. Kacedan.
84-85: A. Philipps, G. Szyttia.
86-87: Ch. Rivière, T. Hill.
88-89: x, J.-M. Kacedan, R. Lindsay, M. Sinier, G. Szyttia.
90-91: M. Pommier. .
92-93: D. Brumaud, F. Cusson, M. Sinier.
94-95: S. Doyle. J.-B. Héron,
T. Townsend .
96-97: Ph. Candé, F. Cusson, R. Lindsay.
98-99: P. Kostel.
100-101: O. Hubert, C. Rose.
102: E. Gillion, M. Sinier.

Itineraries:
151: T. Hill.
153: N. Castle, C. Felloni.
162: D. Brumaud.
164 and 165: J. Chevallier.
166: C. Felloni.
174-175: P. Poirier.
204: P. Kostel.
210: J. Chevallier.
217: J.-B. Héron.
218-219: J.-B. Héron.
224-225: M. Sinier.
238-239: J.-M. Lanusse.
194-195: M. Sinier.
267: J. Chevallier, C. Felloni.
287: T. Townsend.
310 and 311: J.-M. Kacedan.

314: C. Felloni.

Travel notebook:
M. Pommier.

Maps:
V. Brunot, J.-Y. Duhoo, M. Duplantier, E. Gillion, S. Girrel; F. Liéval, S. Serprix.

Coloring:
I.-A. Chatellard

Computer graphics:
E. Calamy, P. Coulbois, A. Leray, K. Chemineau, C. Mallié, P. Merienne.

We would like to thank the following persons and institutions for their help:
Archives départementales des Alpes-de-Haute-Provence, Digne-les-Bains (Mme Hautefeuille conservateur, et M. Magasson), Archives départementales du Var (Mme Martella, conservateur), Archives départementales de Vaucluse, Archives du Palais princier de Monaco (M. R. Boyer, conservateur), Archives de la S.B.M., Monaco, Association des Amis du Vieux Toulon (M. Fontaine, president), M. Alex Baussy (commissaire priseur, Le Cannet), Mme Lucette Bellini, Cannes, M. P. Bennaroche (expert, Aix-en-Provence), Bibliothèque du chevalier de Cessole, Nice (M. J.-P. Potron, bibliothécaire), Bibliothèque Inguimbertine, Carpentras, Bibliothèque municipale, Marseilles (Mme Jacobi, conservateur fonds ancien), Bibliothèque Méjanes, Aix-en-Provence (Mme D. Oppedit, conservateur, M. P. Ferrand), M. P. Bonnet (Dauphin), M. Ch. Bonnin (expert, Béziers), Daniel Brentchaloff (Conservateur du Patrimoine et président de S.E.S.E.V., Fréjus), M. J.-C. Castex, Paris (collectionneur), Musée Calvet, Avignon, Musée de Carpentras, M. Choll (expert Aix-en-Provence), M. Creusveaux (collectionneur, Aix-en-Provence), M. Maryan Daspet, Musée municipal, Digne-les-Bains (Mme N. Gomez, conservateur et Mme J. Richaud, documentaliste), Mme S. Durbet-Giono, Galerie Gérard-Guerre, Hôtel Belles-Rives, Golfe-Juan (Mme Estène Chauvin), Hôtel Métropole, Beaulieu-sur-Mer, Hôtel Negresco, Nice (M. M. Palmer, directeur), Hôtel Westminster, Nice (M. P. Gouirand directeur), M. Fabrice Lepeltier, Galerie Martin-Caille, Paris, M. P. Martin-Charpenel, (collectionneur Barcelonnette), M. Ch. Martini de Châteauneuf, Menton (collectionneur), Mme Mattio, Médiathèque Ceccano, Avignon, M. J.-C. Monotolli (collectionneur, Paris), Mme A. de Montry (expert), M. Mme Montagu (agence Taylor, Cannes), Musée du Veil Aix, Aix-en-Provence (Mme N. Martin-Vignes, conservateur), Musée de l'Annonciade, St-Tropez (M. Monery, conservateur), Musée P.-Arbaud, Aix-en-Provence (Mme M.-C. Rémy, conservateur), Muséon Arlaten, Aix-en-Provence (Mme D. Serena conservateur), Musée d'art et d'histoire de Provence, Grasse (Mme J. Desjardins, documentaliste), Musée d'art moderne et contemporain, Nice (Mme M. Anssens, photographe and M. P. Chaigneau, conservateur), Musée des Arts et Traditions populaires, Draguignan (M. Fattori, conservateur), Musée national biblique Marc Chagall, Nice (Mme S. Forestier, conservateur), Musée camarguais, Arles (Mme M.-H. Sibille, conservateur), Musée de Hyères (Mme Nicolaï conservateur), Musée Cantini, Marseilles (M. Cousinou, conservateur, Musée de la Castre, Cannes (Mme M. Wallet, conservateur), Musée Granet, Aix-en-Provence (M. B. Telay), Musée Grobet-Labadié, Marseilles (Mme D. Maternati, conservateur), Musée d'histoire de Marseilles (Mme M. Morel, conservateur), Musée Fernand Léger, Biot (M. R. Bauquier, conservateur), Musée Masséna, Nice (M. de Lorenzo, photographe), Avignon, Musée du Mont-de-Piété, Avignon, Musée municipal d'Orange, Musée Requien, Orange, Musée Picasso, Antibes, Musée du Vieux Marseille (Mme Sportiello, conservateur), Fondation Théodore Reinach, Beaulieur-sur-Mer, Galerie Schmit, Paris, SOCRA (Périgueux), Mme Elia Surtel, M. Traverso, Cannes, Galerie Varine Gincourt, Paris, Centre Jean Giono, Manosque (Mme A. Vigier, conservateur), M. R. Rocca, Palais du Roure, Avignon, Musée de la Vallée, Barcelonnette (M. P. Coste, Mme H. Homps, conservateurs).

PLM posters were reproduced with the kind permission of ACCOR.

Despite our efforts to trace the original publishers or holders of copyright for all the documents used in the guide we are aware of certain gaps. We apologize for any oversight in this respect and would be pleased to settle any outstanding payments due in the case of rights we were unable to identify.

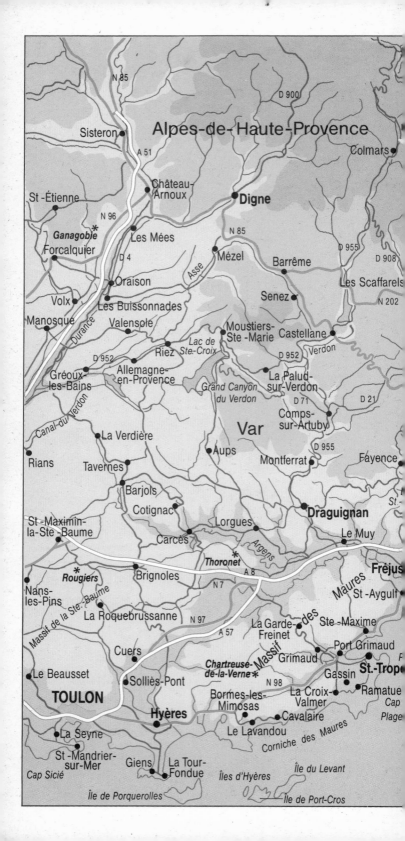